AFTERLIVES

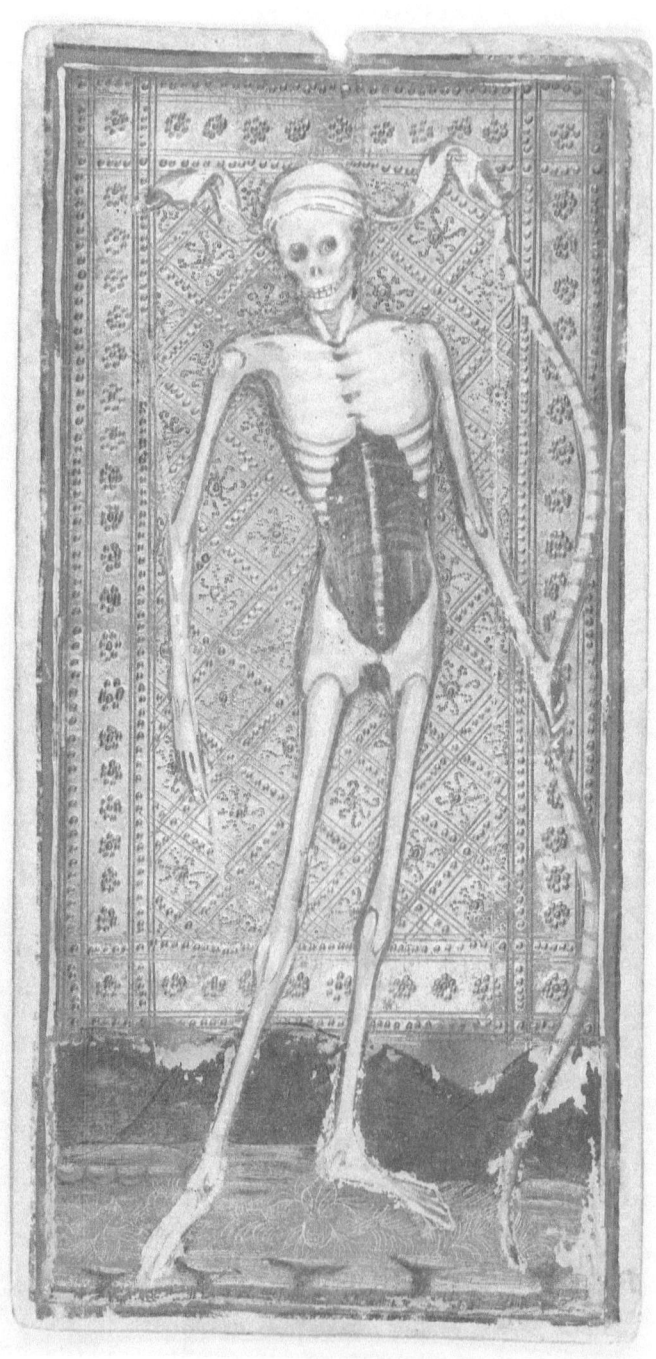

FRONTISPIECE. Death Tarocco Card. Playing card from the Visconti-Sforza Tarot deck, ca. 1451.
Courtesy of the Pierpont Morgan Library, MS M.630, card 12.

AFTERLIVES

THE RETURN OF THE DEAD IN THE MIDDLE AGES

NANCY MANDEVILLE CACIOLA

CORNELL UNIVERSITY PRESS
Ithaca and London

Copyright © 2016 by Cornell University

All rights reserved. Except for brief quotations in a review, this book, or parts thereof, must not be reproduced in any form without permission in writing from the publisher. For information, address Cornell University Press, Sage House, 512 East State Street, Ithaca, New York 14850.

First published 2016 by Cornell University Press
First paperback printing 2017

Printed in the United States of America

ISBN 978-1-5017-1069-8 (pbk.)

Library of Congress Cataloging-in-Publication Data

Names: Caciola, Nancy, 1963– author.
Title: Afterlives : the return of the dead in the Middle Ages / Nancy Mandeville Caciola.
Description: Ithaca ; London : Cornell University Press, 2016. | © 2016 | Includes bibliographical references and index.
Identifiers: LCCN 2015041806 | ISBN 9781501702617 (cloth : alk. paper)
Subjects: LCSH: Death in popular culture—Europe—History—Middle Ages, 600–1500. | Dead—Mythology—Europe. | Future life—Christianity—History of doctrines—Middle Ages, 600–1500.
Classification: LCC HQ1073.5.E85 C33 2016 | DDC 306.9—dc23
LC record available at http://lccn.loc.gov/2015041806

Cornell University Press strives to use environmentally responsible suppliers and materials to the fullest extent possible in the publishing of its books. Such materials include vegetable-based, low-VOC inks and acid-free papers that are recycled, totally chlorine-free, or partly composed of nonwood fibers. For further information, visit our website at cornellpress.cornell.edu.

For my friends and family

Contents

List of Maps and Illustrations   ix

Acknowledgments   xi

Abbreviations   xv

Introduction	1
PART ONE: IMAGINING MORTALITY	19
1. *Mors*, A Critical Biography	23
2. Diagnosing Death	66
PART TWO: CORPOREAL REVENANTS	109
3. Revenants, Resurrection, and Burnt Sacrifice	113
4. The Ancient Army of the Undead	157
5. Flesh and Bone: The Semiotics of Mortality	206
PART THREE: THE DISEMBODIED DEAD	255
6. Psychopomps, Oracles, and Spirit Mediums	259
7. Spectral Possession	302
Conclusion	346

Index   353

Maps and Illustrations

Maps

3.1.	Northern Europe and the Eastern Marches	116
6.1.	Southern France	268
7.1.	The Italian Peninsula	309
7.2.	Portugal	331

Illustrations

1.1.	Lady Death and her handiwork	22
1.2.	Tree of Knowledge of Good and Evil / Tree of Life and Death	27
1.3.	Exhuming the bones of a saint	35
2.1.	Physicians' "Death Prognostic Man"	79
2.2.	Personified Death pierces the vitals of a sick man	85
2.3.	Vigil at a deathbed	86
2.4.	Laying out the corpse	87
2.5.	Human mummy among medical supplies	106
3.1.	General resurrection	132
3.2.	The grateful dead	155
4.1.	Army of the dead attacks the army of the living	190
4.2.	Hellequin accompanying some coffins	202
4.3.	Hellequin and some dead folk participate in a charivari	203
5.1.	Revenant carrying its coffin	216
5.2.	Killing a revenant by beheading	225
5.3.	Vampiric revenant in a backpack	226
5.4.	Legend of the three living and the three dead	228
5.5.	Revenant in an ossuary	230
5.6.	Revenant attack	235
5.7.	Triumph of Death combined with the dance of death	248
6.1.	Ghostly conversation with the soul of Guy of Thurno	295
7.1.	Soul floats away from a dead man	313

🌿 Acknowledgments

The life of this project has already been long and varied, and my debts are many. I must begin by thanking Diane Owen Hughes, who continues to be an inspiration to me as a thinker, writer, and friend. Leigh Ann Craig read a full draft of the manuscript and offered marvelous feedback, then continued to be an excellent sounding board for ideas as I moved forward with revisions. Chris Wickham read a near-final version of the manuscript and offered invaluable feedback that helped me avoid a few errors. Moshe Sluhovsky likewise read a late version and alerted me to implications of the book that I myself had not discerned. Several colleagues generously shared their unpublished work with me, including María de Lurdes Rosa, Iona McCleery, Scott Bruce, Leigh Ann Craig, and Benjamin Saltzmann. Louisa Burnham generously helped me out of tight spots on several occasions, sending page photographs and PDF scans of rare material. Marie Kelleher, among other offerings of friendship and collegiality, oversaw an online writing group with an iron fist in a velvet glove, helping me to complete final revisions. Far-flung medievalist colleagues including María de Lurdes Rosa, Gábor Klaniczay, Éva Pócs, Christian Krötzl, Sari Katojala-Peltomaa, and Louise Nyholm Kallestrup invited me to conferences at which many of the ideas for this book were first formulated and refined. David Frankfurter suggested a key methodological article, and Megan Springate was my touchstone for archaeological references. Ana Grinberg and Miriam Shadis helped out with medieval Portuguese. Michele Greenstein created the beautiful couture maps tailored to my specific needs. Robbi Siegel of Art Resources was a great help to me with many of the images, and Luc Olivier generously shared the use of a photograph.

I sometimes posted ideas and images on social media and benefited from the online brainstormings of many generous minds, including Michael A. Ryan, David Winter, Susan D. Amussen, Meg Worley, Richard Raiswell, Sarah Iles Johnston, Bronwyn Wallace, and Annie Murphy. My University of California, San Diego, colleagues Jack M. Greenstein, Robert Westman, Edward Watts, Ulrike Strasser, and Dayna Kalleres. also provided helpful conversation and support. I would like to thank the Order of the Good Death and especially Caitlin Doughty of Undertaking, L.A., and Jeff Jorgenson of Elemental Cremation and Burial, Seattle, for answering some of my technical questions about postmortem changes in the body.

Cornell University Press has a wonderful team of people, and I thank them for their attention to this book. In particular, my editor, Peter Potter, waited patiently as I finished writing this long work. Peter then recruited two fabulous readers for the Press, each of whom provided incisive, thoughtful, and engaged feedback: I so appreciate the care with which they composed their reports. Karen T. Hwa oversaw the editing and page proofs, and publicist Susan Barnett has displayed continual enthusiasm for this project and its promotion. I thank them all for making the publishing of this volume so gratifying.

Portions of this research were supported by a Faculty Fellowship from the American Council of Learned Societies; a President's Research Fellowship in the Humanities from the Regents of the University of California; and several travel grants from the Academic Senate of UCSD. I am most grateful to these organizations for their ongoing support of the humanities. I also would like to thank the Wellcome Medical Library, the British Library, the Biblioteca Vaticana, the Bibliothèque Nationale de France, the Bäyerische Staatsbibliothek, the Getty Library, and the Pierpont Morgan Library for their generous sharing of manuscript materials. Three long summer weeks spent at the Wellcome was a particularly wonderful interlude during the research for this book.

Certain chapters of this work benefited from the attention and engagement of various audiences who heard early versions delivered orally. A portion of chapter 2 was presented at "Passages from Antiquity to the Middle Ages V: *Infirmitas*. Social and Cultural Approaches to Cure, Caring and Health" at the University of Tampere, Finland, in August 2012. Various sections of chapter 3 were delivered as the keynote address of the 17th Annual Graduate Conference of the Princeton Medieval Studies Program, in April 2010; at the symposium "Heresy, Magic, and Natural Philosophy," at the Medieval Center of the University of Southern Denmark, Odense, in November 2010; and at the conference, "Social Relations and Cross-Cultural Communication in the Medieval and Early Modern Worlds," at the University of Michigan, Ann Arbor, in March 2012.

A project such as this one is never only the product of intellectual community, however. The nurturance of family and friends has been such an important element in my life during the years when this project took shape. My sister, Susan Joan Valcic, has been a constant touchstone, checking in with me weekly as a source of connection and support through the good, the bad, and the crazy. My mother, Eve Mandeville Caciola, first taught me to be curious and bookish, a quality I consider to be a lasting gift. My brother, Gary Caciola, died untimely but not before instilling a profound love of history in me. His best friend and widow Amy Buitenkant remains my link back to him, and I thank her for remaining connected all these years later. Equally as important as my family of blood is my family of choice, however. When I made the unlikely move of joining a performing arts circus a decade ago, I was welcomed by some truly marvelous people who continue to enrich my life. Among these creative souls are Bridget Rountree and Iain Gunn, whose artistic productions continually force me to think in fresh ways, and whose daily friendship sustains me. Xep Levy Campbell introduced herself to me as a diamond that wants to be coal, but she is far too sparkly a treasure for that. I have had the privilege of watching Justine Bethel grow into a woman of spirit and power and I am so proud of her.

Though I initially bonded with Renee Michelle Thompson over snark, fashion, and cocktails, she also made a remark one day in 2013 that inspired me to change my life for the better. For that she deserves my profound thanks. Violet Levy and Gregor Miziumski adopted me as family at first sight: I appreciate their kindness. Amy Wright is my favorite ninja warrior kitty: everyone should have a friend like her. Carrie Rosenberg helped me through some rough times by being an extraordinarily generous listener when I needed it most. Nadya Lev prompted me to think in new ways about art, love, and feminism, and is the amazing photographic talent behind my author photo. Finally, Jack M. and Michele Greenstein are both my oldest and newest friends on this list. I am so very grateful to them for their stimulating conversation, unfailing friendship, and generosity to me in all ways, even when I did not deserve it. I also would like to remember my favorite *daimones*, Enkidu and the late Li'l Peeper, my loving companions throughout the writing of this work.

I surely would not be the woman I am today without the love and support of my friends and family. With sincerity and gratitude, I dedicate this book collectively to them.

ABBREVIATIONS

AASS *Acta Sanctorum, quotquot toto orbe coluntur, vel a Catholicis Scriptoribus celebrantur*, ed. Société des Bollandistes, 68 vols. (Brussels, 1863–87)
CH Caesarius of Heisterbach, *Dialogus Miraculorum*, ed. J. Strange, 2 vols. (Cologne, 1851)
CPM Aurelius Augustinus, *De cura pro mortuis gerenda*, in *PL*, 40, cols. 591–610
GrGr Gregory the Great, *Dialogorum libri quatuor*, in *PL*, 77, cols. 149–428
GT Gervaise of Tilbury, *Otia Imperialia: Recreation for an Emperor*, ed. and trans. S. E. Banks and J. W. Binns (Oxford, 2002)
HRA William of Newburgh, *Historia Rerum Anglicarum*, ed. Richard Howlett, Rolls Series (London, 1884–85)
JF *Le registre d'Inquisition de Jacques Fournier, Évêque de Pamiers (1318–1325): Manuscrit Vat. Latin no. 4030 de la Bibliothèque Vaticane*, ed. Jean Duvernoy, 3 vols. (Toulouse, 1965)
LA Tertullian, *Liber de anima*, in *PL*, 2, cols. 641–752
MJG *Miraculi S. Joannis Gualberti Abbatis*, in *AASS*, 30 (July 12): 363–433
MTC Curial report on the miracles of Thomas of Cantilupe, Paris, Bibliothèque nationale de France, MS lat. 5373A, edited in appendix 1 to André Vauchez, *Sainthood in the Later Middle Ages* (Cambridge, 1997), 540–54
OV Orderic Vitalis, *Historia Ecclesiastica*, ed. and trans. Marjorie Chibnall, *The "Ecclesiastical History" of Orderic Vitalis*, 6 vols. (Oxford, 1969–80)
PCNT *Il processo per la canonizzazione di S. Nicola da Tolentino*, ed. Nicola Occhioni (Rome, 1983)
PCTC *Processus Canonizationis S. Thomae Herefordensis*, Vatican City: Biblioteca Apostolica Vaticana, MS Vat. Lat. 4015
PL *Patrologiae cursus completus, series Latina*, ed. J. P. Migne, 221 vols. (Paris, 1841–66)

TM Thietmar of Mersebug, *Chronicon: Die Chronik des Bischofs Thietmar von Merseburg*, ed. Robert Holzman, Monumenta Germaniae Historica, Scriptores Rerum Germanicarum, n.s. 9 (Munich, 1980)
WA William of Auvergne, *De universo*, in *Opera omnia*, 2 vols. (Frankfurt-am-Main, 1963), 1:593–1074
WM Walter Map, *De nugis curialium*, ed. T. Wright (New York, 1968)

 AFTERLIVES

Introduction

This book charts a history of the unknown: of pure, unslaked curiosity. It seems only appropriate, then, to begin with questions. These are just a few of the many things that medieval people wondered about death and afterlife:

- A priest asks the spirit of a dead man, "What is it like to die?"
- A novice asks a monk, "What makes a death 'good' or 'bad'?"
- A crowd gathers to interview a specter haunting an inn, "Where do you live? . . . Are you alone or in a community? . . . How do you spend your time?"
- An abbot asks a woman visionary, "What does the soul look like?"
- A storyteller wonders, "*Why* do we die?"
- A cleric examining the case of a boy's death muses, "Since the body was intact, how was the determination of death made?"
- A young girl asks the ghost of her favorite cousin, "Where is Gehenna? . . . Do the dead reach their place in the afterlife right away? . . . Do material things feel heavy to you?"[1]

---

1. GT, 771; CH, 2:266; Augustus Potthast, ed., *Liber de rebus memorabilioribus sive Chronicon de Henrici de Hervordia* (Gottingen, 1859), 279; CH, 1:39; Albrecht Wagner, ed., *Visio Tnugdali lateinisch und altdeutsch* (Erlangen, 1882), 8; MTC, 540–54; GT, 764–68.

Death remained strange: it lay beyond the limits of the knowable, a subject of obsessive speculation and uncertainty. The questions above indicate the scope of nonconvergence between available systems of knowledge and human curiosity. Despite the Christian church's confident claims to otherworldly answers, postmortem questions persisted. The popularity of the medieval motif of the postmortem pact, in which friends swear an agreement that the first to die should return and give a full account to the survivor, testifies to the open-ended curiosity of the living for an understanding of the world beyond the grave.[2]

The memory of the dead lingered, hovering at the social periphery yet central to the symbolic systems of medieval culture.[3] Indeed, perhaps more than any other cultural arena, attitudes toward death and the dead reveal how societies think distinctively about what it means to be human. Death is the ultimate translation of self: seemingly in an instant, it transmutes a *person* into a *thing*. Yet at the same time that mortality confronts us with a radical materialist change in the body, so, too, does it involve purely idealist constructions of a perduring self in an afterlife. The very secrecy of the grave—the word "cryptic" derives, after all, from "crypt"[4]—both engenders fascination and fosters imaginative constructions of a world beyond. Death thus opens up a vivid, yet wholly elusive and imaginary, space: it is the heterotopic site par excellence. The dead themselves, as imaginary persons, collectively serve as a fulcrum for broader ideas about how the individual relates to the macrocosms of society and a well-ordered universe. However, this imaginative aspect of the dead was built upon real personalities and real cadavers: thus the history of the dead is necessarily both idealist and materialist. The dead were freighted with significance for the ultimate questions: mortality, eternity, and bloodline; fertility and decay; where one came from and where one ultimately must go.

Patrick Geary has defined the dead in the Middle Ages as an "age class."[5] The phrase is suggestive of a final phase of existence as an ancestor, one who watches over the younger, still-living members of the family or community. The term neatly encapsulates the social reciprocity and continued influence

---

2. Wolfgang Behringer, *The Shaman of Oberstdorf: Chonrad Stoeckhlin and the Phantoms of the Night*, trans. E. Middelfort (Charlottesville, VA, 1998); Renate Blumenfeld-Kosinski, "Philippe de Mézières's Ghostly Encounters: From the *Vie de Saint Pierre de Thomas* (1366) to the *L'Epistre lamentable* (1397)," *Romania* 127 (2009): 168–89.

3. Barbara A. Babcock, "'Liberty's a Whore': Inversions, Marginalia, and a Picaresque Narrative," in *The Reversible World: Symbolic Inversion in Art and Society*, ed. Barbara A. Babcock (Ithaca, NY, 1978), 95–116.

4. Benjamin Saltzmann, *The Limits of Secrecy: A Cultural and Literary History of Concealment in Early Medieval England* (manuscript in preparation), 81–82. I would like to thank Dr. Saltzmann for sharing his work in progress with me.

5. Patrick Geary, *Living with the Dead in the Middle Ages* (Ithaca, NY, 1994), 36.

that the dead were believed to exert over the living throughout medieval society. Preoccupation with the continuing vitality and power of the dead was a characteristic feature of medieval society. We encounter the dead at every turn. After the millennium, in all corners of Europe we find strange accounts of deceased people who seem far from fully extinct. Corporeal revenants (the embodied dead) arose from their tombs to attack their former neighbors,[6] or to celebrate mass in abandoned churches;[7] other undead folk danced joyously in cemeteries and fields.[8] Ghosts arrived from the otherworld to spirit-possess their descendants;[9] Hellequin's dead army marched across moonlit forests and winter skies,[10] and whole royal courts of the dead were discovered (after)living inside hollow mountains.[11] The living, for their part, divided bodies for plural burial,[12] held festivals, wakes, and other rites in honor of the recently deceased,[13] and staged dances of death in graveyards.[14] Some men claimed they snatched their dead wives back from fairy

---

6. Nancy Caciola, "Wraiths, Revenants and Ritual in Medieval Culture," *Past & Present*, no. 152 (1996): 3–45; Jacqueline Simpson, "Repentant Soul or Walking Corpse? Debatable Apparitions in Medieval England," *Folklore* 114, no. 3 (2003): 389–402; John Blair, "The Dangerous Dead in Early Medieval England," in *Early Medieval Studies in Memory of Patrick Wormald*, ed. Stephen Baxter et al. (Burlington, VT, 2009), 539–59.

7. Nancy Mandeville Caciola, "Revenants, Resurrection, and Burnt Sacrifice," *Preternature* 3, no. 2 (2014): 311–38.

8. Elizabeth Barber, *The Dancing Goddesses: Folklore, Archaeology and the Origins of European Dance* (New York, 2013). I would like to thank Jamie M. Marvin for bringing this book to my attention.

9. Nancy Caciola, "Spirits Seeking Bodies: Death, Possession, and Communal Memory in the Middle Ages," in *The Place of the Dead: Death and Remembrance in Late Medieval and Early Modern Europe*, ed. Bruce Gordon and Peter Marshall (Cambridge, 2000), 66–86.

10. Alan Bernstein, "The Ghostly Troop and the Battle over Death: William of Auvergne (d. 1249) Connects Christian, Old Norse, and Irish Views," in *Rethinking Ghosts in World Religions*, ed. Mu-Chou Poo (Leiden, 2009), 115–61.

11. Arturo Graf, "Artù nell'Etna," in *Miti, leggende e superstizioni del Medio Evo*, 2 vols. (Bologna, 1965), 2:301–35; Robert E. Lerner, "Frederick II, Alive, Aloft, and Allayed," in *The Use and Abuse of Eschatology in the Middle Ages*, ed. Werner Verbeke, Daniel Verhelst, and Andries Welkenhuysen (Leuven, 1988), 359–84.

12. Elizabeth A. R. Brown, "Death and the Human Body in the Later Middle Ages: The Legislation of Boniface VIII on the Division of the Corpse," *Viator* 12 (1981): 221–70; Elizabeth A. R. Brown, "Authority, the Family, and the Dead in Late Medieval France," *French Historical Studies* 16 (1990): 803–32; Agostino Paravacini Bagliani, "The Corpse in the Middle Ages: The Problem of the Division of the Body," in *The Medieval World*, ed. Peter Linehan and Janet L. Nelson (London, 2001), 27–41.

13. Nikolaus Kyll, *Tod, Grab, Begräbnisplatz, Totenfeier: Zur Geschichte ihres Brauchtums im Trierer Lande und in Luxemburg unter besonderer Berücksichtigung des Visitationshandbuches des Regino von Prüm (†915)* (Bonn, 1972).

14. Louis Gougaud, "La danse dans les églises," *Revue d'Histoire Ecclésiastique* 15 (1914): 5–22, 229–43; see also consideration in Kyll, *Tod, Grab, Begräbnisplatz, Totenfeier*, 95–101; Florence Whyte, *The Dance of Death in Spain and Catalonia* (Baltimore, 1931); Elina Gertsman, "Pleyinge and Peyntinge: Performing the Dance of Death," *Studies in Iconography* 27 (2006): 1–43; Elina Gertsman, *The Dance of Death in the Middle Ages: Image, Text, Performance* (Turnhout, 2010), 51–100.

rings and even had children with them afterwards: the dead giving life.[15] Of course, everywhere relic cults proliferated for the "very special dead" of recent memory.[16] Concern to assist the dead escalated steeply in monastic and clerical circles, as evidenced by the innovation of necrologies,[17] the increasing formalization of purgatory,[18] and the multiplication of assistance techniques for one's ancestors—the "Church Suffering"—held there.[19] Both medical specialists and regular folk struggled precisely to determine the exact physiological differences between vitality and mortality and to diagnose deaths when someone was unresponsive.[20] Medical writers recommended consumption of powdered human mummy or the blood of executed criminals as health tonics and guarantors of vitality.[21] Finally, in the latter part of the period, macabre iconographies such as the "Three Living and Three

---

15. Claude Lecouteux, *Fées, sorcières et loups-garous au Moyen Âge: Histoire du double* (Paris, 1992); Éva Pócs, *Fairies and Witches at the Boundary of South-Eastern and Central Europe*, Folklore Fellows Communications 243 (Helsinki, 1989); Éva Pócs, *Between the Living and the Dead: A Perspective on Witches and Seers in the Early Modern Age* (Budapest, 1999); Diane Purkiss, *At the Bottom of the Garden: A Dark History of Fairies, Hobgoblins, and Other Troublesome Things* (New York, 2000); Emma Wilby, *Cunning Folk and Familiar Spirits: Shamanistic Visionary Traditions in Early Modern British Witchcraft and Magic* (Brighton, 2005); Alaric Hall, "Getting Shot of Elves: Healing, Witchcraft, and Fairies in the Scottish Witchcraft Trials," *Folklore* 116, no. 1 (2005): 19–36; Laurent Guyénot, *La mort féerique: Anthropologie du merveilleux, XIIe–XVe siècle* (Paris, 2011); Barber, *Dancing Goddesses*.

16. Peter Brown, *The Cult of the Saints: Its Rise and Function in Latin Christianity* (Chicago, 1981). The most recent study in this large field is Robert Bartlett, *Why Can the Dead Do Such Great Things? Saints and Worshippers from the Martyrs to the Reformation* (Princeton, NJ, 2013); see also the unsurpassed André Vauchez, *Sainthood in the Later Middle Ages*, trans. Jean Birrell (Cambridge, 1997).

17. Dominique Iogna-Prat, "The Dead in the Celestial Bookkeeping of the Cluniac Monks around the Year 1000," in *Debating the Middle Ages: Issues and Readings*, ed. Lester Little and Barbara Rosenwein (Oxford, 1998), 340–62.

18. Jacques Le Goff, *The Birth of Purgatory*, trans. Arthur Goldhammer (Chicago, 1984); Aron Gurevich, "Popular and Scholarly Medieval Cultural Traditions: Notes in the Margin of Jacques Le Goff's Book," *Journal of Medieval History* 9 (1983): 71–90.

19. Michel Lauwers, *La Mémoire des ancêtres, le souci des morts: Morts, rites, et société au Moyen Âge (Diocese de Liège, XIe–XIIIe siècles)* (Paris, 1996).

20. Christian Krötzl, "'Evidentissima signa mortis': Zu Tod und Todesfeststellung im Mittelalterlichen Mirakelberichten," in *Symbole des Alltags, Alltag der Symbole: Festschrift für Harry Kühnel zum 65 Geburtstag*, ed. Gertrud Blaschitz, Helmut Hundsbichler, Gerhard Jaritz, and Elizabeth Vavra (Graz, 1992), 765–75.

21. Mabel Peacock, "Executed Criminals and Folk-Medicine," *Folklore* 7, no. 3 (1896): 268–83; Wayland Hand, "Hangmen, the Gallows, and the Dead Man's Hand in American Folk Medicine," in *Magical Medicine: The Folkloric Component of Medicine in the Folk Belief, Custom, and Ritual of the Peoples of Europe and America* (Berkeley, 1980), 69–80; P. Kenneth Himmelman, "The Medicinal Body: An Analysis of Medicinal Cannibalism in Europe, 1300–1700," *Dialectical Anthropology* 22, no. 2 (1997): 183–203; Charles Zika, "Cannibalism and Witchcraft in Early Modern Europe: Reading the Visual Images," *History Workshop Journal*, no. 44 (1997): 77–105; Michael Camille, "The Corpse in the Garden: *Mumia* in Medieval Herbal Illustrations," in *Il Cadavere / The Corpse*, Micrologus 7 (Turnhout, 1999), 297–318; Richard Sugg, *Mummies, Cannibals, and Vampires: The History of Corpse Medicine from the Renaissance to the Victorians* (London, 2011); Louise Noble, *Medicinal Cannibalism in Early Modern English Literature and Culture* (New York, 2011).

Dead," "Triumph of Death," and "Dance of Death" sprung up on church walls,[22] even as churchmen composed guides to dying a perfect death—the *ars moriendi* ("art of dying well").[23] Given this context, it should hardly be surprising that in the 1140s, Peter the Venerable declared appearances of the dead to be *the* characteristic miracle of his time.[24] The struggle to imagine death and afterlife is a recurrent theme in every region, social stratum, and area of cultural endeavor in the Middle Ages.

Some of these phenomena have received attention from scholars: the cult of the saints, in particular, is a flourishing area of inquiry. Yet the overall importance of the dead across medieval culture has been either overlooked or underemphasized by medievalists. When viewed together, however, these beliefs and practices suggest that medieval religion, as experienced on the ground, was dominated by the dead.[25] Indeed, the deceased interacted with

---

22. In addition to the works in n.14, see Philippe Ariès, *The Hour of Our Death*, trans. Helen Weaver (New York, 1981); Emile Mâle, *Religious Art in France: The Late Middle Ages* (Princeton, NJ, 1986); Helmut Rosenfeld, *Der Mittelalterliche Totentanz: Entstehung-Entwicklung-Bedeutung*, 2nd ed. (Cologne, 1968); Wolfgang Stammler, *Die Totentänze des Mittelalters* (Münich, 1922); James Clark, *The Dance of Death in the Middle Ages and in the Renaissance* (Glasgow, 1950); Karl Künstle, *Die Legende der Drei Lebenden und der Drei Toten und der Totentanz nebst einem Exkurs über die Jakobslegende* (Freiburg im Breisgau, 1908); Leonard Kurtz, *The Dance of Death and the Macabre Spirit in European Literature* (Geneva, 1975); Whyte, *Dance of Death in Spain and Catalonia*; Ann Tukey Harrison, ed., *The Danse Macabre of Women: MS. fr. 995 of the Bibliothèque nationale* (Kent, OH, 1994); Jean Batany, "Une image en négatif du functionnalisme social: Les Danses Macabré," in *Dies Illa: Death in the Middle Ages*, ed. Jane Taylor (Liverpool, 1984), 15–28; Peter Walther, *Der Berliner Totentanz zu St. Marien* (Berlin, 1997).

23. Roger Chartier, "Les arts de mourir, 1450–1600," *Annales E.S.C.* 31, no. 1 (1976): 51–75. Still valuable is the classic work of Alberto Tenenti, *Il senso della morte e l'amore della vita nel Rinascimento (Francia e Italia)* (Turin, 1957).

24. Petrus Venerabilis, *De miraculis*, in *PL*, 189, cols. 851–954.

25. Kyll, *Tod, Grab, Begräbnisplatz, Totenfeier*; the entire issue of *Annales E.S.C.* 31, no. 1 (1976); Pierre Chaunu, *La mort à Paris, XVIe, XVIIe, et XVIIIe siècles* (Paris, 1978); Hughes Neveux, "Les lendemains de la mort dans les croyances occidentales (vers 1250–vers 1300)," *Annales E.S.C.* 34, no. 2 (1979): 245–63; Stephen Wilson, "Death and the Social Historians: Some Recent Books in French and English," *Social History* 5 (1980): 435–51; Jacques Chiffoleau, *La comptabilité de l'au delà: Les hommes, la mort, et la région d'Avignon à la fin du Moyen Age (vers 1320 – vers 1480)* (Rome, 1980); Ariès, *Hour of Our Death*; Joachim Whaley, ed., *Mirrors of Mortality: Studies in the Social History of Death* (New York, 1981); Herman Braet and Werner Verbeke, eds., *Death in the Middle Ages* (Louvain, 1983); Taylor, *Dies Illa*; Ronald Finucane, *Appearances of the Dead: A Cultural History of Ghosts* (New York, 1984); Claude Lecouteux, *Fantômes et revenants au moyen âge* (Paris, 1986); Frederic Paxton, *Christianizing Death: The Creation of a Ritual Process in Early Medieval Europe* (Ithaca, NY, 1990); Geary, *Living with the Dead in the Middle Ages*; Jean-Claude Schmitt, *Ghosts in the Middle Ages: The Living and the Dead in Medieval Society* (Chicago, 1998); Paul Binski, *Medieval Death: Ritual and Representation* (Ithaca, NY, 1996); Lauwers, *La mémoire des ancêtres, le souci des morts*; Christopher Daniell, *Death and Burial in Medieval England, 1066–1550* (London, 1997); *La mort et l'au-delà en France méridionale (XIIe–XVe siècle)*, Cahiers de Fanjeaux 33 (Toulouse, 1998); Iogna-Prat, "The Dead in the Celestial Bookkeeping"; *Il Cadavere / The Corpse*; Gordon and Marshall, *The Place of the Dead*; Antonius C. G. M. Robben, ed., *Death, Mourning, and Burial: A Cross-Cultural Reader* (Oxford, 2004); James S. Amelang, "Mourning Becomes Eclectic: Ritual Lament and the Problem of Continuity," *Past & Present*,

the living with far greater frequency than did the divine. God the Father, and even the suffering Christ, were regarded from a greater distance than the knowable figures of the recently passed. Of course, even Christ himself was a deceased human being whose death iconography was central to the Christian religion. Medieval people encountered the dead at every turn, in contexts of veneration, supplication, and fear. In sum, the majority of "ordinary" people who believed that they had had direct experience of the supernatural realm did so in confrontation with other dead human beings.

Imagining Life after Death

The dead are poised in a peculiarly vivid symbolic position. On the one hand, they represent the ancestors or family line from which an individual springs; on the other, they ineluctably present the image of an unknown future, the thickly veiled, imagined realm of postmortem hopes and fears. They are at the intersection of fundamental ideas about identity and society, fertility and decay, temporal limitations and eternal transcendence. In sum, the dead present the perfect screen for human beings' imaginations of themselves and their ultimate values. As such, the dead are quite intimately revelatory of the living.

This book begins from the premise that the social constructs that are built upon the fact of mortality are chief instruments of culture. Mortality and the ways in which afterlives are envisioned are central themes in the history of religion and the study of human society. Of course, the social significance of death is constructed with great variety and complexity within different cultural contexts.[26] For the Middle Ages, the most systematic articulation of a thanatology ("the science of death") was that of formal Christian theology. In doctrinal terms, the body awaited resurrection even as it decayed,[27] while

---

no. 187 (2005): 3–31; Howard Williams, *Death and Memory in Early Medieval Britain* (Cambridge, 2006); Kenneth Rooney, *Mortality and Imagination: The Life of the Dead in Medieval English Literature* (Turnhout, 2011); Frederick Paxton, with the collaboration of Isabelle Cochelin, *The Death Ritual at Cluny in the Central Middle Ages / Le rituel de la mort à Cluny au moyen âge central* (Turnhout, 2013).

26. Cf. Robert Hertz, *Death and the Right Hand*, trans. Rodney Needham and Claudia Needham (Glencoe, IL, 1960); Robert Hertz, "Contribution à une étude sur la répresentation collective de la mort," *Année Sociologique* 10 (1907): 48–137; Maurice Bloch and Jonathan Parry, eds., *Death and the Regeneration of Life* (Cambridge, 1982); Jack Goody and Cesare Poppi, "Flowers and Bones: Approaches to the Dead in Anglo-American and Italian Cemeteries," *Comparative Studies in Society and History* 36, no. 1 (1994): 146–75; Robben, *Death, Mourning, and Burial*; John Clifford Holt, "Gone but Not Departed: The Dead among the Living in Contemporary Buddhist Sri Lanka," in *The Buddhist Dead: Practices, Discourses, Representations*, ed. Bryan J. Cuevas and Jacqueline I. Stone (Honolulu, 2007), 326–44; Martha Lincoln and Bruce Lincoln, "Toward a Critical Hauntology: Bare Afterlife and the Ghosts of Ba Chúc," *Comparative Studies in Society and History* 57, no. 1 (2015): 191–220.

27. Caroline Walker Bynum, *The Resurrection of the Body in Western Christianity, 200–1336* (New York, 1995).

the soul entered one realm of a multitiered afterlife, there to await reembodiment at the end of time.[28] In the meantime, here on earth the sites of Christian worship for the living were simultaneously spaces for the dead—in both interior sepulchers and exterior cemeteries. The Second Council of Nicaea in 787 made the well-established custom of enclosing relics of the saints in Christian altars a formal requirement for every church. Thus the commemoration of the violent death of Jesus, via the Eucharist, took place above the corporeal remains of the holy dead; the altar of worship was literally a tomb. Yet as we shall see, though death and eternal afterlife were central concerns of the Christian religion, its scriptures offered very little guidance to the faithful on such matters. Though belief in an afterlife was the central dogma of the church, there were few guideposts about how this otherworldly afterlife realm was organized or what postmortem existence would be like. In consequence, patristic scholars differed widely on a few key questions. These included whether death was instantaneous or a long-term process, and whether there could be postmortem returns of the dead to this plane of existence. Between the second and the seventh centuries, the Latin church fathers suggested several different answers to these questions of death, afterlife, and postmortem return. The leadership of the church never formally endorsed one position over the others, however, so all were maintained as viable precedents within church tradition. In consequence the Middle Ages inherited a rather broad set of parameters for considering death and afterlife.

This openness to multiple points of view about how to imagine mortality and existence beyond the threshold of the grave continued as the church expanded from its Mediterranean roots into northern Europe. The intersection of Christian eschatology with various pagan afterlife imaginings, from the classical paganisms of the Mediterranean to the Germanic, Slavic, and Scandinavian paganisms indigenous to northern Europe, brought new cultural values about the dead into the Christian fold as the church expanded. For its part, the church was surprisingly open to these influences, absorbing new images of death and afterlife almost indiscriminately. For, quite simply, the chief teaching of the church was that life persisted for eternity, even after death, and that all the dead would someday resurrect to regain their bodies. Thus ghost and revenant stories were simply too useful to reject, for

---

28. Le Goff, *The Birth of Purgatory*; Alan E. Bernstein, *The Formation of Hell: Death and Retribution in the Ancient and Early Christian Worlds* (Ithaca, NY, 1993); Aron Gurevich, *Historical Anthropology of the Middle Ages* (Chicago, 1992), 50–89; Gurevich, "Popular and Scholarly Medieval Cultural Traditions"; Isabel Moreira, *Heaven's Purge: Purgatory in Late Antiquity* (Oxford, 2010). For English translations of primary source documents on purgatory, see Eileen Gardiner, ed., *Visions of Heaven and Hell before Dante* (New York, 1989).

they offered direct, firsthand evidence for the existence of an afterlife beyond this one. Traditional pagan beliefs about the dead interacting with the living seemed like useful tools to Christian evangelizers and clergymen: they saw teaching opportunities in these local traditions about the returned dead. Furthermore, since the doctrinal precedents of the church were themselves multiple and diverse, these motifs, lightly reframed, could be incorporated into Christian texts and Christian preaching with relatively little friction. In many cases it was easy to find loose correlates within Christian tradition. For instance, ghost stories and tales of revenants could be utilized as vivid proofs of the afterlife. Through these means, the church maintained its core doctrinal coherence while permitting continual syncretistic transpositions with other cultural forms.[29] For their part, converts from paganism were enabled to maintain familiar aspects of their ancestral culture under shifting guises and with changed interpretations. Indeed, converts from paganism may also have discerned similarities between some of the church's teachings—particularly relic veneration or the doctrine of resurrection—and their own traditions.

There thus existed a broad space for the persistence, into the Christian culture of the high and late Middle Ages, of originally pagan traditions about the vigorous and active dead. These motifs settled side by side with scriptural references and the teachings of the church fathers. In sum, beliefs about the dead provided particularly active conduits for the circulation of ideas among different groups, and they often evolved in such a way as to function within more than one field of meaning simultaneously. Originally pagan stories about the returned dead were permitted to occupy the capacious middle ground of toleration without endorsement that long had characterized the church's attitude toward this realm of culture. In consequence, the *materia mortalia* of medieval culture was both abundant and often contradictory.

Changing Deathways: Religious Conversion and Afterlife

Intercultural contacts and struggles for hegemony quite often are played out as a series of inchoate negotiations over attitudes toward death, mourning, and burial. Indeed, funerary beliefs and rituals are among those most resistant to total reacculturation in contexts of cultural and religious transformation. Laurent Guyénot has concisely summed up this process in relation to medieval Europe:

> Europe underwent a period of intense cultural brewing and sedimentation up through the end of the eleventh century: the result was a

---

29. Anita Leopold and Jeppe Jensen, eds., *Syncretism in Religion: A Reader* (New York, 2004).

civilization more pagano-Christian than Judeo-Christian. But the elements that filtered through from pre-Christian traditions into the lay religiosity of the twelfth and thirteenth centuries had nothing to do with pagan divinities. Principally, it was beliefs about the dead.[30]

Indeed, medieval Christian authors themselves seem to have been aware of pagans' reluctance to transform their "deathways"[31] when they considered converting to the new religion. Chroniclers and missionaries' hagiographers imagined that death and afterlife played a preeminent role in the minds of potential converts when they weighed the merits of the new rite. Thus when they wrote about conversions from paganism, they placed debates over mortality and the ancestors at the center of their discussions.

Bede's sparrow is a good example. The famous simile recounted in the *Ecclesiastical History of the English People* occurs as part of an account of a lively debate over conversion held in the Kingdom of Northumbria in 627. King Edwin and his court wondered whether to adopt a foreign religion that recently had been brought from the east and that had been making some inroads in Britain. One warrior advised:

> It seems to me, O King, that the life of human beings present here on earth, when considered in light of how uncertain our time here is, is like this: It is as if, some time during winter you were relaxing at dinner with your war band and your ministers, with the fire lit at the center of the dining hall and warming it; while outside, winter tempests of rain and snow were raging away. And then as if a sparrow were to fly straight through the hall ever so swiftly, coming in through one window and just as quickly exiting by another. While it is inside the sparrow is untouched by the winter storm, but the length of this calm span is but a brief moment all the same. Soon it disappears from your sight and goes back: from winter, into winter. This life is a little bit like that: what came before, and what is to come after, we know nothing about. So, if this new teaching brings a more certain knowledge, then I think it seems worth following.[32]

The image of a winter sparrow briefly warmed by its flight through a feasting hall is famed for its stark evocation of the ephemerality of mortal

---

30. Guyénot, *La mort féerique*, 18–19.
31. The word is borrowed from Erik Seeman, *Death in the New World: Cross-Cultural Encounters, 1492–1800* (Philadelphia, 2010).
32. Bede, *Historia Ecclesiastica Gentis Anglorum* 2:13, in *Bede: Historical Works*, ed. J. E. King, 2 vols. (Cambridge, MA, 1979), 1:282–84.

life. And yet, the persuasive force of the simile lies elsewhere: it is the mystery of the sparrow's existence in the drear and cold outside. The unseen and unknowable flight of the sparrow before and after its passage through the firelit hall, in the dark and inhospitable atmosphere beyond the bounds of the familiar, directs attention to the human inability to know what lies beyond life's boundaries: "what came before, and what is to come after, we know nothing about." The grave was a cipher, the ultimate keeper of secrets. Anglo-Saxon kings like Edwin traced their genealogy back to Woden, but what could they expect for the future, after their deaths?[33] As each generation arose and passed away, what was the fate of those who joined the ancestors?

The simile is a pious reconstruction crafted by Bede long after the event. Yet at the same time, and as Bede well knew, it is plausible that the historical deliberations of Edwin's council or *witan* centered, broadly, upon questions of death, afterlife, and eternity.[34] Christianity was dedicated to the memory of a dead man resurrected from the grave; its most powerful claim was indeed that it provided "a more certain knowledge" that pierced beyond the veil of mortality. The new religion likely was compelling to some converts precisely because Jesus' resurrection was regarded as furnishing direct, firsthand answers to the epistemological anxieties of death and afterlife. This was the argument made by the unnamed warrior, and Bede reports that it carried the day for Christianity.

The history of paganism in the Kingdom of Northumbria was far from over, however. A scant five years after his adoption of Christianity, Edwin was killed in battle with a pagan rival, King Penda of Mercia. Edwin's successor, Osric, "ascended with curses against the rites of the heavenly kingdom,"[35] and promptly reestablished paganism as the official religion of the realm. However the next king to take the throne, Oswald, restored Christianity to a firm footing, which persisted through subsequent reigns. Yet even this was not the final religious oscillation: paganism eventually would be reimported to Northumbria via the Viking invasions. The establishment of independent Viking settlements known as the Danelaw with its capitol at York (*Jórvik*) meant that, two centuries after Edwin's conversion to Christ, his kingdom was once again an epicenter for pagan religion and culture. In the ninth

---

33. Richard Fletcher, *The Conversion of Europe: From Paganism to Christianity, 371–1386 A.D.* (London, 1997), 240.

34. Early Christian chroniclers like Bede make extensive use of the rhetorical device of "invented speech" to add drama to the historical scenes they described. Roger Ray, "Bede's *Vera Lex Historiae*," *Speculum* 55, no. 1 (1980): 1–21; S. D. Church, "Paganism in Conversion-Age Anglo-Saxon England: The Evidence of Bede's *Ecclesiastical History* Reconsidered," *History* 93 (2008): 162–80.

35. Bede, *Historia Ecclesiastica* 3:1, in *Bede: Historical Works*, ed. King, 1:326.

century, Anglo-Saxon churchmen were complaining about the veneration of pagan gods in Northumbria;[36] and as late as 1012, Archbishop Wulfstan of York was publicly inveighing against the presence of *wiccan 7 wælcyrian* in the region: "wiccans and Valkyries."[37] The process of conversion could be complex and oscillating.

A contrasting legend comes to us from the conversion of Frisia. As the Christian missionary Wulfram was evangelizing the region, he exerted himself particularly toward converting the local leader, Radbod (ruled 680–719), under the well-tested assumption that gaining the allegiance of a leader ultimately would mean the conversion of his people as well. Radbod, however, regarded Christianity as a foreign faith intimately linked to the expansionist designs of his Frankish neighbors to the south, who already had managed to wrest portions of Friesland from him. Thus Radbod tolerated the missionaries' travels only when he felt in a position of weakness; at other times (particularly after the death of the Frankish leader Pepin of Herestal in 714) he expelled them and tried to root out the religion itself, burning churches and monasteries.

According to Wulfram's *Vita*, however, at one point Radbod asked Wulfram to baptize him, and the two met at a stream. Radbod at first stepped into the water with every indication of acquiescence, but then he hesitated. He thought of all the generations of his ancestors who had lived and died before him as pagans. Their shades, suddenly restless in his mind, gave him pause. So Radbod turned to Wulfram and asked about the fate of his mighty Frisian forbears:

> Where was the great multitude of kings and princes and the nobility of the Frisian people? Were they also in that heavenly kingdom that was being promised to him if he believed and accepted baptism? Or were they in the place Wulfram was calling "infernal damnation"?
>
> Wulfram replied, "Make no mistake, distinguished Prince . . . your ancestors, the leaders of the Frisian people, all of whom died without baptism, have surely received a judgment of damnation. . . ."

---

36. Audrey L. Meaney, "Æthelweard, Ælfric, the Norse Gods, and Northumbria," *Journal of Religious History* 6, no. 2 (1970): 105–32; Audrey L. Meaney, "Ælfric and Idolatry," *Journal of Religious History* 13, no. 2 (1984): 119–35.

37. Neil Price, "Foreword: Heathen Songs and Devil's Games," in *Signals of Belief in Early England: Anglo-Saxon Paganism Revisited*, ed. Martin Carver, Alex Sanmark, and Sarah Semple (Oxford, 2010), xiii. While the precise roles of such persons are ill understood, it is certain that both terms designate pagan individuals with supernatural powers, the latter specifically having to do with assisting the dead in some manner. Price points out that the terms may not be Danish loans, since "we have no way of telling whether the pre-Christian Saxons also had 'proper' Valkyries in the Scandinavian sense" (ibid., x). See also Gerd Tellenbach, *The Church in Western Europe from the Tenth to the Early Twelfth Century* (Cambridge, 1993), 3.

Hearing this the king was incredulous.... He pulled his foot out of the baptismal waters and announced, "I cannot abandon my ancestors and the fellowship of all the greatest men of the Frisian people, in order to live with a motley band of paupers in heaven.... I would rather remain in the places that have been reserved for me and all the Frisian nation from time immemorial."[38]

Radbod was faced with a choice: either abandon his ancestors to their eternal fate, whatever that might be, or else share it with them in lineal solidarity. In the end he remained a pagan precisely in order that he might join his forefathers.

King Radbod's choice to remain among his people in death, as in life, is a salutary reminder: conversion could be perceived as abandonment. It could mean separating oneself from one's blood history forever and entering the next world as a lonely stranger, with no expectation of a joyful greeting from one's parents and ancient forbears. Indeed, it appears that the prospect of an afterlife outside one's genetic and ethnic community, more than that of a life lived in new ways, was a very significant factor in causing potential pagan converts to waver. The above two case studies, though literary, effectively highlight an underlying theme that recurs continually in the conversion of northern Europe: the significance of the ancestors, and the hesitations engendered by the requirement to abandon them for all time when accepting the Christian faith. Some refused this sacrifice; others made it, but ambivalently and with great hesitation. Some new converts sought strategies to bring their dead kin into the fold retrospectively: King Harald of Denmark, for instance, disinterred his pagan father and relocated him to a Christian churchyard after his own conversion in about 960. Presumably, extending the benefit of Christian burial to Harald's kin would, he hoped, permit the family line to remain united even once sundered by his conversion to a new religion.[39] In a similar vein, some church buildings in the Rheinland and in Sweden appear to have been erected directly above the burial sites of important ancestors for the leading local clans, thus consecrating their burial grounds after the fact.[40]

The problem of how to imagine the pagan ancestors of Christian converts remained a vexing one: the newly faithful were reluctant to believe that all the previous generations of their family languished in torment; yet

---

38. *S. Vulfrannus Archiepiscopus Senonensis, Fontanellae et Abbauillae in Gallia, Appendix*, in *AASS*, 6 (March 20), 146–47.

39. Fletcher, *The Conversion of Europe*, 406.

40. Patrick Geary, "The Uses of Archaeological Sources for Religious and Cultural History," in *Living with the Dead in the Middle Ages*, 37–38.

that was the teaching of their new faith. Imagining the fate of the ancient dead was an exercise in peril: either they were damned in the Christian hell, or perhaps lived on in some atavistic, pagan otherworld separate from the Christian afterlife, or worst of all, perhaps they wandered, adrift and homeless, lost between worlds. As we shall see, variations on these alternatives, and syncretistic combinations of them, all appear in medieval sources concerning the afterlife of the dead. As generations of missionaries slowly pushed back the frontiers of Christendom, advancing the faith through all the regions of Europe, they proved unable to exorcise these ghosts of the past. The dead flitted through a landscape in transition, at times appearing as malevolent, demonic presences, at times imagined as retrospectively (if imperfectly) Christianized forbears, and sometimes as both.

Populations in transition, even when they accepted the new religious ideology, did not immediately and irrevocably reorient their lives to conform to new dogmas. Archaeology tends to confirm an image of slow cultural convergence and intermingling, rather than a sudden replacement of one set of rites with another. The latest generation of studies has, for instance, rejected the dispositive value of "grave goods" as indicators of paganism, for far too many excavations contain both Christian religious objects and traditional pagan grave goods for these objects to be indicators of a clear religious preference.[41] Excavations show that originally pagan burial customs continued well into the Christian period, perhaps indicating a desire to "hedge one's bets" when it came to afterlife beliefs. Another recent archaeological study reveals that the pagan ritual of making foundation offerings when constructing homes—vessels containing food, sacrificed animals, small implements, and other tokens—actually *accelerated* after the introduction of Christianity to Poland, as part of the complex cultural process of clinging to past traditions while in the midst of widespread transformation.[42] As material culture,

---

41. Ágnes Cs. Sós and Ágnes Salamon, *Cemeteries of the Early Middle Ages (6th–9th Centuries A.D.) at Pókaszepetk* (Budapest, 1995); Bonnie Effros, "*De partibus saxoniae* and the Regulation of Mortuary Custom: A Carolingian Campaign of Christianization or the Suppression of Saxon Identity?," *Revue belge de philologie et d'histoire* 75 (1997): 267–86; Guy Halsall, "Burial, Ritual, and Merovingian Society," in *The Community, the Family, and the Saint: Patterns of Power in Early Medieval Europe*, ed. Joyce Hill and Mary Swan (Turnhout, 1998), 325–38; Bonnie Effros, *Caring for Body and Soul: Burial and the Afterlife in the Merovingian World* (University Park, PA, 2002); Williams, *Death and Memory in Early Medieval Britain*; Andrew Reynolds, *Anglo-Saxon Deviant Burial Customs* (Oxford, 2009); Carver, Sanmark, and Semple, *Signals of Belief in Early England*; Jo Buckberry and Annia Cherryson, *Burial in Later Anglo-Saxon England, c. 650–1100 A.D.* (Oxford, 2010).

42. Justyna Baron, "Ritual and Cultural Change: Transformations in Rituals at the Junction of Pagan Religion and Christianity in Early Medieval Poland," in *Rytm przemian kulturowych w pradziejach i średniowieczu* [The rhythm of cultural change in prehistory and the Middle Ages], ed. Boguslaw Gediga et al. (Warsaw, 2012), 449–63.

so too, immaterial culture preserved traces of cultural convergence, rather than wholesale replacement.

Thus, even after the assimilation of formerly pagan populations to the Christian church, earlier cultural practices and imaginative constructs persisted, whether as active deeds of resistance or as inheritances of custom and folklore that continued to be considered meaningful. People who venerated saintly relics still thought of their dead ancestors as nearby, active presences; Christians who prayed for the swift salvation of their kinfolk sometimes buried them with pagan tokens or grave goods; many with faith in the resurrected Christ still feared the dangerous dead who might roam from their graves. The pagan dead haunted the new world that was coming into being.

Pagan Survivals in Christian Europe

I am not suggesting that medieval society was cryptopagan, nor that the macabre traditions that we can trace back to various paganisms persisted unchanged. My starting point is, rather, the opposite: these motifs were regarded as unproblematically Christian by the time they were recorded, even when they originated from outside Christian tradition. My project, then, is simply to take seriously the contributions of earlier pagan societies to the distinctively medieval culture that superseded them. Imaginings of the dead permit me to track this cultural process.

Yet, such a project requires a light hand. How might we analyze "survivals" from an antecedent religious tradition into a period when that religion no longer claims adherents or devotees? Some extreme positions have been staked out in answer to this question. In my view, arguments that deny any persistent medieval influence from pagan cultures (for instance, by suggesting that all references to pagan traditions are merely empty repetitions of outdated earlier texts) are equally as reductive as those that present paganism as a full-blown, structured religion that survived underground.[43] Surely the truth lies somewhere between the shoals of these two treacherous extremes. A sensible middle course has been proposed by João de Pina-Cabral. He notes, first, that the modern social sciences tend to "devalue evidences of relative invariance [that] . . . loom in the shadows,"[44] with the result that we

---

43. An influential statement of the former position is Dieter Harmening, *Superstitio: Überlieferungs- und theoriegeschichtliche Untersuchungen zur kirchlichtheologischen Aberglaubensliteratur des Mittelalters* (Berlin, 1979); for the latter, see Margaret Alice Murray, *The Witch-Cult in Western Europe* (Oxford, 1921).

44. João de Pina-Cabral, "The Gods of the Gentiles Are Demons: The Problem of Pagan Survivals in European Culture," in *Other Histories*, ed. Kirsten Hastrup (London, 1992), 49. I am indebted to David Frankfurter for bringing this essay to my attention.

do yet not possess a set of analytic tools that is fully adequate to the evolving meaningfulness of stable beliefs or customs through time. It is necessary to go beyond merely recognizing the existence of certain stories or aspects of popular culture in medieval Christian Europe that descended, in part, from an anterior paganism. If we were to adopt the notion of "pagan survivalism" in a facile way, we might readily fall into romantic notions of a pagan peasantry wholly untouched by the Christian teachings of the elite. This is a characterization with roots in Enlightenment ideology, and one that modern scholars of medieval popular culture have sometimes falsely been accused of maintaining.[45] The language of survivalism, while apposite, can tend to suggest a narrative of wholly nonselective reproduction, leading to slow cultural denaturation, increasing irrelevance, and ossification.

Yet cultural transmission need not be conceived in unconscious, passive terms. We might challenge ourselves instead to think of long-term cultural survivals as both selective and specific, thus foregrounding the agency of the communities that preserved them. What persists is significant and repeated; what withers is deprioritized and neglected. Cultural survivals, then, are consciously and actively *chosen*. From this perspective, we are able to discern the perpetual renewal, relevance, and specificity of those cultural formations that persist fixedly over many centuries and their continued vitality within the communities that sustained them. We can take continuities across time seriously as dynamic expressions of continuously relevant local knowledge—knowledge that is selectively rather than reflexively upheld.

Finally, with full and careful attention to the specificities of temporal change, we can historicize the shifting horizons of meaning embodied in

---

45. The scholarly literature on popular culture is vast. However, a cohesive multilateral debate emerges from these works: Harmening, *Superstitio*; Peter Burke, "From Pioneers to Settlers: Recent Studies of the History of Popular Culture," *Comparative Studies in Society and History* 25, no. 1 (1983): 181–87; Thomas Tentler, "Seventeen Authors in Search of Two Religious Cultures," *Catholic Historical Review* 71, no. 2 (1985): 248–57; John Van Engen, "The Christian Middle Ages as an Historiographical Problem," *American Historical Review* 91, no. 3 (1986): 519–52; Michel Lauwers, "'Religion populaire,' culture folklorique, mentalités: Notes pour une anthropologie culturelle du moyen âge," *Revue d'Histoire Ecclésiastique* 82 (1987): 221–58; Jean-Claude Schmitt, "Introduzione," in *Religione, folklore, e società nell'Occidente medievale* (Bari, 1988), 1–27; Aron Gurevich, *Medieval Popular Culture: Problems of Belief and Perception* (Cambridge, 1988); Rudi Künzel, "Paganisme, syncrétisme et culture religieuse populaire au Haut Moyen Âge: Réflexions de méthode," *Annales E.S.C.* 47, nos. 4–5 (1992): 1055–69; Ludo J. R. Milis, ed., *The Pagan Middle Ages* (Woodbridge, 1998); Carl Watkins, *History and the Supernatural in Medieval England* (Cambridge, 2007), 68–106; Stella Rock, *Popular Religion in Russia: "Double Belief" and the Making of an Academic Myth* (New York, 2007); and the superb overview by Gábor Klaniczay, "'Popular Culture' in Medieval Hagiography and in Recent Historiography," in *Agiografia e Culture Popolari / Hagiography and Popular Cultures: Atti del Convegno Internazionale di Verona (28–30 ottobre 2010) in ricordo di Pietro Boglioni*, ed. Paolo Golinelli (Bologna, 2012), 17–44.

these "survivals." For even as stories and practices persisted beyond pagan societies and into the Christian Middle Ages, their frameworks and meanings evolved radically over time. To ground this point in an example: the motif of an army of wandering shades originated in the Teutonic pagan belief in the *Einherjar*, an army of dead warriors under the command of the god Odin. In the eleventh and twelfth centuries, however, the army of the dead came to be used as an exemplum of purgatorial penance. In one rendering, the army of the dead even becomes a heavenly host sent from above! Clearly the meaning of the motif shifted radically as it moved through different cultural contexts, even as the basic form of the tale remained recognizably intact.

Recovering both the public and the hidden aspects of medieval beliefs thus involves negotiating seen and unseen levels of texts, reading both for what is said too markedly and for what is left unsaid. My primary strategy in the chapters that follow will be to separate as far as possible the interpretations of ecclesiastical authors from the basic "cultural facts" of the stories they recount. By "cultural facts" I mean the most minimal description of what things are reported to have occurred (hence "facts") and were held as true by the community that circulated the report (hence "cultural").[46] Thus I focus upon close readings of individual sources, with particular attention to hybridities, inconsistencies, and multiple meanings. These ruptures, in turn, provide a point of entry into issues of cultural pluralism, unveiling the diversity of cultural strands that are knit together in the sources.

Organization of the Book

The title *Afterlives* has two levels of meaning. On the one hand, this book literally concerns different versions of afterlife, stemming from different cultural and regional milieux. The book takes death and afterlife as a springboard for an inquiry into how cultural attitudes shifted, diverged, and overlapped through varying contexts and social strata. It juxtaposes universalizing discourses such as theology and medicine with regional case studies, in order to cast light upon the multiplicity of cultural traditions in the Middle Ages and their conceptualizations of the human. A secondary resonance of the title *Afterlives* pertains more broadly to historical processes of cultural and religious transformation. Thus the title also refers to the fact that many medieval ways of imagining postmortem existence preserve an afterlife of paganism, so to speak, long after the pagan religions of Europe had become

---

46. This discussion is reprised from Caciola, "Wraiths, Revenants and Ritual in Medieval Culture," 10.

moribund. The words Ronald Hutton penned about witchcraft could equally well apply here: "there remain aspects of the subject which we can only begin to understand properly if they are studied within a framework of diverse and differing regional cultures characterized by belief systems which derived from much earlier traditions."[47] Yet, just as the afterlife of a human person usually is imagined as only a partial survival, involving some form of loss—the soul without a body, the body without an intellect, the spirit without a social persona—so, too the afterlife of medieval pagan cultures, as they emerge in the following pages, is only fragmentary and partial. Much has been left behind, irretrievable, and the fragments of evidence that survive are frequently disconnected and contingent.

The chapters that follow are grouped into three subsections. The pair of chapters in Part One analyze the writings on death of the medieval intellectual classes. Chapter 1 focuses upon scripture and the formative traditions of the church fathers, while chapter 2 shifts focus to medieval medical knowledge as discussed within natural philosophy. Thus this first section of the book is dedicated to universalizing discourses produced by the most educated sectors of society.

Part Two of the book presents three detailed case studies of how return from the dead was imagined within northern Europe. Here, the returned dead were conceptualized as embodied (that is, as revenants) and often as extremely dangerous and violent. Chapters 3 and 4 each trace a different motif in which the dead were imagined as collective groups, conducting their postmortem existence in well-organized societies that mirror those of the living. Chapter 5 turns to a discussion of individual revenants and tries to tease out some of the underlying logic of belief in the medieval undead.

The third section moves to the Mediterranean regions. Here stories about return from the dead took a different form—literally. Rather than imagining the dead returning as embodied beings, as in northern Europe, here tales of postmortem return involved spirits or ghosts. Chapter 6 examines accounts of disembodied shades who appear to one living person, who then learns to act as a spirit medium for the dead. The seventh and last chapter examines individuals possessed by ghosts, usually the spirits of those who died while young adults. Finally, a short conclusion tries to tease out some of the insights to be gained from the above series of focused studies.

A note concerning translations: Most of the quotations of original documents in *Afterlives* are my own translations. The footnotes provide guidelines: in all cases where the cited volume is exclusively in Latin, where it contains

---

47. Ronald Hutton, "Witch-Hunting in Celtic Societies," *Past & Present*, no. 212 (2011): 71.

both a Latin edition and an English translation of the text, or where it is an edition of a medieval vernacular text (e.g., in medieval French, Portuguese, German, or English), then the linked quotation is my own translation into English. Quoted biblical passages have been translated directly from the Latin Vulgate. In cases where a footnoted work presents only an English edition, then the translator of that volume is responsible for the English rendering.

❧ PART ONE

Imagining Mortality

> Of all sources of religion, the supreme and final crisis of life—death—is of the greatest importance. Death is the gateway to the other world in more than the literal sense . . . love of the dead and loathing of the corpse, passionate attachment to the personality still lingering about the body and a shattering fear of the gruesome thing that has been left over—these two elements seem to mingle and play into each other.
>
> —Bronislaw Malinowski, "Magic, Science, and Religion" (2009)

Death remains elusive. For the living it must always be an imagined experience, albeit one regarded with terror. Human cultures ever and always have strived to pierce through mortality's shroud, unearth death's secrets, and see into the shadowy world that is imagined to exist postmortem. How does a living person become an inanimate object? Where does the personality or self go, and what rites are owed to the corpse? As Malinowski's quote so vividly suggests, imagining the dead is a complex process fraught with both love and repulsion.

Medieval Christianity was built upon the memory of a violent death and fueled by a promise of eternal transcendence of death for the faithful. Thus mortality bracketed the religion's founding and its future: any study of medieval thanatologies must begin here. The notion that the human person had a double nature, being comprised of both a spiritual and a material self in intimate union with one another, was central to Christian anthropology. For theologians, then, the chief concern in analyzing life and death was to understand how the soul inhabited the body and how the bond between the two ruptured at death. Likewise, in imagining the afterlife Christian thinkers struggled to determine the exact conditions under which the soul would persist in a disembodied state after death and whether it could interact with those still living. These questions are central to the first part of this book.

Chapter 1, "*Mors*: A Critical Biography," discusses the interrelationships of body and soul from a theological viewpoint. It takes up the foundational Christian mythology of death and resurrection, the formation of the cult of the martyrs in the early church, and patristic debates about death and return from the dead. The focus here is upon the coexistence of multiple strands of interpretation and what this diversity signified within an institution that commonly policed its doctrines with great zeal. Chronologically this chapter, which ends in the seventh century, may be regarded as a prequel to the other portions of the book. It presents the formative traditions that later generations, in the high and late medieval periods, looked to for guidance. The presuppositions about death and afterlife that were established in the early centuries of the church continued to be important touchstones throughout the Middle Ages.

If the harsh reality of death is a key inspiration for religious yearnings, so too is death a chief preoccupation of medical inquiries. Like medieval theology, medieval medicine also was rooted in the idea that a union of body and soul was the fundamental basis for human existence. Once the soul left the body, the latter perished. Thus the second chapter in the pair that comprises this section is dedicated to medical thought. If theology attempted to understand life and death by focusing on the soul, then medicine sought the same answers by focusing on the body. The two branches of inquiry had significant overlaps, even as they focused on differing aspects of human selfhood. In particular, chapter 2 charts developments in the understanding of death engendered by the efflorescence of medieval medical theories that began in the twelfth century. "Diagnosing Death," shows that an increasingly medicalized view of death took hold in medieval culture between the twelfth and the fifteenth centuries; through the analysis of numerous different sources and genres, it explores how death was diagnosed and understood as a physical process. Because this chapter takes us to the end of the medieval period in the fifteenth century, it also suggests a terminus for the history of death in this period. The rising authority of scientific epistemologies is one of the most important developments for understanding the culture of the later Middle Ages, and the history of death is no exception. By the end of the period, the prestige of such approaches to death had increased to the point that medical definitions were coming to the forefront of broader conversations about death and afterlife.

Medieval theology and medicine represent two distinct but ultimately harmonious intellectual approaches to death. Medical theorists were also, of course, literate and well-educated Christians: they looked to the Bible as well as to the body for instruction. In fact, these thinkers also voraciously read pagan and Arabic writings on human physiology, taking inspiration from as many sources as they could find. Yet theology and medicine had something else important in common as well: both were universalizing discourses that presented themselves as authoritative interpretations of reality for all times and places. Understanding the debates and areas of consensus that emerged within these two translocal discourses, then, is a necessary prelude to investigating more local cultural formations. Hence this first section provides a basis for comparison for the later sections of this book, which will focus upon more uniquely regional macabre motifs and ways of imagining the dead. For now, let us turn our attention to death as a "gateway to meaning," to paraphrase Malinowski, within some broadly shared discourses of the Middle Ages.

FIGURE 1.1. This fourteenth-century fresco of "Lady Death" was painted in the wake of plague in the region. It is quite unusual in showing death as an allegorical living figure rather than as a corpse. She is labeled *Mors* and is surrounded by her handiwork: heaps of corpses. St. André Church, Abbey of Lavaudieu, France, 1355.
Courtesy of Luc Olivier Photography.

Chapter 1

Mors
A Critical Biography

A 1355 fresco from the Abbey of Lavaudieu portrays *Mors* as an allegorical figure: Lady Death (figure 1.1). She triumphantly clutches arrows in each fist and stands surrounded by heaps of fresh corpses. She might almost be a nun but for the vivid red of her dress, which is topped by a white cloak and black veil. The latter is pulled low over her eyes, emphasizing that Death is blindly indiscriminate in her targets. This representation is unique in portraying Death as a living figure, rather than as a skeleton or emaciated corpse. The message of death's universality is conveyed with absolute clarity.

Yet that all humankind inevitably should perish was *not* a plain and self-evident fact according to Christian teaching. Beginning with the Apostle Paul, a long succession of Christian theologians taught that human mortality was not a necessary but a contingent, even an *unnatural* fact of existence. As William of Auvergne summed up this tradition in the thirteenth century, the body "is not mortal by nature; the fact that it is mortal came about through circumstance [*accidenti*]."[1] To perish was neither the natural nor the inevitable destiny of the human race. Rather, mortality was something foreign to human nature as originally constituted: death was introduced into the fabric of creation at a particular moment in time. Furthermore, death

---

1. William of Auvergne, *Cur Deus homo*, in *Opera Omnia*, 2 vols. (Paris, 1674), 1:556.

someday would cease to afflict the human race. The Resurrection of Jesus had changed the future of death, upending its relationship to humanity for a second time. In the future, mortality would be extinguished and annihilated; immortality would again take up its rightful place as the natural destiny of humankind. In short, the Christian church taught that death was not a fact, but a developing narrative: it had a history and a future.

This chapter unfolds in two stages. First I explore attitudes toward death in the primitive church, examining the chief biblical passages having to do with death, afterlife, and resurrection. I observe that Christianity early developed a strong and distinctive thanatology that came to be at the center of its narrative of human history and salvation. This thanatology told a story of abrupt shifts and reversals: from deathlessness to mortality and back again. Moreover, the Christian church was from its origins a religion built upon veneration of the violently killed. First Jesus and then the martyrs were the central focal points of Christian reverence. To outsiders the new religion seemed unusually macabre, even a cult of death. The congregations of the faithful were known to gather in funereal locations such as cemeteries, in order to be near the sepulchers of the martyrs. And, as the religion gained more public prominence, Christians increasingly brought the bodies of their heroic dead—the relics of the saints—into the spaces of the living and exalted them at the center of their religious architecture. Thus death and corpses were central, both symbolically and literally, to the Christian religion.

The second half of the chapter unpacks some of the collective representations of death and afterlife in some of the most influential patristic writings.[2] The church fathers were the foundation of medieval Christian theology; these authorities set the parameters for what was thinkable and tolerable in later centuries. Yet the fathers were not in agreement about certain questions pertaining to death and afterlife; they set forth taxonomies of mortality that were at odds with one another in important ways. The two most prominent early Latin Christian theologians were both North Africans: Tertullian of Carthage (ca. 160–ca. 225) and Saint Augustine of Hippo (354–430). I emphasize these men's attempts to shed older ways of thinking about mortality and to formulate a distinctively Christian approach in line with scriptural teachings. Their view of death emphasized the instantaneity of mortality: death as *event*. However, a later generation of formative Christian thinkers

---

2. For general background on the thanatologies of ancient Rome and the patristic era, see Jaroslav Pelikan, *The Shape of Death: Life, Death and Immortality in the Early Fathers* (Nashville, 1961); Jon Davies, *Death, Burial, and Rebirth in the Religions of Late Antiquity* (New York, 1999); Catharine Edwards, *Death in Ancient Rome* (New Haven, CT, 2007); Valerie Hope, *Death in Ancient Rome: A Sourcebook* (London, 2007).

made a different set of assumptions about death and afterlife. The understanding of mortality advanced by Pope Gregory the Great (ca. 540–604) and the encyclopedist Isidore of Seville (ca. 560–636) represented an alternative tradition to their forbears from North Africa: death as long-term *process*. These two systems of thought, though incommensurable in important ways, each continued to inform learned opinions throughout the medieval period; neither ever achieved full dominance within the church. Indeed, the tension between them was to continue for centuries, in shifting forms. The purpose of this chapter, then, is to emphasize the fundamentally heterogeneous and fluid character of the church's imaginings of death and the world beyond in the formative epoch of its history.

The Birth and Death of Death Itself

Death was born in the fecund garden of paradise. As the book of Genesis relates, God crafted the first humans as the culmination of his six-day labor of Creation. He breathed into Adam's nostrils, filling the first man with the spark of life, the vital spirit that animates each human body from within. Adam and his spouse Eve were furnished with a living space of ease and delight, a fecund garden where their needs effortlessly were met without labor or striving. Yet a prohibition also was placed upon the first human beings: they were forbidden to consume the fruit of the Tree of Knowledge of Good and Evil. "In the day that you eat of it," God promised, "you shall die with a death [*morte morieris*]" (Gen. 2:17). In disobeying this commandment Adam and Eve introduced mortality into the world—and thus into the very fabric of human nature for all their descendants. After this transgression the Creator exiled Adam and Eve from paradise, specifically in order to prevent their continued access to another supernatural plant, the Tree of Life. Early Christian commentators taught that eating the fruit of this tree would have conferred continued immortality upon the pair, in contravention of God's new mandate that human bodies become mortal. And so, generations of human beings arose and passed away, subject to the cycle of birth and death.

In the first century CE, a new religious movement added another chapter to this myth of death's origin. Christianity was engendered by a violent death: the Crucifixion of the Jew Jesus of Nazareth some time around 30 CE. Even more important than Jesus' execution, however, were reports of his Resurrection from the grave, which came to be the emotional core of the new religion. To be Christian was to believe that Jesus, alone among all the generations of humanity, had transcended mortality: he overcame the curse of our first parents. Further, to believe this paradox, to hold it as a tenet of faith, was to participate in a promise of immortality for oneself. Death not only had been overcome in one instance, it was to be reversed for all the faithful. As Jesus had counseled a potential disciple who wished to see to his parent's funeral, "Let the dead bury the dead" (Matt. 8:22). The injunction suggests that death pertains only to those outside the community. Those in Jesus' new movement, by contrast, have moved into the sphere of eternal life and need no longer concern themselves with mortality, nor even with funeral rites for their kinfolk.

In the First Letter to the Corinthians, the Apostle Paul presented Jesus as a figural reembodiment of the first man, Adam, and his Resurrection as a reversal of Adam's introduction of mortality into human nature. Jesus recovered humanity's natural, prelapsarian immortality.

> For as by a man came death, so by a man has come also the resurrection of the dead. For as in Adam all die, so also in Christ shall all be made alive! . . . The last enemy to be destroyed is death. . . . The first man was from the earth, a man of dust; the second man is from heaven. . . . Just as we have borne the image of the man of dust, we shall also bear the image of the man of heaven. . . . When the perishable puts on the imperishable and the mortal puts on immortality, then shall come to pass the saying that is written: Death is swallowed up in victory. O death where is thy victory? O death where is thy sting?
>
> (1 Cor. 15:21–22, 26, 35, 45, 47–49, 54–55)

Paul suggests that Adam and Jesus were figural forms of one another and patterns for subsequent humanity as well. Just as Adam's introduction of mortality into human nature was an inheritance for the whole human race, so Jesus becomes the basis for a re-formed humanity inheriting the promise of his immortality: the "man of dust" gives way to the "man of heaven." Jesus' obedience unto death and reward of resurrection is an antithesis and reversal of Adam's fatal disobedience.

A late fifteenth-century missal from Salzburg captures these ideas nicely in a visual representation (figure 1.2). At right, Eve accepts the fruit of the Tree of Knowledge of Good and Evil from the serpent and hands it off to a crowd of waiting men and women, her progeny through the ages. Though the fruit she holds is luscious, a skull peers down through the leaves of the tree, showing that the fruit will lead the human race to "die with a death." Meanwhile, looming over Eve's left shoulder is a blackened corpse who holds aloft a scroll reading *mors est malus*

FIGURE 1.2. The Tree of Knowledge of Good and Evil is simultaneously the Tree of Life—and of Death—in this illumination. While Eve distributes the forbidden fruit to the generations of her progeny, thus subjecting them to Death (who looms over her shoulder), Mary distributes Eucharistic Hosts plucked from the same tree. Illumination, Missal, ca. 1478–89. Bayerische Staatsbibliothek, München, MS Clm 15708 III, fol. 61v.
Courtesy of Bayerische Staatsbibliothek.

vitam hominis inde, "death is thenceforth the bane of human existence." The fruit, Eve's punishment, and her newfound knowledge are all one in death. To the left, however, a symbolic reversal of this scene is portrayed. Mary, the "new Eve" and symbol of the church, stands before a crucifix nestled in the boughs of the same tree. She plucks a different type of fruit from the branches: Eucharistic Hosts, which she distributes to the faithful behind her in a frank appropriation of a male clerical role. Her scroll, in an inversion of Eve's, notes that the "angelic bread" she distributes is a token of eternal life. The Tree of Knowledge is thus also the Tree of Life—and of Death. Adam, meanwhile, sits passive and somnolent beneath the tree, as though recently awakened from the sleep in which God placed him when creating Eve.[3]

Contained in this transformative anthropology was a promise that the resurrection body would be fundamentally different in some way: the return to life guaranteed by Christian faith occurred in a body made ready for eternity.[4] Paul notes in his Corinthian correspondence, "some will ask, 'How are the dead raised? With what kind of body do they come?'" (1 Cor. 15:35). The underlying concern appears to have been fear that the revivification Paul preached was some kind of necromancy, a reanimation of unchanged corpses.[5] Gentiles imagined eternal life not as postmortem resurrection but as apotheosis: being swept up into heaven *without* ever undergoing the horror of death. Paul's preaching, then, was frightening and new insofar as it involved coming back to life after first having become a cadaver, a thing regarded as loathsome and polluting throughout the ancient world. Implicit in Paul's letter is a suggestion that some either doubted the resurrection entirely (1 Cor. 15:12) or else were alarmed by the prospect of corpses arising from the grave. Then as now, imagining the living dead was fraught with dread rather than reassurance. Evidently in response to these fears, Paul instructs the congregation at Corinth that, though believers must first die in order to gain eternal life, the resurrection body is *not* merely a reanimated carcass: "What is sown is perishable; what is raised is imperishable. It is sown in dishonor; raised in glory. It is sown in weakness; raised in power. It is sown a physical body; raised a spiritual body" (1 Cor. 15:42–44).

If Jesus' resurrection was a pivotal event in the history of death—a hinge upon which mortality opened and closed—this was only because the world itself was about to be radically transformed. Intrinsic to the promise of resurrection through faith was a temporal consciousness that was thoroughly eschatological and otherworldly. Christian concern about the brief window of time remaining to the familiar order of creation is evident throughout the New Testament and is intimately related to the Christian expectation of resurrection and postmortem reward—a set of hopes known as the Parousia. The so-called little apocalypse, a sermon attributed to Jesus, likely circulated in Jewish-Christian oral tradition before being interpolated into the synoptic

---

3. For further background on the portrayal of the creation of Eve from Adam, see Jack M. Greenstein, "The Body of Eve in Andrea Pisano's *Creation* Relief," *The Art Bulletin* 90, no. 4 (2008): 575–96.

4. Caroline Walker Bynum, *The Resurrection of the Body in Western Christianity, 200–1336* (New York, 1995).

5. I am grateful to my colleague Dayna Kalleres for her suggestions about this passage.

tradition beginning with Mark around 70 CE.⁶ The segment, which appears in the thirteenth chapter of Mark, in Matthew 24–25, and in Luke 21, is rife with Jesus' assurances of his imminent return to judge the living and the dead, to institute the Kingdom of God, and to restore immortality to humanity. "This generation shall not pass away," preaches Jesus, "before all these things take place" (Mark 13:30). Yet Jesus' contemporaries *did* pass away without those things taking place. Unsurprisingly, as the first generation of converts began to age and die, survivors experienced a sense of cognitive dissonance in regard to this failed prophecy.⁷ The very earliest book of the New Testament, Paul's First Epistle to the Thessalonians, composed between 50 and 52 CE, testifies to the community's anxieties about the unexpected persistence of death. Paul assured the congregation at Thessalonika that loved ones who had passed away before the Second Coming merely had undergone a temporary form of mortal surcease, a sleep from which they would awaken to life once more. "Since we believe that Jesus died and rose again," Paul consoled them, "even so, through Jesus God will bring with him those who have fallen asleep" (1 Thess. 4:14). Elsewhere, Paul uses the same metaphor of death as somnolence, in a passage that likely preserves an early hymn:

> Arise, you who are sleeping!
> Rise up from those who are dead
> and Christ will illuminate you.
> (Eph. 5:14)

Thus from the earliest generation of people entering into the Jesus Movement, the core promise of the new religion was transcendence of mortality: "Christ Jesus has set me free from the law of sin and death" (Rom. 8:2). Death will be vanquished, its bitter sting no longer felt. Jesus and Paul promised that these events would transpire sooner, rather than later. In chapter 7 of First Corinthians, Paul urged members of the community not to seek to change their lives: not to marry, nor pursue ambitions; not to start new businesses or undertakings, nor to seek to change their social status. Do not worry about what is to come, Paul wrote: "I mean, brethren, the appointed time has grown very short. . . . For the form of this world is passing away" (1 Cor. 7:29, 31). Because time is winding down, Paul suggested, it is not worthwhile to lay plans; better to look to the next world and await the

---

6. Bernard McGinn, *Antichrist: Two Thousand Years of the Human Fascination with Evil* (New York, 1994), 38.
7. Leon Festinger, Henry W. Riecken, and Stanley Schachter, *When Prophecy Fails* (Saint Paul, 1956).

imminent apocalypse. The First Epistle of John echoed the point in the 90s, "Do not love the world or the things that are in the world. . . . The world is passing away, along with its desires; but he who does God's will abides in eternity. Children: it is the last hour" (1 John 2:17–18).

Yet inevitably, as each successive generation *did* pass away without the prophesied Messianic return, the postponement of the Second Coming became an issue of escalating concern and doubt. Scholars refer to this situation, and the theological and existential responses to it, as "the delay of the Parousia": how to maintain faith in a promise unfulfilled, a hope that had held together the intellectual edifice of the young religion. The apocalyptic consciousness of the primitive church was given a compelling descriptive form in the final text of the New Testament, the book of Revelation, composed at the close of the first century. As is characteristic of apocalyptic writing the author "write[s] future history as if it were in the past"—that is, with a strong level of certainty and vivid detail.[8] The book lays forth a prophetic vision of the second coming of Christ, which takes place amid a cosmic war with the forces of evil. Humanity will suffer various plagues, persecutions, and martyrdoms ending in the triumph of the just, universal resurrection, and judgment of the good and the evil. Finally, a glittering city will descend from the skies as a new home for all the faithful: the Heavenly Jerusalem. In a reversal of the book of Genesis, at the center of the holy city there is "the tree of life, with its twelve kinds of fruit, yielding its fruit each month" (Rev. 22:2). Thus the celestial home is not only the New Jerusalem, it is the New Eden: the garden turned city, with the immortal tree at its center. After the general resurrection, the just are guaranteed a steady diet of immortality, the fruit of the tree denied Adam and Eve in punishment for their transgression. The last book of the Christian Bible thus reverses the first: Genesis and Revelation bracket a history of mortality that unfolds like a vast palindrome inscribed upon the human body.

Around the same time that the book of Revelation was composed, the Gentile author known to us as Luke was composing his gospel and a sequel, the Acts of the Apostles. The Gospel according to Luke contains the sole New Testament passage that addresses the postmortem condition of the soul *before* resurrection. The teaching unfolds as a story:

> There was a rich man dressed in purple and fine linen who lived in luxury every day. And there was a beggar named Lazarus who lay at his

---

8. J. Gordon Melton, "Spiritualization and Reaffirmation: What Really Happens When Prophecy Fails," in *Expecting Armageddon: Essential Readings in Failed Prophecy*, ed. Jon R. Stone (New York, 2000), 145.

gate, covered with sores and longing to eat the crumbs that fell from the rich man's table.... In time the beggar died and the angels carried him to the bosom of Abraham. The rich man also died and was buried in hell [*sepultus est in inferno*]. Raising his eyes from where he was in torment, he saw Abraham far off with Lazarus in his bosom. So he called to him, "Father Abraham, have pity on me and send Lazarus to dip the tip of his finger in water and cool my tongue, for I am tormented in this fire." And Abraham said to him, "Son, remember that you received good things in your lifetime, while Lazarus received bad things. Now, however, he is comforted here and you are tormented. And in all ways, between us and you a great chasm has been set in place, so that those who want to go from here to you cannot, nor can anyone cross over from there to us."

(Luke 16:19–26)

Thus according to Luke the souls of the dead live on postmortem in another world where they are recompensed for their life's deeds. A bifurcated system of reward and punishment inverts the fortunes of this life. In a passage that seems closely aligned with the radical ethos of Jesus' Sermon on the Mount, Luke imagines an otherworld in which the heedless wealthy are tormented while the abject are comforted. Moreover, those condemned to the place of torment can gain neither relief nor release. The righteous and the unjust cannot interact, though they can see one another across a great chasm.

Luke goes on, in the next verses, to discuss whether the shades of the dead may visit those who are still alive. The rich man next asks Abraham for a special boon: the visit of a ghost to his surviving loved ones. He wishes Lazarus to appear to his family in order to warn them, so that they may not end up in torment like himself. Abraham replies that his family members should heed Moses and the prophets and reform of their own volition. But the rich man stresses the probative value of an apparition from the dead: "Father Abraham, if someone from the dead will go to them, they will repent" (Luke 16:30). The patriarch continues to refuse, however, stating that the living should have faith without proof. Here, Luke's teaching suggests that ghosts are not impossible (Abraham never suggests that Lazarus cannot go) but that they remain unlikely in the normal course of events (Abraham refuses to provide this proof of an afterlife). This ambiguous status for the return of the dead permitted a wide latitude of subsequent interpretation, as we shall see.

Glorious Relics and Unclean Cadavers

Christianity was slow in becoming "a full-service religion."[9] Because of its otherworldly focus and apocalyptic expectations, the early church did little to develop specifically Christian rites of passage marking mundane events such as births, marriages, deaths, grieving, changes between seasons, and so forth. In consequence, most Christian converts simply maintained the customs of their ancestors in these matters of social life while awaiting the Second Coming of Christ. They celebrated weddings according to long-standing traditions, with jubilant feasts and entertainments, and they sometimes married across religious lines (like Saint Augustine's parents) without second thoughts. They educated their children in the traditional pagan classics as well as in the Christian scriptures. Christian practices such as shrine incubation (in hope of receiving a healing or a vision) derived from pagan antecedents, as did the custom of leaving ex-votos in gratitude. The veneration of holy objects—salt, water, blood, and phylacteries or amulets—likewise borrowed from existing norms of the broader Greco-Roman world. Even the dress of the higher clergy—the impressive silken robes and miters—was modeled on imperial court costumes. From the earliest spread of the Christian religion, church leadership consciously permitted, even cultivated, borrowings from local cultures.[10] Thus did the new religion replicate many norms of the existing world while awaiting the rewards of the next.

Likewise, Christians initially buried their "sleeping" coreligionists next to their pagan ancestors, in the same cemeteries and with similar kinds of sarcophagi. The faithful honored their dead with festive meals and commemorations at regular intervals throughout the year, just as their pagan ancestors had always done as part of the grieving process. Custom called for commemorations to be held at the gravesite at regular intervals after interment; archaeological excavations of ancient cemeteries have found widespread use of feasting *mensae* (stone tables) atop burial plots, which served as gathering places for these commemorative picnics. These *mensae* often were fitted with libation tubes that funneled offerings of drink from the tabletop down

---

9. Ramsay MacMullen, *Christianity & Paganism in the Fourth to Eighth Centuries* (New Haven, CT, 1997), 154.

10. Ramsay MacMullen, *Christianizing the Roman Empire, A.D. 100–400* (New Haven, CT, 1984); MacMullen, *Christianity & Paganism*; Ramsay MacMullen, *The Second Church, Popular Christianity, A.D. 200–400* (Atlanta, 2009). For the subsequent historical period, see Valerie I. J. Flint, *The Rise of Magic in Early Medieval Europe* (Princeton, NJ, 1991); James Russell, *The Germanization of Early Medieval Christianity: A Sociohistorical Approach to Religious Transformation* (Oxford, 1996); Bernadette Filotas, *Pagan Survivals, Superstitions and Popular Cultures in Early Medieval Pastoral Literature* (Toronto, 2005).

through the enclosing sarcophagus to the head of the corpse down below, who thus could participate in the festivities personally.[11] The dead were said to be thirsty, and offering drink to them was an act of piety on the part of their descendants. Augustine of Hippo explicitly noted this process of transfer of older traditions into the church, noting that earlier generations of Christian evangelists had permitted converts to maintain their ancestral customs, including lavish funerary parties on the death anniversaries of the saints: "Our forebears either tolerated or did not dare to forbid the excesses of an unthinking people . . . [and] thought it best to make a concession for the time being to [pagan converts'] weakness and to permit them to celebrate, instead of the feasts they had renounced, other feasts in honor of the holy martyrs—not with the same sacrilege, but with the same elaborateness [*luxus*]."[12] Augustine deplored this approach to conversion, believing that it had introduced vulgar, materialist customs into what should be the spiritual purity of the Christian community.[13] Decades later Caesarius of Arles (ca. 468–542) made a similar complaint about "the wretches who dance and caper about before the churches of the saints . . . [they] appear during Church to be Christians, yet they leave as pagans, for that custom of dancing still is with us from pagan ritual."[14]

It appears that Christians buried and commemorated the martyrs much like other dead folk. The Christian cult of the martyrs was among the most

---

11. Victor Saxer, *Morts, martyrs, reliques en Afrique Chrétienne aux premiers siècles: Les temoignages de Tertullien, Cyprien, et Augustin à la lumière de l'archéologie africaine* (Paris, 1980); Umberto Fasola, "Un tardo cimitero cristiano inserito in una necropoli pagana della via Appia," *Rivista di archeologia cristiana* 60, no. 2 (1984): 7–42, plus tavola 1 (site plan). Photographs of Christian funerary *mensae* are reproduced in Noël Duval, "Bréves observations sur l'usage des *Mensae* funéraires dans l'Illyricum," *Rivista di archeologia cristiana* 60, no. 2 (1984): 259–75. See also MacMullen, *The Second Church* and *Christianity & Paganism*, passim; Michel Lauwers, *Naissance du cimitière: Lieux sacrée et terres des morts dans l'Occident medieval* (Paris, 2005).

12. Augustine, Epistle 29.8ff., quoted in translation in Macmullen, *Christianity & Paganism*, 114–15.

13. However, as Peter Brown has pointed out, Augustine likely was incorrect in this perception. By his time these practices had a long history of acceptance within Christian communities without being considered cryptopaganism. Likewise, there is little evidence for mass conversions in a brief space of time, which might have forced accommodations with older customs as Augustine implies. To take the example of the saint's own town of Hippo, the archaeological record offers "no support for Augustine's picture of the expansion of the Christian congregations." Absent the pressures of large-scale conversions all at once, then, it seems that earlier generations of Christian leadership simply failed to see any cause for concern about the adoption of such feasts and celebrations. It was, rather, Augustine who was the innovator, attempting to bring Christian communities around to a more abstemious standard of behavior. Peter Brown, *The Cult of the Saints: Its Rise and Function in Latin Christianity* (Chicago, 1981), 29.

14. Caesarius of Arles, Sermon 13:4, quoted in translation in MacMullen, *Christianizing the Roman Empire*, 74–75.

ancient traditions of the church, going back to the book of Revelation. The latter text likely was inspired, in part, by the memory of Nero's persecution of the Roman Christian community in 64; it promoted martyrdom over civic conformity, depicting special rewards for those who were "beheaded for their testimony" (Rev. 20:4). At the center of the new religion, then, were deeply interlinked ideas about death, voluntary self-sacrifice, and immortal life. And indeed, Christians early achieved a reputation among the surrounding pagan society for their striking "contempt of death . . . [which] is patent to us every day," in the words of the second-century physician Galen.[15] The contemporary essayist Lucian explained why: "the poor wretches have convinced themselves that they will be absolutely immortal and live for ever; and in consideration of this they despise death and commonly offer themselves of their own accord [for martyrdom]."[16] What differed was the degree of attention the martyrs' burial sites came to receive: the sepulchers of the saints became a shared, quasi-public space for gatherings of the Christian community. Congregants went out from the cities to gather at suburban cemeteries in order to retell the violent passion stories of the martyrs at the sites of their tortured remains, to make offerings and pour out prayers in their presence, to eat meals and share the Eucharist above their gravesites. In short the sepulchers of the saints soon evolved into a network of gathering points for the Christian community, fulfilling social and religious functions unknown to purely private, familial gravesites.[17] Ultimately the relics of the saints—from the Latin *reliquiae*, "things left behind"—constitute one of the most significant types of object to receive the veneration of the faithful, second only to the celebration of the altar. The symbolic terrain of early Christianity was a grid of graves.

After Christianity gained official status within the Roman Empire in the fourth century, these suburban tomb-shrines grew in grandeur and prestige, eventually becoming new city centers in themselves. The remains of saints became sanctifiers of place, guarantors of the holiness of particular buildings and the grounds attached to them.[18] At the same time, however, the remains of the martyrs were exhumed and relocated with increasing frequency—"translated" is the official term—to new locations, often being installed in chapels and churches within the city confines. The cult of relics,

---

15. Ramsay MacMullen and Eugene N. Lane, *Paganism and Christianity, 100–425 C.E.: A Sourcebook* (Minneapolis, 1992), 168.
16. Ibid., 167.
17. Brown, *Cult of the Saints*, 23–24; Robert Bartlett, *Why Can the Dead Do Such Great Things? Saints and Worshippers from the Martyrs to the Reformation* (Princeton, NJ, 2013), 621–22.
18. Lauwers, *Naissance du cimitière*, 56.

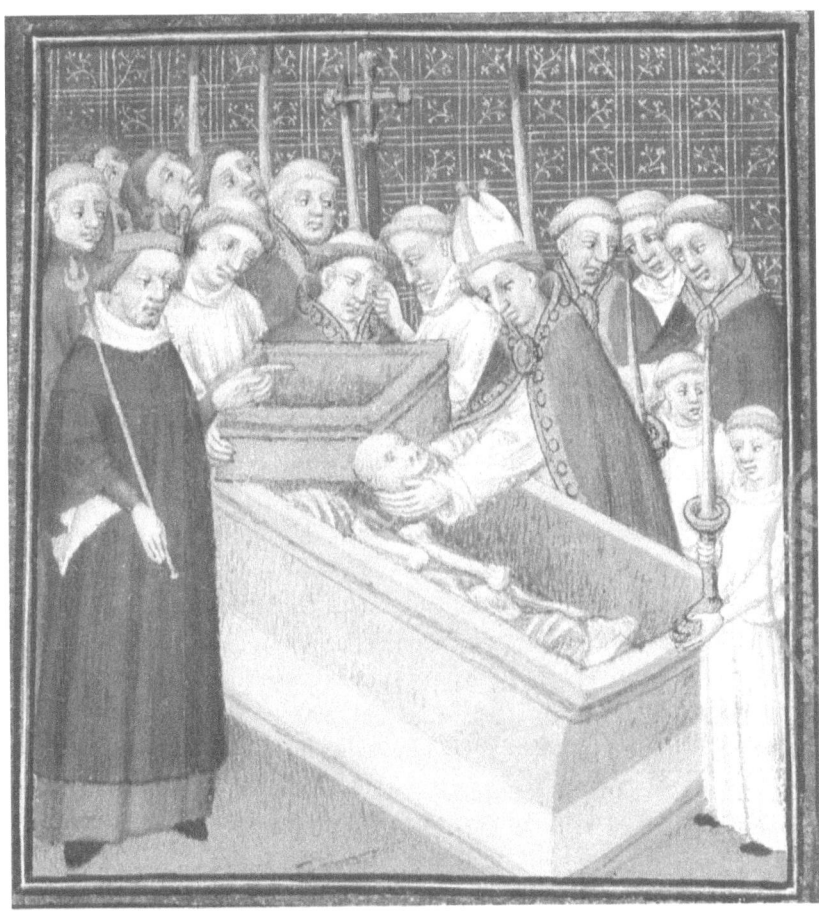

FIGURE 1.3. The exhumation of the bones of King Louis IX of France for his canonization. The veneration of relics in medieval Europe was persistent and widespread. Scenes such as this one would have recurred throughout the period. Miniature, fifteenth century. Bibliothèque Mazarine, Paris; no catalog information available.
CCI / The Art Archive at Art Resource, NY.

always a defining feature of Christianity, flourished. From the fourth century onward, and throughout the Middle Ages, whole bodies as well as bones, teeth, and other fragments of saints' holy bodies circulated as objects of pious transfer and trade.[19] Larger portions of bodies were subdivided in order to create more holy objects; saints were exhumed upon canonization and their bones or bodies placed on display. The scene portrayed in figure 1.3, showing

---

19. Patrick Geary, "The Ninth-Century Relic Trade—A Response to Popular Piety?" and "Sacred Commodities: The Circulation of Medieval Relics," both in *Living with the Dead in the Middle Ages* (Ithaca, NY, 1994), 177–93 and 194–220, respectively.

the exhumation of the bones of Saint Louis of France, exemplifies a type of pious event that was enacted continuously from Late Antiquity through the end of the Middle Ages. The saint's sepulcher lies open and surrounded by a crowd of candle-bearing prelates and aristocrats, who look on as a bishop gently lifts out the skull of the dead saint, gazing reverently into its eye sockets. Saints' cadavers were among the holiest objects on earth.

Early on, the custom of placing relics inside altars grew increasingly common, thus twinning the imagery of corporeal self-sacrifice both above and below the table of God.[20] And once relics were acquired, their installation in a chapel could be a grand affair, replete with ceremonies of inclusion in special sepulchers or precious boxes, sacral processions with holy cadavers winding through the urban cityscape, and public readings of passion narratives filled with gruesome details to edify the faithful. In 401 the Sixth Council of Carthage prescribed the destruction of altars that did not contain relics; by the time of the Second Council of Nicaea in 787, bishops who consecrated altars without relics were to be deposed.[21] Thus the core Christian ritual, the Eucharist, commemorated the violent death of Jesus through a sharing of his fragmented body, and the central action of this rite took place upon an altar that was a tomb. Death was central to Christianity in ways that transcend the symbolic to embrace the literal.

Meanwhile, Christian families increasingly sought to bury their own dead as close as possible to the relics of the saints. The practice, known as burial *ad sanctos*, was predicated upon the notion that proximity to the saintly dead would provide an advantage for the ordinary dead at the Day of Judgment. By the third century, funerary rites and the precise locations and conditions of burial became central to Christian identity.[22] Believers took increasingly elaborate—and competitive—steps to protect the afterlife fates of themselves and their loved ones, expending vast sums of wealth in the process. They endowed lavish tombs and chapels, commissioned costly reliquaries for the saints, and fostered a new ethos in which worldly wealth might be used to advance otherworldly salvation.

Yet Christians' impulse to honor the corpses of their dead was deeply in conflict with the values of the surrounding pagan society. To bring the dead into the daily places of the living was a thing foreign to the classical pagan

---

20. Lauwers, *Naissance du cimitière*, 57.

21. Lauwers, *Naissance du cimitière*, 59; H. Schroeder, trans., *Disciplinary Decrees of the General Councils: Text, Translation and Commentary* (St. Louis, 1937), 148.

22. Peter Brown, *The Ransom of the Soul: Afterlife and Wealth in Early Western Christianity* (Cambridge, MA, 2015).

imagination, for corpses were putrid and unclean. Christians now routinely violated this deeply rooted taboo; the pagan perspective has been aptly presented by Peter Brown as the "full charnel horror of the rise of Christianity." Repulsed by the attention given to the cadavers of the saints, the last pagan emperor Julian complained, "You have filled the whole world with tombs and sepulchers!" He likewise responded to processions of the martyrs' relics with appalled disbelief: "[They carry] corpses of the dead through a great assembly of people, in the midst of dense crowds, staining the eyesight of all with ill-omened sights of the dead."[23] His contemporary Eunapius of Sardis likewise observed the Christians' propensity for "collecting the bones and skulls of those who had been condemned for many crimes" and then "defiling themselves at their tombs."[24] He further notes that these criminals were given a special name, "martyrs," by Christian believers and that they were thought to convey prayers to the deity. In fact, the martyrs' fervent embrace of death in testimony to their faith was cathected through violence, not diminished by it.

An important aspect of Christian devotion to the saints was the sense that relics were imbued with the very presence of the holy man or woman.[25] To pray to a saint's body, to kiss or to touch a relic, rendered the supernatural tangible. Relics were the embodied presence of the saint, even after death; it was this quality that made them special and different from other corpses. And it was this that made them powerful. Christians early on found comfort in adopting saints as friends and patrons, making them the most universally accessible point of entry for supernatural contact. The relics of the saints were said to smell sweet and to resist decay, an indicator of their continuing vitality beyond the threshold of death. Likewise, they possessed consciousness: relics heard the orisons of faithful; they expressed their will in various ways, gave blessings, and occasionally cursed the reprobate. Thus the souls of the martyrs often were imagined both as present in their relics and as simultaneously existing in the presence of God.

But let us shift our focus now to the vast anonymous mass of the ordinary dead. The remainder of this chapter sets forth some of the dominant paradigms for thinking about death and afterlife advanced in the patristic era. As we shall see, the viewpoints put forward can broadly be sifted into two dominant paradigms: death as event versus death as process. I examine each in turn.

---

23. Both quotes in Brown, *Cult of the Saints*, 7. For a respectful critique of some of Brown's positions, see Charles Pietri, "Les origines du culte des martyrs (d'après un ouvrage récent)," *Rivista di archeologia cristiana* 60, no. 2 (1984): 293–320.

24. Bartlett, *Why Can the Dead Do Such Great Things?*, 623.

25. Brown, *Cult of the Saints*, chap. 5, 86–127.

Toward a Christian Thanatology: Tertullian and Augustine

In the early third century the North African theologian Tertullian composed a short treatise titled *Liber de anima* (*Book on the Soul*).[26] A considerable portion of this work is dedicated, unsurprisingly, to mortality. As the first major Latin theologian, Tertullian's influence on medieval thought was significant. While he was not as widely referenced in the Middle Ages as some other patristic writers, he was known, and he was an important touchstone for thinkers who *were* very widely cited, like his later compatriot Aurelius Augustinus, bishop of Hippo. Both men spent much of their lives in the area around Carthage in North Africa, a center of fervent Christian piety known to scholars as the "Bible Belt of the Mediterranean."[27] Both thinkers also favored a kind of elegant facility and clarity in matters of mortality. The following pages are dedicated to unpacking the ways in which these two formative Christian thinkers imagined death and the otherworld.

Little is known about the life of Tertullian. He likely was born into a pagan family around 160 CE, adopted Christianity around 198, and may have died around 225. From the much later vantage point of the fourth century, Jerome reports that Tertullian's father was a proconsular centurion and that he himself became a presbyter; the fourth-century church historian Eusebius adds that he was learned in law. However, the late provenance of all these statements casts doubt upon their reliability, leaving us little firm data about Tertullian's background. We do not know why he converted, only that he considered this event to be a transformative and definitive break with his earlier life. We know that Tertullian married and that around 206, he became interested in a form of Christianity known as the "New Prophecy," a group that considered the process of Christian revelation to be open and ongoing.[28] Scholars are divided as to how deeply and for how long Tertullian was committed to the New Prophecy, which also is known as Montanism. While some suggest he wholly embraced the movement, others argue that he never left the orthodox church, merely incorporating some Montanist viewpoints where he found them compelling. Whatever the case may be, Tertullian's writings nonetheless attained a very high degree of prestige. He became the first significant theologian of the Latin church, penning thirty-one surviving

---

26. Timothy Barnes, *Tertullian: A Historical and Literary Study* (Oxford, 1985); David White, *Tertullian the African: An Anthropological Reading of Tertullian's Context and Identities* (Berlin, 2007). Cf. also Saxer, *Morts, martyrs, reliques*.

27. Paula Fredriksen, "Tyconius and Augustine on the Apocalypse," in *The Apocalypse in the Middle Ages*, ed. Richard K. Emmerson and Bernard McGinn (Ithaca, NY, 1992), 21.

28. Christine Trevett, *Montanism: Gender, Authority, and the New Prophecy* (Cambridge, 2002).

treatises, as well as others, now lost.[29] His thought was to be formative for many early theological and practical debates within the emerging church, which was still actively developing doctrines and an institutional hierarchy at this time.

The North African convert is one of our best early sources for Christian attitudes in the Latin West during one of the early persecutions, in North Africa ca. 202–3. Tertullian surely heard a great deal about the deaths of the martyrs Perpetua and other Christians in 203 in the arena in Carthage; certainly, he was aware of their execution and of Perpetua's reputation as a seer, for he mentioned both her martyrdom and her visions of paradise in his *Book on the Soul*. He argues that the souls of the martyrs, uniquely, enter paradise directly after death, concluding with the counsel, "The sole key to unlock paradise is your own life's blood."[30] Thus violent death is presented as a path to immediate salvation. Yet, from another perspective, he argues that *all* deaths are violent: since Adam and Eve were created as immortals, the introduction of death into the world was an abrogation of humanity's natural state. Since body and soul were formed and grew together in the womb as in the world, the intimacy and interdependence of their bond was deeper than any other form of human relationship. Death's severing of their connection, then, could only be an unnatural and invasive event; this accounts for its intrinsic sense of violation.

For Tertullian mortality was simple to define: the subtraction of the soul from the body. Death was a highly circumscribed, discrete event. He argued vigorously against any conceptualization of death as gradual or of the body as possessing any vital capacities in its own right. The latter ideas were widespread in the ancient world, but Tertullian wished to craft a definition of mortality that was more closely informed by a Christian anthropology, predicated upon the union of a purely spiritual soul-self enlivening a corporeal shell. Thus, it is important to note that Tertullian's work on the soul is not an ossified treatise describing a consensus viewpoint, but an emergent polemic actively engaged in debate with a pagan worldview that was still alive—indeed, dominant and vigorous—in his day. Thus he adopted a somewhat confrontational tone in setting forth his own ideas, in contrast to the prevailing assumptions of his contemporaries:

> The operation of death is in essence the separation of body and soul. Some, however . . . choose to believe that some souls cleave to the body

---

29. Barnes, *Tertullian*, 55.
30. *LA*, col. 745.

> even postmortem. Indeed, to support this idea Plato . . . tells about the unburied cadaver of a certain person that was preserved a long time without any decay because the soul was not divided from the body. Likewise Democritus observes the growth of the nails and hair in the grave for a considerable time. . . . But not even a little bit of the soul can possibly remain inside a [dead] body, which is itself destined to disappear. . . . Death, if it is not complete, is not death; if any part of the soul remains, it is life. Death will no more mix with life than will night with day.[31]

There could be no partial death, no gradual death, no interim term between vitality and mortality. Tertullian's instinctual approach, throughout his discussions, was to reduce complexities and to prune back extra categories, arguing that death was a simple binary term opposed to life. Death was a bounded event; there was no need to pile on further abstractions and set forth types of deaths or processes of mortality.

In keeping with this preference the African father rejected the contemporary distinction, widespread in Mediterranean cultures, between natural and violent deaths. This was a false dichotomy, argued Tertullian; all deaths inherently are violent because all violate the original integral condition of the self, conceived in the womb as a union of body and soul. Moreover, all deaths go against the original prelapsarian design of humankind as a union of soul and body: to fracture this unity, to perish, is inherently a violent event, no matter what the circumstances. Once again, Tertullian's argument was framed against contemporary opinions:

> Setting aside the question of fate or chance, the operation of death, that is the separation of flesh and soul, has been divided into two types in human thought: ordinary and extraordinary. A person who has an ordinary death goes gently and according to nature; an extraordinary death is seen as going against nature, such as cases of violent death. But we, who know about the first man: we boldly assert that death is *not* the natural destiny of men, but that it arises from sin and is unnatural. . . . If man had been created mortal, then of course death would be part of human nature. . . . [But] if [humanity] had not transgressed then humans would never have died. . . . A thing cannot be considered natural if it came about through the exercise of free choice, rather than from established governing laws or from necessity. In short: even though there are as many ways to die as there

---

31. *LA*, cols. 736–38.

are a variety of kinds and causes, we affirm that no death is so gentle as to be without violence. The very fact of death is, simply stated, a form of violence.[32]

Since death by definition rends the soul-body unity of the human person, it is an inherently violent subversion of personal integrity. Thus it followed for Tertullian that even a tranquil expiry—aged, at home, and in bed—was violent. No death ever occurs in gentle increments; it is always a discrete event, contingent upon that one final moment that fractures the unity of body and soul:

> A rapid death such as decapitation lays open all at once a wide outlet for the soul . . . nor does a death like this painfully linger moment by moment. However, in the case of a slow death, the soul withdraws from each member bit by bit. And yet the soul is not, in such a case, divided up, but withdrawn; and the withdrawal may only be regarded as complete when it goes out from the final part.[33]

Paradoxically, even as Tertullian stressed the agony that always was inherent in shedding the mortal coil, he also utilized the peaceful simile of slumber as an image of death. He sees sleep as a figura for death: the dead who await resurrection are merely slumbering. In life, sleep is a daily reminder of the kind of state the body will experience after the soul withdraws:

> [God] uses images and shadows to assist us. . . . He therefore shows you the human body overtaken by the friendly power of sleep, lying down with a sweet need for rest and remaining immobile . . . just as it will lie down postmortem. . . . And just as the body awakens after its rest is done, shakes off its slumber, so this affirms the resurrection of the dead for you. . . . If only you would see [sleep] as the image of death, you would grow in faith, you would meditate upon hope, you would learn both how to die and how to live, and how to be awake while you sleep.[34]

Thus on the one hand, death is against nature, something violent and alien that deprives one and all of joy and pleasure; on the other hand, it is likened to sleep, which is kindly, friendly. This seeming enigma both acknowledges fear and offers hope; as Tertullian concludes, it undergirded Christian attitudes toward life, death, and ultimately, resurrection.

---

32. *LA*, cols. 738–39.
33. *LA*, cols. 740–41.
34. *LA*, cols. 723–24.

If Tertullian was the earliest Christian theologian to define death thusly, his later compatriot Augustine was to be the most prestigious and widely read disseminator of this idea. Born in 354 (about 120 years after Tertullian's death) Aurelius Augustinus also came from the area around Carthage. He was the product of a mixed marriage between a Christian woman and a pagan father but was raised in the faith of his mother. Yet Augustine fell away from the church for much of his youth, finding the simple piety of his unlearned mother unchallenging, and searching for intellectual and spiritual fulfillment in philosophy and non-Christian religious systems—notably, Manicheeism, a dualistic religion widespread in the ancient Mediterranean as well as throughout Asia. In his early thirties, Augustine reconverted to Christianity, ultimately becoming the most important theologian in the early Christian church. He died in 430, after authoring an autobiography, the *Confessions*, numerous short letters and treatises, and his masterwork, a broad compendium of Christian doctrine and theological history titled *The City of God against the Pagans*.

Like Tertullian before him, Augustine utterly rejected the thought that death might be a process or that there existed any transitional state between life and death that somehow partook of the qualities of both. In *The City of God against the Pagans*, Augustine discusses this question in book 13, chapter 11. The chapter is titled "Whether someone can be living and dead at the same time?" Augustine begins on an irritable note, complaining, "It is quite absurd that a person, before he dies, is said to be 'in death' . . . particularly since it is the height of insolence to suggest that one can be called living and dying at the same time. It is the same as the fact that one cannot be simultaneously asleep and awake."[35] A body cannot be animate and defunct at one and the same time. There can be no form of partial or gradual death: vitality and mortality are dichotomous, diametrically opposed states of being that cannot coexist within a single organism. Indeed, the bishop of Hippo continued, building upon Tertullian's core argument, the actual moment of death was so infinitesimal as to be nearly nonexistent. Though one might speak of a "dying person," the *dying* nevertheless were *living*.

> So the question must be posed as to when a person is "dying." For, before death will have come the person is not dying but living. But when death arrives, then the person is dead and not dying. The first case is pre-death and the second, post-death. So, when is a person in

---

35. Aurelius Augustinus [Augustine of Hippo], *The City of God against the Pagans*, 7 vols., Loeb Classical Library 411–17 (Cambridge, 1966), 4:166–68. My translation from the Latin.

the state of death itself? That is to say, when is a person dying? For we have three terms: pre-death, in death, and post-death; and these can be correlated to three states: living, dying, and dead. It is very difficult to define when someone is dying, for while in death one is neither alive (the state pre-death), nor dead (the state post-death), but actively dying (the state *of* death).

The fact is, as long as the soul is inside the body, and especially if the person is conscious, then certainly he is alive, for the living state is defined as soul plus body. For this reason such a person is still pre-death, not in death. However, when the soul is cut off and steals away with all the bodily senses, then the person is already post-death and referred to as dead.[36]

The expiring body yet remains alive up until the very instant of its transmutation into a corpse. Thus the human being always is in a premortem or a postmortem state; there is no way to identify the event of dying as a third term in this binary. And since one cannot be alive and dead at the same time, then the moment of death itself is so instantaneous as to be impossible to distinguish; it would seem almost not to exist. Yet of course, death not only exists but is of profound significance, for in this mere flash or glimmer of time, this unmeasurable flicker, the person passes forever to the otherworld.[37]

Augustine and Tertullian on Postmortem Return

Augustine and Tertullian also addressed questions about whether the dead might bridge the gap between the otherworld and this one. Wandering shades of the dead were common presences throughout the ancient world; indeed, classical pagan cultures took for granted not only that death might be gradual, but that certain individuals among the dead might linger on in some way among the living. Reports of encounters with the dead, and apotropaic technologies geared toward warding off any harm that the dead might inflict, were intrinsic aspects of late antique Mediterranean religious cultures—as indeed, they are of many cultures worldwide.[38] As we have seen, in Tertullian's day many people assumed that the dying only slowly disengaged

---

36. Augustine, *City of God*, 4:168.
37. Cf. Tullio Gregory, "Per una fenomenologia del cadavere: Dai mondi dell'immaginario ai paradise della metafisica," and Jackie Pigeaud, "La question du cadavre dans l'antiquité gréco-romaine," in *Il Cadavere / The Corpse*, Micrologus 7 (Turnhout, 1999), 11–42 and 43–72, respectively.
38. Sarah Iles Johnston, *Restless Dead: Encounters between the Living and the Dead in Ancient Greece* (Berkeley, 1999).

from the body, from life, and from the world of the living. The lingering dead could be perceived in various ways: they sometimes were envisaged as corporeal presences (recall the growing nails and hair of a corpse, mentioned by Tertullian); sometimes as insubstantial ghosts or spirits. If a dead person remained present on the worldly plane of existence, classical paganisms usually attributed this either to an untimely, violent death or to a lack of proper funerary rites. Ancient societies tended to be cultures of multiplicity in regard to questions of mortality and postmortem persistence: some people might return after death, in a variety of ways and for a variety of reasons, while others might not return at all. Tertullian and Augustine rejected the possibility of postmortem return. In so doing they were rebutting ideas that had long been held as self-evident truths.

One phenomenon that widely was ascribed to the ghosts of the untimely dead was spirit possession of the living. Tertullian complained that some people argued that the shades of those who die through violence continued to wander the earth until the time appointed for them to die, had they not been untimely ripped from this world. He suggested that this misapprehension arose from the fact that demons sometimes possessed the bodies of the living and then, when exorcised by Christian holy men, pretended to be ghosts of the dead in their "confessions." Tertullian, however, was firm in his insistence that the spirits of the dead had passed on to another dimension, while the possessing spirits that sometimes invade human bodies were fallen angels, rebellious creatures transmuted into demons through a primordial sin of pride. Indeed, Tertullian rejected any belief in ghosts whatsoever. He disbelieved tales of necromancy (including even the biblical story of Saul and Samuel), and he scoffed at rumors of the dead appearing to the living in visions, dreams, or other visitations. He ridiculed any reports that suggested that cadavers of the ordinary dead might grow or change in ways other than normal putrefaction. The dead, Tertullian argued, immediately moved beyond the purview of the living.

Tertullian's comments, while firm, were not particularly systematic. It was left to Augustine to craft a mutually exclusive thanatology and demonology. The bishop of Hippo agreed with Tertullian that death separated the dead from the living and that this gulf between worlds could never be bridged by shades or shadows. There were no evil dead, no possessing shades, no haunting ghosts or necromantic souls. In *De cura pro mortuis gerenda* (*On the Care to Be Taken for the Dead*), Augustine argued that burial rites had no salutary effect upon the souls of the dead at all; they are, rather, purely a solace for the living. As for those who claimed to see apparitions of the dead, Augustine reminded his readers that many people see visions, in dreams, of the living as well, but that this certainly does not mean that those living people are present in the dreamer's room.[39] Likewise, then, in the case of the deceased: a vision of a dead person does not mean that the individual is present. The human imagination can summon to mind many *similitudines*—"likenesses"—that may vividly evoke the presence of someone who is in fact absent, whether through the distance of space or of mortality. Such likenesses or images of the dead originate in the mind of the living individual, coming to consciousness either in dreams, during frenzies, in bouts of madness, in episodic private visions, or else they may, on very rare occasions, be produced by means of angelic mediation.[40] However, according to Augustine these images definitively were not the dead themselves. Those who have perished move wholly beyond this sphere of existence and are unconscious of its worldly vicissitudes. Augustine included a bittersweet personal reflection on the theme:

> It is enough to say this: If the souls of the dead became involved in the affairs of the living, and we in theirs when we see them and converse together with them in dreams, then my faithful mother would never desert me myself for a single night, she who followed me over land and sea in order to live with me. Perish the thought that a happier life has made her so cruel that she would not console her sad son (whom she loved above all others) whenever anything troubled his heart: for she never wished to see me upset.[41]

Readers of the *Confessions* no doubt will quickly recognize the justice of this argument, for Augustine's mother Monica was uncommonly protective of him in life. He concluded,

> If even our relatives desert us, how can they be involved in our cares and affairs? And if our relatives are not involved, then who else among the dead would follow what we do, the things we undergo? . . . Therefore, in the place where the spirits of the dead are, they do not see anything that is done or that occurs in this life.[42]

At the same time that Augustine (like Tertullian before him) rejected apparitions of the ordinary dead, however, he embraced the cult of the martyrs. Thus, while the earliest Latin fathers distanced themselves from the common ancient belief in wandering spirits of the vengeful dead, they

---

39. *CPM*, cols. 600–601.
40. *CPM*, cols. 602–4.
41. *CPM*, col. 604.
42. *CPM*, col. 604.

enshrined veneration of dead saints' relics as important sources of power and spiritual intervention. Both Tertullian and Augustine venerated the cult of their local Carthage martyrs Perpetua and Felicitas, for example, and Augustine accepted the possibility that martyrs might intervene in the life of the living (though he admitted that it escaped his understanding precisely how they did so).

Augustine preferred to think of these interventions as both rare and remote, however. He conceded that healings at the shrines of martyrs did occur. The common practice of shrine incubation at the tomb of a martyr was becoming an increasingly important part of late antique Christian cult devotion, and reports of miraculous healings were widely accepted by clergy and laity alike. Common opinion ascribed the healings that were said to occur in these cases to the direct power of the martyrs themselves, displaying their personal *virtus* through their corporeal remains or relics. Yet Augustine was quick to reinterpret this phenomenon: it is not the dead saints themselves who procure such healings, either through their miraculously preserved corpses or even through their attentive souls. No: though martyrs' relics may be present when healings occur, it is not through their own power that such events transpire. They are, rather, channels for divine power; being dead, they have no power of their own to affect the human condition:

> It is not on this account to be thought that the dead can in any manner involve themselves in the affairs of the living, just because during certain healings or assistances the martyrs were present. Rather it should be understood that the martyrs are involved in the affairs of the living only through divine power; the dead cannot become involved in the affairs of the living in their own right.[43]

Augustine was eager to forestall speculation that such healings might indicate some kind of regular continuing vitality and engagement on the part of the dead. Rather, Augustine argues that even the interventions of the saints only occur through a divine suspension of the normal laws of creation. Even the saints were subject to the laws of death.

In sum, for thinkers like Tertullian and Augustine death was an event, not a process. It was not a drawn-out transition, involving an incremental withdrawal of the soul in pieces; rather, the moment of death was so instantaneous as to be difficult to pinpoint. This glimmer of an instant was nearly nonexistent in its rapidity yet hugely transformative in its effects. And the dead, once departed, are wholly and utterly removed from this worldly

---

43. *CPM*, cols. 606–7.

sphere. The notion that the dead might persist on this plane of existence as active personalities, engaged with the world and able to interact with the living, was anathema to the stringent logic of separation between body and soul, this world and the next, advanced by Tertullian and Augustine. Ghosts were impossible given the line of interpretation presented by these thinkers, for death was an immediate and complete separation. The deceased cannot be sensed by the living, nor make their effects felt in any way. Efforts undertaken by the living on behalf of the dead—prayers, burial rites, alms—do not benefit the departed, but only succor the hearts and consciences of their survivors. The living cannot reach across the void of mortality to assist the dead. Conversely, the dead cannot ordinarily bridge this gulf from their side either. Visions of ghosts and apparitions of dead loved ones are merely likenesses produced by natural or, perhaps, angelic means; they are not really the mourned and longed-for person. The veil between worlds is thick and cannot be thrust open from either side.

Yet, as the suspension of such laws in the case of the martyrs suggests, Christian traditions about the dead were complex. Debates over whether it was relevant how a person died, whether the dead could see the living or the living see the dead, and whether there could be any interaction across worlds were ongoing and to some degree contradictory. This is not the place to trace the persistent influence of this strand of interpretation in any detail, but it is important to note, albeit briefly, that what I shall henceforth term the "Augustinian position" was to become a major touchstone for later generations of medieval writers and thinkers, particularly those working in theological traditions and to some degree in natural philosophy. Intellectuals who wrote theological works primarily for an audience of other intellectuals followed Augustine's and Tertullian's lead. For example, the notion that the dead could never return to this world after death was frequently cited by moralists; as one such writer phrased it, "after death there is no means of gaining merit. . . . Afterwards, there is no possibility of returning to the body or to the world."[44] Likewise, the understudied but important early thirteenth-century theologian and bishop William of Auvergne, examining anecdotal reports of ghosts, firmly sustains the Augustinian ideal. In his *De universo* he writes,

> If [the dead] are in the society of the blessed and sublime spirits, then why would they descend . . . from the joys of blessedness? If, however,

---

44. Vincent of Beauvais, *Speculum morale* (Duaci, 1624; repr. Graz, 1964), II, I: IV, 710–11. The work, while attributed to Vincent of Beauvais, is likely the work of another, pseudonymous thinker.

they are in the infernal prison or the purging fire, then in either case they would seem to be confined and incapable of leaving.[45]

There is no need for an overabundance of citations and examples. The immense prestige of Augustine was sufficient to guarantee the relevance of his ideas for many centuries after his own mortal end. The Augustinian model was a highly influential reading of death for many centuries.

Yet this model was not the singular position of the church; nor did it reign unchallenged. Various countercurrents of opinion continued to be put forward by other thinkers. By the late sixth and early seventh centuries, leading Christian intellectuals were putting forth a view of mortality and afterlife that revisited the core questions of manner of death, connections between the living and the dead, and the possibility of postmortem return. The binary between life and death that Tertullian and Augustine had constructed was frequently ignored in the thought of this later generation of Christian writers, who were living on the cusp of the transition from Late Antiquity to the early medieval period. The two most influential thinkers in this reevaluation were an evangelical pope, Gregory I, "the Great," and a bishop and highly influential natural philosopher, Isidore of Seville. Let us begin with Gregory, the slightly older of this contemporary pair.

Death as Process: The *Dialogues* of Gregory the Great

Born around 540 to a noble Roman family, Gregory grew to adulthood amid disease, violence, and political instability.[46] During the previous century, western Europe had been carved into various smaller kingdoms presided over by Germanic rulers; shortly before Gregory's birth, the emperor Justinian initiated a campaign to regain these western provinces, which formerly had been united under Roman governance. The resulting wars were particularly severely felt in Italy, as Gothic and imperial forces continually clashed. As a young man, Gregory entered public life, holding the office of urban prefect, but by 573 he had turned to a monastic vocation, transforming one of his inherited family properties into a cenobitic foundation. Yet Gregory remained active in the world, representing the church on various diplomatic missions. In 590, he was elected pope, an office he was to hold until his death in 604. It was during this period of his life that Gregory

---

45. WA, 1069.
46. Carole Straw, *Gregory the Great: Perfection in Imperfection* (Berkeley, 1991); R. A. Markus, *Gregory the Great and His World* (Cambridge, 1997).

likely composed his *Dialogues*; though some modern scholars have debated whether this work is genuinely Gregorian, the weight of opinion seems to be in favor of authenticity.[47] In the Middle Ages, Gregory's authorship was not questioned—indeed, the work held a high prestige and was widely referenced, in part because of its papal pedigree.

Gregory the Great may justly be called the father of the Christian ghost story. The fourth book of the *Dialogues*, with its vivid stories of postmortem encounters, demonstrates the consequences of an incomplete separation of the dead from the living. Gregory appears actively to have collected this type of motif: in his *Dialogues* he recounts quite a number. In so doing, Gregory also was inaugurating a new evangelical strategy for the church: he is the first writer in the Christian tradition to use ghost stories as probative tools for Christian teachings about the afterlife. His insightful realization was that ghosts could be an extremely useful tool for proving the core truth-claims of the Christian church: that the soul lived on eternally either in torment or bliss. Thus, far from trying to reject ghosts, as earlier writers had done, Gregory sought out ghosts—Christian ghosts. In baptized form, the old notion of the lingering dead could testify, compellingly and firsthand, to the *real* nature of life after death. Gregory the Great understood, as none before him had done, that the very best proof of Christian cosmology was refugees from the otherworld beyond the grave. Much like the rich man in the Gospel of Luke, who begged for an apparition to visit his surviving family—"if someone from the dead will go to them, they will repent!"—so, too, Gregory intuited that firsthand accounts, drawn from direct, experiential evidence of the afterlife, would be the most compelling argument to those who doubted the otherworldly doctrines of the Christian faith. Testimony from beyond the grave, he sensed, would be an excellent means of rebutting materialist and empiricist objections to the Christian doctrine of the soul's immortality. The pope thus inaugurated a strategy of utilizing ghost stories as evidence to convert skeptics and gentiles, one that would flourish for many centuries, among many different populations. In Gregory's imagination, death could be imagined as partial or processual, and he recounted episodes of return from the dead with relish. Yet, though Gregory and others of his generation imagined mortality in ways that contrasted with their earlier forebears, their conceptualizations were hardly new. In fact, they were very old: these thinkers presumed the continuing relevance of quite ancient notions about mortality and a this-worldly afterlife for the soul. Thus, ideas that Tertullian

---

47. See Markus, *Gregory the Great and His World*, 15–16, for an encapsulation of the debate.

and Augustine had forcefully repudiated lived on nonetheless. By the seventh century, these notions were becoming a canonical part of Christian tradition. Ultimately, they provided an alternative model for the mortal imaginary.

The *Dialogues* fulfills its title: the book is composed as a conversation between two men. It pulses back and forth between the poles of empiricism (voiced by Peter, the skeptical interlocutor) and faith (represented by Gregory himself, the respondent). The question of death and how to define it arises early in book 4. Peter begins the conversation by commenting that he has never seen a soul, even though he specifically has looked for them at opportune moments. For this reason, he doubts its existence:

> PETER: It happened once that I was present when a brother died. Suddenly, while he was talking, the vital breath went out. He had just been speaking to me and then I saw he was dead. But I did not see whether his soul went out or not. It seems very hard to believe in something that no one can see.
>
> GREGORY: Why marvel, Peter, if you did not see the soul coming out? . . . The nature of the soul is invisible; therefore it departs invisibly from the body.[48]

Peter's starkly empiricist and rationalist stance demands visible proof of the soul's existence; we will see this attitude recur in later times. Though Gregory concedes that the soul itself normally remains invisible to the human eye, he goes on to argue that the soul's effects may readily be identified, providing clear evidence for its existence. More specifically, Gregory argues that the presence of a soul inside a living person, and its departure at death, may logically be inferred from the changes that occur in the human body when it perishes. He suggests that the inertness of a cadaver constitutes visible proof of the invisible soul: the quietude of a corpse after death demonstrates that human life depends upon a vital force that animates the living body. When this entity departs the individual loses all sense, vital functions cease, and the body collapses and falls still. There must, then, be some animating principle, and this force or entity we call the soul.

Peter concedes the merit of this argument, yet still he hesitates concerning the principle that this animating entity, the soul, necessarily lives on after the death of the body. As he points out, something called "soul" may indeed vivify the flesh, and it may well cause death by exiting the corporeal shell. Yet this does not prove that the soul itself does not perish at the same moment of separation. Thus Peter demands further proofs: of the soul's eternality and

---

48. GrGr, col. 328.

of the existence of the otherworld. "All this is rightly said," Peter stubbornly reiterates, "but the mind refuses to believe in something that cannot be seen with the bodily eyes."[49] The invisible must be made evident and sensible in order for Peter to believe in it.

Having thus far failed to dissuade Peter from his materialism vis-à-vis the soul, Gregory shifts tactics, employing ghost stories to counter Peter's skepticism. In the next several chapters of the work Gregory shares tales of those who witnessed what Peter himself did not: souls exiting the body in visible form at the moment of death. These are, in essence, fleeting ghosts who immediately fly off to their destined afterlife. He declares that certain individuals with a high level of faith and purity have, through assiduous prayer, gained the power to witness the transits of souls, though they normally remain invisible to others. For instance: Saint Benedict saw, from a distance, the soul of Bishop Germanus shoot heavenward as a fiery globe;[50] several other saintly individuals beheld the ghosts of holy persons leaving their bodies as well.[51] Another witnessed a dove fly from the mouth of a holy companion at the moment of decease,[52] and an innocent child saw saints from heaven arrive in a blaze of light to retrieve the soul of the bishop of Reati.[53] In one case, the souls of two monks martyred by the invading Lombards lingered near their bodies for some time after death. The monks' souls, though invisible, were heard to sing sweetly from amid the branches of the tree upon which their bodies were hung.[54] Other accounts offered by Gregory focus on angelic presences, sweet smells, blazing lights, heavenly melodies, and other indications of celestial welcome extended to the saintly at the moment of their passing.

After Gregory concludes his lengthy discourse on the deaths and rewards of the just, Peter finally pronounces himself satisfied: he concedes the existence of the soul, its persistence beyond the death of the body, and the rewards of blessed souls in heaven. He even volunteers, spontaneously, that since logic demands moral balance in the afterlife, there must be a place of punishment for sinners just as there is a place of delight for the saintly. Yet, Peter confesses, he still finds it difficult to conceive of hell very clearly: How can a disembodied soul be tormented by material fire and other discomforts? Would Gregory care to provide some enlightening aperçus about the retributive

---

49. GrGr, col. 329.
50. GrGr, col. 332.
51. GrGr, cols. 332–33.
52. GrGr, col. 336.
53. GrGr, col. 340.
54. GrGr, col. 353.

afterlife for which sinners are destined?[55] Gregory, of course, obliges. The subsequent portions of the *Dialogues* contain the most vivid of Gregory's stories about return from the dead.

These tales of postmortem return may be sorted into a taxonomy of three types that become progressively more individualized and localized. First, Gregory recounts a handful of anecdotes about people who died temporarily and then returned to life. The afterlife in this group of tales is portrayed as a vast otherworldly bureaucracy that swallows up huge numbers of souls and assigns them punishments appropriate to their sins. As with any vast institutional system, the administrators of hell occasionally make mistakes. For example, Gregory tells of a man named Stephen who visited the infernal realms but was returned to his body when the managerial class of hell realized that there had been a mix-up: a different Stephen had been the one slated to die that day.[56] Stephen and other protagonists of this motif type are framed as living individuals who are able to give first-person accounts of the reality of hell and the terrors of its punishments. This relatively simple type of story is a topos with a lengthy literary history. Stories involving the temporary death of a person, who thereby garners a tour of the afterlife during the period he lies dead, begin with the Apocalypse of Peter, dating from the early second century, and continue with unabated vigor through Dante and beyond.[57]

Moving on to the next category of story, we find some portrayals of a highly localized afterlife: Mount Etna in Sicily. In two lengthy narratives, unrepentant souls are seen to enter into the tartarean flames of this volcano at their deaths. Thus the flames of Etna provide a material, this-worldly access point to the spiritual realm of hell. In the first story, Gregory relates how some sailors once stopped at the island of Lipari, off Sicily, and there encountered an isolated hermit. To their surprise, the man informed them that King Theodoric of the Ostrogoths had just died. Startled, the sailors responded that Theodoric had been alive when they left the mainland; how could news of his death have traveled to this remote place ahead of them? The hermit responded, "He is indeed dead. For yesterday at the ninth hour Theodoric was led here. . . . shoeless and belt-less and with his hands bound together, he was thrown into Vulcan's cone [*olla*]."[58] The king was thrown into the

---

55. GrGr, col. 365.
56. GrGr, cols. 381–85; tales with a similar moral are told in the next two chapters as well.
57. Jacques Le Goff, *The Birth of Purgatory*, trans. Arthur Goldhammer (Chicago, 1984); Carol Zaleski, *Otherworld Journeys: Accounts of Near-Death Experience in Medieval and Modern Times* (New York, 1988). A compilation of texts, including the Apocalypse of Peter, is translated in Eileen Gardiner, ed., *Visions of Heaven and Hell before Dante* (New York, 1989).
58. GrGr, col. 369.

volcano, the hermit further explained, by two of his victims, righteous men whom he had killed and who now appeared from beyond the grave in order to conduct their nemesis to his punishment. In the original Latin, the chief meanings of the unusual word Gregory chooses to designate the interior of Etna—*olla*—cement this vision of the volcano as a place of fiery postmortem torment. *Olla* is not normally a term used to designate the cone of a volcano; rather, the term's most common Latin meaning is a clay cooking-vessel or pot. This usage aptly suggests that Theodoric is about to be cooked or roasted in a fiery volcanic afterlife. A second meaning of the word is a funerary urn, thereby compacting the future fate of Theodoric into a single term: he will be roasted, cremated, entombed as ashes in an urn for eternity.

A few chapters later, Gregory explains more about the link between hell and Etna. He recounts the last moments of a young man who, lying upon his deathbed, saw a vision of a great ghostly ship arriving, ready to transport him and a neighbor to Sicily. He therefore sent a messenger to summon the neighbor to board the ship with him, but as the messenger was en route between the homes, both his young master and the neighbor perished at the same instant. Though the story is presented by the character of Gregory as self-evidently intelligible, Peter nonetheless voices some obvious questions: Why a ship? And why Sicily? Gregory explains that though the disembodied soul does not actually require a material vehicle in order to travel, when it is still in the body it is unable to conceive of such spiritual transport and thus imagines that its journey will take place through a material conveyance. As for the destination, Gregory comments,

> As for why he said that he was to be led to Sicily, what else can be meant, except that in certain places in the geography of that land, volcano cones [*ollae*] lie open and spew forth the flames of torment? . . . Omnipotent God wished to display these places in this world as a rebuke to the living, so that the minds of the faithless who do not believe in the torments of Hell might *see* the places of torment that they refused to credit by oral reports.[59]

This identification of the afterlife with this-worldly topographical features, most particularly with isolated volcanic mountains, was not culturally new. However Gregory was the first major thinker to bring it into Christian tradition. It is likely that the association of mountains with the places of the afterlife had been brought to Italy by Germanic peoples like the Goths, from whom King Theodoric had sprung. Eventually the association between

---

59. GrGr, col. 380.

mountains and either hell or purgatory was to become a common theme in Christian visionary literature, most spectacularly in the case of Dante's *Divine Comedy*. And though nothing in scripture associates the afterlife specifically with mountains, the "lake of fire" that figures prominently in the book of Revelation (19:20; 20:10, 14–15; 21:8) would seem to be aptly embodied by the liquid lava visible at the opening of a volcano. Of course, mountains figure in the sacred topographies of both Judaism and Christianity, most often as the setting for significant moments of revelation of the Godhead, from Yahweh's appearance as a burning bush on Mount Horeb (Exod. 3) and revelation of the Ten Commandments on Mount Sinai (Exod. 10), to Jesus' most lengthy teaching, the Sermon on the Mount (Matt. 5–7) and his ascent to heaven after his Resurrection from the Mount of Olives (Acts 1:9–12).

Most importantly, the lesson to be drawn from the two Etna tales is that the realms of death and of life overlap. The otherworld occupies the same spatial plane as this world and this life; thus the strict boundaries and separations that thinkers such as Tertullian and Augustine had attempted to erect between life and death were eroded in the thought of Gregory the Great. This is most particularly the case in the last type of motif to be considered here, one in which the veil between worlds was lifted entirely. In this final type of story, Gregory tells of shades who return to the places of their former existence in order to undergo torment on the surface of the earth. Here, hell becomes coterminous with the dimensional plane of the living. These dead folk are punished with individualized torments in places that are frequented by the living: the public baths. Significantly, such presences were conceived as corporeal revenants in Gregory's tales: able to grasp, talk, and interact with the living in a fully material manner. Differences between the living and the dead are thus muted; the deceased act and speak just as the living do, and it literally is impossible to tell the difference between them until the dead ones themselves confess their postmortem status. They recount their sins and the manners of their expiries; they explain that they are conducting penance in the here and now, through material means. These tales are the most individualized and localized of all; rather than revealing a vast otherworld teeming with thousands of anonymous souls, these revenants conform to the "classic" ghost story type of this-worldly presences who haunt the places of their former lives.

The relevant anecdotes occur in chapter 40, where Gregory recounts the case of a certain Paschasius the Deacon, and in chapter 55, which treats of an unnamed sinner. Paschasius was to all appearances a good and holy man: author of a treatise on the Holy Spirit, abstemious in personal habits, a generous almsgiver and humble lover of the poor. He was even credited with a miraculous healing: after his death, while his body lay publicly upon a bier, a demoniac was healed by the touch of his garment. Yet, some time after Paschasius's death the bishop of Capua, Germanus, was astonished to encounter him, moving and speaking and acting for all the world like a living person. While visiting a hot spa, the bishop found himself being waited upon by Paschasius, whom he had known in life and instantly recognized. "Seeing him, he was struck with abject terror."[60] Inevitably, however, curiosity overcame fear and Germanus began to converse with Paschasius, asking how and why he came to be a spa attendant after his death. Paschasius explained that he obstinately had preferred the antipope Lawrence over the true pope Symmachus. "But I beg you," Paschasius continued, "pray to God on my behalf; you will know that your prayers have been heard if when you return here, you do not find me."[61] Moved by compassion for this dead man forced to serve as a lowly body servant in the hot pools, Germanus fulfilled his request and, returning, found the deacon gone. Comments Gregory, since Paschasius had sinned out of ignorance rather than malice, he was permitted to purge himself after death and to benefit from the offerings of others. Thus the story, though putatively concerned with the postmortem punishments of hell, anticipates the doctrine of purgatory.

A second, similar tale concerns a priest who was accustomed to go to the baths, and who was waited upon by the same body servant each time he visited. The man tended his needs with great care, watching his shoes and clothes, proffering a towel to him as he exited the hot pool, and helping him re-dress. After a number of visits, the priest decided to reward this faithful bath valet with a gift, bringing two loaves of consecrated bread as a reward. Yet the loaves were mournfully refused with these words: "Why do you give these to me, Father? This is holy bread, and I am unable to eat it."[62] The servant then revealed that he was, in fact, deceased: "Behold, I formerly was the manager of this place, but for my sins I have been sent here after my death. If, however, you wish to give me a gift, then offer this bread to omnipotent God on my behalf, in order that you might thus intercede for my sins."[63] Though unable to eat the holy bread—the verb utilized, *manducare*, has the literal sense of "to chew"—the dead man certainly was embodied. He was able to touch and move clothes, shoes, and towels; in all respects, he appeared and acted like a living man to the generous priest. After the encounter, the

---

60. GrGr, col. 397.
61. GrGr, col. 397.
62. GrGr, col. 417.
63. GrGr, col. 417.

priest devoted himself to a week of tears and masses for his bath servant and then returned to the spa to see if he still haunted the premises. The man was nowhere to be found, demonstrating the efficacy of masses for the dead; no wonder, then, that "the spirits of the dead ask for them from the living."[64]

For Gregory the Great, then, the boundaries between this world and the next are not fixed, but porous, brittle, and thin. The dead continually appear in his *Dialogues*: some have corporeal capabilities; others may be more numinous apparitions. Righteous souls are seen to shoot from their dying bodies in various forms; unhappy souls are glimpsed after their death in human form, bound and led into mountainous infernos; individuals die and return to life with detailed reports about their experiences; still others persist for long periods of time on the face of the earth as physical revenants, fulfilling lowly existences as body servants in the baths. Many dead men converse with the living, offering vivid information about the afterlife that functions as moral instruction to the faithful—a function Gregory values highly in his debates with the skeptical Peter. By the end of book 4, Peter pronounces himself convinced; the ghost stories have fulfilled their intended function. Thus Gregory established a tradition that was to have a lengthy afterlife of its own: using ghost stories to "prove" the eternality of the soul and the existence of a complex afterlife realm. Indeed, this was a key point of appeal for such anecdotes: ghost stories offer firsthand evidence about eternity beyond the threshold of the grave.

A Hierarchy of Deaths: Isidore of Seville

The last important light of the guttering patristic era was the encyclopedist Isidore of Seville. A younger contemporary of Gregory the Great, Isidore was born around 560 near Cartagena in Spain.[65] We know few details of Isidore's biography. He was orphaned young and likely received his expansive education in the monastic environment in which he was raised thereafter. At around age forty, in the year 600, Isidore became bishop of Seville after the death of his brother, who previously had held the position. He was to occupy the see of Seville until the end of his life in 636.

As a bishop and keen observer of the natural and social worlds, Isidore authored several encyclopedic and historical texts. The twenty-book

---

64. GrGr, col. 417.
65. A sketch of Isidore's life is in the "Introduction" to *The Etymologies of Isidore of Seville*, trans. Stephen A. Barney et al. (Cambridge, 2006), 7–10; see also John Henderson, *The Medieval World of Isidore of Seville: Truth from Words* (Cambridge, 2010).

Etymologies, or *Origins*, was his most influential composition; it would become a basic instructional textbook and reference work for centuries to come. Throughout this vast and comprehensive text, Isidore explored things through words, which he presented as direct signifiers of their referents' essences. The bishop's approach was to suggest direct equivalences between a given word's proposed etymology and the necessary qualities of the phenomenon it signified. In a religious culture that revered scripture, that called its God "the Word," and whose myth of origin involved creation of the universe and of all that exists therein through divine speech acts,[66] this methodology was compelling indeed. The work ranks among the most copied of all manuscripts throughout the Middle Ages, a vital reference work for any library or collection. Embracing such diverse subjects as the liberal arts, theology, medicine, geography, shipbuilding, animal life, and history, the *Etymologies* promiscuously intermingles ideas drawn from theology, classical culture, and what might best be termed "common sense."[67] In the words of Ernst Curtius, it became "the basic book of the entire Middle Ages. . . . It not only established the canonical stock of knowledge for eight centuries but also molded their thought categories."[68]

The *Etymologies* provides a semiotics of mortality in book 11, dedicated to "The Human Being and Portents." In a passage that would be widely cited for many centuries, Isidore presents three alternative etymologies for the word "death" then goes on to suggest a taxonomy for different types of mortality, according to age:

Death [*mors*] is so called because it is bitter [*amara*]; or else *mors* is from Mars, who is the bringer of death; alternatively, *mors* is from the bite [*morsu*] of the first human being, for by biting the apple of the forbidden tree he incurred death. There are three kinds of death: sharp, untimely, and natural. The death of a child is sharp; of a young man, untimely; of an old man, worthy, that is, natural.[69]

---

66. J. L. Austin, *How to Do Things with Words* (Cambridge, MA, 1975).
67. Clifford Geertz, "Common Sense as a Cultural System," in *Local Knowledge: Further Essays in Interpretive Anthropology* (New York, 1983), 73–93.
68. Ernst Curtius, *European Literature and the Latin Middle Ages*, trans. Willard R. Trask (New York, 1953), 496–97. Not least among Isidore's contributions to later culture is his vision of the spatial arrangement of the world, which he described as a material record of salvation history progressing from Eden in the east to humanity's then-contemporary position at (as he believed) the western limit of the world. This vision of the world was given form in the famous Isidorean T-O map, the most common form of world map before Columbus. Dante placed the famous bishop of Seville in paradise, beside Bede and Richard of Saint-Victor.
69. Isidori Hispalensis Episcopi, *Etymologiarum sive originum libri XX*, ed. W. Lindsay, 2 vols. (Oxford, 1911), 2:25.

Isidore's word associations cover a broad semantic terrain. The first etymology is a commonsense evocation of fear of the unknown: human beings instinctually cling to life and find the inevitability of death to be a bitter thing. The second etymology, rather oddly for a Christian text, derives mortality from the name of the Roman god of war, Mars. Certainly, the presence of a pagan etymology beside—even before—a Christian derivation is at first surprising, but it is likely that this reference to a pagan god came with the territory of Isidore's own sources. By this time the ancient Roman gods were beginning to be regarded by some learned Christian authors as euhemeristic avatars for their areas of influence. Hence, Mars can stand metonymically for the violence of war. Finally, Isidore concludes the series with an association between death and the fall from grace. In fact this third, Christian-based etymology is sometimes missing from the early manuscript tradition, suggesting that it may have been a later interpolation.[70] Regardless, this section, which so neatly reifies into the word *mors* itself the Christian mythological narrative about death and its place in the material world, was widely invoked by later authors and was very well known in medieval tradition. Whether the sentence was original to Isidore or not, then, is somewhat immaterial, since it was important to later generations. The etymology of *mors* from *morsu* functions as a sort of mnemonic device, continually making present the birth of death in the fall from grace.

The second half of the quotation goes on to provide a taxonomy of mortality, discriminating among three different types of death according to age. The longer the lifetime, the less grievous the passing. What is important to note is that not all deaths are equal: to die "before one's time" was a peculiarly fraught category of mortality, and the longer the gap between one's time of death and one's expected life span, the more negative the death. Early deaths were "marked" in a particular way, as ones in which the deceased were yet attached to this life. Such deaths ran counter to the usual and expected course of nature, and thus the untimely dead were thought to preserve an attachment to this world for some time. The untimely dead would, of course, include the martyrs, those killed before their time in testimony to their faith. Perhaps it is not so surprising, then, that they were the Christian category par excellence of postmortem vitality.

Contemporary understandings of the physiological changes that underlay growth, maturation, and aging dovetailed with this general observation. The humoral system taught that the vital heat, force, or *virtus* of the individual

---

70. The editor, Lindsay, places brackets around this portion of the text, indicating that not all manuscripts consulted contained this portion.

first waxed and then waned throughout the course of a normal lifetime, along the line of a bell curve. This vital heat, which was a product of one's humoral balance and state of health, was in some sense the basis of life itself: loss of heat meant ill-heath, lethargy, weakness, and in the end, cold death. In terms of age, one's maximal heat and vitality was achieved in the late twenties to early forties; the very young and the very old were "cooler," that is, lacking in the intrinsic vital warmth that fueled the energy of a person at his or her peak.[71] In this way, the aged were explicitly paralleled to the young: as the elderly diminished in intellectual acuity and physical strength, they slowly became reduced to a childlike, more dependent and vulnerable state. The bodies of the very young were fragile; of the very old, moribund.

Thus, the deaths of elderly persons were regarded as natural and expected transitions into the next "age class" of the dead. As such, a specific intervening cause for a death in old age was seldom sought; to die of old age meant simply that one had used up one's vital heat and animating energy. Turning to the death of a child, we find that the formulaic term used is that such a death is "sharp," *acerba*, denoting something painful and hard to bear. Yet however poignant the adjective, nevertheless the estimated infant mortality rate of 40–45 percent for the medieval period suggests that the experience of grieving the death of a baby or toddler was shared by nearly all families.[72] However acutely mourned, then, the perishing of a young child was commonplace, something every parent expected to undergo at some point. Until a child survived beyond the dangers of toddlerhood, she or he was not securely lodged in this world. Like the aged person, the child lived in intimacy with mortality. And like the elderly, in the case of very young children, a specific cause of death often was not required. It was known that sometimes infants simply failed to cling to life and might die in their cribs quietly and without any obvious cause.

Isidore's hierarchy of death types was to be extremely influential on later medieval works. It is invoked in the Cistercian monk Caesarius of Heisterbach's collection of exempla, the *Dialogus miraculorum*, as well as in the thirteenth-century Franciscan Bartholomew the Englishman's *De rerum proprietatibus*, to give only two examples.[73] Age was always a preeminent factor in evaluating deaths and positing causes for them. Individuals at the extremes

---

71. Shulamith Shahar, "The Old Body in Medieval Culture," in *Framing Medieval Bodies*, ed. Sarah Kay and Miri Rubin (Manchester, 1994), 160–86.

72. David Herlihy and Christiane Klapisch-Zuber, *Les Toscans et leurs familles: Une étude du catasto florentin de 1427* (Paris, 1978); David Herlihy, *Medieval Households* (Cambridge, MA, 1985).

73. CH, 2:266–67; Bartholomeus Anglicus (Bartholomew the Englishman), *De rerum proprietatibus* (Frankfurt, 1601), 234.

of the age spectrum—the very young and the very old—were characterized by a tenuous condition of corporeal embodiment. Children and the elderly dwelt at the borders of the human life span, the first having just entered into the world, and the second being very close to exiting it. Both groups struggled to hold on to a life that was mere months removed from the unthinkable void of disembodiment that surrounded human existence. As the thirteenth-century Dominican Vincent of Beauvais was to write in his *Speculum naturale*, "Like flowers, a human being springs forth from the unknown and suddenly appears in the world [*in publico*]; then just as suddenly he is drawn back, by death, from this world to the unknown."[74]

What of deaths in the central adult years, then? Isidore and those who referenced him designated the death of a young adult as "untimely," a term that connotes something unnatural or against expectation. The sudden interruption of the life force in full flow was troubling to people in the ancient and medieval worlds alike. The question that ineluctably arose in such cases was, what happened to the "energy still unexpended,"[75] which suddenly was cut short by an early decease? The spirit of the deceased, evacuated too soon from its accustomed fleshly home, might be angry or confused by this sudden and intense alteration of the terms of its existence. Indeed, such souls might actively resist the mortality that had overtaken them, attempting to maintain some form of contact with the people, places, and things that they cherished in life. Because the category of early death was defined as intrinsically a form of unnatural death, brutally severing the life force in medias res, an atmosphere of violence and terror clung to the memories of those who died thusly. And this symbolic association, in turn, rendered these dead a group that was feared by the living. They often were regarded as the dangerous dead, the ones who came back with ill intent. The ancient world was rife with haunting spirits of those who had expired before their "natural" span.[76] The *Etymologies*' elaboration of the different kinds of death thus reopened a door that some of the earliest Latin fathers had attempted to slam closed. Though Tertullian—and after him, Augustine—had attempted to uproot this belief, centuries later it was still resonating with Christian thinkers like Isidore.

The learned bishop next goes on to discuss the various types of dead bodies. The discussion arranges them according to precise degrees in the fulfillment of funerary rites: an unburied corpse is a different category of

---

74. Vincent of Beauvais, *Speculum naturale* (Graz, 1964), col. 2373.

75. Lester K. Little, *Benedictine Maledictions: Liturgical Cursing in Romanesque France* (Ithaca, NY, 1993), 151.

76. Johnston, *Restless Dead*. For further discussion, see chapter 7.

dead person than an interred one; various moments in the funeral require different words for the body. This section of text has particularly fascinating ramifications for the understanding of mortality:

> Every body that is dead is either a *funus* or a *cadaver*. The body is a *funus* if buried: it is called that because of the ropes [*funis*] set on fire that were carried before the bier. . . . The body is a *cadaver* if it lies unburied: *cadaver* is from "falling down" [*cadendo*], for at that time it cannot stand upright. When the *cadaver* is being carried, we call this a funeral procession [*exsequiae*]; what is left after it has been cremated are the "remains" [*reliquiae*]; and after it is in the ground, it is "interred" [*sepultum*]. . . .
>
> A defunct person [*defunctus*] is so named because he has completed the task of life. For we say that a task has been fulfilled [*functus*], when the duties that are required for it have been completed . . . therefore, the person is "de-funct" because he has been taken away from the task of life, or else because he has fulfilled his days.[77]

It is important to note that several discrete steps are necessary to fulfill before one is defunct. One who dies untimely, before having completed a full life span, is *not* immediately defunct. Full expiration of the self is contingent upon reaching the terminus of a complete and full life. In consequence, one who is cut down in the midst of existence, before fulfilling life's basic tasks (reaching adulthood, setting up a household and a career, engendering and raising children, settling into a venerable old age) will not attain the quietude implied by the term "defunct." Indeed, even after death, Isidore suggests, there is a further set of requirements: the fulfillment of proper funeral exsequies is necessary. Proper treatment and honor to the corpse must be undertaken before the dead person is fully separated from the living. Thus, an as-yet-unburied body occupies a distinctly different status than the buried body, and each step between "falling to earth" and final interment is set forth and named. These thoughts are in continuity with Isidore's general ideas about age and death, in which earlier deaths are considered more lamentable than those in old age. In sum, not every death is equal; not every death is expected; and finally, not every death is complete. Many deaths are gradual and processual in nature, rather than singular events.

The rationale that underlies Isidore's meticulous attention to these details is not difficult to fathom. Despite the determined efforts of the earlier Latin fathers to intervene in ancient afterlife beliefs, despite Augustine's

---

77. Isidori Hispalensis, *Etymologiarum sive originum*, 2:25–26.

prestige and Tertullian's clarity, their writings had failed to overturn ancient common sense regarding the processual shift of life into death. Late antique culture was yet filled with hauntings and apparitions, for the inheritance of the dead was not an easy one to divest. As Gregory the Great had testified, corporeal ghosts still wandered both landscape and cityscape. The unquiet dead especially were attracted to topographical features such as mountains and rivers; they likewise returned to haunt their homes and places of business; they appeared to their survivors, both in dreams and as apparitions to the wakeful; and they lingered near cemeteries, crossroads, and boundaries, where they accosted strangers and friends alike. Likewise, Isidore's conceptualization of the dead was neither avant-garde nor retrograde. The *Etymologies* is an encyclopedia in the classic sense of being a broad compendium of generally accepted contemporary knowledge. Though Isidore's ideas about the semiotics of death were ancient, at the same time they were fully of his own day, as his close contemporary Gregory the Great likewise attests. Moreover, this set of ideas was to live on, long after this generation perished.

Biblical scripture from Genesis to Revelation charted a story of death's past and future that was complex and open to manifold interpretations. It was a story of abrupt changes and reversals, of mortality's introduction into an originally deathless world, through human trespass, of the death and transcendence of a human God who altered the prospects of human mortality for all time, and of an expectation of resurrection and eternal life to come. Death, in this theological narrative, was not an inevitable fact of life but a contingent condition that right-thinking people could overcome through faith. The resulting Christian contempt of death led to some spectacular deaths of uncompromising believers: the cult of martyrs developed relatively early within the history of the church. The remains of such individuals were honored by all the faithful, and their tombs became public gathering places and, ultimately, sites for the construction of shrines. Most Christians believed that the relics of the saints possessed consciousness and could extend healings to the faithful. Thus for Christians, the perfected dead were also vital and conscious, still actors within this world. Though cults for the cadavers of the saints were troubling to pagan observers, they became increasingly central to Christian life and worship. The church was, in many ways, a religion focused upon death above all else: stories of deaths, remains of the dead, were central to Christian identity and ritual.

At the same time, patristic thinkers were striving to theorize death and its contemporary meaning, given the delay of the Parousia. A first phase of development was characterized by church fathers who strove to forge a distinctively Christian deathway,[78] set apart from the values of the surrounding pagan culture. Tertullian in the third century and Augustine in the fifth pioneered a new model of death for the new religion they served. In this imagining of mortality, death was a discrete, unidirectional event. This viewpoint, which for convenience's sake I designate as "Augustinian" in honor of its most famous proponent, claimed that mortality occurred instantaneously as the soul left the body and that, thenceforth, the shades of the dead were transferred to an otherworldly realm from which there could be no—or at least, exceedingly rare—returns. In making this argument these two thinkers rejected—and in Tertullian's case, explicitly refuted—the phantom-filled world of Roman paganism, which tended to see fearsome spirits and shades in every cemetery and topographical feature.

Yet the Christian conversation about death and the afterlife was far from closed. In the seventh century a later generation of church fathers embraced a different approach. Pope Gregory the Great's *Dialogues* confronted the possibility of skepticism about the eternality of the soul and the retributive nature of the afterlife by invoking the firsthand testimony of the dead to "prove" Christian doctrine: thus was the Christian ghost story born. As a rhetorical tool for persuading materialists of the reality of the unseen otherworld, the ghost story was exceptionally useful. Just as Gregory confronted the fictional skeptic "Peter" in the fourth book of his *Dialogues* with "evidence" from the returned dead, so successive generations of bishops and evangelists would utilize this same technique to try to persuade potential converts of the truth of the Christian promise of eternal life. Gregory's younger contemporary, Isidore of Seville, added another layer to the recovery of the ghost for Christian purposes. He revived yet another set of classical ideas, concerning which manner of death was most conducive to postmortem hauntings and apparitions. Isidore's thoughts on the bitterness of death, the natural length of a human life span, and its fulfillment, as well as his stress on the importance of funerary rites, set forth a precise set of conditions for restful versus restless deaths. As such, Isidore's ideas complemented and extended Gregory's, providing an underlying logic for the full, extended process of death, as well as a rationale for why some deceased individuals returned whereas others did not. I call this model, which construes death as a long-term process of detachment from the world of the living, the "Gregorian" model, in distinction from the "Augustinian" model.

---

78. A term borrowed from Erik Seeman, *Death in the New World: Cross-Cultural Encounters, 1492–1800* (Philadelphia, 2011).

What is most striking and important to note, as this chapter reaches its close, is that these divergent, even mutually contradictory, ideas were allowed to persist side by side within accepted, canonical church tradition. Indeed, for an institution that jealously guarded the integrity and coherence of most of its doctrines, the Catholic Church was exceptionally expansive in its admittance of all these different conceptualizations of death into its authoritative tradition. These different thanatologies had long and active afterlives in the Middle Ages. That having been said, however, we can observe some clear patterns about the contexts within which the Augustinian versus Gregorian models were most appealing, for as a general rule, these differing views on death and the possibility of postmortem return appealed to different groups. The Gregorian model of death as a long-term process, and of the afterlife as accessible to this world, was favored by missionaries, itinerant preachers, and other clerics charged with direct pastoral responsibilities. Indeed, this connection was embodied in Gregory himself, for he was an important patron of the missionaries who evangelized Britain, and he instructed them to accommodate local beliefs and practices as far as possible when teaching the Good News. This pragmatic spirit seems likewise reflected in his appropriation of the gossip of ghost stories into his *Dialogues*, to further the message of postmortem existence, and it prefigures the adoption of similar ghost tales into later literatures concerned with conversion and instruction. The thoughts of Isidore of Seville could readily be combined with Gregory's ideas: Isidore's taxonomies of mortality as "better" or "worse," depending upon one's age and readiness for death, were frequently used as justifications for understanding why certain shades did not rest quietly but wandered as earthly presences. It harmonized well with the cult of the martyrs, who were characterized above all by their untimely, violent deaths—and by their tendency to remain active presences in the world afterward. Likewise, this hierarchically ranked way of thinking about death, though adopted from the classical cultures of the Mediterranean, was also consonant with the values of the Celtic, Teutonic, and Slavic cultures that dominated northern Europe. As the church imported its foreign faith into new regions over the next several centuries, the Gregorian and the Isidorean outlooks provided points of entrée into a conversation about mortality with the indigenous populations of the north. We shall see this dynamic at work in section two.

Likewise, this model also was useful in contexts of doctrinal innovation about the afterlife—most notably, in teaching lay populations about the doctrine of purgatory. This notion, though rooted in early church tradition, only gradually made its way into formal dogma. Since tales of the returning or lingering dead could readily be reframed as stories about souls in purgatory, some writers attempted to promote the doctrine through appropriation of local ghost folklore. Eventually, however, such uses of the Gregorian model came to be hotly disputed. Though ghost stories still seemed useful to some, the Gregorian model nevertheless lost ground after the epoch of Christian conversion and came to be less and less appealing to new generations of church leadership. As the church came to be dominated by contemplatives and philosophers, rather than evangelizers and men of action, the mortal imagination of the church's leadership shifted decisively toward the Augustinian pole. Thus we can make out a general chronological evolution in the church's approach to death and afterlife over time. As formerly pagan regions came to be more securely folded into the Christian imperium, one by one, and as university training began to produce a sophisticated new generation of theologians in the thirteenth century, the Augustinian model gradually achieved dominance over the Gregorian paradigm. The Augustinian model of death as a discrete event was one that appealed principally to theologians and intellectuals whose audience was other Christian intellectuals, not pagans or the undereducated laity. Moreover, the logical training of such thinkers was bound up, in large part, with an Augustinian revival in the schoolroom. Thus Augustine's formulation ultimately eclipsed, though never entirely displaced, the Gregorian view.

CHAPTER 2

Diagnosing Death

The Thrice-Dead

On July 24, 1224, a woman named Christina died in the town of Saint Trond in the Low Countries. She was in her midseventies, an age people of her time seldom attained; most would have perished some time earlier. And so in fact did Christina: the summer of 1224 marked her third death.

Christina expired for the first time in 1182, after a prolonged illness. Her two older sisters lamented her passing and brought her still body to church. The funerary rites were well under way when suddenly Christina's corpse raised itself up on the bier and, "in the manner of a bird," levitated up to the rafters of the nave.[1] When she returned to earth and to her senses, Christina explained that during her death she had received a special vision. Her soul had been conducted by angels through a tour of hell and purgatory, then brought to heaven and presented before the throne of God. She recognized many acquaintances among the suffering souls of the afterlife. Thus when the Lord offered her the opportunity to return to life in order to torment herself, thereby conducting vicarious penance on behalf of purgatorial souls, Christina readily agreed. As the vision faded, her soul reinserted itself into her body; thenceforth, she would utilize the latter as an instrument

---

1. Thomas of Cantimpré, *De S. Christina Mirabili Virgo*, in *AASS*, 32 (July 24), 649–60.

of harsh, self-inflicted penitence. The torments she sought out—jumping into freezing rivers or scorching hot ovens—mimicked the penitential sufferings medieval people imagined took place in the tormenting regions of the afterlife.

Forty-two years later Christina died again. As the now elderly nun grew frail and her religious sisters kept vigil at her bedside, one named Beatrice begged her not to depart this life without revealing certain secrets. However, as it transpired, Christina passed on while her friend was not present. Upon her return, Beatrice was displeased to find Christina's "body lying lifeless on the ground, laid out in the manner of dead people." Determined to satisfy her curiosity, Beatrice forcefully recalled Christina's soul back into her body:

> Putting her face to the mouth of the dead woman, she said, "O Christina! You always were obedient to me in life! I now therefore beg you . . . to return to life and tell me the things I asked you about so intently while you were alive!" A marvelous thing! Scarcely had Beatrice shouted like this into the dead woman's ears than Christina returned into her body, heaving a great sigh.

The scene suggests that there was a period of time during which the soul hovered nearby, ready to reenter the recently abandoned body if necessary. After this, her second revival, Christina answered Beatrice's importunate questions, blessed the community, shared a few final words of advice, and then, "she who experienced death thrice, died for the third time."[2]

Christina was regarded as a saint by some, a demoniac by others.[3] Her hagiographer Thomas of Cantimpré presented her as living between worlds: she readily could slip over the boundary separating this life from the next. Indeed, Thomas subtly presented Christina as a living dead person: a still-embodied soul undergoing the torments of the afterlife while yet in this world. Her religious vocation to offer vicarious suffering on behalf of others in purgatory required that she remain poised between life and death. Like the bodies of the early martyrs, like a living relic, her body was both privately her own and available for broader salvific purposes. Christina's transition to the next world thus was gradual and proceeded by stages over the course of most of her adult life; hers was a clear exemplar of death as a process, rather than death as an event.

Nearly 250 years after Christina's final expiration another thrice-dead religious woman achieved public notice, in this case with a radically different

---

2. Ibid., 659.
3. Cf. Nancy Caciola, *Discerning Spirits: Divine and Demonic Possession in the Middle Ages* (Ithaca, NY, 2003).

denouement. A comparison serves to highlight some important changes in the intervening time period. In early December 1430 a nun named Magdalena Beutlerin, living in a convent at Freiburg, received a revelation foretelling her coming death.[4] It was to be her second: Magdalena already had died as a girl of three or four, while living with her pious widowed mother. After laying the child out in her funerary garments, Magdalena's mother went to church to pray for her revivification, vowing that, should the girl return to life, she would place her in a cloister as a sacrifice to God.[5] Returning home, the woman rejoiced to find Magdalena sitting up and entirely recovered. Magdalena's mother kept her vow, but by the age of twenty-three Magdalena had become a polarizing presence in her Clarissan nunnery. For some, she was a holy visionary and potential saint; yet her hagiography also notes that there were frequent murmurings against her in the community from those who doubted her sincerity and disapproved of her extremism. Magdalena appears to have believed that foretelling her own death would confirm her sanctity and set the stage for her postmortem veneration.

According to Magdalena's own account of her revelation, she would undergo "a temporal death" precisely thirty-seven days later, on Twelfth Night during Epiphany 1431.[6] The date fell on Friday, January 7, that year.[7] The death Magdalena had in mind would be a grand affair worthy of great public notice. Magdalena informed her sisters; the convent informed the town council; the town council informed the local religious institutions and clergy. Rumors of the nun's coming public death soon spread throughout Freiburg and the surrounding region. The Clarissan convent, though usually enclosed, busily prepared to host a major festival for the occasion. Magdalena, for her part, stoked public interest by claiming that witnesses

---

4. A hagiographical version of her life is the "Magdalena-Book," City Library of Mainz, cod. II 16 (M), from 1491; University Library, Freiburg, cod. 185 (F), from 1656/57. For a partial translation, see Karen Greenspan, trans., "The Life of Magdalena Beutler," in *Medieval Women's Visionary Literature*, ed. Elizabeth Alvilda Petroff (New York, 1986), 350–54. See also Karen Greenspan, "Erklaerung des Vaterunsers: A Critical Edition of a Fifteenth-Century Mystical Treatise by Magdalena Beutler of Freiburg" (PhD diss., University of Massachusetts–Amherst, 1984). Magdalena also is discussed in Ioannis Nider, *Formicarium Ioannis Nider S. theologiae doctoris et ecclesiasticae praestantissimi in quinque libros*, 3:8 (Douai, 1602), 229–35. For background on Nider, see Michael Bailey, *Battling Demons: Witchcraft, Heresy, and Reform in the Late Middle Ages* (University Park, PA, 2003); Gábor Klaniczay, "Entre visions angéliques et transes chamaniques: Le sabbat des sorcières dans le Formicarius de Nider," *Médiévales* 44 (2003): 47–72; Gábor Klaniczay, "Learned Systems and Popular Narratives of Vision and Bewitchment," in *Witchcraft Mythologies and Persecutions*, ed. Gábor Klaniczay and Éva Pócs, Demons, Spirits, Witches 3 (Budapest, 2008), 62.
5. Greenspan, "Erklaerung des Vaterunsers," 22.
6. Ibid., 69.
7. Greenspan, "Life of Magdalena," 351.

to her public expiration would escape hellfire through this act of devotion. In consequence, "as the appointed day neared, a great crowd arrived from the surrounding regions in carriages, on horseback, and by foot; nobles and peasants, clerks and monks, laity and not a few ecclesiastics, all desirous of witnessing this thing."[8]

The culmination of the event was to be Magdalena's funeral, an affair she planned personally down to the last detail. A new, elaborately carved coffin was prepared and placed in the convent chapel, in readiness for her freshly "martyred" corpse. A large quantity of candles and other ornaments surrounded the sepulcher, and plans were made for her funerary procession to tour the dioceses of Constance, Argentina, and Basel, in order to edify the maximum number of people and produce abundant miracles. Johannes Nider, the Dominican friar who is one of our chief sources for this event, describes himself as "rather amazed" at these preparations. He deputed "a trustworthy man, a devoted procurator of [Nider's own] convent,"[9] to travel from Basel to Freiburg, a journey of about one full day. Nider instructed his proxy to be attentive to all that transpired and to be ready with a detailed report about Magdalena's passing (if indeed it should occur) upon his return. Other local convents did similarly, as did the secular authorities. The town council of Freiburg deputed sober witnesses, wise laymen who sat upon the council. Magdalena's hagiography meticulously recorded all these officials' names and credentials:

> The following people, both worldly and religious . . . had been appointed to observe this matter clearly, to witness and to listen. These are the individuals by name: Graf Bernhart von Tierstein; Junker Hans Erhard von Schefenberg; the Deacon of Freiburg; the Deacon of Rheinfelden; the reading-master of the Augustinians; the holy Lords Prior of the Carthusians of Freiburg and Prior of the Carthusians of Basel; the Burgermeister of the city, Junker Heitze Kichle; plus Junker Jerg von Kipppenheim, who was the former Burgermeister. In addition, the foremost men of the city council: Ulrich Ruber; Haman von Todnau; Rudolf von Kilchen; Master Paul Gloterer, a doctor; Haman Schnidke, the city secretary; Anders Henenberg; and Erhart Hesle.[10]

Clearly, there was a great deal of excitement about the prospect of Magdalena's public exsequies: the notion that one might foresee and control death,

---

8. Nider, *Formicarium*, 231.
9. Ibid., 231.
10. Greenspan, "Life of Magdalena," 352.

rather than being snatched from life unwillingly, seems to have been intriguing to all. The attendance by so many secular and religious notables tells us that this event was being taken very seriously. Of particular note is the mention of the medical doctor, one Master Paul Gloterer, whose name and presence likewise were noted by Johannes Nider. Master Paul appears to have been instructed by his fellow town councilors to monitor Magdalena's pulse and to verify for the crowd the much-anticipated moment of her passing.

On the morning of Epiphany the convent chapel was packed with people spilling out into the street. Finally the hour arrived. Magdalena, entering before the crowd, rested her head in the lap of one of her sister nuns and lay still for a long time. The crowd waited and watched and eventually began to murmur with impatience. Master Paul approached and took the nun's pulse, then declared that life was still present. Before the crowd could react to this announcement, however, Magdalena suddenly rose up and cried out dramatically, and in a strangely coarse voice, *To the coffin!*[11] Yet though she swiftly was transferred to the sarcophagus that had been prepared to her specifications, still no signs of death appeared. The crowd was becoming increasingly restless. Nider's account states that Magdalena eventually sat up in the sarcophagus and plaintively asked for some food. Her *Life*, by contrast, has the provincial of the Franciscan Order intervening in what was fast becoming an embarrassing debacle for the order. He repeatedly adjured her, by her vow of obedience, to explain herself, and he ordered her removed from the coffin since it was clear that she was not dying.[12] In fact, Magdalena would continue to live for another twenty-seven years, until 1458.

Magdalena eventually explained that she had misunderstood her original vision: the prophesied death was to be spiritual and symbolic, rather than physical and bodily. The trance state from which she had just been roused, she suggested, had been a symbolic death, which culminated in her deposition into the coffin; her subsequent recovery was a spiritual rebirth to demonstrate an even greater miracle to believers. Thus she suggested the terms of the prophecy had indeed been fulfilled; she simply had died in a different form. Yet few others endorsed this interpretation. Though Magdalena's Clarissan sisters already were composing a hagiography in her honor, the project was left in a fragmentary and unfinished state, possibly in recognition of the fact that her reputation had been damaged irretrievably by this debacle. For the crowd expecting an edifying and macabre spectacle, for Master Paul the doctor and the other members of the Freiburg town council, for the

---

11. Nider, *Formicarium*, 231; Greenspan, "Life of Magdalena," 352.
12. Nider, *Formicarium*, 231; Greenspan, "Life of Magdalena," 352–53.

Franciscan provincial, for the representatives of various local religious houses, and for Nider and his informant, Magdalena was either a deluded failure or a demonic fraud.

Death is not just *a* but *the sole* source of possible meaning in Magdalena's story. A trance state or visionary journey was not deemed an acceptable alternative by anyone outside Magdalena's community. Life and death were conceived as diametrically opposed; there could be no partial death, no positioning between worlds. Death, in fifteenth-century Freiburg, was a medically certifiable, physiological event; not a metaphor, a symbol, or a ritual performance.

These two stories of aspiring visionary women and their multiple deaths open up a set of questions about precisely how deaths were evaluated, particularly when the deceased was young and vigorous. Both Christina and Magdalena were young women in the prime of life when their ambiguous deaths took place. Their careers raise questions about how medieval observers concluded that an *inert* body was in fact a *dead* body—and how they reacted if such a body later revived. Furthermore, the differing outcomes of these two cases also signal some important changes over time: procedures for diagnosing death changed between the twelfth and the fifteenth centuries. It is clear that by 1431, the borderline between life and death had shifted considerably from its location in 1182. Magdalena was not accepted as a visionary poised between the realms of the living and the dead, as was Christina; the sole fact of overweening importance was Magdalena's failure to physically expire in a medically certifiable manner. This was a hardening of conceptual boundaries that earlier had been seen as more porous. Magdalena could attempt to "save" her original revelation by harkening back to older models of thought, in which trances and death were assimilated and overlapping, in which life and death could coexist, sometimes, for those special few beloved of God. However, few others accepted this counter-interpretation.

One important reason for the divergence between Christina and Magdalena, of course, was that the latter was examined by a medical doctor whose professional expertise was held as authoritative. Master Paul, the doctor, was the arbiter of Magdalena's state, and he relayed his judgment to a crowd that is portrayed, in both documents, as passive and awaiting an expert opinion. At the time of Christina's initial death in 1182, by contrast, doctors seldom were called in to certify deaths; such decisions typically were made by family and community consensus. However, theoretical medicine was beginning to take off as a new branch of natural philosophy in certain monastic centers. This new branch of thought adopted the theological idea of the soul as the basis for life and sought to translate it into physiologically legible terms. In so doing, this system ultimately construed life and death as wholly incommensurate, dichotomous states with no overlaps and no third terms. In consequence, by the end of the Middle Ages mortality had become a much clearer, neater object of apprehension than it earlier had been. The remainder of this chapter charts the ways in which death achieved this epistemological status. I seek to understand how death become clarified, defined, and medicalized and to chart some of the effects of this evolution.

Body and Soul

"Why do we die?"[13] As we have seen, in the religious tradition the answer was simply that the bond between body and soul had been severed. Christian anthropology reaching back to Tertullian in the third century held that the soul was the guarantor of life. In its absence, the body fell to earth, the breath ceased, the senses failed, and the individual perished. However, exactly *how* the soul animated the body was unclear in traditional theological writings. How could an immaterial essence interact with corporeal matter so intimately and in such a transformative way?

In the late twelfth century, a systematic answer to this question was offered for the first time. Central to medieval theories of life was the notion of *spiritus* as the principle of human vitality, a sort of adhesive device between the body and the soul:[14]

> Since the soul is so subtle it cannot be conjoined to the body, which is so gross and impure, except through some intermediary thing. Spirit became the intermediary. Since it is a body, it can interact with a bodily nature; but since it is a nearly incorporeal body, it seems almost similar in kind to the soul. Thus it is an appropriate link on both sides. However, when the spirit leaves the two are separated from one another.[15]

---

13. Albrecht Wagner, ed., *Visio Tnugdali lateinisch und altdeutsch* (Erlangen, 1882), 8.
14. M. D. Chenu, "*Spiritus*: Vocabulaire de l'ame au XIIe siècle," *Revue des sciences philosophiques et theologiques* 41 (1957): 209–32; Ruth Harvey, *The Inward Wits: Psychological Theory in the Middle Ages and in the Renaissance* (London, 1975); G. Verbeke, *L'Évolution de la doctrine du pneuma du stoicisme à S. Augustin* (New York, 1987); Nancy Siraisi, *Taddeo Alderotti and His Pupils: Two Generations of Italian Medical Learning* (Princeton, NJ, 1981); James J. Bono, "Medical Spirits and the Medieval Language of Life," *Traditio* 40 (1984): 91–130; Danielle Jacquart and Claude Thomasset, *Sexuality and Medicine in the Middle Ages* (Princeton, NJ, 1988); Nancy Siraisi, *Medieval and Early Renaissance Medicine: An Introduction to Knowledge and Practice* (Chicago, 1990).
15. Brian Lawn, ed., *The Prose Salernitan Questions: An Anonymous Collection dealing with Science and Medicine written by an Englishman c. 1200* (Oxford, 1979), 44–45.

Without the spirit, in other words, there would be no way for the soul to use the body as an instrument. The will could have no physical outcome or effect; the senses could not relay information; memory would have no emotional force; even speech would be impossible. *Spiritus* was the means through which consciousness was seated within the material plane. Thus the theory of spirit permitted transferences between the immaterial aspects of the self or soul and the grossly corporeal realm of the senses, humors, organs, and limbs. And of course, without the intermediation of spirit, soul and body were separated from one another and death would occur.

Though rooted in older, Galenic models, the idea of the vital spirit was enhanced after the twelfth century by Arab influences. *Spiritus* was said to be manufactured in the left ventricle of the heart from inhaled air, and thence diffused throughout the body via the arteries.[16] Thus it was intimately linked to the breath and to the beating heart at the core of the body. In consequence, "when the heart stops the pulling-in of air and the expulsion of air, without this traction the person cannot breathe, and then the person must die according to nature."[17] In the process of moving throughout the living body, *spiritus* regulated the other vital signs as well as the heartbeat: pulse, respiration, and maintenance of proper body temperature.[18] Thus rather than being an abstract or numinous entity, the *spiritus* was a material, albeit highly refined and subtle, substance within the body, one that interacted with the body's internal organs and moved along its interior pathways. Medically defined, *spiritus* constituted the principle of life itself. With the last breath, the spirit was exhaled from the mouth.

By contrast, in traditional theological parlance the soul was held to be the principle of life. Yet leading medieval intellectuals desired to harmonize the natural and the divine orders. As a result, theologians increasingly broadened the definition of *spiritus* so as to assimilate it to the soul. They thus united the presuppositions of theology with those of medical thinkers. As Alcher of Clairvaux phrased it in *De spiritu et anima* (*On Spirit and Soul*), "the soul is called 'anima' because it animates the body for living: that is, it vivifies."[19] He expatiates further,

> It is called soul when it vivifies; spirit when it contemplates; a sense when it perceives; consciousness when it knows; when it understands,

---

16. Siraisi, *Taddeo Alderotti and His Pupils*, 166.
17. *MTC*, 546.
18. Siraisi, *Medieval and Renaissance Medicine*, 107.
19. Alcher of Clairvaux, *De spiritu et anima*, in *PL*, 40, col. 784. In addition, see Hugh of Saint-Victor, *De unione corporis et spiritus*, in *PL*, 177, cols. 285–94; Isaac de Stella, *Epistola ad quemdam familiarem suum de anima*, in *PL*, 194, cols. 1875–90; Richard of Saint Victor, *De statu interioris hominis*, in *PL*, 196, cols. 1115–60.

mind; when it discerns, reason; when it remembers, memory; when it consents, will. These are not, however, differences of substance, but of names, for all these things are a single soul: diverse properties, but one essence.[20]

Thus, though the spirit was a useful construct in terms of medical discourse, theologians were anxious to define it as a function of the life-giving soul inside the body.

Vital Signs and Mortal Signs

The theory of the *spiritus* provided an integrative explanation for the vital signs of heartbeat, pulse, respiration, and body warmth. Works of a more clinical character—natural philosophical texts as well as treatises generated by and for practicing physicians—built upon this basic system. They discussed how to assess irregularities in the vital signs, and they complemented these discussions with analogous lists of the "mortal signs": physical symptoms through which a patient's imminent or present death might be diagnosed.

Lists of the mortal signs stemmed from several different roots, many traceable back to the Hippocratic corpus. This vast body of fifth- and sixth-century Greek medical writings (only some of which were actually composed by Hippocrates of Cos) were disseminated widely throughout the medieval Greek and Arab worlds in an unbroken chain of cultural transmission from the classical past. Major intellectuals of the Arab world commented on these texts and knew them intimately. In the early medieval Latin West, by contrast, only small portions of the corpus were available in Latin translation. Parts of the *Aphorisms* were translated in the sixth century, but the Hippocratic corpus remained largely unknown in the post-Roman world.[21] However, as western European and Arabic cultures began to interact more fully starting in the twelfth century, more and more medical texts arrived in western Europe. The new translations included hitherto-unknown ancient Hippocratic texts as well as their Arabic commentaries, introduced either from al-Andalus or else southern Italy via North Africa. The process of translation continued into the thirteenth century, as the scholastic milieu that dominated universities consciously sought to mine the usable knowledge of other cultures. The increased interest in Arabic natural philosophy and classical Greek thought fed into the revival of Hippocratic theories of health and of death.

---

20. Alcher of Clairvaux, *De spiritu et anima*, cols. 788–89.
21. Joan Cadden, *Meanings of Sex Differences in the Middle Ages* (Cambridge 1995), 15–16.

The Hippocratic tradition taught that disease arose from imbalances in the humors; scrutiny of the body's appearance, temperature, and excreta could help diagnose this imbalance and suggest appropriate cures through diet or medical compounds. The Hippocratic corpus includes various prognostic means for apprehending death, intended for physicians' use. For example, a version of the Hippocratic signs of death, rendered into Latin hexameter verse, was a popular addition to physicians' herbals and handbooks. The British Library holds a twelfth-century versified herbal by Macer Floridus, which interpolates classic Hippocratic content on the signs of death:

> First turn the face to yours: it is the first thing to be examined:
> For in it is a sign through which the crisis of disease will be indicated.
> If the eyes are rolled back, or if they just shrink back from light
> These signs reveal that the prick of death is in the entrails.
> If the eyes are bruised, or else suffused with red,
> They betoken a coming death, with a very diminished vitality.
> If the flesh of the ears is hard, the brow, dry, and the temples, flat;
> If the nose sharpens, movement is labored, and sleep is fleeting;
> If the extremities are cold but there is dry heat in the lower parts
> When you see these things: Give up and bring help to someone else.[22]

This counsel derives, in some line of transmission, from the *Prognosis*, a Hippocratic text dedicated to teaching doctors how to diagnose death so as to avoid being blamed for it.[23] Nearly identical hexameter verses are likewise found in some manuscripts of the *Flos medicinae* (*Flower of Medicine*), also known as *Lilium medicinae* (*Lily of Medicine*), and as the *Regimen sanitatis Saleritanum* (*Salernitan Health Regimen*). This was a late twelfth- or early thirteenth-century tract of the Salernitan school dedicated to practical medicine and

---

22. "Prima tibi facies occurrit prima notetur / in se signum gerit quibus aegri crisis largeretur / Lumina si lateant vel si fugiant modo lumen / litera designunt ventre mortis acumen / Livida si fuerint, vel sint suffusa robore / signum serunt mortis, nimio districta vigore / Auris pulpa rigens, frons arida, timpora plana / naris acuta, labor in motu, sompnia vana / Algor in extemis, sitis et calor interiorum / hiis visus abeas: curam geras aliorum." London, British Library, MS Royal 12 B. III, fol. 65ᵛ. The pseudonym "Macer Floridus" has puzzled scholars, and little is known of the author. He likely was French and active around 1070–1112. See Bruce P. Flood Jr., "The Medieval Herbal Tradition of Macer Floridus," *Pharmacy in History* 18, no. 2 (1976): 62–66. Two published versions of the *Flos medicinae* have slight variations from this verse. Since each manuscript is different, I draw upon both: Andrea Sinno, ed., *Regimen sanitatis: Flos Medicinae scholae Salerni* (Salerno, 1987), 342–44; and Salvatore de Renzi, ed., *Flos medicinae Scholae Salerni*, in *Collectio Salernitana* (Naples, 2001), 1:491. A Middle English translation of the verse is in London, British Library, MS Add. 37786.

23. G. E. R. Lloyd, ed., and J. Chadwick and W. N. Mann, trans., *Hippocratic Writings* (New York, 1983), 170–71.

healing. There they appear under the heading "Signa mortis" ("Signs of Death"). This text adds further information culled from the Hippocratic corpus, however, with some manuscripts incorporating longer discussions than others. For example, though both published editions incorporate a version of the versified hexameter lines quoted just above, one version expands upon this information with several additional paragraphs. Portions titled "Another Reading" suggest,

> If you read these things often, you will be able to be a prognosticator:
> If the brow temples redden, the nose twists and whitens
> If the eyes water and tears fall from the pupils,
> If the nose grows cold and the teeth chatter in the mouth;
> And if the eyebrows of the forehead droop downwards,
> And if the mind fails, if the body cavity rattles
> If the sweat of the forehead and the breath of the mouth
> are cold: recognize that the patient shows the sign of death.
> I judge that when the testes and the penis shrink it is a sign of death
> . . . .
> Dearest sons, grasp the correct signs of death
> so that you may recognize them shrewdly and note them
> in many sick people, particularly acute cases.[24]

This subsection goes on for several pages, repeating some of the most commonly cited signs of approaching death from the Hippocatic tradition. A shorter paragraph on "The Signs of Certain Death" focuses on the death struggle of the final moments:

> The vigor of the lungs, of the heart, of the stomach fails;
> He clings on, anxious; he raves and perspires, blood flows from
> his nose without any trauma; he stiffens, is jaundiced, feels cold and distant.
> Thirsty, his mouth groans, he cries, he wastes down to nothing.
> Lividity appears in the extremities, with the front yellow-green
> There is little urine, and raw food gets liquefied.
> A very reliable sign is the contraction of the testicles
> Or the retraction of the private part, the virile member:
> These are signs through which the expectation of death is suggested.[25]

---

24. Sinno, *Regimen sanitatis*, 344.
25. Ibid., 348.

Finally, both versions of the text come back into correlation with one another with the next section titled "The Semiotics of the Dying":

> By these signs you may confidently recognize when a sick person is dying:
> First by the forehead, which will redden,
> and by the feet, which will become cold.
> Then, as the end approaches, the brow relaxes,
> the mind cuts out, the left eye tears up,
> hearing stops, and the nose whitens up to the tip.
> Freely weeping, he announces the hour of death.
> Before he goes, the pulse moves with great exertion.
> Keep watch night and day over a suffering child;
> But if an old person sleeps, it means he will die that night.[26]

Both versions of the *Flos medicinae* give great attention to symptoms of approaching death diagnosed from the excreta. A section on "The Semiotics of Urine," for instance, instructs that if the urine is either too pale or tending toward a dark color of black, it is a sign of death; "The Semiotics of Stool" advises that a greenish-black color betokens death.[27] "The Semiotics of Let Blood" explains that blood that is "sulfuric, that quickly splits and breaks apart" should be read as an indication that the person is coming to the terminus of life.[28] The section on "The Semiotics of Sweat" notes that a cold sweat indicates the unraveling of life (*vitam detexit*). "The Semiotics of Dreams" suggests that a good night's rest, filled with dreams, conduces to health; but if sleep and dreams refuse to come, it is a sign of an "intense or painful death."[29] "The Semiotics of Farts" is more restrained in its prediction, noting that "a little fart with no sound augurs better than one that is noisy . . . a buzzing one that is out of control portends frenzy and suffering."[30]

Lists of the mortal signs occasionally circulated as independent tractates. Thus the chapter on the mortal signs of John of Mirfield's *Breviarium Bartholomei*, an encyclopedic medical handbook, sometimes was copied separately. A surviving version is in London, British Library, Lambeth MS 444.[31] Occasionally, such independent texts were illustrated with drawings

---

26. De Renzi, *Flos medicinae Scholae Salerni*, 1:491; cf. Sinno, *Regimen sanitatis*, 348–50.
27. De Renzi, *Flos medicinae Scholae Salerni*, 1:492, 494; cf. Sinno, *Regimen sanitatis*, 360–62.
28. De Renzi, *Flos medicinae Scholae Salerni*, 1:493; cf. Sinno, *Regimen sanitatis*, 356–58.
29. De Renzi, *Flos medicinae Scholae Salerni*, 1:494; cf. Sinno, *Regimen sanitatis*, 358–60.
30. De Renzi, *Flos medicinae Scholae Salerni*, 1:491; cf. Sinno, *Regimen sanitatis*, 362.
31. Rossell Hope Robbins, "Signs of Death in Middle English," *Mediaeval Studies* 32, no. 1 (1970): 282.

of human figures, showing areas of the body to check for particular indicators. A manuscript held at the Wellcome Medical Library in London shows a "Death Prognostic Man" (figure 2.1). The accompanying text guides the interpretation of the figure: "Here are the signs of death discovered by Hippocrates."[32] Circles on the figure's body show where to look for particular signs, with the expected focus on the brow, ears, face, feet, and pulse points. Various swellings, tender points, and inflammations from classic Hippocratic prognostics are also shown. The lessons of Death Prognostic Man are supplemented by other diagnostic images. These include "Wound Man," "Disease Man," "Pain Tree," and a colored chart for urinomancy: green and black flasks of urine in the lower right zone designate death, in line with Hippocratic teaching.

Hippocratic lists also occasionally made their way into literary works, where the deaths of characters were described in similar terms. An apt example is *Tundale's Vision*, a widely disseminated tale from the mid-twelfth century. It is the story of a man who dies, receives a tour of the afterlife by turns terrifying and edifying, and then returns to his body in order to do penance and share his experiences. Though fictive, the story circulated as a true account. Tundale's death scene includes a checklist of the most commonly cited mortal signs:

> The signs of death were present: his hair whitened, his forehead hardened, his eyes wandered, his nose sharpened, his lips grew pale, he became unconscious, and all the parts of his body became rigid. . . . From almost the tenth hour of the fourth day up to the same hour on Saturday he lay dead, with no signs of life remaining in him, except that those who diligently took care to palpate his body detected a little heat in his left chest. For this reason, they did not want to bury his body.[33]

Tundale later revived and gave an account of his tour of heaven and hell. Like his real contemporary Christina Mirabilis, his visionary experience was coded as a death and resurrection, rather than as a trance or illness.

Aside from the handbooks of medical professionals, university men versed in scholastic methods were also familiar with Hippocratic medical traditions. A passage in Vincent of Beauvais's enormously popular encyclopedia is one of the most extensive treatments of how to determine a death in a scholastic

---

32. "Haec sunt signa mortis inventa per Ipocratem," London, Wellcome Medical Library, MS 49, fol. 40r. For background, see F. Saxl, "A Spiritual Encyclopedia of the Later Middle Ages," *Journal of the Warburg and Cortauld Institutes* 5 (1942): 82–142.

33. Wagner, *Visio Tnugdali lateinisch*, 8.

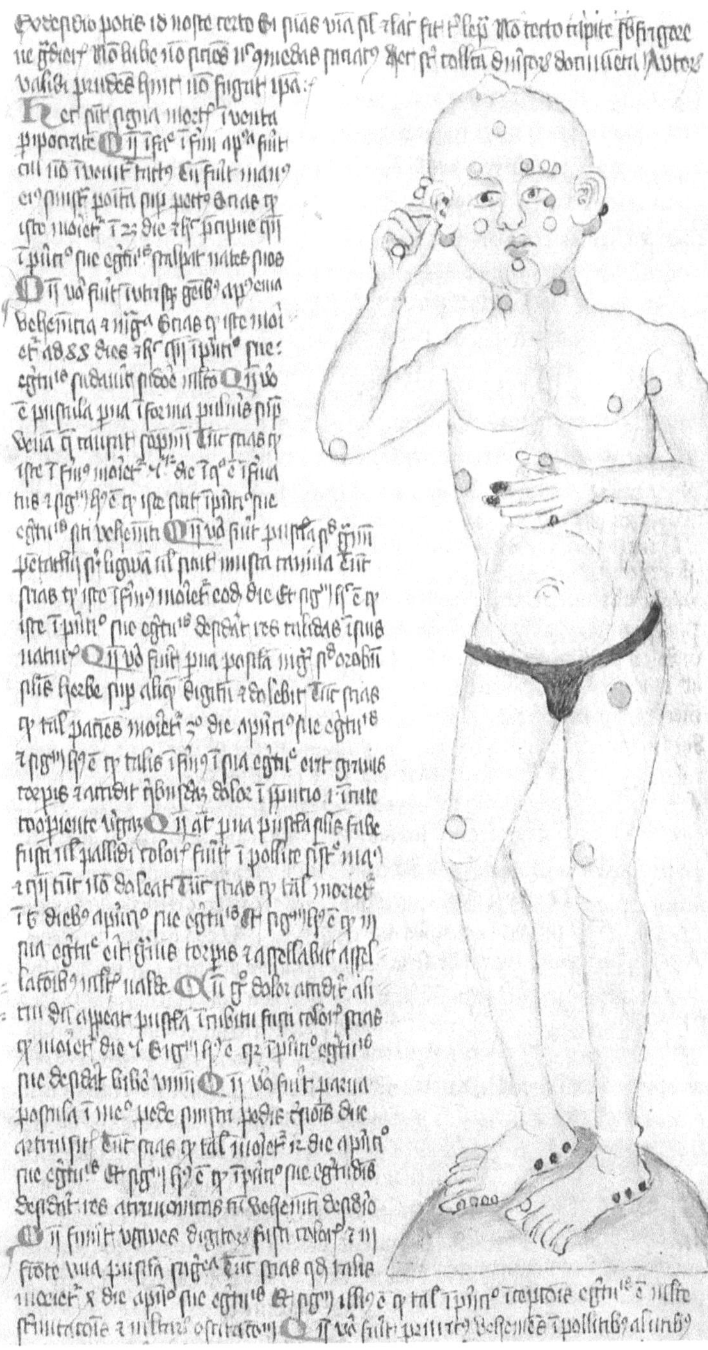

FIGURE 2.1. This "Death Prognostic Man" accompanies a text about the Hippocratic signs of death. The figure is marked with circles and lesions showing the physician where to look for certain signs and symptoms. Wellcome Medical Library, London, MS 49, fol. 40r, fifteenth century.
Courtesy of the Wellcome Library, London.

work of natural philosophy. Vincent (1190–ca. 1264) was comprehensive in his research, drawing upon several different sources for the latest information and scattering it across his massive work, the *Speculum majus* (*Great Mirror*). The latter is comprised of three large volumes—the *Speculum naturale*, *Speculum doctrinale*, and *Speculum historiale*—and in total includes eighty books and 9,885 chapters. It was rightly regarded as the most extensive summa of all knowledge of its day.[34] For our purposes, the *Speculum naturale* is the most useful volume of Vincent's work. Book 31 includes extensive discussion of the signs of death. Vincent's originary source is Hippocrates as mediated by Muhammed ibn Zakariya al-Razi, a Persian physician of the tenth to eleventh centuries. In keeping with the scholastic approach of thirteenth-century university learning, Vincent was happy to mine other cultural traditions, like this translated Arabic work, for useful knowledge. Al-Razi's *Book of Medicine Dedicated to Mansur* had been translated by Gerard of Cremona in twelfth-century Toledo and ultimately became one of the most influential works of medicine in the Latin West.[35] Al-Razi, in turn, came from a cultural tradition in which the Hippocratic *Aphorisms* and other anatomical and medical treatises were the subjects of extensive commentary.

In the chapter on the signs of death, Vincent immediately introduces al-Razi as a leading authority and quotes him at length:

> *Al-Razi in al-Mansur, part eight, writes:* At that time the face will have collapsed, the eyes will appear sunken, the temples will have caved in, the ears will have become cold and turn yellow (and their end parts that hang down will have shrunk), and the facial skin will appear slack.
>
> Besides these things, if the patient passes anything the color yellow, or else green or black, then the ill person will not last long past the evacuation: all these are signs of death. In particular black urine, black saliva, or black stools are signs that indicate death.
>
> Furthermore, if there are greatly burning fevers these are strong indicators of death. Likewise, foul-smelling breath and mouth in the course of an acute illness is a sign of death. Again, breaking out in a labored sweat on the forehead, and weakness of the pulse and movements, is a

---

34. Gregory G. Guzman, "The Encyclopedist Vincent of Beauvais and His Mongol Extracts from John of Plano Carpini and Simon of Saint-Quentin," *Speculum* 49, no. 2 (1974): 287–307. The *Speculum morale*, sometimes attributed to Vincent, is spurious.

35. H. Ritter and R. Walzer, "Arabische Übersetzungen griechischer Ärtze in Stambuler Bibliotheken," *Sitzungsberichte der Preussischen Akademie der Wissenschaften*, 1934, 907; Luis García-Ballester, "A Marginal Learned Medical World: Jewish, Muslim, and Christian Medical Practitioners, and the Use of Arabic Medical Sources in Late Medieval Spain," in *Practical Medicine from Salerno to the Black Death*, ed. Luis García-Ballester et al. (Cambridge, 1994), 353–94.

sign of death. Similarly, a glazed eye that does not move, and shudders that do not stop but that seem almost to overlap there are so many, are signs of death. . . . If an abscess arises on any body part, accompanied by either pain or followed by foaming, and burning or thirst, things look bad. If at the same time there is a tremor in the heart, it will be fatal.

Mentioning the names of dead people is a bad sign; strong thirst accompanying a cold sweat is very bad; and cold breath with diminishing strength signifies that the patient is near death. A cold sweat with a high fever is worst of all: if shivering follows a sweat, it is a bad sign.

The strengths of these signs ought to be compared with one another: if there is one good strong sign, it may outweigh many bad signs.[36]

Vincent's thorough presentation of al-Razi's gloss demonstrates that he was well attuned to contemporary trends in theoretical medicine. The chief element of the above list that is out of place is the advice that "mentioning the names of dead people is a bad sign." This sign—which may actually be al-Razi's interpolation, rather than Vincent's—seemingly derives from a religious, rather than a medical, purview on death; it suggests that the dying were believed to be seeing into the next world and greeting already-dead acquaintances by name. It is a unique inclusion that I have not found in other lists of mortal signs.

Having discussed al-Razi in some detail, Vincent then moves on to a direct presentation of Hippocrates. It is unclear whether Vincent was even aware that the al-Razi text he quoted was a commentary on the very same Greek medical writings.

Hippocrates in the book of Aphorisms: An illness in which sleep is labored will be fatal. And if in the course of any illness . . . black bile comes out either below or up top, it will be fatal. If the patient has fevers along with other symptoms, and if the eyes tear up involuntarily, that is unfortunate. In cases of acute sickness, coldness of the extremities is bad. Likewise, if the flesh around the bones of the patient is livid, that is bad. The same goes for a rattle while vomiting, and redness in the eyes, and stiffness while sweating. Whoever has immoderate pain in the brain will die within three days; if the pains disappear, he will be healed.[37]

It should be clear by now that the various symptoms described under the rubric of mortal signs actually covered a spectrum of diagnostic situations,

---

36. Vincent of Beauvais, *Speculum naturale* (Graz, 1964), col. 2372.
37. Ibid., cols. 2372–73.

from predicting the course of acute illnesses to prognosticating fatalities to recognizing the processes of dying in the moribund. While the last category is the element of greatest interest for my purposes, discussions of this factor were inextricably bound up with the other two.

Vernacularization of the Mortal Signs

As we have seen, investigations into the physiology of life and death first emerged in the twelfth-century monastic milieu, which worked to correlate the patristic theology of the soul with the medical anatomy of the spirit. In the later part of the twelfth century this discourse was taken up by medical professionals, who incorporated knowledge of the Hippocratic mortal signs into their handbooks, and in the thirteenth century by university scholars like Vincent of Beauvais, who brought in the latest translations and Arabic commentaries. Thus far, I have focused upon elite Latinate discourses consumed by monastic intellectuals, university scholars, and (at a somewhat lower social level) professional physicians who were literate. There also are indications, however, that this knowledge was at least partially disseminated to broader segments of the population as well. By the fourteenth century, many of these texts were passing into different vernaculars. In theory, then, many of the ideas discussed above were available to a broader populace in the later Middle Ages.

The Latin version of the *Speculum naturale* of Vincent of Beauvais, for example, often was recopied and excerpted. The work was also translated into an array of vernacular languages including English, French, German, Catalan, Spanish, and Dutch.[38] And when movable type became available in the latter part of the fifteenth century, the entire, three-volume *Speculum majus* was swiftly printed, appearing three times in incunabula editions.[39] This text very likely constituted one of the main lines of transmission of medical ideas outside the university context. Indeed, we can tentatively discern some lines of reception. The mid-twentieth-century scholar Pauline Aiken, for example, meticulously traced a number of Chaucer's ideas, most especially his understanding of medicine, back to Vincent's *Speculum naturale*.[40] The English version of this work very likely provides a genealogy for

---

38. Guzman, "The Encyclopedist Vincent of Beauvais and His Mongol Extracts."
39. Ibid.
40. Pauline Aiken, "Vincent of Beauvais and Dame Pertelote's Knowledge of Medicine," *Speculum* 10, no. 3 (1935): 281–87; Pauline Aiken, "Arcite's Illness and Vincent of Beauvais," *Publications of the Modern Language Association* 51, no. 2 (1936): 361–69; Pauline Aiken, "Vincent of Beauvais and the Green Yeoman's Lecture on Demonology," *Studies in Philology* 35, no. 1 (1938): 1–9; Pauline Aiken, "Vincent of Beauvais and Chaucer's Knowledge of Alchemy," *Studies in Philology* 41, no. 3 (1944): 371–89; Pauline Aiken, "Vincent of Beauvais and the 'Houres' of Chaucer's Physician,"

many of Chaucer's discussions of illness and medicine. The herbal of Macer Floridus, quoted above, was also translated into the vernaculars of nearly every European language group: German, French, Italian, Catalan, Middle Dutch, and Middle English.[41] *Tundale's Vision*, the twelfth-century vision text that includes a death scene enumerating the mortal signs, was wildly popular in translation: the text is found in fifteen different vernaculars, from Icelandic to Belorussian.[42]

We have a fascinating fragment of evidence for the reception of these ideas in the *Fasciculus Morum* (*Cluster of Customs*), a fourteenth-century preacher's aid composed by an anonymous English Franciscan. The work is chiefly in Latin but breaks into Middle English in the middle of a discussion of the mortal signs, attributing the information to hearsay. This detail suggests that this set of Middle English verses of the mortal signs already was in circulation in that language and recorded by the preacher from oral sources. The section begins in Latin:

> Note that according to blessed Jerome, the signs of death are these: the nose grows cold, the face turns pale, the eyes darken, the ears grow deaf, the nerves and the veins rupture, and the heart is split in two.
>
> There is nothing viler or more abominable than a dead cadaver. It is not allowed to stay in the house, lest the people there should die from the stench. . . . Therefore someone has said in English:

> When þe hede quakyth
> And þe lyppis blakyth
> And þe nose sharpyth
> And þe senow stakyth
> And þe brest pantyth
> And þe breþe wantyþ
> And þe teþe ratelȝt
> And þe þrote roteliþ
> And þe sowle is wente owte
> þe body ne tyt but a clowte
> Sone be it so stekenn
> þe sowle all clene ys forȝetenn.[43]

Studies in Philology 53, no. 1 (1956): 22–24. See also W. K. Wimsatt Jr., "Vincent of Beauvais and Chaucer's Cleopatra and Croesus," *Speculum* 12, no. 3 (1937): 375–81.

41. Flood, "Medieval Herbal Tradition of Macer Floridus," 65. The Middle English translation in the British Library is MS Add. 37786.

42. Robert Easting, *Visions of the Other World in Middle English* (Cambridge, 1997), 70–71.

43. Siegfried Wenzel, ed. and trans., *Fasciculus Morum: A Fourteenth-Century Preacher's Handbook* (University Park, PA, 1989), 718–21.

The Middle English verse translates thusly:

> When the head trembles
> And the lips turn pale
> And the nose sharpens
> And the sinews stiffen
> And the breast shudders
> And the breath is wanting
> And the teeth chatter
> And the throat rattles
> And the soul has gone out
> Then the body is nothing but a lump.
> Soon it will stink so badly
> That the soul will be completely forgotten.

The passage provides clear evidence that lists of the Hippocratic mortal signs were circulating from Latin to vernaculars and back. Furthermore, the fact that the list existed in this particular form—translated, versified, and rhymed—suggests that it likely functioned as a popular mnemonic device. The rhyming form in Middle English suggests an oral "checklist" of things to remember to look for when presented with an uncertain death.

We also find the death signs referenced in artistic portrayals of deathbed scenes. For example, figure 2.2 shows a personified Death looming over a moribund man. Death pierces his victim's heart with a lance, signaling that the vital signs must soon cease as the moment of death has arrived. At the foot of the bed, a physician glumly contemplates a flask filled with dark urine in his right hand and grasps a phlebotomy knife in his left. Another man checks for the pulse while a woman joins her hands in prayer. All these actions align with the ways in which life and death were diagnosed in medieval medicine.

Likewise, a sequence of miniature illumination scenes from the 1434 *Hours of Catherine of Cleves* takes the viewer through the process of death and burial, step by step.[44] The set accompanies the Monday Office of the Dead and begins with an image of man on his deathbed (figure 2.3). The man lies limply, his eyes closed and his head drooping to the side. The doctor holds aloft a flask filled with vivid green urine—a negative sign. Other figures surrounding the dying man include a priest for the last rites; the man's wife, dressed in mourning and reading prayers; some women who

---

44. For background, see John Plummer, *The Hours of Catherine of Cleves* (New York, 2002).

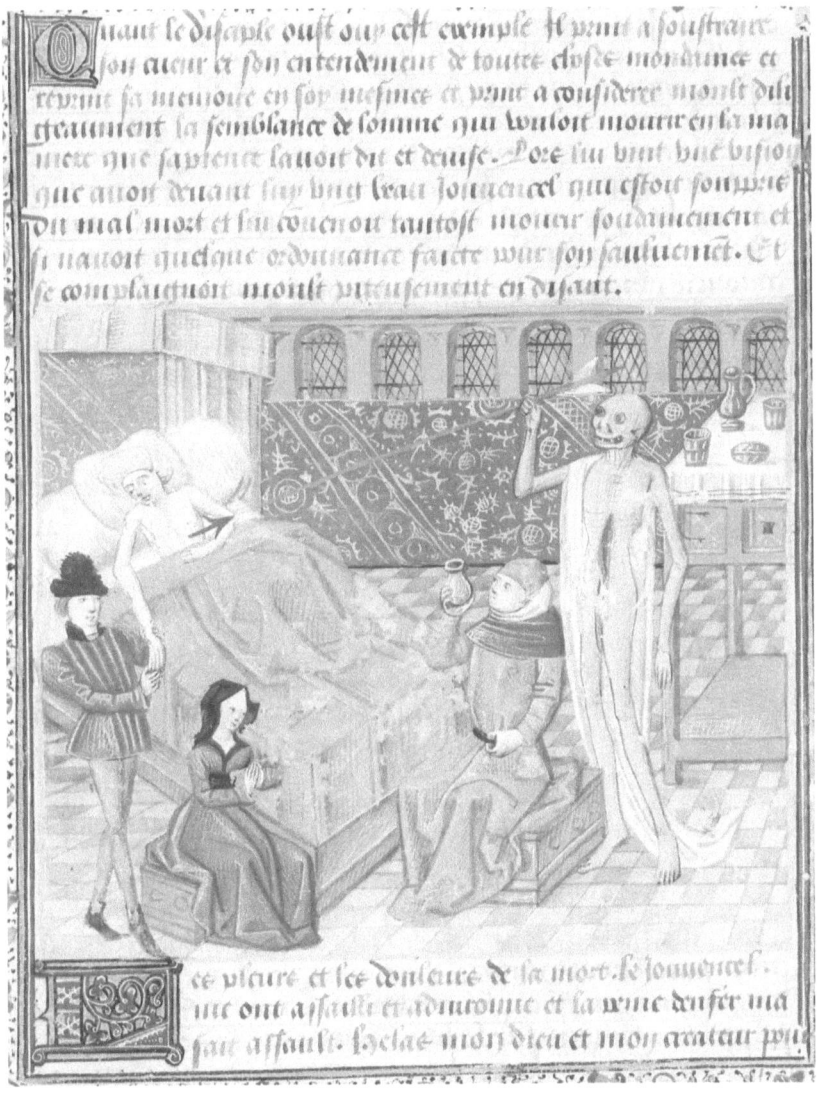

FIGURE 2.2. In this illumination Death is personified as an animate cadaver piercing the heart of a sick man with a long lance. A physician sits nearby with a urine flask and a phlebotomy knife, while another man checks the victim's pulse. Illumination from *Le Trésor de Sapience* (*Treasure of Wisdom*) by Jean Gerson, France, fifteenth century.
Musée Condé, Chantilly, France, MS 146, fol. 2v. © RMN-Grand Palais / Art Resource, NY.

soothe the man's forehead and place a lit taper in his right hand; and two garishly dressed youths bouncing into the room, clearly the heirs eager to acquire their inheritance. One of the latter also appears in the lower margin, gleefully opening a chest of coins.

FIGURE 2.3. As an older man passes away, his family sits vigil and prays. At the back of the room, the physician inspects the victim's green urine, a sure sign that he is soon to die, while some women place a taper in his hand. Meanwhile, two well-dressed young men, the heirs, joyfully enter the room. In the bottom margin, one of these youths is shown opening a coffer filled with coins. Illumination from the *Hours of Catherine of Cleves*, 1434.
Courtesy of the Pierpont Morgan Library, MS M.917/945, p. 180.

DIAGNOSING DEATH   87

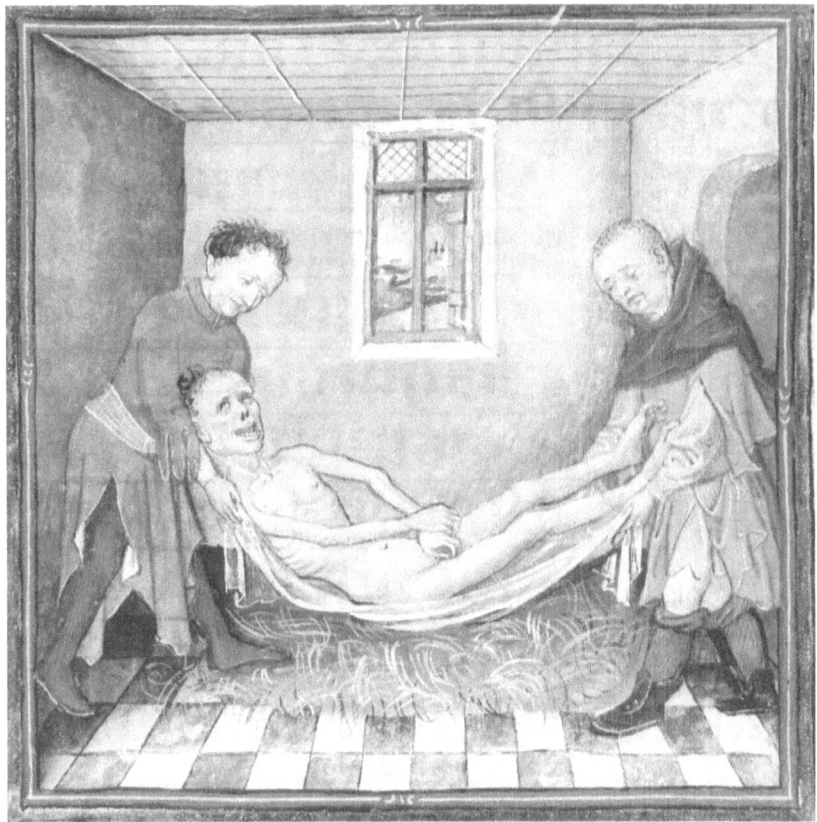

FIGURE 2.4. The same man shown in figure 2.3 is now dead and his bedchamber has been emptied of furniture. Two men lay the corpse on the floor, over a pallet of straw, until it can be transported to church for the funeral. The dead man's stiff pose and rictus grin are vivid details. Illumination from the *Hours of Catherine of Cleves*, 1434.
Courtesy of the Pierpont Morgan Library, MS M.917/945, fol. 99v.

A subsequent illumination displays the pathetic spectacle of the man's body after his passing (figure 2.4). This scene is set in the same room as the death vigil, but the furnishings have been removed and the windowpanes thrown open for ventilation. The nude cadaver of the now-dead man is transported on an ad hoc litter—a sheet held on either side by two men—and is set to rest on a pallet of straw placed on the floor to catch any effluvia. The rictus grin, hollow eyes, and stiff limbs of the figure clearly represent some of the signs of death. It was customary to place a corpse on the floor, rather than to leave it on a bed, in the lead up to the funerary rites. Additional images in the sequence show the coffin in church during the funeral mass, the interment, and a requiem mass.[45]

Inert but Intact

Some deaths, however, were particularly difficult to diagnose. The most complicated category of deaths were the untimely deaths of young adults in the fullest vigor of life, without any clear trauma or violence. A kind death, a gentle death of a person in the prime of life, was puzzling. In order for death to be clear and evident, there had to be visible corporeal signs of death's ravages. And here we reach a vitally important point in the diagnosis of death: any death that involved evident signs of disease, or else extensive tissue destruction and/or blood loss, would be certain and self-evident. Corporeal trauma—whether through violent injury or accidents, serious illness, or natural disasters like fire or famine—made it abundantly clear that a body could no longer sustain life; the damage was evident and readily apprehensible as a cause of death. Conversely, subtle deaths due to internal illnesses or injuries could be ambiguous and difficult to evaluate. Faced with a young body that was inert but intact, observers sometimes were flummoxed about how to proceed.

In a detailed discussion of burial norms, for example, William Durandus considered the case of individuals who die "for no apparent reason, but only through the judgment of God."[46] Until the corpse of such a person began to putrefy and break down, mortality could be difficult to certify. Putrefaction—another form of tissue destruction—was an incontrovertible and solid proof of death; as we have seen in previous chapters, the absence of putrefaction—in the case of the saints or the recently dead—was sometimes linked to an assumption that the cadaver still possessed some vitality. As one source mused, "Why would a body be considered dead, in the absence of injuries [*fractura*]?"[47] It was a question that would be repeated often.

From the thirteenth century onward, medical writings about mortality began to include attempts to discriminate between deaths and other, similar-seeming states. These alternatives are articulated and described as confusingly similar to death, and attempts were made to delimit the boundaries between mortality and other states. As noted earlier, this was a fairly new set

---

45. Plummer, *Hours of Catherine of Cleves*, 44–46.
46. *The Rationale divonorum officiorum of William Durand of Mende: A New Translation of the Prologue and Book One*, trans. Timothy M. Thibodeau (New York, 2007), 58.
47. *MTC*, 548.

of juxtapositions. Though trances and deaths existed as separate categories, they had been allowed to bleed into one another rather often. As we have seen in the case of Christina Mirabilis and Tundale, earlier writers were not particularly concerned to sort out the differences between trances and death, between visions and dreams, or between feverish insights and revelation. Departed souls might journey to other realms, then return to the body again—yet meticulously categorizing these experiences from hindsight and setting them off from one another was unimportant to observers. Increasingly, however, these were becoming points of concern for intellectuals, at least, who understandably wished to set forth clear boundaries for death. The thirteenth- to fourteenth-century *medicus* Pietro d'Abano, for example, noted that apoplectic seizures could deceptively produce a deathlike state, in which the life signs were faint and nearly undetectable.[48] Another deathlike syndrome noted in various medical texts was "syncope," a trance state in which "motion and sensation are removed from the body for the greater part, through weakness of the heart; and the word 'syncope' is synonymous with 'little death.'"[49] Here we see a clearer delimitation of trances as wholly natural states in which the sufferer remained alive, rather than being seen as temporarily dead.

Scrupulous ruling-out of alternate states that mimicked death was important for several reasons. First, of course, standard tools for recognizing death were useful. The fear of misdiagnosing death, leading to premature burial, seems to be a perennial one found in many times and places. The decision to bury often engendered considerable doubt and trepidation, as in this illuminating anecdote from the early thirteenth-century *Flowers of History*:

> In the morning . . . when the brothers were rising for Prime and were crossing before the chapter-house on their way to church, they saw this brother . . . lying prostrate and barefoot, with his face intent and fixed on the floor. . . . Seeing this, the astonished brothers came running. When they tried to raise him, they found that he was unconscious and lacked any motion in his body. His eyeballs were turned back in the sockets and these seats of light as well as his nose were flecked with blood. After the pulses of his veins, which at first had been very far apart, ceased almost entirely, then everyone agreed that he had died. At

---

48. Cited in Maaike van der Lugt, "The Incubus in Scholastic Debate: Medicine, Theology, and Popular Belief," in *Religion and Medicine in the Middle Ages*, ed. Peter Biller and Joseph Zeigler (Woodbridge, 2001), 175.

49. John of Gaddesden, *Rosa anglica sive rosa medicinae*, ed. and trans. Winifred Wulfe (London, 1923), 122.

long last, they discerned some breath, albeit faint, so they washed his neck, chest, and hands with cold water. And lo! At first they saw his whole body shudder slightly, but he soon became restful and remained entirely still.

For a long time they did not know what to do, for they could scarcely figure out whether he was dead or if he was improving at all. Finally, after a debate, they carried him into the infirmary, placing him on a bed where some designated caretakers might maintain a careful watch over him. Next, they placed plasters on his chest and pricked the soles of his feet with needles but could not discover any sign in him that seemed to indicate a living man.[50]

The passage emphasizes the real confusion of the monk's brothers: "for a long time they did not know what to do, for they could scarcely figure out whether he was dead. . . . Finally, after a debate. . . ." These lines suggest an agonized perplexity over how to determine whether the monk was living or dead. One is reminded of the similar scene in the story of the visionary knight Tundale. The first recourse in any case of unclear death seems to have been to check for breath, pulse, and heartbeat. At the same time, however, medieval people realized that these indicators of life could sometimes be faint and difficult to detect, particularly if a person was ill or otherwise weakened. Erring on the side of caution, the monk was transported to the infirmary and placed under vigil, a custom similar to that of a wake: the living kept watch by the insensible body for several days and nights following a possible death, but before final burial. We see a similar action in a miracle story attributed to Saint Nicholas: when a child sickened he "lay as if dead for three days, such that his relatives and the other people present did not know whether he was living or dead."[51] The custom of the vigil served as a reasonable waiting period before an immobile and unreactive person would be considered definitively deceased. During this time, a constant rotation of vigil keepers would have kept watch for any significant activity, such as movements, sighs, or moans that would indicate the lingering presence of life. Various revival measures would be attempted as well. In the case of the comatose monk, this was done first through a cold washing of his chest, neck, and hands and later via an application of plasters, presumably in an effort to stimulate the

---

50. Roger of Wendover, *Chronica, sive flores historiarum*, ed. Henry O. Coxe, 4 vols. (London, 1851), 3:98.
51. Christian Krötzl, "'*Evidentissima signa mortis*': Zu Tod und Todesfeststellung im Mittelalterlichen Mirakelberichten," in *Symbole des Alltags, Alltag der Symbole: Festschrift für Harry Kühnel zum 65. Geburtstag*, ed. Gertrud Blaschitz et al. (Graz, 1992), 770.

circulation or perhaps awaken the sense of smell. As a last resort, the brothers finally stabbed his feet with pins in the hopes of stimulating a pain reaction. This test for life is one with a long history; it is frequently attested in hagiographies, for example, which likewise portray observers of entranced visionaries subjecting them to pinpricks and pinches, in order to see whether or not they could be roused from their raptures or lethargies.[52] Archaeological evidence of the practice exists as well, albeit from a somewhat later period.[53]

Some monasteries had designated individuals who were trained to recognize death. The death ritual at Cluny, for instance, refers to specialists who were in charge of diagnosing the onset of death: "when servants who are well trained and highly skilled in such matters see that the hour of his death is now imminent, they spread a hair shirt on the ground and sprinkle ashes on it in the shape of a cross. Then they raise the sick man out of his bed and place him on the hair shirt."[54] The sick brother would then be watched carefully until it was clear that the moment of his passing had arrived. At that point the person who was "well trained and accustomed to the particular task" would make the determination of death and rouse the whole community by beating a tablet.[55] It remains unclear precisely what sort of training such a person would have received, but it seems likely that he might have worked in the infirmary and had wide experience of the course of various illnesses and the approach of death.

Outside the monastic context, the process of determining death was rooted in local community consensus. It was fully expected that everyone would have an opinion. Gossip spread quickly through medieval communities, and crowds gathered in case of any unwonted event. In consequence, determining deaths was often a community affair at the local level. As one source offhandedly comments: "After everyone had arrived and examined him throughout two daylight hours, it seemed he was completely dead, having no sign of life."[56] In another case, a woman's debilitating illness was the subject of local discussion for some time, for her case was "followed publicly by everyone." As her condition worsened, her husband wished to give her the last rites and to have someone in a position of authority present. He traveled

---

52. Daniel Bornstein, "Violenza al corpo di una santa: fra agiografia e pronografia. A proposito de Douceline di Digne," *Quaderni Medievali* 39 (1995): 31–46.

53. Georges Leonetti et al., "Evidence of Pin Implantation as a Means of Verifying Death During the Great Plague of Marseilles (1722)," *Journal of Forensic Science* 42, no. 4 (1997): 744–48.

54. Frederick Paxton with the collaboration of Isabelle Cochelin, *The Death Ritual at Cluny in the Central Middle Ages / Le ritual de la mort à Cluny au moyen âge central* (Turnhout, 2013), 90–91. The text includes a Latin edition of the death ritual.

55. Paxton, *Death Ritual at Cluny*, 92–93.

56. Krötzl, "'*Evidentissima signa mortis*,'" 772.

from his rural parish to Stockholm in order to recruit a Dominican friar for this purpose; the friar, in his turn, felt it was appropriate to consult with the neighbors before declaring her dead. As the friar later remembered the scene,

> At length, consumed by illness, she reached her last breath: she was foaming at the mouth, and since she had her eyes closed and all her members were rigid, it seemed to me to be a clear indication of her passing, that her body had been quit by her soul. So I called together the grieving neighbors and asked for their advice about this problem. After they all arrived, they relocated the body from the bed to the floor, in the manner of a funeral.[57]

The customary period of waiting before burial might also give time for two other changes that are normally undergone by dead bodies to be observed. The first is livor mortis or lividity, a discoloration of the corpse caused by the gravitational pooling of the blood in the lowest portion of the body once the heart stops pumping it throughout the circulatory system. Livor mortis normally sets in between thirty minutes and three hours postmortem; afterward, the portion of the body positioned lowest will appear bruised and the upper part pale.[58] Some of the mortal signs mentioned in medieval texts are known side effects of livor mortis, such as "sharpening of the nose" and "flattening of the temples," caused by the deplumping of the flesh after the settling of the blood.[59] In addition, rigor mortis, a temporary contraction of the muscles that begins a few hours after death and that lasts two to three days, would likely be observable during the period of a wake.

Professionalizing Death

Making sure that a person was truly dead and not suffering from some other ailment or condition was part of a broader project of firming up the boundary between nature and supernature in the later medieval centuries.

---

57. Gregorius, *Miracula Sanctae Crucis Stockholmiae seculo XV ineunte* (Upsala, 1725), 38–39.

58. Dick Teresi, *The Undead: Organ Harvesting, the Ice-Water Test, Beating-Heart Cadavers—How Medicine Is Blurring the Line between Life and Death* (New York, 2012), 236. Though livor mortis is common at death, it seems not to have been universally understood. Orderic Vitalis recounts how an abbot's corpse was divided in half by color postmortem: "the color of lead" on the right side and "snowy white" on the left. This suggests that the abbot died while lying on his right side, which then became darkened as a result of the blood pooling there. Orderic states that the bicoloration "struck terror into all who saw it" and that many debated its origin and meaning. OV, 4:162.

59. I am indebted to professional mortician Caitlin Doughty for providing this information in a series of personal communications, April 2013. See now Caitlin Doughty, *Smoke Gets in Your Eyes, and Other Lessons from the Crematorium* (New York, 2014).

Medicine was an integral part of this process. The increasingly common inclusion of doctors in artistic portrayals of deathbed scenes, for instance, indicates that mortality was coming under the aegis of a professionalized guild of experts, who had the authority to establish life or death. Extremely talented medical practitioners might even gain reputations for acquiring their skills via supernatural dealings, as was the case for the Portuguese physician Gil de Santarém, considered variously as either a saintly doctor or a covert necromancer.[60] Such developments indicate the mysterious quality of doctors' diagnostic and healing skills to lay observers.

In the twelfth century, the first specific university training centers were being established at locations like Salerno, Bologna, or Toledo, largely for theoretical specialists. (Surgery remained a distinct subspecialty practiced both by the learned and by largely untrained barbers and bloodletters.)[61] It was only natural that physicians would eventually come to be employed by the power structures of medieval Europe; this was increasingly the case from the second half of the thirteenth century on. The rise of professional medicine prompted the establishment of legal inquests and coroners' offices, for instance. In later medieval England, a formal inquest was opened in the event that a person died "from a death other than their rightful death."[62] In such cases, whether by murder, suicide, or accident, the testimony of witnesses would be correlated with the condition of the corpse, with medical specialists examining the body for physical evidence to confirm or deny the eyewitness accounts. Coroners would be asked not only to determine the *fact* of death, but also to offer an explanation of the *cause* of death: Which wound, stemming from which circumstance, was responsible for the mortal injury? Juridical processes could hang on the outcome.

For example, in 1296 in the Crown of Aragon, a surgeon was called to testify in a murder case. He explained that he had looked for the pulse of the victim on his neck but determined that there was none: the victim was dead by the time of his arrival. Then he examined the victim's body, finding a wound that he considered to be the cause of death, and he investigated it manually. When asked what might have caused a wound of that depth and

---

60. Iona McCleery, "Saintly Physician, Diabolical Doctor, Medieval Saint: Exploring the Reputation of Gil de Santarém in Medieval and Renaissance Portugal," *Portuguese Studies* 21 (2005): 112–25.

61. P. Kenneth Himmelman, "The Medicinal Body: An Analysis of Medicinal Cannibalism in Europe, 1300–1700," *Dialectical Anthropology* 22, no. 2 (1997): 189.

62. Reginald Sharpe, ed., *Calendar of Coroners Rolls of the City of London, A.D. 1300–1378* (London, 1913), xiv. I have been unable to consult the new, in-depth study of coroners' procedures by Sara M. Butler, *Forensic Medicine and Death Investigation in Medieval England* (New York, 2015).

shape, he offered that to his "expert touch" it felt like the wound of a small sword or dagger.[63] In France, the procedure of investigation was similar. In 1336 in the Provençal town of Manosque, a barber and a surgeon were interviewed by the court as expert witnesses and asked to examine the corpse of a murder victim. "Having stripped the cadaver, turned it over, thumped it, probed it with a small wax candle, and the other things that are customary in such cases," they determined that a chest wound was the cause of death.[64] The reference to probing the cadaver with a candle, at first puzzling, is clarified by another case from the year 1322, which explains that candles were used to measure the depth of a wound and to check for any involuntary flinching without inflicting further injury.[65] (They also, when lit, might be utilized to detect a flicker of breath before the mouth or nostrils.) Cases such as these could be multiplied: from the thirteenth century onward, the office of coroner was swiftly becoming an important aspect of royal institutions of justice, peacekeeping, and (potentially) the establishing of inheritances.

A fascinating case study of this professionalizing process may be seen when we turn to the last set of sources I want to introduce: canonization dossiers. Clerics and medical doctors alike (including Pietro d'Abano) advised that in order to authenticate reputed resurrections by saints, the patient must first definitively be proven dead: without death, there could be no resurrection. This injunction was taken very seriously in cases for canonization. Thus the impulse to precisely define death and to differentiate it from other states found a crucial application here. Indeed, as a particular category of saintly miracle, resurrections gained in importance after the late thirteenth century,[66] a phenomenon that is directly related to the concurrent rise of professional medicine and the use of medical practitioners by dominant authorities. Materials relating to resurrection miracles in hagiographies and canonization dossiers are thus among the richest sources available for studying how death was debated and determined. Furthermore, since such sources include the direct testimony of both medical professionals and nonprofessionals, clergy and laity, literate and illiterate, they provide access to the thought processes of a wide cross-section of medieval society. These texts show that medieval people, even those without any medical training, often had a very good grasp of the physical changes attendant upon a death. Thus as one witness testified

---

63. Marie Kelleher, *The Measure of Woman: Law and Female Identity in the Crown of Aragon* (Philadelphia, 2010), 42–43.

64. Joseph Shatzmiller, "The Jurisprudence of the Dead Body," in *Il Cadavere / The Corpse*, Micrologus 7 (Turnhout, 1999), 227.

65. Ibid.

66. Vauchez, *Sainthood in the Later Middle Ages*, 467.

at such an inquiry, a child "demonstrated that he was deceased through clear enough signs. That is: he lacked the vital breath; his face was discolored by bruising and pallor, and his whole body was seized with stiffness."[67] Local communities debated and formed their own opinions, as always. However, the canonization documents also show how the authority of professionals with expertise in diagnosing death was gaining in importance.

Intact Deaths and Miraculous Resurrections

A uniquely useful source for miraculous resurrections derives from the cult of Thomas of Cantilupe, bishop of Hereford. Thomas died in odor of sanctity in 1282 and was soon credited with numerous resurrection miracles. Among them: a little girl, Joan, whose playmate pushed her into the fishpond of a tavern while her parents were drinking inside; a little boy, Nicholas, who fell into a river and drowned while looking after the family cow; a small boy named Walfrid whose head was run over by a cart; a hanged political rebel, William Cragh; a toddler, Roger, who fell into the ravine around the local castle one night because he did not know the drawbridge was up; and more.[68] Moreover, this canonization cause generated two particularly intriguing documents.

The first document is the transcript of the inquiry *in partibus* examining Thomas's life and miracles. The inquiry was held in London in 1307; local witnesses from the area around Hereford were interviewed in their native languages—chiefly English, but a few in Welsh or French—and their testimony recorded in Latin.[69] The English dialect in the region of Hereford was difficult for the papal commissioners: partway through the testimony, the scribe noted that two new interpreters arrived from a minorite convent who possessed better knowledge of the local "vocabulary, which differs in the

---

67. *De B. Bernardo Poenitente Audomaropoli in Belgio*, in *AASS*, 11 (April 19), 697a.
68. Valerie Flint, "The Saint and the Operation of the Law: Reflections upon the Miracles of St. Thomas Cantilupe," in *Belief and Culture in the Middle Ages: Studies Presented to Henry Mayr-Harting*, ed. Richard Gameson and Henrietta Leyser (Oxford, 2001), 342–57; Valerie Flint, "Magic in English Thirteenth-Century Miracle Collections," in *The Metamorphosis of Magic from Late Antiquity to the Early Modern Period*, ed. Jan N. Bremmer and Jan R. Veenstra (Leuven, 2002), 117–31; Jussi Hanska, "The Hanging of William Cragh: Anatomy of a Miracle," *Journal of Medieval History* 27 (2001): 121–38; Robert Bartlett, *The Hanged Man: A Story of Miracle, Memory, and Colonialism in the Middle Ages* (Princeton, NJ, 2004); Leigh Ann Craig, "Describing Death and Resurrection: Medicine and the Humors in Two Late Medieval Miracles," in *The Sacred and the Secular in Medieval Medicine*, ed. Barbara Bowers and Linda Migi Keyser (Farnham, forthcoming). I would like to thank Dr. Craig for sharing this article with me in advance of its publication.
69. See Meryl Jancey, ed., *St. Thomas of Cantilupe: Essays in His Honour* (Hereford, 1982).

diocese of Hereford from many other dioceses in the English realm."[70] They went on to re-interview some earlier witnesses in order to clarify a few points. The scribe also occasionally doodled small portraits of local witnesses: a friar, an old bearded man, a cowled peasant, and two women with fancy hair (one wearing something akin to an early gable headdress) appear, as well as several portraits of Bishop Thomas himself.

Second, after all the evidence was gathered it was sent to the papal curia, where a panel of cardinals evaluated the testimony of the witnesses, resolved perceived problems and contradictions, weighed various explanations for the events that had occurred, and then made a determination about which miracles might be considered indisputably authentic. The document presenting their findings was produced quite a bit later, sometime between 1318 and 1320.[71] This second source nicely complements the original inquiry *in partibus*: examining both the notarial transcription of original oral testimony and the curial evaluation of the same allows us to trace attitudes toward particular deaths through different social and educational strata.

The testimony given at the London inquest shows that in the early fourteenth century lay people had a basic knowledge of the signs of life, of rigor mortis, of the significance of the evacuation of the bowels, and a somewhat more limited understanding of coloration changes after death, or livor mortis. Witnesses at the canonization inquiry were examined closely about how and why they had determined the deaths of individuals who later were claimed to be the recipients of resurrection miracles. Even after detailed testimonies about the lack of vital signs, however, the commissioners pressed for more details about the corpse's condition, seemingly in a bid to establish extensive damage to the body, when possible. This could offer an independent proof of death, aside from the potentially flawed death diagnoses of untrained lay observers. The witnesses' testimony is vivid and often poignant.

Let us begin with the child Walfrid, tragically overrun by a cart while napping in the middle of the trail. The adults who found him brought him to a nearby home, laid him on a bed, and kept vigil over him while hoping for a revival. "He remained in the bed until the half hour between nine and vespers, and from the moment they placed him in the bed this witness and the aforementioned Letitia were frequently palpating him and putting their hands over his heart and near his mouth and nostrils. They did not detect any motion or breath in him, and his body had become cold and rigid, and

---

70. "vocabula diversitatur in diocesi heresfordiensis a pluribus aliis diocesibus regni anglie." *PCTC*, fol. 129r.

71. Vauchez, *Sainthood in the Later Middle Ages*, 540.

there was no sign of life in it."[72] Despite this very clear and exhaustive evidence of death, the cardinals leading the canonization inquiry seem to have been looking for extensive visible physical damage as well. Presumably this attitude stemmed from the assumption that if the child's head was severely crushed, then the death could not be in the least ambiguous. "[The witness] was asked if, from that concussion with the cart's wheel, blood was flowing from his mouth, ears, nose, eyes, or from any other part of Walfrid's head; and if the skin and bones of the head had been broken?"[73] The answer was no.

In another case, that of a drowned boy named William, the commissioners asked follow-up questions that likewise seem oriented toward absolutely certifying the death and thus the resurrection. First, they simply inquired about William's passing, and the witnesses meticulously listed the absent signs of life. A typical testimony runs thus: "No sign of life appeared in him: his body was cold and his limbs were so stiff that they could not be flexed except through violence; his teeth were clenched against one another, and his lips were pulled back; his eyes were open, and the pupils were covered with a kind of veil such that one could not see the pupils themselves. There was no hope," this witness concluded, "that William could arise again naturally."[74] Yet despite this strong testimony, the commissioners still wondered whether there might have been any "fraud or fiction or hoax employed so that William might feign being dead, and so was not resurrected? Or if any sorcery or incantation or invocation of demons was employed for the resurrection? Or if anything, natural or artificial, aided or cooperated in the resurrection?"[75] The witness affirmed that nothing of the sort had happened.

Witnesses were usually confident about their judgments of death. In the case of a little drowned boy named Nicholas, the victim's father testified

---

72. "Mansit in dicto lecto usque ad horam mediam inter ix et vesperam et frequenter ipse tesis et dicta Letitia ex quando collocaverant eum in predicto lecto palpanted ipsum et manus apponentes circa cor et curca os et nares nullum motum nec a[nhe]litum senserunt in eo et corpus fuit effectum frigidum et rigidum et nullium in se signum vite habebat." *PCTC*, fol. 166r. A detailed study of this miracle has been made by Craig, "Describing Death and Resurrection." I thank Dr. Craig for kindly sharing with me an advance version of this article.

73. "Requisitur si ex dicta concussion rote plaustri emanavit sanguinis per os aures nares oculos vel per aliquam aliam partem capitis ipsius Galfridi; et si pellis et ossa dicti capitis fuerunt confracta." *PCTC*, fol. 166v.

74. "Quod nullum signum vite aperiebat in eum et habebat corpus frigidum membra adea rigida quod non poterant plicari vel violenter dentes ad invicem constrictos labia retracta oculos apertos et pupillam oculorum ex quadam tela opertam ita quod non poterat videri ipsam pupillam et nullam spes adesset quod ipse Willelmus naturali resurgere posset." *PCTC*, fol. 148r.

75. "fraus vel fictio vel machinatio uteretienerunt ut dictus Willelmus fingeretur mortuus vel resurrectio non esset; et si pro eius resurrectione sint tunc fari aliquod sortilegium vel aliquod incantatio vel invocatio demonum et si aliques res naturales vel artificales fuerunt adhibete vel cooperate in resurrection predicta?" *PCTC*, fol. 142v.

movingly that he was very sure his son was deceased. "I believed at this point that my son was dead. For his body was completely cold and rigid and ashen, that is, livid and the color of lead. And he held his eyes open, and they were covered with a sort of veil. I was thinking about the burial of my son. And so in order to prepare his corpse for burial, I placed two fingers on his eyelids. I wanted to close his eyes, so I tried to do so."[76] The action awoke the boy, however, who began to groan.

In one of the most compelling cases in the entire collection, a little girl named Joan drowned in the artificial fishpond of the local tavern. The day had started out well. It appears that the majority of the village was enthusiastically drinking at this local establishment all day. Joan followed her parents to the tavern, found some playmates outside, and ended up being accidentally pushed into the pond by another child. She drowned, and her body remained in the pond. Meanwhile, as the day wore on, the adult gathering became progressively merrier: "they led a dance in the middle of the tavern and all the way out into the public street. They led the dance there and then afterward they led the dance back to the house and garden all the way until sunset."[77] When the first witnesses spied Joan's pale garments floating in the water of the murky fishpond, they pulled her out, but it was quickly determined that she was beyond assistance. Joan's parents were called from inside the tavern. "Seeing his young daughter dead, without the least sign of life, both her mother and many other people standing there began to wail and cry around her," testified the father.[78] The group cut Joan's belt, for her stomach was bulging with water. Then the bystanders tried to recompose Joan's expression into one of greater repose: "They began to push the girl's tongue back into her mouth, since for the most part it extended outside her mouth, and it was black and swollen."[79] As in the case of Nicolas, these witnesses did not make attempts to revive Joan, for they were certain that she was beyond human assistance. Rather, they simply tried to make her look more peaceful in death and to alleviate the condition of her body.

---

76. "Et ipse reputaret ad huc dictum filium suum mortuum. Qui habet corpus totus frigidus et rigidus et suppallidum seu lividum ad modum plumbi et teneret oculos apertos et quadam tela velatos. Cogitans ipse testis de sepultam predicta filii sui. Et quoad ipsum corpus ad sepultam preparetur appositis duobus digitis ad palpebras oculorum ipsi. Michi voluit et tenptaverit clauderre dictos oculos." *PCTC*, fol. 158v.

77. "Duxerunt coream per mediam tavernam usque in viam publicam et in ea duxerunt coream illam et postea revertentes duxerunt coream in domo et gardino usque ad occasum solis." *PCTC*, fol. 137v.

78. "Videns dictam filiam suam . . . mortua esse et ullatena in se signum vite habere et matrem ipsius puelle et multos astantes plangere et flere circa eam commotis." *PCTC*, fol. 125r.

79. "Chonabatur reducere in os dicte puelle linguam eius que pro magna parte protendebatur extra os puelle et erat niger et inflata." *PCTC*, fol. 125r.

If an individual was thought to be alive but in extremis, however, various revival measures would be undertaken. Thus in the Cantilupe hearings one witness dramatically described his efforts to test for the vital signs and even to give mouth-to-mouth resuscitation to a little boy named William. I have not found this procedure referenced often, but apparently it was known: "The witness applied his mouth and cheeks to William's mouth, and several times he placed his finger inside William's mouth. Finally [William] closed on the finger with his teeth, and he felt some breath. Placing his hand on William's chest, near the heart, he felt the heartbeat, just as a heart pumps when drawing breath for a person. Everyone present, seeing these signs of life in William, praised and glorified God."[80] However, the crowd's optimistic hope for William's condition took a turn for the worse when he began to groan, an event that they interpreted as a death rattle. This mortal sign in particular was thought to be of signal importance in indicating the transition from living to dead. Whenever witnesses heard a near-dead individual groan loudly, far from interpreting this as a sign of revival, they usually became convinced that the individual had perished. Thus, several days after the resuscitation, while William still lay ill in bed, "he gave forth a great groan, and with that groan he closed his eyes. Everyone said he was dead."[81] A similar interpretation of a loud moan as a final death rattle prevailed in the case of the little girl Joan, who drowned in the fishpond: "The girl's mouth was open and there was heard, by this witness and by others standing there, a certain moan from inside the girl's body. One of those standing near, the late Walter de Pirebrok, said, 'If any breath of life remained in that girl, now it has been completely breathed out.'"[82]

"How can a body be declared dead, when there is no injury?"

Since extreme physical trauma to the body was an excellent indicator of death, the commissioners' interest in the violent bodily details of an accident, or the gruesome condition of a corpse, makes sense. More puzzling for these

---

80. "Testis aplicut os suum et genas suas ad os dicti Willelmi et posuit digitum inter os dicti Willelmi pluries et finaliter strinxit cum dentibus dictum digitum et sensit a[nhe]litum et apponens manum ad ventrem circa cor ipsius Willielmi sensit ipsius cor palputare sicut palpitate cor homines attrahentes a[nhe]litum et omnes astantes videntes predicta signa vite in dicto Willielmo laudaverunt et glorificavant deum." *PCTC*, fol. 148v.

81. "Idem Willelmis emisit magnum rugitum et cum dicto rugiu clausit oculorum tunc astantes dixerunt ipsum esse mortuum." *PCTC*, fol. 148v.

82. "Aperto ore memorate puelle sic auditur ab ipso teste et ab aliis astantibus quidam rugitus in corpore dicte puelle et unus de astantibus scilicet Walterus de Pirebroke quondam dixit si erat alliquis flatus vite in puella nunc ex toto exalavit." *PCTC*, fol. 124r.

evaluators were instances in which the corpse was intact yet inert. Such was the case for Roger of Conway, who died in the early morning hours of September 6, 1303. The testimony about this miracle is particularly fascinating because of how many different groups of people—from villagers to the local constable to the royal coroners—examined his body and discussed the probability that he was dead. The various investigations of little Roger's death and resurrection bring together many of the themes of this chapter, from the appropriation of medical knowledge for legal purposes, to the determination of death on the part of lay observers, to the consideration of death from learned religious and medical points of view.

Aged two years and three months, Roger woke up in the middle of the night and missed his father. The latter was employed at the local castle, seemingly working with the local constable, and he slept there most nights. Roger set off to find him. The toddler knew the way to the castle from his home, but what he did not realize was that the drawbridge was pulled up at night. Stepping out into thin air where the drawbridge would have been, Roger tumbled into the gorge that ringed the castle, an eighteen-foot drop. Though it was the first week in September, the night was quite cold. The next morning, September 7, 1303, a man named John of Gistyn spied him lying upon the frozen bank of the castle moat, a bit of snow drifting over his body. John immediately went into the castle in order to inform the constable and Roger's father, as well as another man present, that Roger lay dead under the drawbridge. The group went out and looked out over the bridge:

> They saw Roger's body and then John of Gistyn, on order of the constable, climbed down into the ravine to determine whether Roger was dead. While they all watched, he palpated Roger's body, and picked him up from the bank in his arms; then he called up that he was dead. And this witness himself, along with the others, saw from his condition that he was dead, for he did not cry out or emit any sound; and his body looked rigid, with one leg up and the other one folded underneath him.[83]

For these witnesses, it was enough to determine Roger's death from a distance of eighteen feet or more. The fact that he was so still and stiff, with

---

83. "Quo viso dictus Johannes de Gysstyn de mandato predicti constabularii descendit in fossatum ad iudicandi si esset mortuus Rogerus supradictus et eis videntibus palpavit corpum predicti Rogeri et ipsum elevavit de rupe in manibus suis et dixit eis quod mortuus erat et ipsi tesi et aliis predictis ex aspectus fuit visus quod esset mortuus quare nec flebat nec emittebat aliquem vocem et aparebat rigidus tenens unam tibyam erectam et aliam incurvatam." *PCTC*, fol. 189v.

the position of his legs unaltered even as John of Gistyn picked him up, was surely one reason why the crowd considered him to be dead. Likewise, the fact that he emitted no cry or moan even when palpated appears to have been important to witnesses. The men are depicted as coming to a judgment very quickly, led by John of Gistyn's report. In fact, they were certain enough about Roger's death such that they decided to call the coroners:

> However, when John of Gistyn wanted to remove him from the ravine, John of Boys told him that he could not to do so until the king's coroners had arrived, for it was their right of office to inquire into the death, whenever someone was found dead from an accident or else killed. And without them, a dead body or a killed person should not be removed from the place in which they were first found dead or killed. So John of Gistyn left Roger in the place where he found him.[84]

The legal obligation to "raise the clamor," inform other people and most especially the coroners, is referenced often throughout the miracle inquiry. For example, in the case of the little girl who drowned in the fishpond, Joan, there seems to have been some delay in raising the clamor, but one witness volunteered to do so: "he wanted to raise the clamor according to the custom of the land, which requires that whenever people are found murdered or drowned or otherwise accidentally killed, it should be reported right away."[85]

Turning now to the actions of the coroners: as death professionals, the situation Roger presented required careful scrutiny. Their job was to make an initial judgment of death and also to try to determine the cause of death. This was not immediately clear in Roger's case, for though he had fallen a far distance, his body bore few marks of trauma. The testimony of the witness above continues by describing their detailed inspection of Roger's body:

> Stephan of Ganvy and William of Nottingham, the royal coroners, and a cleric named William, who was the secretary for the coroners, arrived in order to examine Roger lying in the ravine, after being informed of the fall through the constable who was then resident in the village. They went down to him in the ravine, and they covered him, and then

---

84. "Cum autem dictus Johannes de Gysstin vellet eum extrahere de fossato memoratus Johannes de Boys dixit ei quod non faceret quousque venirent coronatores regii ad quorum officiis pertinet quando aliquis invenirere casualiter mortuus vel interfectus inquirerer de dicta morte et sine eis mortuus vel interfectus non debet levari de loco in quo primo est mortuus vel interfectus et tunc dictus Johannes de Gisstyn dimiserat in loco in quo invenerat dictum Rogerum." *PCTC*, fol. 189v.

85. "Voluit levare clamorem secundum consuetudinem patrie que servatur quando interfectu vel submerse vel alias casualiter mortui primo reperiuntur." *PCTC*, fol. 134v. Similar language was used by a witness to the case of the drowned boy named William: *PCTC*, fol. 146v.

they palpated him and checked (as is required by their office) to see if he had any wounds, and measure how long and wide and deep they were and to record it in writing to send to their superiors. And they did not find any wound on him: neither any crushing of limbs or breaking of bones, nor any bleeding or emission of blood, nor any piercing of the skin. However, he did have a large bruise on his left chest, where he had been laying and had got stuck to the ground, which this witness had seen before the coroners arrived. But no other part of his body seemed harmed or had suffered any sign of damage. The witness states that he saw this while standing on the bridge and looking down on the coroners and watching their doings, as described above.[86]

The coroners first needed to definitively establish that there *was* a death, and thus they, like John of Gistyn earlier, palpated Roger to see whether they could revive him. This was a measure that professional medical specialists like coroners also commonly enacted. This overlap of technique between coroner's protocols and the action of a local man suggests that the villagers may have been learning how to think about death, how to recognize it, and some techniques for revivals by observing coroners at work.

It also was the coroner's duty to determine *why* Roger had died, however, and this was considerably more difficult. They carefully examined him all over for bruises, wounds, scrapes, fractures, crushed areas, and bleeding, as their secretary made notes to be relayed to their superiors, but they found no evident injuries. Indeed, the witness goes on to note that after the examination, they "retired a little distance away from Roger's corpse so that they might sit down and convene their inquiry; and they had the relevant things written down that pertained to their office."[87] These men were trained to look for physical causes of death and to compose a report, but in this case

---

86. "Stephanus de Ganvy et Willelmus de Notingham coronatores regii et Willelmus clericus et scriptorem dictorum coronatorum significato eis predicto casu per prefatum constabularium qui errant tunc in predicta villa vel prope venerunt presente ipso teste ad videndum dictum regerum iacentem in fossato. Et descenderunt ad ipsum in fossatum et tetigerunt et palpaverunt eum perquirentes prout pertinet ad officium eorundem si habebat aliquam plagam cuius quidem plage longum latum et profundum debent distincte secundum eorum officium rediret in scriptis ad referendum superioribus suis. Et non invenerit aliquam plagam in eo nec confractionem pellis nec confractionem alienus membris nec alicujus ossis nec effusione vel emissionem sanguinis. Habebat tamen in maxilla sinistris super quam iacebat et adherebat rupi qui ipse testis ante adventeum coronatorum viderat cum magnum livorem sed in aliqua alia parte corporis suis non apparebat in eo aliqu aliud signum lesionis violenter sibi illatae vel ab eo suscepte. Et dicit se vidisse idem testis existens in ponte predicto coronatoribus circumspicientibus et agentibus supradicta." *PCTC*, fol. 189v–190r.

87. "Elongassent se aliquantulum a corpore dicti Rogerii ut sedentes formarent inquisitionem ut scribi facerent circa premissa pertinentia ad officium eorundem." *PCTC*, fol. 190r.

there appeared to be nothing but a large hematoma on the child's left chest. Yet, if they could not determine a cause of death, could they be certain of the fact of his death at all?

We do not know what the coroners wrote in their report—indeed, since Roger was resurrected, perhaps they never filed one. Thirteen years later, however, the question of how to determine death in the case of an intact but inert body persisted. In this year, Roger's case was analyzed by a member of the papal curia, our last layer of evaluation. The anonymous author wondered whether the lack of injury to Roger's body should disqualify his case from consideration as a miracle. Perhaps he had not really died, in which case no miraculous resurrection would have occurred:

> How can a body be declared dead, when there is no injury? . . . It can happen from the interior concussion of the members and parts, which must have been caused by the fall. In addition, the coldness and rigidity of his limbs attests to the truth of his death, as does the pooling of fluids in his body, his lack of movement and of the use of his senses, the cessation of breathing, and the length of time these signs of death persisted.[88]

The curial writer then introduced a parallel case from memory, of a boy who fell fifty feet and who suffered from internal pains thereafter, with the suggestion that internal injuries, even though unseen, can be grievous and possibly cause death. Thus, Roger's expiry was proven with great attention. The scientific symptoms of death—coldness, rigidity, and so forth—were carefully enumerated; a cause of death—internal damage—was posited and underscored with a supportive comparison to a similar instance of a fall. This author was determined to prove Roger's death, to eliminate any possibility of lingering life, and to utilize medical authority in order to do so.

This was typical of his approach. In the case of a girl who suffocated, a similar issue arose: an intact but inert body, with no injuries.

> Though she *appeared* to be physically dead—given the immobility of her body and limbs, the inflexibility of her joints, her coldness at all times, the cessation of breathing, her lack of the use of her senses—it might be doubted as to whether these were sufficient indications of a true death, and whether her body ought to be considered dead on the strength of these things.

---

88. *MTC*, 548.

In this case, there was no question of interior mangling. Instead, the curialist took the lack of vital signs as sufficient evidence of what he calls "a true death." In line with contemporary medical-theological discourse on the relationship of the soul to the body, he responds to the potential objection:

> The above symptoms demonstrate the absence of all vital operations; . . . hence, her soul cannot have been united to her body . . . and since the separation of the soul and body is what constitutes death, we therefore conclude that these things are reliable indicators of a real death.[89]

The argument here is somewhat tautologous: the lack of vital signs indicates the absence of the soul, and the absence of the soul explains the lack of vital signs. Regardless, we see the importance, to this curial analyst, of the idea that death must be entirely distinct from life, that alternatives must be considered and excluded, and that death is evidenced, above all, by the lack of vital signs, indicating the departure of the soul.

By the early fourteenth century, medical and theological ideas about life and death were beginning to penetrate into some nonliterate sectors of society. The approach to Roger's death evidenced by different social groups is telling. The coroners are the middle term, here: medical professionals making a skilled judgment in service to the realm. The villagers appear to be somewhat informed by previous contacts with coroners. Such contacts likely supplemented common sense garnered through their life experience, dealing with the deaths of people and animals. They knew some basic signs of death, they placed a high significance on the death rattle, and they had learned about the technique of palpating the heart. At the other extreme is the curial writer, who clearly is aware of medical definitions of life as based on the vital signs, but who also gives preeminence to the soul. There are differences of sophistication among these groups, but there are also important areas of consensus.

Harnessing Postmortem Vitality

Thus far, this chapter has charted broad trends in the definition of life and death over the course of the high and late Middle Ages, arguing that this boundary became firmer over time. Yet it would be untrue to suggest that this was a unidimensional trajectory. For there always existed important

---

89. *MTC*, 549.

exceptions to this broad trend: dead bodies that behaved in living ways, or dying bodies whose powers could be harnessed to heal.

First and foremost in this category were the relics of the saints. Conceptually, relics existed between worlds. Though they were bones or fragments of corpses, they nevertheless were suffused with abundant vitality that could overflow and could shower benefits upon the faithful. Their perceived power was intimately linked with their purported lack of decay: for a cadaver to remain intact was to signal to an observer that the corpse, though dead, was still pervaded with vital energy that might be shared out with the living as healing power. In fact, relics were not the only powerful, preserved bodies credited with healing properties. Ground up Egyptian mummy was thought to function similarly; the unusual preservation of such remains was taken as a sign of these bodies' overabundant vital power.[90] Thus ingestion of ground up *mummia*, a foul, black excretion that "sweated" from mummified bodies, was thought to transfer that vitality to another person.[91] It was a luxury medicament. Since ancient mummies were expensive imports in short supply, however, recipes for the preparation of "fresh" mummy from the corpses of recently killed criminals also circulated in medieval medical works.[92] An illuminated leaf from a luxurious 1470 French version of the *Book of Simple Medicines* shows mummy among other apothecary supplies (figure 2.5). Such practices of medical cannibalism, or uses of body parts, form intriguing parallels to the tradition of seeking healings at saints' tombs. Both types of incorruptible bodies were divided, circulated, and commodified for these reasons.[93]

In sum, life could be captured from death and then transferred to another body. In a similar vein, other kinds of human remains were sometimes prescribed as medicine in the Middle Ages. For example, the fresh blood of a healthy executed criminal was considered an extremely nourishing tonic. The spirit-rich blood of an executed criminal, flowing from

---

90. Himmelman, "Medicinal Body"; Michael Camille, "The Corpse in the Garden: *Mumia* in Medieval Herbal Illustrations," *Il Cadavere / The Corpse*, 297–318; Richard Sugg, *Mummies, Cannibals, and Vampires: The History of Corpse Medicine from the Renaissance to the Victorians* (London, 2011); Louise Noble, *Medicinal Cannibalism in Early Modern English Literature and Culture* (New York, 2011).

91. Camille, "Corpse in the Garden."

92. Noble, *Medicinal Cannibalism*, 6.

93. Katharine Park, "The Life of the Corpse: Division and Dissection in Late Medieval Europe," *Journal of the History of Medicine and Allied Sciences* 50 (1995): 111–32; Katharine Park, "The Criminal and the Saintly Body: Autopsy and Dissection in Renaissance Italy," *Renaissance Quarterly* 47 (1994): 1–33.

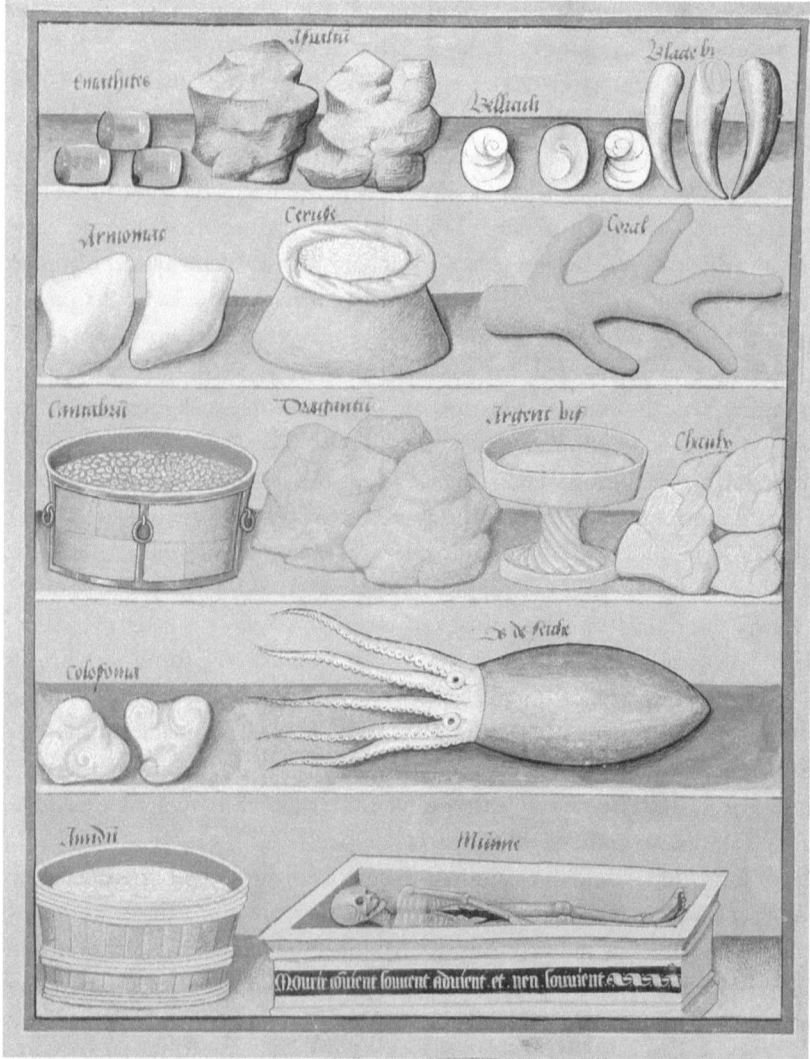

FIGURE 2.5. Egyptian mummy was used as a luxury medicament in the Middle Ages. Here it is shown amid other medical supplies and labeled, *mummia*. National Library, St. Petersburg, MS Fr. Fv VI #1, fol. 166v. Illustration by Robinet Testard (fl. 1470–1523) from the *Book of Simple Medicines* by Matthaeus Platearius (d. ca. 1161), ca. 1470 (vellum).
National Library, St. Petersburg, Russia / Bridgeman Images.

the veins of a person killed before his time, presumably would contain some of the individual's life force, which then could be transferred to a weakened body and utilized for healing. Folk customs preserved such ideals for an extremely long time, as seen in the long-lived custom of seeking personal healing through the laying upon oneself of the hand of an executed criminal.[94] Similarly, ingestion of pulverized human bone, particularly dust from a human skull, was recommended by many medieval medical authorities for the treatment of epilepsy.[95] The thirteenth- to fourteenth-century physicians John of Gaddesden and Arnold of Villanova both recommended burned and powdered human skull for treatment of these neurological disorders. "For epilepsy make this approved powder: take of the bones of the human head, especially from the anterior part, burned, . . . and give them in drink."[96] Water from a human skull was sometimes used as a love philter, as in the case of a Florentine sorceress named Giovanna, who successfully bound her lover Giovanni to herself by these means.[97]

This chapter has sketched out a chronology in which, beginning in the twelfth century, medical and theological authors worked to harmonize the physiology of life and death with the religious ideology of the soul. The resulting system of knowledge was in line with Augustinian thanatologies, which construed vitality and mortality as distinct and dichotomous states. This was a decisive battle in the history of death; interest in making careful distinctions about death was part of a new set of priorities concerned to mark off death from other kinds of intense and enlightening experience. Up until the twelfth century, the categories of deaths, trances, ecstasies, dreamful sleep, and illnesses were allowed to bleed into one another; now, however, medical specialists began to categorize death as definitive and permanent, not processual and sometimes temporary. Death was an event, not a process; there could be no living dead, no temporary deaths, no returns from beyond across a porous natural border. By the fourteenth century, such ideas were fairly well disseminated through various social strata. The Gregorian model, conversely, stood on ever-eroding ground in the later Middle Ages.

---

94. Wayland Hand, "Hangmen, the Gallows, and the Dead Man's Hand in American Folk Medicine," in *Magical Medicine: The Folkloric Component of Medicine in the Folk Belief, Custom, and Ritual of the Peoples of Europe and America* (Berkeley, 1980), 69–80. The hands of executed criminals likewise were used for magical purposes, such as the "Hand of Glory," a candle formed around the mummified hand of an executed person, which was believed to put others to sleep when the owner lit the wicks. It is unknown how early this tradition developed, though it appears in woodcuts from the 1590s. Charles Zika, "Cannibalism and Witchcraft in Early Modern Europe: Reading the Visual Images," *History Workshop Journal*, no. 44 (1997): 77–105.

95. Valentina Giuffra and Gino Fornaciari, "Pulverized Human Skull in Pharmacological Preparations: Possible Evidence from the 'Martyrs of Otranto' (Southern Italy, 1480)," *Journal of Ethnopharmacology* 160 (2015): 133–39.

96. Arnold of Villanova, quoted in Giuffra and Fornaciari, "Pulverized Human Skull in Pharmacological Preparations," 136.

97. Gene Brucker, ed., *The Society of Renaissance Florence: A Documentary Study* (New York, 1971), 271.

PART TWO

Corporeal Revenants

As Christianity expanded into northern Europe from its origins in the eastern Mediterranean it came into contact with many different populations that sustained distinct religious pantheons and cultural practices. Converting these societies was a long-term process of cultural exchange, convergence, and assimilation. The civilization that emerged in the High Middle Ages was formed from a rough patchwork of divergent cultures stitched together by the common thread of conversion to the Christian religion. The borders of a unified Christendom still embraced persistent regional variation through the end of the medieval period; this culture possessed both broadly shared and locally specific elements.

This second section of *Afterlives* shifts its focus away from universalizing discourses such as theology and medicine in order to examine a broad regional pattern of thought about death and the afterlife endemic to northern Europe. My core geographic focus is chiefly (though not exclusively) the septentrional regions along the Baltic, the North Sea, and the North Atlantic, from England to central Europe. These regions were home to a number of Slavic and Germanic tribal peoples as well as some Celtic groups to the west; they practiced a variety of pagan religions. The Germanic tribal migrations of the fourth and fifth centuries created a diaspora that spread their culture west and south across Europe. Soon thereafter, however, a reverse cultural movement began, one that imported Christianity from its Mediterranean base to the north and east. Christian missionaries claimed France in the fifth century, England in the seventh through tenth centuries, the North Sea regions in the ninth and tenth centuries, and the Baltic area across the Elbe river in the tenth through twelfth centuries.

Despite a variety of different gods and pantheons, traditional Slavic and Germanic cultures appear to have held relatively similar attitudes toward their ancestors. The evidence indicates that a basic cultural presupposition of the broader region was that life and death existed as part of a longer continuum of states, with many points in between that shared some characteristics of each. The liminal state between life and death was depicted as an embodied one: when medieval northern Europeans thought about the dead returning among the living, they imagined revenants. That is, they visualized cadavers arising from their graves and physically interacting with the world. Until the flesh dissolved fully, and the corpse was reduced to bare bones, the dead might remain active. The living often feared these corporeal shades, especially when they were the bodies of folk who had died young or through violent means. They told stories about the dead attacking the living, and sometimes they imagined the dead as forming armies or aggressive cohorts. At other moments, however, the living portrayed the dead as feasting, dancing, or simply living their (after)lives underneath mountains, conducting themselves in much the same way that the living did atop the surface of the earth. These motifs illuminate the persistence of alternate ways of imagining death and afterlife in medieval Europe, ideas that sprang from anterior, non-Christian cultural roots. Indeed, such collective representations are the afterlife of earlier cultural systems that ultimately syncretized with Christian teachings.

Part 2 illuminates the merging of pagan and Christian cultures over time as shown through revenant motifs. The three individual chapters spiral around common themes and frequently find points of overlap, though without charting a strictly linear progression. Chapter 3, "Revenants, Resurrection, and Burnt Sacrifice," begins in the early eleventh century in the German marches of central Europe, a pagan Slavic region then being colonized by the Ottonian emperors of Germany. This was the frontier of Christendom at the time, and the historical context for the chapter is that of a mixed pagan and Christian society actively in the process of religious transition. The chapter seeks to highlight the active intermingling of cultures that was ongoing at this moment through a close analysis of local motifs about the returned dead. The next chapter in this section, "The Ancient Army of the Undead," focuses upon a particular folklore motif that was endemic to Norman regions of Europe. This study shows how an atavistic story type with pagan origins was recuperated by Christian thinkers for their own religious purposes, and by secular authors for more worldly agendas, well into the High Middle Ages. Thus, the historical context for this chapter is one more step removed from the originally pagan background of revenant tales; it demonstrates a process of folklorization of these motifs, as they were reframed within Christian popular culture. Finally chapter 5, "Flesh and Bone: The Semiotics of Mortality," dissects the underlying logic of revenant belief. It demonstrates how revenancy functioned within medieval popular culture and explores some of the different interpretations of life and death that were attached to revenant stories. The chapter brings to the fore several important patterns, such as the importance of remaining flesh on the bone to postmortem vitality and the significance of a "bad death" as a predictor for postmortem return. This chapter likewise analyzes a number of images that present visual evidence for understanding the contours of revenant beliefs.

Taken together, these chapters outline a trajectory along which ideas about the living dead are observed to migrate through dramatically changing cultural contexts. As João de Pina-Cabral has suggested, persisting cultural forms are chosen, not merely passively reproduced, and those that survive are often those that best lend themselves to new significances.[1] Revenants retained their forms even as they evolved their meanings in shifting historical circumstances. What began as a feature of the pagan imagination of the dead lived on as an aspect of regional, Christian popular culture.

---

1. João de Pina-Cabral, "The Gods of the Gentiles Are Demons: The Problem of Pagan Survivals in European Culture," in *Other Histories*, ed. Kirsten Hastrup (London, 1992), 49.

CHAPTER 3

Revenants, Resurrection, and Burnt Sacrifice

When, in the first quarter of the thirteenth century, Snorri Sturluson began to compose his *Heimskringla* (*History of the Kings of Norway*), he wrote a preface in order to introduce his project. He explained that he wished to set down in writing all the available historical information concerning the ancient royal chieftains of the Norse, availing himself of legends, genealogies, and oral histories. "Although we do not know for sure whether these accounts are true," he noted, "yet we do know that old and learned men consider them to be so." Snorri concluded by offering a taxonomy for the successive epochs of Norse history:

> The first age is called the Age of Cremation. In that age it was the custom to burn all the dead and to raise memorial stones after them. But after Frey was laid to rest in a burial mound at Uppsala, many chieftains erected burial mounds as often as memorial stones to commemorate their departed relatives. However, after Dan the Proud, the Danish king, had a burial mound made for himself and decreed that he was to be carried into it when dead, in all his royal vestments and armor,

---

Portions of this chapter have appeared as "Revenants, Resurrection, and Burnt Sacrifice," *Preternature* 3, no. 2 (2014): 311–38.

CHAPTER 3

together with his horse, fully saddled, and much treasure besides, and when many of his kinsmen did likewise, then the Age of Sepulchral Mounds began. However, the Age of Cremation persisted for a long time among Swedes and Norwegians.[1]

Snorri's preface betrays a fascinating set of cultural and historical priorities. So central are funerary customs to his worldview, he uses them as the organizing rubric for his understanding of history. Epochs of the Scandinavian past are not, for Snorri, best differentiated by battles won, lands conquered, marriages made, or wealth gained. Rather, social change is best charted by innovations in funerary practices: the Age of Cremation gives way to the Age of Sepulchral Mounds. In keeping with this finely attuned consciousness toward disposal of the dead, Snorri explains in exquisite detail the origins of this centrally important shift: which chieftain was the first to abandon cremation and use a burial mound; where the practice started; the first imitators; the first king to direct that armor, wealth, and animals should be placed in his mound alongside him, thus formally initiating the new age; and finally, how the custom spread and where the older form persisted. All in all, the passage displays an extraordinary attention to disposal of the dead as the chief defining element of culture. Funerary rites are the hinges of history.

Of course, Snorri's preface interprets the far past from the vantage point of the thirteenth century. Nevertheless, we know that burial customs had long been of signal importance to the pagan cultures of the broader Scandinavian and Baltic region. Readings of archaeology in tandem with correlative texts suggests that funerals for major chieftains could be lengthy affairs, "ten days of feasting, drinking, music and sex" in the words of Neil Price, the leading authority on the subject.[2] Elaborate rituals of sacrifice, careful emplacement of various objects and bodies (both animal and human) around the main corpse, and laborious actions such as burying entire ships suggest that funerals could be a very high-investment activity, at least for important individuals. At the same time, the archaeological record shows a wide diversity of concurrent practices, as well as indicating some funerary customs that remain completely unattested in written sources.[3]

As Christianity made inroads in these regions, converts from paganism sometimes invented creative strategies to bring their ancestors into the

---

1. Snorri Sturluson, *Heimskringla: History of the Kings of Norway*, trans. Lee Hollander (Austin, TX, 1992), 3–4.
2. Neil Price, "Mythic Acts: Material Narratives of the Dead in Viking Age Scandinavia," in *More than Mythology: Narratives, Ritual Practices and Regional Distribution in Pre-Christian Scandinavian Religions*, ed. Catharina Raudvere and Jens Peter Schjødt (Lund, 2012), 25.
3. Neil Price, "Dying and the Dead: Viking Age Mortuary Behavior," in *The Viking World*, ed. Stefan Brink in collaboration with Neil Price (London, 2012), 257–73.

Christian fold retrospectively through manipulations of burial space. King Harald of Denmark, for instance, exhumed his pagan father and reburied him in consecrated ground after his own conversion in about 960. Harald likely hoped that this action would keep the family line together in the afterlife.[4] The *Penitential of Theodore*, widely known in German lands, proscribed the consecration of such a church:

> In a church in which the bodies of dead unbelievers are buried, an altar may not be sanctified; but if it seems suitable for consecration, when the bodies have been removed and the woodwork of it has been scraped or washed, it shall be re-erected. . . . if there is a pagan [buried there] it is better to cleanse it and cast [the corpse] out.[5]

There were alternative strategies than simply importing the bodies of pagan kin into Christian spaces. For example, some early churches in the Rheinland and in Sweden were constructed atop existing pagan burial sites. Thus important ancestors of the leading local clans were "saved" despite themselves. An example is the parish church of Flonheim, which was erected over an early Germanic row-cemetery; the structure seemingly was designed to include ten pre-Christian graves, which likely all belonged to the same important bloodline. One exceptionally rich pagan burial was found under the main church tower.[6] Christian sacred structures thus enclosed pagans in their foundations, even as they enclosed the relics of the saints in their altars. Some converts simply ignored the question of consecrated ground entirely. Even as late as 1428, the Council of Riga was trying to stamp out the continuation of earlier pagan funerary customs, both in terms of burial choices and in the ways in which ancestors were honored and remembered by the living:

> We greatly desire to abolish the ancient pagan custom that abusively is maintained by many people (especially the country people of this land). Despising consecrated cemeteries, they choose instead to be buried in woodland places with the wild beasts, or else in other profane places where their relatives and friends from pagan times were buried. Also, they often hold parties in the churches and consecrated cemeteries,

---

4. Richard Fletcher, *The Conversion of Europe: From Paganism to Christianity, 371–1386 A.D.* (London, 1997), 406.
5. John McNeill and Helena Gamer, trans., *Medieval Handbooks of Penance: A Translation of the Principal Libri Poenitentiales* (New York, 1990), 199.
6. Patrick Geary, "The Uses of Archaeological Sources for Religious and Cultural History," in *Living with the Dead in the Middle Ages* (Ithaca, NY, 1994), 37–38.

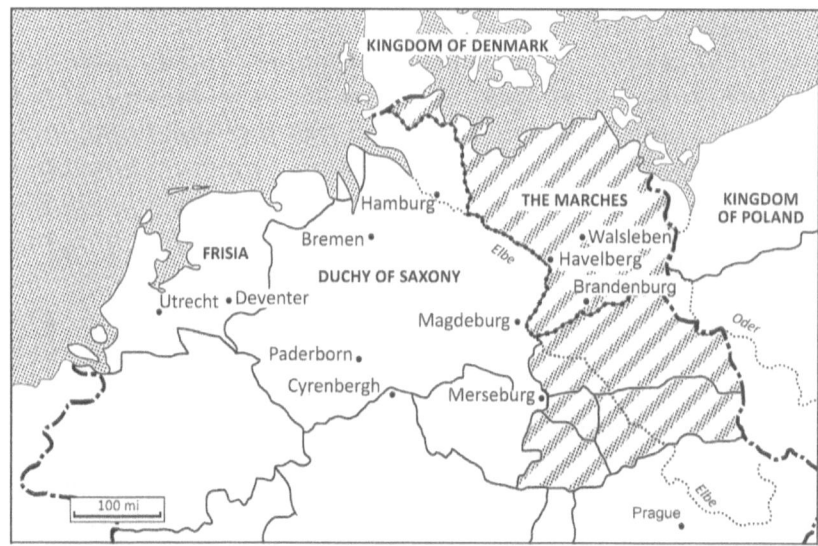

MAP 3.1. Northern Europe and the Eastern Marches. The region between the Elbe and the Oder rivers was hotly contested between German Christian and Slavic pagan forces in the late tenth and early eleventh centuries. The borderline shown along the Oder, at the east, demonstrates the extent of German hegemony under Otto I, in 972. By 1030 this boundary was pushed back to the line shown along the Elbe, at the west. Many of the important towns and villages mentioned in this chapter are marked.

at which they offer food and drink to their dead relatives and friends, believing that this gives the dead comfort.[7]

The reason for such attention to burial was, of course, that such observances were linked intimately to cultural concepts about the status of the dead in the next life, and therefore the ability of the living to conduct their affairs with the tacit benevolence of their ancestors guaranteed. Careful attention to the dead after they passed on to another form of existence bespeaks both a strong sense of lineal attachment stretching into the past, as well as a sense of expectation about a continued form of existence beyond the grave. Snorri was describing a distant pagan past from within a Christian present, but the afterlife of this epoch remains vivid in his mind. Presumably the same could be said of the people targeted by the Council of Riga. In short, Snorri's introduction opens a vista onto a telling set of clues about the continuing afterlife of the pagan dead, lingering on in the medieval memory of a Christianized society.

---

7. "Statuta provincial concilii Rigensis," 1428, #19, *De sepulturis*, reprinted in Willhelm Mannhardt, *Letto-Preussische Götterlehre* (Riga, 1936), 155–56.

Perhaps not surprisingly, then, the eastern European marches along the Elbe, a site where Scandinavian and Slavic paganisms met, also was the site for the earliest collection of ghost stories to come down to us from the Middle Ages. This group of horror tales dates from just after the turn of the millennium, a time when the region still was in conversion transition. They were recorded by a Christian bishop.

A Frontier Bishop

All good ghost stories must begin with an act of violence. In the year 929 the town of Walsleben was attacked without warning and "all its inhabitants, that is to say an innumerable multitude," brutally slaughtered.[8] Walsleben was one of a series of fortified towns along the Elbe River, protecting the northeastern marches of the expanding realm of the Ottonian king Henry I (r. 876–936). Thus German power structures were being established in lands that were pagan in religion and Slavic in ethnicity and culture. Our chief source for this event, Widukind of Corvey, reports in his *Deeds of the Saxons* that other "barbarous nations" of Slavs likewise began to rebel when they saw the successful devastation of this revolt, led by a group known as the Redarii.[9] The spread of rebellion was checked, however, when Henry I seized the Slavic fortress of Lenzen.[10]

The strike at Walsleben lived on as an act of infamy inscribed in Widukind's Saxon chronicle. However, the mass killing at the town also spawned a legend, passed along through oral transmission for an unknown length of time until it, too, finally found its way into the written record. In 1013 another proud Saxon, Thietmar of Merseburg, took up his pen and began to write his eight-volume *Chronicon*, a work he continued until his death in 1018. He belonged to an old missionary family—his ancestors had been instrumental in converting the eastern Saxons—and he understood the local Slavonic tongue.[11] Born around 975 of an exalted warrior bloodline, Thietmar had served as a military advisor to Henry II (r. 972–1024), was educated at Magdeburg, and eventually became the second bishop of Merseburg.[12]

---

8. Widukind von Corvey, *Res gestae Saxonicae / Die Sachsengeschichte: Lateinisch/Deutsch*, I:36, ed. and trans. Ekkehart Rotter and Bernd Schneidmüller (Stuttgart, 1981), 81–82.
9. Widukind, *Res gestae Saxonicae*, 82.
10. David Bachrach, *Warfare in Tenth-Century Germany* (Woodbridge, 2012), 198–99.
11. Fletcher, *Conversion of Europe*, 425.
12. Helmut Lippelt, *Thietmar von Merseburg: Reichsbischof und Chronist* (Cologne, 1973); David Warner, "Thietmar of Merseburg: The Image of the Ottonian Bishop," in *The Year 1000: Religious and Social Response to the Turning of the First Millennium*, ed. Michael Frassetto (New York, 2002), 85–110; Bachrach, *Warfare in Tenth-Century Germany*, 70–71.

In setting forth his history, which also functioned as a glorification of the Ottonian dynasty his family had served for generations, Thietmar noted the devastation of Walsleben toward the beginning.[13]

Yet as soon as Thietmar's quill formed the strokes of the name Walsleben, his thoughts seem to have drifted from history to memory. First to arise was a personal remembrance enshrined in his family's history: Walsleben prompted him to note proudly that two of his great-grandfathers had perished at the seige of Lenzen.[14] Then Thietmar recalled something else he had heard about Walsleben, an uncanny tale set in a haunted church:

> So that no one who is faithful to Christ may doubt the future resurrection of the dead, but may proceed to the joy of blessed immortality zealously and through holy desire, I shall confide certain things that I have verified as true and that occurred in the town of Walsleben when it was rebuilt after its destruction.
>
> The priest of that church used to sing matins there at the first blush of dawn. But when he arrived at the cemetery for the dead he saw in it a great multitude of them, making offerings to a priest who was standing at the doors to the sanctuary. At first he stopped in his tracks but then, fortifying himself with the sign of the holy cross, he tremblingly went through the whole crowd to reach the oratory, without acknowledging any of them. One of them, a woman whom he knew well and who had died recently, asked him what he was doing there. After he told her why he had come she returned that everything had already been taken care of by them, and also that he did not have long to live. He reported this to his neighbors and it turned out to be true.[15]

The memory of this tale opened a floodgate for Thietmar. He was interested in reports of the returned dead, and he immediately went out of his way to recount several similar stories in the pages following. These form a rather lengthy digression from the narrative of early Ottonian triumph with which he had begun his work.

Thietmar's tales of revenants at worship form one of the richest and most fascinating collections of ghost stories (or more properly, revenant stories, since they concern the embodied dead) in any medieval text. They are a

---

13. TM, 14–16. The volume presents facing-page editions of two slightly variant Latin manuscripts: Codex One is reproduced on even-numbered pages; Codex Two may be found on odd-numbered pages. I note divergences in the notes when relevant.
14. TM, 14–16.
15. TM, 16–17.

cohesive and unique corpus: these tales of the undead are the first significant grouping of such accounts since the sixth century, the era of Gregory the Great. And like Gregory, Thietmar presumes that in certain circumstances the dead might appear to the living from beyond the grave, and in material form. Though Thietmar's *Chronicon* often has been consulted by scholars of Ottonian political, military, and social history,[16] his revenant tales have attracted scant attention from historians of medieval religions or conversion.[17] Yet Thietmar's chain of mental associations, entwining rebellion, revenants, and resurrection, opens up a rich space for inquiry into such questions. In the following pages, I take Thietmar's chronicle as a point of entry into three intertwined historical issues.

First, we may use these tales to excavate some of the features of local traditions about the potential afterlife of the body. Thietmar's tales feature dead folk who climb out bodily from their graves, every night, in order to engage in communal worship. They are tomb dwellers who secretly return to the spaces of the living at night. Thietmar's tales of revenants unveil a set of presuppositions about the continuing consciousness and capabilities of the corpse that spring from non-Christian sources.

Second, Thietmar's rationale for including these stories touches upon another form of afterlife: the resurrection. He introduced the story set in Walsleben by suggesting that it provided a refutation to skeptics of the doctrine of resurrection, and this is a theme to which he returns continually. Thietmar was attempting to appropriate these local legends to evangelical purposes: indeed, he tells us explicitly that the local Slavic populations did not understand the idea of resurrection properly and that he hoped his stories might serve as useful corrective. This appropriation was only made possible, of course, because of the capaciousness of the church's tolerance toward reports of life after death. Thietmar could appropriate these legends because the precedent of Gregorian ghost stories permitted their recuperation.

---

16. Bachrach, *Warfare in Tenth-Century Germany*; David Bachrach, "Memory, Epistemology, and the Writing of Early Medieval Military History: The Example of Bishop Thietmar of Merseburg (1009–1018)," *Viator* 38, no. 1 (2007): 63–90; Karl Leyser, *Rule and Conflict in an Early Medieval Society: Ottonian Saxony* (Oxford, 1979); Albrecht Finck von Finckenstein, *Bischof und Reich: Untersuchungen zum Integrations-prozeß des ottonisch-frühsalischen Reiches (919–1056)* (Sigmaringen, 1989); Heinrich Fichtenau, *Living in the Tenth Century: Mentalities and Social Orders* (Chicago, 1991); David A. Warner, "Ritual and Memory in the Ottonian Reich: The Ceremony of Adventus," *Speculum* 76, no. 2 (2001): 255–83; Warner, "Image of the Ottonian Bishop."

17. Brief treatments include Jean-Claude Schmitt, *Ghosts in the Middle Ages: The Living and the Dead in Medieval Society* (Chicago, 1998), 36–39; Patrick Geary, *Phantoms of Remembrance: Memory and Oblivion at the End of the First Millennium* (Princeton, NJ, 1994), 72–73.

Third, and following upon the previous point, there is an issue of cultural and religious afterlife at stake in these tales. Thietmar's society was a pluralistic, frontier context that intermingled different cultural traditions, ethnicities, and religions. The region was bordered on the north by the Baltic, on the east by the Elbe/Saale, and on the west by the Oder.[18] Many peoples living in this region, particularly those in and around Thietmar's city of Merseburg, practiced traditional forms of Slavic cult, including a cult for the ancestors. Scandinavian religions, present at the northern limits of this region, likewise practiced veneration of the deceased and believed them to be active after death. At the same time, the relatively new, foreign religion of Christianity had won significant numbers of converts in this area as well. Lastly, and most importantly for my purposes, there existed informal syncretistic admixtures: paganized Christian and baptized pagan traditions, in which new and old ideas and symbols intermingled. Thietmar's ghost stories, I will argue, are hybrid formations of this kind. They express a pagan logic about life after death, but somewhere along the line of transmission they were adapted to a Christian semantic field. The higher implication of this argument is a key point: acculturation processes are always inherently mutual. Though we tend to assume that processes of conversion or social transformation flow unidirectionally toward the pole of greater power, in fact such shifts are better conceived as reciprocal exchanges.[19]

---

18. Ildar H. Garipzanov, Patrick J. Geary, and Przemysław Urbańczyk, *Franks, Northmen, and Slavs: Identities and State Formation in Early Medieval Europe* (Turnhout, 2008).

19. A. Leopold and J. Jensen, eds., *Syncretism in Religion: A Reader* (London, 2004). My thoughts have also been influenced by James C. Scott, *Domination and the Arts of Resistance: Hidden Transcripts* (New Haven, CT, 1990); Jacques Berlinerblau, "Towards a Sociology of Heresy, Orthodoxy, and Doxa," *History of Religions* 40, no. 4 (2001): 327–51; and Bruce Lincoln, *Authority: Construction and Corrosion* (Chicago, 1994). Useful medievalist studies, not necessarily confined to this direct region, include Ruth Mazo Karras, "Pagan Survivals and Syncretism in the Conversion of Saxony," *Catholic Historical Review* 72, no. 4 (1986): 553–72; Robert Bartlett, "The Conversion of a Pagan Society in the Middle Ages," *History* 70 (1985): 185–201; Rudi Künzel, "Paganisme, syncrétisme et culture religieuse populaire au Haut Moyen Âge: Réflexions de méthode," *Annales E.S.C.* 47, nos. 4–5 (1992): 1055–69; James Russell, *The Germanization of Early Medieval Christianity: A Sociohistorical Approach to Religious Transformation* (Oxford, 1994); Ian Wood, "Pagan Religions and Superstitions East of the Rhine from the Fifth to the Ninth Century," in *After Empire: Towards an Ethnology of Europe's Barbarians*, ed. G. Ausenda (Woodbridge, 1995), 253–79; Ludo J. R. Milis, ed., *The Pagan Middle Ages* (Woodbridge, 1998); Martin Carver, ed., *The Cross Goes North: Processes of Conversion in Northern Europe, AD 300–1300* (Woodbridge, 2005); Kurt Villads Jensen, "Sacralization of the Landscape: Converting Trees and Measuring Land in the Danish Crusades against the Wends," in *The Clash of Cultures on the Medieval Baltic Frontier*, ed. Alan Murray (Surrey, 2009), 141–50; Justyna Baron, "Ritual and Cultural Change: Transformations in Rituals at the Junction of Pagan Religion and Christianity in Early Medieval Poland," in *Rytm przemian kulturowych w pradziejach i średniowieczu* [The rhythm of cultural change in prehistory and the Middle Ages], ed. Boguslaw Gediga et al. (Warsaw, 2012), 449–63.

In sum, Thietmar's ghost stories are rife with internal contradictions that hold up a mirror to the tensions, the cultural pluralism, and the ongoing transformations of his time and place. Carefully unpicking the seams of these stories will enable us to see the pattern pieces, thus gaining insight into the movement of ideas between different groups as they acculturated to one another. Exploring Thietmar's ghosts can thus provide a revealing study of how traditional forms of local, oral common sense came to be incorporated into a Christian text, ultimately enshrining divergent models of life and death within the written tradition of the medieval church. This was possible because the church already had such a broad array of acceptable thanatologies enshrined within its own patristic tradition. The Gregorian model of postmortem return permitted an opening for stories like those told by Thietmar.

Pagan and Christian

Before proceeding further, however, a further unpacking of Thietmar's religious context in early eleventh-century Merseburg is necessary. I write of pagans and Christians, Germans and Slavs, and it is important to address what I mean by these terms, which are not as transparent as they might at first seem. The earliest historiography of this period was intimately bound up with nineteenth-century German nationalism, thus setting in place a vocabulary that served a teleological narrative of "civilizing" German expansion that is now badly outdated. In reaction to this, Henrik Janson has sensibly suggested that "we should be a bit reluctant" to employ these words too facilely; he suggests that they introduce into our writing social divisions that were of limited impact or meaning in their original context.[20] Janson's challenge is gracefully formulated and demands consideration.

As a starting point, it is worth noting that the two dichotomies at issue here—German/Slavic and Christian/pagan—really reduce to one multifaceted cultural distinction. The expansion of German lordship was implicitly bound up with bringing the Christian religion to new peoples. Indeed, the Ottonian dynasty mythologized itself as the legendary "Last World Emperors" who would bring about the conditions for the Second Coming of Christ by reviving the Roman Imperium and expanding the reach of the

---

20. Henrik Janson, "Making Enemies: Aspects of the Formation of Conflicting Identities in the Southern Baltics around the Year 1000," in *Medieval History Writing and Crusading Ideology*, ed. Tuomas M. S. Lehtonen et al. (Tampere, 2005), 149. The notion that such differences were of limited significance was first formulated by Carl Erdmann, *Die Entstehung des Kreuzzeugsgedankens*, Forschungen zur Kirchen- und Geistesgeschichte 6 (Stuttgart, 1935).

church throughout the known world.[21] In particular, Otto I's long reign (936–73) established the policy that acceptance of tributary status to the empire meant at least openness to Christian teachings with a view toward accepting baptism. Otto likewise established a series of bishoprics along the Elbe—the most important was Magdeburg, in 968—to facilitate conversion efforts and provide structure for what he hoped would be growing communities of new Christians. At the same time, however, these episcopal seats were fully fortified towns, strongholds that both established and protected German hegemony in the region. Thus when we speak of eastward imperial expansion we are also, implicitly, discussing an expectation of gradual religious acculturation and conversion in the colonized regions. The German emperors had long used the strategy of suppressing local religious identity, most particularly as expressed through funerary custom, as a means of cementing their political authority. In an earlier century, Charlemagne had initiated this practice when expanding into Saxon territory.[22] Conversely, of course, when we speak of Slavic rebellions against German encroachment we should acknowledge that since German lordship was intimately bound up with Christianity, resistance to one entailed resistance to the other. Christian administrative centers were, quite simply, German power centers and vice versa. The process of political expansion into new ethnic and cultural territories was inherently fraught with violence; undoubtedly the resentments of rebelling groups were complex and many.

Unsurprisingly, the most successful revolt against Ottonian overlordship was led by the Slavic group that also was most resistant to Christian conversion: the Wends, also known as the Liutzi or Luticians. To speak simply of "Slavs" in the trans-Elben region is to conflate several distinct groups under a single term: different Slav polities had divergent diplomatic and acculturation histories with the empire.[23] Yet when we unbundle these terms it becomes

---

21. The mythology of the Last World Emperor was popularized by the revelations of Pseudo-Methodius, composed in the seventh century but attributed to a fourth-century figure: see G. Reinink, "Pseudo-Methodius und die Legende vom römischen Endkaiser," in *The Use and Abuse of Eschatology in the Middle Ages*, ed. Werner Verbeke, Daniel Verhelst, and Andries Welkenhuysen (Leuven, 1988), 82–111. As Janson notes, the idea was also present in Adso of Montier-en-Der's letter on the antichrist, composed for Otto I's sister Gerberga around 950 at her request. See Janson, "Making Enemies," 145–47.

22. Bonnie Effros, "*De partibus Saxoniae* and the Regulation of Mortuary Custom: A Carolingian Campaign of Christianization of the Suppression of Saxon Identity?," *Revue belge de philologie et d'histoire* 75 (1997): 267–86.

23. Erdmann, *Entstehung des Kreuzzeugsgedankens*; F. Dvornik, "The First Wave of the Drang nach Osten," *Cambridge Historical Journal* 7 (1943): 129–45; Bartlett, "Conversion of a Pagan Society in the Middle Ages"; Friedrich Lotter, "The Crusading Idea and the Conquest of the Region East of the Elbe," in *Medieval Frontier Societies*, ed. Robert Bartlett and Angus MacKay (Oxford, 1989),

even clearer that rebellion against foreign hegemony was imbricated with resentment against Christianity. The Wendish rebellion began during Thietmar's childhood; initiated in 983, it pushed back the frontier of German influence and was succeeded by a period of intermittent skirmishes along the Elbe. Thietmar, eight years old at the time, later looked back on the event with horror. Centers of German power, which were, of course, also Christian religious centers, were targets for attack. These included the Cathedral of Havelburg and the bishopric of Brandeburg, where the remains of the last bishop (Thietmar tells us he had been assassinated by his flock) were dragged from his tomb and despoiled.[24] The nunneries of Kalbe and Hillersleben also were not spared, showing that institutions with predominantly religious, rather than political, associations were targeted as well.[25]

By the time Thietmar began writing in 1013, tensions at the most visible level had died down, though battles along the Elbe were still within living memory. Moreover, the Wends among whom Thietmar lived were religious holdouts who rejected Christianity, though many other Slavic groups had begun to adopt it. For the aristocratic classes, political expediency often took precedence over religious differences: Henry II made military alliances with the still pagan Wends when it suited him, including even against other Christian rulers. Yet this by no means suggests that the ultimate desirability of converting these peoples was mooted. Capitulation to stubborn reality should not be read as respect for divergent viewpoints or commitment to religious pluralism; it was, rather, a case of choosing one's battles wisely.

Indeed, the battle for Slavic souls was a protracted one that persisted long past Thietmar's lifetime. In 1066, the frontier collapsed for a second time; the sees of Oldenburg and Ratzenburg remained unoccupied for nearly a century thereafter. Adam of Bremen, a chronicler of the later eleventh century, records the frequent provisional conversions of the Slavs along the Elbe and their backslidings to paganism. Speaking of the missionary Gottschalk, for instance, he considers it a great success that he converted back to Christianity "nearly a third" of those who had abandoned the new religion two generations earlier,

---

267–306; Roman Zaroff, "Perception of Christianity by the Pagan Polabian Slavs," *Studia Mythologica Slavica* 4 (2001): 81–96; Geneviève Bührer-Thierry, "Les 'réactions païennes' dans le nord de l'Europe au milieu du XIe siècle," *Actes des congrès de la Société des historiens médiévistes de l'enseignement supérieur public* 33 (2002): 203–14; Christian Lübke, Christianity and Paganism as Elements of Gentile Identities to the East of the Elbe and Saale Rivers," in Garipzanov, Geary, and Urbańczyk, *Franks, Northmen, and Slavs*, 189–204; Przemysław Urbańczyk, "Slavic and Christian Identities during the Transition to Polish Statehood," in Garipzanov, Geary, and Urbańczyk, *Franks, Northmen, and Slavs*, 205–22.

24. TM, 118–19.
25. Fletcher, *Conversion of Europe*, 422.

in order to return to the paganism of their ancestors.[26] Likewise, as Thietmar himself testifies, many smaller churches and congregations underwent a period of abandonment in the aftermath of pagan rebellions; monasteries were emptied out and plundered, their inhabitants killed or expelled and not replaced. As one account of the Christianization process in this region concludes, "Because Christianity was so bound up with alien lordship, the uprisings of 983 and 1066—and lesser ones in between, which for simplicity's sake I have omitted—were anti-Christian. The Wends had developed a pagan faith of their own which was both militant and organized."[27]

Meanwhile, when Christians took the offensive and attempted to expand into new territory, pagan shrines became, in their turn, targets of spoliation, destruction, or repurposing by Christian missionaries. Yet the tactic was not always successful. Adam of Bremen tells of some missionaries eager to destroy a pagan temple in Uppsala, who were dissuaded from doing so precisely because it was thought likely to retard, rather than to advance, their goals: "everyone who now believed would quickly relapse into paganism, as they could see had lately been the case in Slavia."[28] It seems that pagan populations in this broader region were willing to experiment with Christianity, as long as they could also maintain their traditional rites and sacred places. When Christian clergy became militantly aggressive toward pagan holy places, or in contexts where they were perceived as furthering the political aims of foreign princes and lords, the response was often revolt and religious recidivism. Roman Zaroff has pointed out that Christian missionaries frequently acted in ways that pagans read as fanatical and intolerant, rather than as an invitation toward conversion and assimilation. Moreover, Christian theology itself seemed alien and forbidding: Slavs wondered why the Christian God (whom they may well have perceived as a Germanic ethnic deity) was so exclusivist, so sexually puritanical, and so joylessly obsessed with evaluating every activity for sin.[29] While some Slavic groups, like the Obodrites, converted with little resistance,[30] others held out fiercely. Archaeological evidence demonstrates that new pagan sanctuaries still were being built and maintained in the area between the Elbe/Saale and the Oder rivers well into the twelfth century.[31]

---

26. Adam of Bremen, *History of the Archbishops of Hamburg-Bremen*, 3:19 (20), trans. Francis J. Tschan (New York, 2002), 130.
27. Fletcher, *Conversion of Europe*, 437.
28. Adam of Bremen, *History of the Archbishops of Hamburg-Bremen*, 4:30 (29), p. 210.
29. Zaroff, "Perception of Christianity by the Pagan Polabian Slavs," 85–88.
30. Ibid., 89–93.
31. Leszek Paveł Słupecki, *Slavonic Pagan Sanctuaries* (Warsaw, 1994) offers the most comprehensive review of the archaeological and textual evidence.

Ultimately, the Wends were converted only by means of a twelfth-century crusade.[32]

If the intertwined nature of religion and politics must complicate our understanding, so too is it difficult to provide a stable meaning for the terms "paganism" and "conversion." Paganism is, of course, a very general word that designates a broad array of beliefs and traditions, pantheons and practices. Even within a fairly restricted region, there could be many different cults and observances. Furthermore, recovery of these systems is complicated by the fact that they are "lost" religions that died out entirely long ago, and thus lack a history of interested parties who might preserve their traces in systematic form.[33] At the same time, however, it is clear that despite the diversity of northern European paganisms, most especially in terms of their pantheons of higher gods, there were significant areas of commonality as well. This is evident when we examine pagan cultural attitudes toward lesser spirits and, most particularly, the cult of the dead. European paganisms widely shared some basic presuppositions about what constituted a "good" or a "bad" death, the kinds of postmortem existence that might be available to the dead, and the ritual duties owed by the living to the ancestors.[34]

As for "conversion," adoption of the new faith could be fleeting or fluid; many individuals who accepted baptism nevertheless continued to practice their traditional rites alongside Christian worship. At other moments, converted persons or groups chose to reject the new religion and returned exclusively to their ancestral observances (the Wends were among them).[35] A key

---

32. Erdmann, *Entstehung des Kreuzzeugsgedankens*, 91–98; Lotter, "Crusading Idea"; A. P. Vlasto, *The Entry of the Slavs into Christendom: An Introduction to the Medieval History of the Slavs* (Cambridge, 1970); Eric Christiansen, *The Northern Crusades: The Baltic and the Catholic Frontier, 110–1525* (London, 1980); Murray, *Clash of Cultures on the Medieval Baltic Frontier*.

33. Hilda Ellis Davidson, *The Lost Beliefs of Northern Europe* (London, 1993); cf. the important methodological articles of Peter Buchholz, "Perspectives for Historical Research in Germanic Religion," *History of Religions* 8, no. 2 (1968): 111–38; Bartlett, "Conversion of a Pagan Society in the Middle Ages"; Künzel, "Paganisme, syncrétisme et culture religieuse populaire au Haut Moyen Âge."

34. Hilda Roderick Ellis, *The Road to Hel: A Study of the Conception of the Dead in Old Norse Literature* (New York, 1968); Nikolaus Kyll, *Tod, Grab, Begräbnisplatz, Totenfeier: Zur Geschichte ihres Brauchtums im Trierer Lande und in Luxemburg unter besonderer Berücksichtigung des Visitationshandbuches des Regino von Prüm (†915)* (Bonn, 1972); Régis Boyer, *La mort chez les anciens Scandinaves* (Paris, 1994); Alan Bernstein, "The Ghostly Troop and the Battle over Death: William of Auvergne (d. 1249) Connects Christian, Old Norse, and Irish Views," in *Rethinking Ghosts in World Religions*, ed. Mu-Chou Poo (Leiden, 2009), 115–61.

35. A famous instance of the former situation is the comment by Widukind of Corvey that the Danes, though Christian, "nonetheless preserved their pagan idol cult." *Res gestae Saxonicae*, 216. The backsliding of the Wends is analyzed by Fletcher, *Conversion of Europe*, 435. On conversion more generally in this region, see, in addition to the works cited in note 23, James Westfall Thompson, "The German Church and the Conversion of the Baltic Slavs," *American Journal of Theology* 20, no. 2 (1916): 205–30; Archibald R. Lewis, "The Closing of the Mediaeval Frontier

point is that the term "conversion" mainly becomes legible within the context of Christian writings and Christian rhetoric. It was the church and her representatives, after all, that both asserted the universality of their faith and demanded exclusivity for their rite. From the point of view of polytheists, conversion could often be more akin to incorporation into a more expansive religious sensibility. Looking at religious change on the ground, then, we should expect to find untidy syncretic admixtures and hybrids, rather than a clean break from old gods to new. The old persisted, haunting the new world that was coming into being. An intriguing material representation of this situation might be the so-called Merseburg Charms, short, rhythmic invocations of valkyries, Phol, Wodan, and Frija composed in archaic German, but carefully transcribed onto a leaf of an otherwise entirely Christian manuscript found in the library of the Cathedral of Merseburg.[36] It is pleasing to think that, decades after they were written down, Thietmar himself might have encountered them there. The decision to commit these charms to writing suggests an active interest, on the part of evangelizing Christian clergy in the area, to understanding something about local beliefs and practices. Thietmar's text likewise provides a testimony to how the imported religion of Christianity interacted with older indigenous traditions. Let us return now to his revenants.

Rebellion and Revenants

In the tale set in Walsleben, an early rising priest finds a group of dead parishioners in his church one morning, just finishing up their own mass and giving offerings to their priest. Though horrified, the priest moves through the crowd and is informed by a dead woman of his acquaintance that he will soon join them in death. The prophecy turns out to be true.

1250–1350," *Speculum* 33, no. 4 (1958): 475–83; Vlasto, *Entry of the Slavs into Christendom*; Murray, *Clash of Cultures on the Medieval Baltic Frontier*; Pavlína Rychterová, "Holes in the Tapestry: Eastern and Northern European Conversion Histories," *Early Medieval Europe* 19, no. 1 (2011): 91–105. On missionaries (with a broader purview than central Europe), see Ian Wood, *The Missionary Life: Saints and the Evangelization of Europe, 400–1050* (Harlow, 2001); M. de Reu, "The Missionaries: The First Contact between Paganism and Christianity," in Milis, *Pagan Middle Ages*, 13–38. A Latin-English edition of the *Lives* of saints active in central Europe is Gábor Klaniczay, *Vitae sanctorum aetatis conversionis Europae centralis (saec. X–XI) / Saints of the Christianization Age of Central Europe (Tenth–Eleventh Centuries)* (Budapest, 2013).

36. Susan D. Fuller, "Pagan Charms in Tenth-Century Saxony? The Function of the Merseburg Charms," *Monatshefte* 72, no. 2 (1980): 162–70; Bill Griffiths, *Aspects of Anglo-Saxon Magic* (Norfolk, 1996), 171–72, gives the full text of the charms in the original early German and in English translation.

A number of things in this tale are worthy of further comment. First, and as a precondition for everything else, the returned dead, rather than being translated to another plane of existence cut off from the living, instead conduct their nightly activities here, in this world. Indeed, it appears that they remain close to the familiar places they occupied during life and persist in the same activities. During the day, they "live" in their graves: they are tomb dwellers who arise at night. As corporeal revenants with physical capabilities to sing, to grasp, and to speak, they decidedly are not phantoms or insubstantial specters. Second, the dead folk appear to be pious Christians who congregate together, beyond the threshold of death, for a formal worship service. The deceased in these tales behave much like a living congregation: there is a multitude of dead laypeople, led in services by a dead cleric; the laity, in departing, furnish material offerings to their priest. They are Christians joined together in postmortem community and maintaining a regular devotional schedule in the rebuilt local church—the same holy precincts in which their bodies had been interred after their deaths. Just as the holy saints looked down with special alertness to the location of their bodily relics, so too did the revenant dead remain attached to their home parish.

Yet there are some very perplexing and irreconcilable elements in this narrative, which become even more exaggerated in some of Thietmar's subsequent tales. Such inconsistencies are, I would suggest, highly revelatory. However, in order to richly complicate our evidence we must isolate, as far as possible, interpretation from story, ideology from narrative. As James Scott remarks, "any analysis based exclusively on the public transcript is likely to conclude that subordinate groups endorse the terms of their subordination and are willing, even enthusiastic, partners in that subordination."[37] Recovering both the public and the hidden aspects of medieval mentalities involves negotiating seen and unseen levels of texts, reading both for what is said too markedly and for what is left unsaid. Thus in the following pages I focus upon close readings of individual stories, with particular attention to hybridities, inconsistencies, and multivariant meanings. These ruptures, in turn, provide a point of entry into the question of cultural pluralism, unveiling the diversity of cultural strands that are knit together in the sources.

---

37. Scott, *Domination and the Arts of Resistance*, 4.

First, there is a striking juxtaposition of piety and violence: these revenants project a strong aura of menace. The sight of the dead congregation is a blood-curdling moment for the living priest, despite their innocuous, even praiseworthy, engagement in prayer. He crosses himself and picks his way through the crowd gingerly. Indeed, one wonders whether the detail that the priest was able to see them for the first time that day, though he always sung matins in the church at that time, suggests that his own approaching death endows him with the ability to see the community of the dead that he is about to join. This appears to be a theme of some antiquity: indeed there is one earlier attestation of a similar motif in Gregory of Tours's *Book on the Glory of the Confessors*, composed from 587 to 588 (and thus, roughly contemporaneous with Gregory the Great). The chapter is titled "On the cemetery of the city of Autun."

> The cemetery in Autun used to be called a city, in the Gallic language, because there were so many cadavers interred there. . . . I heard from two local inhabitants that once, while they pleasantly wandered through the holy places praying, they heard the sound of psalms coming from the basilica of Saint Stephen, which was adjacent to this cemetery. Wondering at the sweetness of the tones, they approached the portals of the church to find out which religious men were celebrating the vigils. They went inside and enjoyed the prayers for a very long time. Then they got up and looked around at the choir of singers, and there was no light in the church except for the personal brightness with which the whole group seemed to glow. However, they did not recognize any of them. At last, as they stood there astonished and struck with amazement, one of the singers approached them and said, "You have done a despicable thing! How dare you stay while we perform the secrets of our worship to God! Leave now! Flee from our home or else you will leave this world!" One of the men, hearing this, left. The other, however, remained in that place, and a few days later he passed from this world.[38]

The presence of a similar story in a much older text from Frankish Gaul suggests that the motif of dangerous encounters with groups of the dead—even when they are encountered at prayer in a Christian church—is one of some antiquity and persistence. Some of its elements very likely were rooted in a broadly shared set of attitudes, common to both Germanic and Slavic

---

38. Gregory of Tours, *Liber de Gloria Beatorum Confessorum*, in *PL*, 71, col. 881.

cultures, that were brought by the Frankish peoples to Gaul in the immigrations of the fourth and fifth centuries.

The atmosphere of dread and danger that encompasses Thietmar's account of the revenants is heightened, of course, by the intimations of who they really are, or *were*: the massacred inhabitants of Walsleben, victims of a rebellion that also devastated and temporarily deconsecrated the church that they now claim each evening. Yet these physically risen dead men and women fulfill a logic of postmortem existence that only partially overlaps with Christian teachings about the afterlife. As we have seen, the idea of the physically embodied dead remaining upon this plane of existence has an ancient Christian pedigree. This likely was one reason the story seemed usable to Thietmar. Other aspects of the tale evade Christian logic, however, and represent the persistence of cultural concepts originating outside Christian teachings. These include the notion that the dead might dwell on in their tombs, which served as a sort of postmortem home base, and that the dead continued, in the afterlife, the same activities and forms of socializing that they had enjoyed while alive. We shall return to this point later. Another ancient notion was the belief those who were subject to a "bad death" that was violent or sudden were unlikely to lay quietly in their graves.[39] While we have seen Christian versions of the belief that an untimely death is marked or special in some way in the *Etymologies* of Isidore of Seville, here such a death engenders a specific consequence: the slaughtered men and women of Walsleben return as corporeal revenants. Undoubtedly the generation of the Walsleben legend (which likely was in oral circulation for some time before Thietmar "verified [it] as true" and recorded it for posterity) was intimately linked to the memory of violent mass deaths that took place in this burg. Behind a mild pious facade lie the violently killed—and thus, intrinsically dangerous—dead.

Revenants and Resurrection

Thietmar, however, wished to recuperate this legend for Christian purposes. For the bishop, the fact that this group had physically risen from the dead provided evidence that the Christian doctrine of universal bodily resurrection at the end of time is true. Indeed, his introductory words to the story

---

39. Nancy Caciola, "Wraiths, Revenants and Ritual in Medieval Culture," *Past & Present*, no. 152 (1996): 3–45.

make clear that he legitimized its inclusion in his chronicle precisely because it could serve as a vivid contemporary proof of this dogma: "so that no one who is faithful to Christ may doubt the future resurrection of the dead," he writes, "but may proceed to the joy of blessed immortality zealously, I shall confide certain things that I have verified as true." Indeed, the resurrection is a point to which Thietmar returned often as he went on to recount more tales about the living dead: it is the refrain that gives meaning to these stories for the bishop of Merseburg.

Hence a few paragraphs later, as Thietmar added in some rather pallid anecdotes about the dead garnered from his own personal experience (mysterious grunts emanating from a cemetery; overheard conversations among persons unseen), he raised the theme of resurrection a second time: "I have written down these things that happened in very recent times so unbelieving people may learn that the words of the prophets are true. One of them says, 'Lord, your dead will live!' Another, 'the dead in their graves will rise, hear the voice of the Lord, and rejoice.'"[40] And finally, after recounting a few more lengthy ghost stories (examined below), Thietmar concluded the entire sequence with yet a third insistence that these sorts of tales make the resurrection visible and self-evident. This time, he addressed his words more sharply to a particular audience: "I speak to the uneducated and most especially to the Slavs, who believe that everything finishes with temporal death, firmly indicating to the faithful the certainty of our future resurrection and recompense according to merits."[41] Thus Thietmar framed this entire group of tales as testimonies to the resurrection: the first words of the first tale introduced the theme as such; he returned again to this point midway through his recitations; and he concluded the series with yet another suggestion that congregations of the living dead, in contemporary times, demonstrate the truth of the general resurrection at the end of time. As someone charged with pastoral responsibilities in an area where paganism still was vital, it is easy to see why Thietmar would have found these legends appealing for evangelizing purposes. After all, they provided compelling entertainment mingled with a frisson of fear and pity, were rooted in local oral traditions and memories, foregrounded devout parishioners united in worship, and are premised upon the continuing life of the physical body. Thus in some ways it makes perfect sense that he would point to them as a rejoinder to pagans, recent converts, and others who might doubt

---

40. TM, 18–19.
41. TM, 20–21.

the doctrine of resurrection. In short, Thietmar was utilizing a traditional local belief about living corpses as a sort of wedge to introduce the dogma of resurrection.

In fact, I would suggest that one reason why stories such as this were so very appealing to men like Thietmar was because, quite simply, the main idea about death that the church wished to promote to the laity, one so important that it overwhelmed all other considerations, was that there *was* life after death. Doubt about the afterlife was a highly threatening area of unbelief for those charged with evangelical and pastoral duties. Annihilation: this was the unthinkable, for immortality is the central promise of Christian faith. Thus stories about ghosts and revenants were simply too useful to reject, for they offered direct, firsthand evidence for the afterlife. Looking back, we have seen the origins of this strategy in Gregory the Great's appropriation of classical pagan ghost motifs for his *Dialogues*, in defiance of the earlier Augustinian approach to postmortem return. In brief, local legends about ghosts and revenants were recounted in Christian sources in large part because they served the church's broader acculturative projects. They provided a form of epistemic proof relating to two key Christian doctrines: the persistence of the soul beyond the death of the body, and the future physical return of the dead in the general resurrection.

On a deeper level, however, Thietmar's reasoning is transparently tendentious. Just how, exactly, do contemporary groups of revenants, in 1013, establish the truth of the general resurrection of all humanity at the end times? Thietmar undoubtedly means to suggest that the moving, animate cadavers of these dead folk provide a pattern of possibility: proof that the mortal coil may transcend corruption, rise, and live again. We see this viscerally portrayed in figure 3.1: whitened bones lie scattered about a cemetery as the dead arise from tombs deep in the earth. In the foreground, a skeletal figure underground takes on flesh, while above him a woman emerges to kneel in prayer. This image suggests how Thietmar may have visualized the living dead in his stories. Yet the fallacy of Thietmar's proposition is manifest: there is no necessary correlation between the evidence he presents and the conclusions he draws. The doctrine of resurrection is more than the paradox of life returned to a defunct body; it plays a specific role within the unfolding of universal history and the process of human salvation. It takes more than a few undead corpses to do it justice. I shall set aside this theme for the moment, but (like Thietmar himself) I will return to it again.

FIGURE 3.1. This fresco shows the dead arising from their graves at the general resurrection at the end of time. Then the bodies of all the dead will arise to reunite with their souls and be rewarded or punished for eternity. Detail of a fresco by Giovanni Canavesio, 1491. Chapel of Notre-Dame-des-Fontaines, La Brigue, France.
Photo from Wikimedia Commons.

The Sacrifice of the Altar

Thietmar's first tale led him to recall two others of a similar type in the following chapter, in both cases oral legends that he collected from other people. The first one concerns a brief sighting, from a distance, of a dead congregation in the churchyard of Magdeburg's merchants' church. Thietmar himself had been educated in the cathedral school of this city, which was one of the key centers of Ottonian power in the region. He began living there at age fifteen, in 990, and remained a prebend afterward until his elevation to the see of Merseburg at the age of thirty-four, in 1009. He writes that he heard the following story while in residence there:

> During my time in Magdeburg . . . the guards of the merchants' church, while keeping watch at night, experienced phenomena similar to what I have described, by sight and by hearing. So they brought some of the foremost citizens and, having set themselves a far distance from the cadavers' cemetery, they watched as lights were placed in the candelabras. Then they faintly heard two parts singing the invitatory and completing all the morning lauds in proper order. However, afterward when they approached they discovered nothing.[42]

By comparison with the Walsleben incident, the texture of this tale is less dense: the witnesses watch and hear only from afar; they do not directly interact with the dead. In fact, the dead themselves are never glimpsed; the sight of the candelabras being lit, seen from across the churchyard, is the only visual accompaniment to the antiphonal singing of the mass. There is no mention of a priest accepting offerings from the laity, and no new deaths are associated with the event. The chief interest of the tale, however, is a very significant one: it suggests that the religious use of church premises by the dead is something that occurs in many different places and that it occurs regularly every night. Thus, when the guards notice a nighttime service in the cemetery, they are reliably able to invite a group of important local notables to witness the event on a subsequent evening. The cadavers of the dead, it seems, arise after sunset each night in order to conduct a service in many churches with attached cemeteries.

Finally, Thietmar came to his third, and most disturbing, variant of the motif of the dead congregation. He received this version from his niece, an abbess named Brigit. Her tale is set in the see of Utrecht, farther west. This was originally an area inhabited by Frisians; it had been converted to Christianity earlier than the trans-Elben region, though not without struggle and

---

42. TM, 18–19.

backsliding.[43] Yet here, too, there were rumors of eerie encounters in dark churches:

> The next day, I told my niece Brigit about [the episode in Magdeburg] . . . and I received this reply from her: "During the eighty years or more when the great man Baldric held the Holy See of Utrecht, he renovated a church that had fallen into ruin from old age, in a place called Deventer. He consecrated it and commended it to the care of one of his priests.
>
> "One day when [the priest] was going to the church very early in the morning, he saw dead people in the church and cemetery making offerings, and heard them singing. The priest informed the bishop immediately. He was ordered by the latter to sleep in the church. However the next night he was thrown out by the dead, along with the bed he lay on.
>
> "Terrified on account of what had happened, the priest complained to his superior about these things again. But the latter ordered that he should cross himself with saints' relics and be aspersed with holy water, but that he should on no account stop guarding the church. The priest, obedient to the bishop's command, tried to sleep in the church again, but he was struck with terror and so lay wide awake and watchful. And lo! at the accustomed hour the dead arrived. They picked him up; they placed him upon the altar; and they incinerated his body with fire down to a fine ash.
>
> "When the bishop heard about this, he ordered a three-day fast to be held for the succor of the dead man's soul. I could say much more, my son, about all these things if my illness did not prevent me. As day is to the living, so night is conceded to the dead."[44]

Though Brigit's report is of the same general type as the two previous stories, her version was recounted with considerably more flair and suspense—and, of course, the denouement is also more horrifying. We know that priests often slept in their churches (for their own convenience as well as to protect the building) but could sometimes be nervous about spending the night alone there, right next to the graves of the dead. This was particularly the case if there had been recent violence there. After a murder in the cemetery of the church of Aix, for instance, "it was said that a tumult used to be heard at night coming from the cemetery of Aix, after that man Valentino was

---

43. Richard E. Sullivan, "The Carolingian Missionary and the Pagan," *Speculum* 28, no. 4 (1953): 705–40; Fletcher, *Conversion of Europe*, 197–98, 239, 242–43; Wood, *Missionary Life*, 57–78.
44. TM, 17–19.

killed there. As a result the priest, for terror, did not dare to remain abed in that church at night."[45] In the case of the unfortunate priest of Deventer, this terror was not misplaced.

Revenants are crepuscular creatures: they awaken in their tombs as night falls. In Deventer, as in the Walsleben and the Magdeburg stories, they move from their graves in the cemetery into the church building itself, a structure that, again like the church of Walsleben, had once fallen into a deconsecrated status. This would have allowed them a foothold in the building, according to medieval thoughts about sacred space. William Durandus wrote in his *Rationale divinorum officiorum* (*The Reasons for Divine Customs*) that the church is a consecrated space precisely because it has been purged of all unwelcome spirits and demonic presences.[46] Sacred buildings might fall into deconsecrated status for three reasons according to Durandus: first, if the walls were mostly burned down (as likely was the case in Walsleben); second, if the original building had completely fallen into ruin and was rebuilt with new materials (a principle that applies in Deventer); and third, if the original consecration were in doubt.[47]

Most intriguingly, the dead of Deventer are devout yet murderous revenants. They are jealous of their privacy, and they resent the intrusion of the living during their rightful nighttime hours. Understandably, the priest is reluctant to return after his first encounter with the revenants, who made known their displeasure at his intrusion by throwing him out of the building. When ordered to return, he takes a blessing from relics, thus attempting to avail himself of the protective power of the "good" dead against the "bad" dead he justifiably fears. The Christian cult of the holy dead here appears as the logical symbolic counterpart to the threat of the unholy dead. Yet the gesture is of no use: the revenants do not hesitate to immolate the priest when they find him back in the church the next evening. Interestingly, the form of killing undertaken by the living dead would prevent this priest from joining their ranks, for his body was entirely destroyed to a "fine ash." Thus he would have no physical basis with which to rise from the churchyard like the others: he remains separated from their community by a vast gulf in death as in life.

This tale, so rife with gestures of piety and worship, also is deeply strange and unsettling. Its transgressive narrative of fatal violence suffered by a priest at the hands of the living dead is difficult to reconcile with the Christian interpretation Thietmar insistently proffers. If, as he argues, tales of revenants

---

45. JF, 1:151.
46. *The Rationale divonorum officiorum of William Durand of Mende: A New Translation of the Prologue and Book One*, trans. Timothy M. Thibodeau (New York, 2007), 61–62.
47. *Rationale divonorum officiorum of William Durand of Mende*, trans. Thibodeau, 70.

provide proof of the dogma of resurrection, then it is a bewildering resurrection indeed: a rise to violence and the infliction of horrific martyrdom upon an obedient clergyman. As it stands, the tale hardly is legible as an edifying moral exemplum: its inconsistencies are too striking, its motifs too irreconcilable with Christian visions of afterlife. Let us turn, then, from Thietmar's own fraught interpretations of the dead congregations to some other possibilities that might make sense for this time and this place.

The Religious Rites of Revenants

The rapidity with which the revenants of Deventer turn from prayer to slaughter is at first glance puzzling. That is, unless worship and killing were one and the same thing for this congregation of cadavers. If so, of course, then they could no longer be characterized as a group of Christian undead, at Christian worship. Certainly, though the tale is set in a church, these dead folk do not behave as good Christians ought to do, whether in this life or the next. How ought we to understand these revenants then?

The best point of entry for exploring this question lies in the details of *where* and *how* the dead folk killed the priest. According to a revelatory detail of Thietmar's omniscient narrative, the dead folk went to some trouble to kill the priest in a specific part of the church. They did not set upon him as he lay upon his pallet, but picked him up bodily and transported him to the spot best suited to their intent: the altar. Likewise, these undead corpses killed the priest in a specific way. Unlike the story set in Walsleben, they did not simply prophesy the priest's imminent, natural death; nor did they slaughter him with weapons, or rend and bruise him with bare hands. They "incinerated his body with fire down to a fine ash." In short, the revenants lay the priest upon the high place of sacrifice and there immolated him, flesh and bones, until nothing remained. Thietmar's revenants, in other words, enacted a traditionally pagan form of worship by making of the living priest a burnt offering, a sacrificial victim reduced to nothingness and rendered as incense for the delectation of the gods—or ancestors. And this, in turn, alerts us to the fact that these living cadavers are not fully or self-evidently the good Christian dead: they seem to worship more in the style of the local pagans.

Human sacrifice and burnt offerings had long been associated with northern European paganisms. The textual tradition describing pagan burnt sacrifice is lengthy, extending back to barbarian ethnographies composed by classical Roman observers. Julius Caesar's *Gallic War* includes a description of the custom of sacrificial immolation to the gods: the northern barbarians, he asserts, craft giant figures of wicker, which they fill with both animals and humans, then set alight so that the victims die amid the flames and the conflagration consumes their remains.[48] Tacitus likewise notes in his *Germania* that the Semnones—his term for the Slavs settled along the eastern bank of the Elbe—assemble in groves for their religious rites, which they open "by slaying a man on behalf of the people."[49] In the late eighth century, Charlemagne had prohibited the Saxons, Thietmar's own ancestors and neighbors of the Wendish Slavs, from the practices of cremation and of human sacrifice: "If anyone should sacrifice a human being to a devil and make of him a victim offered unto demons, according to pagan custom, let him be sentenced to death."[50] Thietmar was undoubtedly familiar with the ancient literary tradition and possibly some more recent testimonies as well.

However, we should not mistake this motif for a literary fiction reproduced through the inherent conservatism of medieval textual norms. In fact, this appears to be a case in which a long-standing textual tradition is not an empty letter, but strongly correlated with ongoing, real practices. Scholars of paganism in the eastern European and lower Scandinavian regions agree that burnt sacrifice of animals and humans was indeed offered to gods, ancestors, or both for centuries until Christianization eliminated the practice piecemeal. Jerzy Kloczowski frames it best: "the extremely elaborate and active cult of ancestor worship carried a special significance as the expression of solidarity between the living and the dead.... For several centuries the Slavs made burnt offering to the dead, a practice that ceased only after the arrival of Christianity."[51]

Given all this, it is hardly surprising that three paragraphs after concluding his final revenant tale Thietmar's mind turned from resurrection to the pagan custom of burnt sacrifice. He was a highly associative thinker and transferred his chains of association to the page. As with his first mention of Walsleben, which

---

48. Caesar, *The Gallic War: A New Translation by Carolyn Hammond*, 6.16 (Oxford, 1996), 127–28.
49. Tacitus, *Germania*, 39, trans. J. B. Rives (Oxford, 1999), 93.
50. Charlemagne, *Capitulatio de partibus Saxoniae*, in *Capitularia regum Francorum*, vol. 1, ed. Alfred Boretius, Monumenta Germaniae Historica (Hannover, 1883). See also Effros, "*De partibus Saxoniae* and the Regulation of Mortuary Custom."
51. Jerzy Kloczowski, *A History of Polish Christianity* (Cambridge, 2000), 9. See also Ken Dowden, *European Paganism: The Realities of Cult from Antiquity to the Middle Ages* (London, 2000), 167–85, 277–89; Wood, "Pagan Religion and Superstition," 259–60; Słupecki, *Slavonic Pagan Sanctuaries*; Prudence Jones and Nigel Pennick, *A History of Pagan Europe* (London, 1995), 172–73; Leszek Paweł Słupecki and Roman Zaroff, "William of Malmesbury on Pagan Slavic Oracles: New Sources for Slavic Paganism and Its Two Interpretations," *Studia Mythologica Slavica* 2 (1999): 9–20; Nora Berend, ed., *Christianization and the Rise of Christian Monarchy: Scandinavia, Central Europe and Rus' c. 900–1200* (Cambridge, 2007); Lars Jørgensen, "Norse Religion and Ritual Sites in Scandinavia in the 6th–11th Century," in *Die Wikinger und das Fränkische Reich: Identitäten zwischen Konfrontation und Annäherung*, ed. Kerstin P. Hofmann, Hermann Kamp, and Matthias Wemhoff (Paderborn, 2014), 239–64. A good study of the piecemeal survival of a traditional ancestor cult is Kyll, *Tod, Grab, Begräbnisplatz, Totenfeier*.

led to a whole chain of associations about ghost stories, his account of the sacrifice of the priest led him to muse on the contemporary pagan practice of burnt offerings. Thietmar is considered by most scholars of the eleventh-century religious scene to be a fairly reliable observer of pagan customs and cult sites, in part because his descriptions are not formulaic reproductions dependent upon earlier antecedents.[52] He reports on the subject of pagan worship in these words:

> Since I have heard marvelous things about their ancient sacrifices, I do not wish to pass over these without mention. . . . Every nine years in the month of January . . . they gather and offer to their gods a burnt offering of ninety-nine men, and an equal number of dogs and cocks and hawks. They believed with certainty that these sacrifices would serve the dead below [*inferos*].[53]

It is striking that so very soon after describing the immolation of a living man upon an altar, "down to a fine ash," Thietmar should offer this description of burnt offerings and human sacrifice as a distinctively pagan sacral rite. The connections can hardly have been lost upon him, especially given the fact that this action had long been the preeminent image associated with pagan worship in the minds of Christian observers.

Other testimonies can fill out a sketch of human sacrifice among medieval central European pagan populations. Though the custom took somewhat different forms in different times and places, as a general practice it was both widespread and persistent. Adam of Bremen, writing a few decades after Thietmar, discusses it in book 4 of his history of the eastern and northern marches: every nine years at a pagan temple in Uppsala, quantities of male animals and of men, up to seventy-two creatures, were offered in sacrifice to the gods.[54] The *Chronicle of the Slavs* by Helmold of Bossau testifies to the 1066 ritual sacrifice of a Christian missionary and former pagan prince, Gottschalk, along with a priest named Eppo, to the Slavic deity Sventovit: the victims were "immolated on the altar."[55] Sventovit's cult is well known to have involved burnt sacrifice, but other Slavic deities appreciated such offerings as well. Elsewhere Helmold mentions the passion of Bishop John

---

52. The principle that we may place greater confidence in observations couched in fresh language was advanced in Buchholz, "Perspectives for Historical Research in Germanic Religion."
53. TM, 22–25; in this case there are minor divergences between the two versions; I have translated the Codex 2 version, on the odd pages.
54. Adam of Bremen, *History of the Archbishops of Hamburg-Bremen*, 4:27, pp. 207–8.
55. Helmold of Bossau, *Chronica Slavorum*, trans. Francis Tschan, *The Chronicle of the Slavs* (New York, 1935), 97.

of Mecklenburg, whose death was offered to the god Redigast.[56] Likewise, a thirteenth-century chronicler of Prussia, Peter of Duisburg, includes a paragraph on the custom, which he describes as an outmoded one in his day. His words associate burnt sacrifices to the dead specifically with afterlife as an embodied revenant. Like Thietmar long before him, Peter presents belief in revenancy as a perverse variant on the doctrine of resurrection:

> The Prussians used to believe in the resurrection of the flesh, but not as they ought to have. They used to believe that if a person was noble or not, rich or poor, powerful or without power in this life, he would be the same after resurrection in his future life. This is why armor, horses, servants . . . [etc.] were put at the disposal of dead nobles. With non-nobles, they burned whatever was appropriate to their station. They believed that things when burned would rise again with them and serve them as previously.[57]

Such sacrifices were widespread throughout the Slavic pagan world. Centuries later, Jan Dlúgosz offers this fifteenth-century testimonial to the practice, concerning a region that was among the last to convert to Christianity:

> It was an ancestral custom and ceremony of the Lithuanians while the murk of paganism possessed them to . . . offer to their ancestral gods, over a three-day period . . . animals, both as sacrificial victims and to be burned whole. . . . And bringing back a triumph or booty from enemy territory, too, on their return they constructed a woodpile or pyre . . . and burned the most outstanding and notable of the captives, thinking their gods were most pleased and gratified by this sort of burnt offering.[58]

In sum, the close association between paganism and burnt sacrifice forms a thinly veiled subtext for Thietmar's tale of revenants immolating a living man upon an altar. The dangerous dead are portrayed in this particular tale as enacting a pagan ritual that involves the offering of gifts—including living beings—to gods or the dead. The custom not only was widespread in the broader region for centuries, it consistently was the focus of Christian comment and contempt, to the degree that paganism itself was defined by this

---

56. Helmold of Bossau, *Chronica Slavorum*, 98; Here, Helmold lifted his information from Adam of Bremen, *History of the Archbishops of Hamburg-Bremen*, 3:50 (49), p. 157.

57. Peter of Duisburg, *Chronica terre Prussie*, ed. Jaroslaus Wenta and Slavomirus Wyszomirski, Monumenta Poloniae Historica, n.s. 13 (Cracow, 2007), 52–53; also excerpted in Mannhardt, *Letto-preussische Gotterlehre*, 88.

58. Mannhardt, *Letto-preussische Götterlehre*, 143, translation from Dowden, *European Paganism*, 287.

act in the Christian imagination. Thus to give an account of a burnt human sacrifice upon an altar would, in Thietmar's time and place, be impossible without simultaneously invoking the specter of pagan worship. Finally, it bears pointing out that the actions of the revenants not only can be read as a traditional form of pagan sacrifice, they are also, de facto, a way of reclaiming for themselves the space of a once deconsecrated, then reconsecrated, church. Homicide is the only additional circumstance that can plunge a church—and most especially, an altar—into the polluted status of deconsecration. Though, as noted above, William Durandus identified fire, ruin, and doubt as the chief criteria through which a church might need to be consecrated anew, he later returns to this question and adds a fourth circumstance to his list: the intentional homicide of a living man, with or without an effusion of blood.[59] By murdering the priest, the living dead not only would appear to be performing a pagan sacrifice upon the altar, they also are thereby reclaiming the church yet again. The building continually moves in and out of consecrated status in this tale, in a way that echoes the vacillations of the region itself, and the population, between pagan and Christian allegiance. And in the end, it seems, the pagan dead win.

This society's connections to its ancestral dead were difficult to displace, even as other aspects of the surrounding culture evolved. Instead, traditional legends of dangerous corpses accreted new details and new settings, amalgamating the new with the old. Thus the tales portray a group of imperfectly assimilated ancestors who haunt a Christian church but kill a Christian priest, who make offerings upon an altar in the form of burnt, rather than Christian, sacrifice. Generations of the dead, persisting at the fringes of consciousness of their descendants, are imagined as pagans in their sacred rites, even though they have been brought (both metaphorically and physically) into the church. The living priest, the vicar of Christ, is not a mediator of the Eucharistic sacrifice that normally would be offered upon the altar for the benefit of the community, but rather an embodiment of pagan sacrifice to appease the gods and ancestors.

Tales in Two Registers: A Comparative Case

We might usefully compare Thietmar's testimonies with a similar motif about the returned dead found in the *Historiae Memorabiles* (*Memorable Histories*), a thirteenth-century compilation of material gathered by the Dominican

---

59. *Rationale divonorum officiorum of William Durand of Mende*, trans. Thibodeau, 73–74.

preacher Rudolf von Schlettstadt (or in French, Sélestat) in Alsace. Like some of Thietmar's stories, this one also involves the dead rising in a churchyard, lighting lamps, and singing; it also, conceivably, can be read as making reference to the provision of afterlife goods. The entry is headlined "On the Rector of the Church of Basel, who Reported that He Saw Dead People." This man held several benefices and was in the course of visiting each of his churches:

> Finally, he arrived at a church whose vicar had a house bordering the cemetery. . . . He slept well and, after having had sweet dreams up until the hour of eleven, he awoke and got up to ease his bladder. Afterward he returned to bed, with the window that looked out onto the cemetery still open, in order that he might see the calmness of the sky and winds. Then suddenly he saw many men in the cemetery, running to and fro with little torches and lamps, while others were leading a ring-dance and singing this song together in a deep voice:

> If I were still in the brief-home,
> As I am in the lengthy-home,
> Then I would, before my end,
> Gather many good things,
> And send them for myself.[60]

The verse is included in the text in Middle High German and is even set to musical notation. The use of a vernacular language in this context is a tantalizing clue to the story's oral foundation. Where did the collector of these tales hear the song in its original tongue and jot down the tune? These questions must remain unanswered. What is clear, however, is that the verse derives from some local community where it was performed specifically as a song of the dead. The references to the "brief-home" (*kurtzhaim*) and the "lengthy-home" (*langkhaim*) identify the singers with the dead and also indicate how parallel the worlds of the living and the dead were felt to be: each has its proper "realm" or home, with distinct names and customs. Though the two realms overlap, they are also, in some sense, separate, like transparent scrims that are layered together but do not touch. Interestingly, the verse, of indeterminate antiquity, "works" in either a pagan or a Christian context,

---

60. Rudolf von Schlettstadt, *Historiae Memorabiles: Zur Dominikanerliteratur und Kulturgeschichte des 13. Jahrhunderts*, ed. E. Kleinschmidt (Cologne, 1974), 72. The verse is in vernacular German, as follows: "wer ich da zw kurtzhaim / als ich bin zw langkhaim / so wölt ich vor meinem ende / gütz vil beywenden / und für mich sendern."

depending on how one understands the penultimate line. If we understand it as Christian, then the dead folk are Christians interred in the cemetery, condemned to some form of postmortem judgment, and therefore lamenting not having piled up more good *deeds* to weigh in their favor. Yet the revenants do not appear to be in any state of torment, infernal, purgatorial, or otherwise. Rather, they are dancing, an activity frowned upon by Christian authorities and prohibited in a long series of canons and regulations.[61] The fact that these revenants are joyously dancing in a ring-dance, in corporeal form, might incline us to look toward an interpretation of the story as a vestigial trace of earlier pagan beliefs, albeit with shifts in their meanings. In such a case, the good *things* that the dead have neglected to send ahead for themselves would be material in nature: grave goods, interred treasures, and burial sacrifices. The ability of the song to function in more than one cultural register at the same time would likely be an important reason for its preservation through time.

Can a similar analysis be applied to Thietmar's tales? The answer is a qualified yes. Thietmar's ghost stories interweave pagan and Christian elements promiscuously, though perhaps only partially consciously. Whether the bishop recorded these stories exactly as he heard them or altered them to suit his own purposes we cannot know for certain; yet the jarring inconsistencies among some elements, and the ill-conceived interpretations Thietmar himself placed upon them, favor the former possibility. One sincerely hopes that, if Thietmar were seeking to craft anecdotes with self-evidently Christian moral content, he would have been able to do better. (Moreover, as we shall see, he later would revise his initial thoughts about revenants and resurrection, moving to a diametrically opposite position.) Working under the premise, then, that Thietmar put these stories into writing in much the same form as he heard them, we are confronted with a motif that appears to have circulated widely in oral transmission. Thietmar heard versions of these stories in several different locations, and from different sources; likewise his niece observed that she knew of many similar tales. Given the context of the surrounding society, it is likely that these stories continuously moved between pagan and Christian populations in the region. As is characteristic of legends circulating for some time in oral form, the stories likely

---

61. Louis Gougaud, "La danse dans les églises," *Revue d'Histoire Ecclésiastique* 15 (1914): 5–22, 229–43; Louis Backman, *Religious Dances in the Christian Church and in Popular Medicine* (London, 1952); Elina Gertsman, *The Dance of Death in the Middle Ages: Image, Text, Performance* (Turnhout, 2010), 51–75. A more popular treatment of ecstatic dance is Barbara Ehrenreich, *Dancing in the Streets: A History of Collective Joy* (New York, 2006). See also chapter 5.

incorporated new elements as they moved through various gossip networks and were recounted by different narrators. They thus incorporate elements from both pagan and Christian cultures, while fully belonging to neither. I would contend, however, that the core elements of the motif are pagan in origin and indigenous to the regional culture and that they are overlaid with an accretion of Christian detail in terms of framing and setting. The latter elements served to render the motif nominally palatable—even, bizarrely, edifying—to audiences like Brigit the abbess and Thietmar the bishop.

If we unstitch the seams of Thietmar's basic story type we can better discern the underlying pattern pieces that make up the narrative, showing how disparate pieces are fitted together. The individual elements of the tales may be separated out from one another for further analysis, as follows.

First, a set of essential ideas having to do with the terms of existence for the dead. These would include the belief that the dead live on as tomb dwellers attached to their place of burial, that they form social groups and are active chiefly at night in places familiar to them in life. As a consequence of the dead's existence on this worldly plane, it is possible for the living to encounter them bodily. A related belief, in this context, is that a living person who sees the dead will shortly join them. These elements of the motif, while clearly originating within traditional northern European pagan culture, can be transferred into a Christian context without significant cognitive dissonance. Gregorian and Isidorean writings about the dead provide warrant for all these notions except tomb dwelling.

Second, a set of contingent elements that provide a specifically Christian context or framing for the stories. Such aspects include the setting of the stories in a consecrated church or cemetery, the fact that the dead are said to perform mass, led by a dead cleric, and the Christian, often clerical, identity of the living interloper. These are inessential elements of the motif, however: the narrative would be equally as dramatic in another setting or with slightly different details. Certainly, rumors about encounters between the living and the dead would have been in circulation locally before the expansion of Christian influence there. As the landscape changed and churches were built and then destroyed in the ensuing conflicts, these sites offered particularly evocative settings for tales of haunted encounters right next to burial places. Thus, in some sense we may say that bringing the dead into a Christian precinct worked to baptize the unquiet pagan dead retroactively and, by implication, the motif itself. However, since Christianity also privileges the theme of life after death, the resulting story can function very well within a Christian semiotic frame. Indeed, as Thietmar intuited, the motif might serve as an excellent point of entry for pastoral instruction.

Third and last, however, we come to those elements that confect internal conflict in Thietmar's accounts, to the point of producing some incoherence. These facets of the narrative include Thietmar's frequent editorial interventions to the effect that such stories somehow "prove" the doctrine of resurrection. As well, there is the juxtaposition, in the final tale, between the distinctively pagan form of worship portrayed (sacrificial killing and burning) and the setting of the story in a church of variable consecration status. The preservation of such inconsistencies is the best argument, in fact, for regarding Thietmar as a faithful recounter of the legends as he heard them: such irreconcilable elements are natural to accounts that circulate orally, accreting new variants and details as they move from mouth to ear to mouth, through different communities and contexts.

There is more that can be plumbed from the depths of these stories, however. There remain more details to be dissected and observed, juxtapositions with other texts to be made, allusions to be suggested, inconsistencies to be noted and judged. Having reached a point of apparent equilibrium in my analysis, it is time, now, to complicate matters further. Let us shift our gaze, then, in a slightly different direction, moving past the confines of the story itself in order to examine the "daily life"—or, more accurately, "nightly afterlife"—of the dead as imagined in this medieval society. Thietmar himself repudiates the belief that "certain pagans maintain that [the dead] maintain the same activities in the next world as in this one."[62] Yet, in Thietmar's ghost stories, that is *precisely* what they do: they worship and gossip just like any living group. The afterlife of the dead mirrors the life of the living for Thietmar, as much as for any pagan Slav.

The Social Life of the Dead

The next section of my analysis is, perhaps, more provocative than probative. It relies largely upon a technique of triangulation with other texts, often, it is true, from widely spaced times and places. I do so under the presumption that recurrent patterns of representation of the living dead gesture, albeit inchoately, toward an originally more coherent set of beliefs, which persists only in fragmentary form. The nature of the motif's significance is difficult to identify in any single case; it is the synthetic process of layering texts and observing the congruences among them that suggests a grasp of something larger than any individual piece of evidence. These fragments function in some ways like the brushstrokes in a pointillist painting: each

---

62. TM, 20–21.

stroke individually is just a smudge, but when layered together and viewed from afar, a picture begins to emerge.

Thietmar's dead congregations do indeed act very similarly to the living. The stories he recounts preserve at their core an ancient pagan idea about the dead forming complex communities in parallel to the living, in the here and now, rather than in another world. The dead are not quiescent: they live underground, in their tombs, during the day; at night they act and walk on the surface of the earth; they use their bodies for singing and grasping; they worship; they know one another; and they live in community. Indeed, there even are hints, in Thietmar's stories, that the dead have much fuller existences than even these things, that the activities at which they are busy when espied by the living are but a small part of a rich afterlife world of experience. Though depicted mainly at worship in cemeteries and sanctuaries, there is warrant for imagining them engaged in other kinds of worldly activities as well.

It is a small detail that provides the best opening for my purposes here: Thietmar reports in passing that the defunct congregations give offerings to their priest at the doors of the sanctuary, a detail that occurs in both the Walsleben and the Deventer stories (the one set in Magdeburg, recall, is only witnessed from afar). This small feature, which might quickly be glossed over, seems to me quite significant; it suggests that the dead *own* things. In other words, the dead have material wealth and an economy of exchange. In the Middle Ages, offerings at mass would normally be in the form of coins, food supplies, or small trinkets of value given directly to the celebrating priest after the conclusion of the mass. These informal gifts, distinct from the more formally mandated tithe, were used for miscellaneous parish expenses, including support for the mass, and as a supplementary sustenance for the lower clergy. Thus it is tempting to suggest that the alms of the dead are helping to support intercessions on their own behalf: masses, prayers, and offerings were beginning to be part of the regular *memoria* of the dead in the eleventh century; by the twelfth, some dioceses had weekly masses for the dead, usually on Mondays.[63] At the end of the story set in Deventer, the bishop orders a fast to succor the murdered priest's soul.

Yet the detail of the offerings also implies something else intriguing: the dead must pursue other activities outside of the communal worship at which they habitually seem to be surprised by the living. Out of sight, then, the lay

---

63. The choice of this day was dictated by the belief that the dead were given relief from their punishments on Sundays. Masses were thought to ease their transition back to torment on Monday. Michel Lauwers, *La Mémoire des ancêtres, le souci des morts: Morts, rites, et société au Moyen Âge (Diocese de Liège, XIe–XIIIe siècles)* (Paris, 1996), 379.

dead must have secular engagements that produce goods or wealth, which they then share with their local dead cleric—just as they did in life. In short, the detail of the offerings opens up a vista onto a fuller postmortem existence: it puts the life in afterlife. In order to flesh out this suggestion, however, we must triangulate Thietmar's accounts with other evidence that suggests a fuller horizon of worldly existence for the dead than formal Christian doctrine allowed.

And this, in turn, prompts a new set of questions and observations. Life is characterized above all by change, by shifting temporal rhythms. Indeed, one significant difference between this life and the next is the continually shifting nature of vitality: the successive occurrence, and then the passing away, of people and events. The afterlife of the Christian imagination, by contrast, is static in its eternity. Since the world to come is perfect and under direct divine governance, there is no possibility for change. The realms of the otherworld, within formal Christian doctrine, generally lacked the texture of continual events—only graduation from purgatory and, eventually, resurrection. Yet as we have seen, in Thietmar as elsewhere, the distinction between vitality and mortality was not always very sharp in the imaginings of medieval people; the dead are often shown as having identical capabilities and customs as the living. In short, the dead are imagined as an "age class"[64] of those who have passed on, but who yet remain organized in a complex society with an economy, worship, social distinctions—and all the vicissitudes of change that that implies.

As we have seen, tales of the restless dead were a particularly active conduit for the circulation of ideas among different sociocultural groups in the Middle Ages. These motifs frequently were drawn from earlier cultural antecedents yet were suffused with an explicitly ecclesiastical ideology; they were thus able to function within more than one field of meaning simultaneously. For instance, we already have had a glimpse of the dead dancing together in a ring and singing a song about their longing for the benefits of "good things" in their afterlife—whether material comforts or spiritual virtues is unclear. Of course, burying the dead with an array of everyday objects or grave goods for their continued use has long been associated with pagan burial custom. Scholars now realize, however, that the presence of grave goods is not a reliable indicator of paganism, for Christians were sometimes interred with objects too, especially in regions that were transitioning between the two religions, and recent trends in medieval archaeology suggest that such

---

64. Geary, *Living with the Dead in the Middle Ages*, 36.

deposits may have been a type of theatrical tableau created in service to the emotional needs of the living, rather than for the benefit of the dead.[65] Just as Christian dead folk sometimes were buried with objects or grave goods, Thietmar's stories tell us that they sometimes were imagined as participating in an afterlife economy of wealth exchange.

Likewise, the living sometimes witnessed the dead engaged in favored pastimes beyond the grave, pastimes that were much the same as those the living enjoyed. The dead were glimpsed at tournaments, at the hunt, at table, or flirting and dancing at parties. These testimonies provide a glimpse into imaginings of dead societies that are complementary to Thietmar's: they portray the dead in similar terms—as conscious, embodied revenants—but we see them engaged in a wider array of activities than just worship services. In many parts of Europe, postmortem courtly societies were imagined as headed by King Arthur. In an anecdote collected from the other end of Europe—Scotland—a bishop encounters Arthur's court in a remote mansion hidden in the forest of his own episcopal lands. While enjoying a fine meal, the bishop asks his host's name and learns that he is feasting at the home of long-dead Arthur and his courtiers. He asks for a sign so that he might prove to others the truth of his encounter. Arthur bestows upon him an unusual gift: whenever he closes his right hand and reopens it, a butterfly will flutter forth. The man thenceforth was known as the "butterfly bishop."[66]

More typical is the story recounted by Étienne de Bourbon, in which a peasant follows a crowd of the dead back home into Mont du Chat in Savoy. Inside, he finds King Arthur and the rest of his long-dead court inhabiting a sumptuous palace: "There, knights and ladies were playing and dancing, drinking and eating gourmet foods. Finally, he was told to go to bed and was led to a room with a bed made up with most precious things. On it lay a woman who appeared wondrously beautiful."[67] Gervaise of Tilbury and Caesarius of Heisterbach also both speak of Arthur's glittering court of the

---

65. Ralph Merrifield, *The Archaeology of Ritual and Magic* (New York, 1987); Bonnie Effros, *Caring for Body and Soul: Burial and the Afterlife in the Merovingian World* (University Park, PA, 2002); Howard Williams, *Death and Memory in Early Medieval Britain* (Cambridge, 2006); Howard Williams, "The Emotive Force of Early Medieval Mortuary Practices," *Archaeological Review from Cambridge* 22, no. 1 (2007): 107–23; Roberta Gilchrist, "Magic for the Dead? The Archaeology of Magic in Later Medieval Burials," *Medieval Archaeology* 52 (2008): 119–59; Andrew Reynolds, *Anglo-Saxon Deviant Burial Customs* (Oxford, 2009).

66. Joseph Stevenson, ed., *Chronicon de Lanercost MCCI – MCCCXLVI e codice Cottoniano nunc primum typis mandatum* (Edinburgh, 1839), 23.

67. Étienne de Bourbon, *De septem donum spiritus sancti*, ed. A. Lecoy de la Marche, in *Anecdotes historiques, légendes, et apologues tirés du recueil inédit d'Étienne de Bourbon* (Paris, 1877), 321.

dead inside a mountain: Etna (also sometimes called Gyber or Stromboli).[68] The figure of King Arthur was particularly popular in Norman Italy: an 1163 pavement mosaic in the Cathedral of Otranto, for example, portrays the royal legend riding a goat and brandishing a club. Indeed, Caesarius has several tales about different groups of the dead happily residing inside Etna and welcoming new arrivals as they die. Thomas of Eccleston, by contrast, reports that it is the German emperor Frederick II who rules over the dead inside Mount Etna, an idea he gathered from local gossip while sojourning in the region.[69]

To be sure, there are strong literary elements in this group of stories; yet the precise form this narrative takes—of the dead forming complex societies inside a mountain—is significant. The topos is also common in Scandinavian literature. *Eyrbyggja Saga*, for instance, features a conflict surrounding

> a mountain held so sacred by Thorolf that no one was allowed even to look at it first without having first washed himself, and no living creature on this mountain, neither man nor beast, was to be harmed until it left of its own accord. Thorolf called this mountain Helga Fell, and believed that he and his kinsmen would go in to it when they died.[70]

The name means "Holy Mountain";[71] it is later portrayed as opening up to receive some of Thorolf's kin, who had recently been lost at sea. A shepherd sees

> the whole north side of the mountain opened up, with great fires burning inside and the noise of feasting and clamor over the ale-horns. As he strained to catch particular words, he was able to make out that Thorstein Cod-Biter and his crew were being welcomed in to the mountain, and that Thorstein was being invited to sit in the place of honor opposite his father.[72]

Surely, the traditional sepulchral mounds referenced by Snorri Sturluson in the opening pages of this chapter were intended to recall these imposing features of the natural landscape: the human-raised mounds reference this traditional location for the afterlife. William Durandus also makes the

---

68. Arturo Graf, "Artù nell'Etna," in *Miti, leggende e superstizioni del Medio Evo*, 2 vols. (Bologna, 1965), 2:301–35.
69. Robert Lerner, "Frederick II, Alive, Aloft, and Allayed," in Verbeke, Verhelst, and Welkenhuysen, *The Use and Abuse of Eschatology in the Middle Ages*, 359–84.
70. Hermann Pálsson, trans., *Eyrbyggja Saga* (New York, 1972), 29–30.
71. Ibid., 30, n. 4.
72. Ibid., 38. Cf. Magnus Magnusson and Herman Pálsson, trans., *Njal's Saga* (New York, 1960), 38.

connection in his discussion of Christian cemeteries: "The nobles used to be buried on mountains, and in the middle of mountains, or at their base and on their own estates."[73] The dead were conceived as living in a parallel society underground; mountains provided a convenient topographical identification of places where the dead might have room to congregate. These places bulging up from the earth were imagined as filled with subterranean cities of the dead. (Indeed, in the next chapter we will visit one such place.)

Perhaps the richest portrayal of postmortem society as complex and changeable, and as living inside mountains, may be found in the fourteenth-century chronicle of Henry of Erfurt. A ghost named Reyneke, though largely an immaterial specter, was perceptible to the living as a single "little human hand, soft and elegant." The floating hand appeared in the town of Cyrenbergh (modern Zirenberg), quite close to Thietmar's see of Merseburg, though long after Thietmar's lifetime. The dead have here been abstracted, with just one hand left to refer to the embodied nature of revenants in traditional belief. Reyneke's hand was "touched and felt by perhaps a thousand people, though no other part of him could ever be touched or seen."[74] His hoarse voice, however, was clearly heard by all, and gossip about the haunting spread quickly. Accordingly, a crowd gathered at the hand's location, an inn, and began to question it intently about the form and customs of the afterlife:

> When it was asked what or who it was, it replied, "Truly, I am a man just like you, a Christian just like you, baptized in the town of Göttingen. . . ."
> "Are you alone?"—"No, there is a large population of us."
> "What do you do?"—"We eat, we drink, we take wives, we have children; we arrange the weddings of our daughters and the marriages of our sons; we sow and we reap, and various other things just as you do."
> "But where do you live? Here?"—"No, we live inside the mountain of Cyrenbergh."[75]

This is quite a peculiar conversation. Reyneke seems at pains to reassure his interlocutors that he is a faithful baptized Christian just like them, only dead. Reyneke's society includes sowing and reaping in the fields and eating and drinking the fruits of these labors. Moreover, he goes on to explain, inside another nearby mountain, Berenberg, there is a rival civilization of different

---

73. *Rationale divinorum officiorum of William Durand of Mende*, trans. Thibodeau, 57.
74. Augustus Potthast, ed., *Liber de rebus memorabilioribus sive Chronicon de Henrici de Hervordia* (Gottingen, 1859), 279.
75. Ibid.

dead folk, the evil dead who are aggressive and who "invade others' land." Thus, there is one mountain for the society of the good dead, and one mountain for a group of the bad—though neither is called heaven or hell.

Most astonishing of all, however, is the theme of fertility that runs through Reyneke's description of his kind's afterlife in Mount Cyrenbergh. There is marriage and reproduction among the dead, points that the shade mentions as he describes his family-centered afterlife: "we take wives, we have children; we arrange the weddings of our daughters and the marriages of our sons." The dead, in other words, are fecund: they are imagined as sexual beings whose numbers are replenished not simply by more deaths from among mortal men and women, but through their own self-sustaining fertility. They are a fully parallel society that draws some of their numbers from the living, yet that also creates new life on their own. The progeny of the dead grow up in turn, find spouses, and then create a new generation of, one supposes, living dead infants. Thus the dead have an afterlife cycle. In Reyneke's world, the dead do indeed lead lives of change rather than impassibility, of temporality rather than static eternity, of production and reproduction rather than sterility and decay. Life after death is imagined as exactly parallel to this life.

An English folk ballad of indeterminate antiquity, known as *The Demon Lover*, replicates the system described by Reyneke: the afterlife is composed of one mountain for the good and another for the evil.

> "O what hills are yon, yon pleasant hills,
> That the sun shines sweetly on?"
> "O yon are the hills of heaven," he said,
> "Where you will never win."
> "O whaten a mountain is yon," she said
> "All so dreary wi' frost and snow?"
> "O yon is the mountain of hell," he cried,
> "Where you and I will go."[76]

Similarly, a long tale interpolated into a Sélestat manuscript of the *Book of the Miracles of Saint Foi of Conques* some time in the first half of the twelfth century concerns two groups of the dead encountered by a nobleman one night. One group is dressed in white, the other in red. A conversation ensues between the living man and one of the Whites. The latter, it transpires, have nearly completed penance for their sins and are soon to be led to salvation.

---

76. Lowry Charles Wimberly, *Folklore in the English and Scottish Ballads* (Chicago, 1928), 132.

The Reds, however, are journeying "as far as Nivelles, to the infernal flames inside a certain mountain."[77]

Yet if heaven and hell were sometimes assimilated to mountains, by far the most common association in this regard for Christian thinkers was the youngest afterlife place, purgatory. First elaborated in the 1170s and formalized into doctrine at the First Council of Lyons in 1254, purgatory was very commonly imagined as located inside a mountain upon the surface of the earth, the best-known exemplar of the tradition being, of course, Dante's *Purgatorio*. Mount Etna often was identified as an earthly entrance into this otherwordly dimension; Saint Patrick's Purgatory in Ireland was likewise associated with a cavern in the side of a hill. Jacques Le Goff has charted these conceptual connections at some length.[78] Yet purgatory was not just a doctrinal solution to the theological problem of how to envision the eternal fates of those who were "not entirely evil" and "not entirely good" (to borrow Augustine's phrasing). Le Goff has argued that though the moral and doctrinal warrant for purgatory was laid forth in the patristic era, the "birth" of purgatory did not occur until, in the 1170s, it was imagined as a place (rather than a process) and designated by a proper noun, *Purgatorium*. Yet this latter development was not such a new imaginative vista after all: the terms in which Purgatory was envisioned were, in fact, quite an old way of thinking about the postmortem home of most dead folk. The features of the pagan afterlife were thus syncretized with the Christian otherworld.

Revenants, Resurrection, and Demons

Thus far, this chapter has wandered through a diverse set of references to the dead in community. We have seen groups of them praying, giving offerings, killing, singing, dancing, working, marrying, even having children. All these reports stem from the physically embodied character of the dead: they are no mere shades or spirits, but corporeal presences that can interact with their material world, with the living, and with one another. Indeed, the bodies of the dead act much like the bodies of the living: they farm food and they eat; they marry, they have sex, and they have children; they earn money and they give offerings; they worship and they kill. And despite the fact that certain elements of these stories ill comport with Christian theology, we have found

---

77. *Liber miraculorum sancte Fidis*, ed. A. Bouillet, Collection de textes pour servir à l'étude de l'histoire 21 (Paris, 1897), 275.

78. Jacques Le Goff, *The Birth of Purgatory*, trans. Arthur Goldhammer (Chicago, 1984); see also Isabel Moreira, *Heaven's Purge: Purgatory in Late Antiquity* (Oxford, 2010).

all these stories in Christian sources, reported by bishops, preachers, and chroniclers, seemingly without any perturbation or cognitive dissonance.

Yet dissonant they were. Thietmar of Merseburg eventually came to realize this himself. Consider the following passage from book 7 of his work:

> In a certain province of the Swabian region . . . an astonishing and rather terrifying thing occurred. A married woman passed away, struck down by the grip of a sudden death. After her body was washed and prepared, it was taken to the church by her sorrowing friends and relatives. Suddenly, she raised herself up on the bier! Everyone fled! . . . It often happens that the cunning enemy of humanity takes on the image of dead people, in this way trying to delude us. Fools believe that such things really happen thus. I would truthfully proclaim . . . that following the commendation of the soul and completion of the solemn office of burial, no corpse will rise from the dead before the resurrection of all flesh.[79]

Thietmar likely composed book 7 four or five years after he wrote book 1: the entire chronicle was finished between 1013 and 1018. By then, he had changed his mind about how best to explain movements of corpses and appearances of the dead. The cadavers of the deceased lie quiet in the ground after they receive the solemn rite of burial; they do not, on any account, wander forth from their graves. What, then, of reports of dead people interacting with the living? Now, Thietmar had a ready answer to explain the cadaver's movement: demonic deceptions that fools believe verily to be the return of the dead.[80] More fool he, then.

Thietmar underwent a significant shift in his interpretation of corpses that rise and move, from believing in the reality of contemporary revenants as proofs of the ultimate resurrection, to flatly denying the possibility of any reanimation of the dead before the resurrection. Of course, blaming evil spirits for mimicking the dead was to become the strategy of choice for Christian skeptics called upon to explain reports of ghosts or revenants. As we shall see, churchmen across medieval Europe who wished to deny the return of the dead qua dead always would resort to a convenient theory of demonic mischief. Either unclean spirits possessed cadavers and used them to attack and to terrify Christian men and women, or else they molded their aerial bodies into the appearance of the dead and wreaked havoc

---

79. TM, 436–39, for this and the quotation in the next note.

80. Yet Thietmar was unwilling to deny the possibility of return from the dead entirely, suggesting that there may be exceptions: "on special occasions, in instances of particular merit, and especially if the glorious life of the departed has caused the world to blossom."

through these impersonations. The beauty of this explanation is that it conceded some real power to the contested entity while undermining its moral authority and encouraging resistance to believing that things were as they seemed.

Having concluded by around 1017 that only unsophisticated fools believe ghost stories, Thietmar nevertheless neglected to go back and re-edit book 1 to bring it into line with his newly skeptical outlook. From book 7's perspective, then, the nature of reality has been grossly misrepresented in book 1; those groups worshipping in cemeteries and churches at night, those shadowy forms that incinerated the priest: these must have been evil spirits, not the human dead. The meanings of ghostly visions proliferate within Thietmar's own text, contradicting one another openly.

Here, Thietmar shifts his interpretation to abandon his hitherto Gregorian style of interpretation, in order to come into line with an Augustinian outlook, the one more dominant in intellectual, rather than pastoral, circles. Thus we can trace, even within the pages of a single text composed over a block of several years, an evolution of attitude and approach. More importantly, we see Thietmar's introduction of an invisible level of reality, which in turn becomes the interpretive key to the event of postmortem activity. The woman's return to life appears to be one thing (dead coming back to life), but in fact *is* something else entirely—something due to an unseen motivating force whose presence must be posited, rather than directly sensed. In introducing this new layer of understanding, Thietmar also shows us a divergence—his own religious interpretations pulling him away from taking the event at face value.

Once again, we can triangulate the motif of demons impersonating dead congregations with other texts. Consider, for example, another anecdote from the later chronicle of Henry of Erfurt: A village in a war zone experienced an invasion of restless dead folk. Word spread and people began to avoid the area; no one would go near the church at night especially. Thus far the tale is familiar: a haunted church, especially fearsome after dark. Regardless, one night a priest and his servant on a journey stay in the building and witness the baptismal water splashed all about and "a multitude of spirits and of devils dancing" in it.[81] We also find an explicitly demonized variant of the motif in the thirteenth- to fourteenth-century *Chronicle of Lanercost*. The story is set in England, in the village of Dalton, near Richmond. An

---

81. Potthast, *Liber de rebus memorabilioribus*, 270.

"impious man" named John Francis skipped Sunday mass and went for a stroll. At length,

> he reached a remote spot filled with powers of the air, all of them small like dwarfs and with deformed features, and dressed as abbots of the Holy Church (a lying illusion)! They followed one taller than the others, who was dressed as a priest. Immediately, they called out to this astonished layman . . . insisting that he should attend their Sunday service. They began with cackles in place of a song and a dreadful mumble instead of a chant. . . . Finally it came time for the aspersion of holy water, so the leader went round and sprinkled all his comrades in iniquity as a punishment for their guilt. Coming to the living man last of all, he gave the fool not water droplets but blows.[82]

Yet despite these demonic elements this tale, too, was almost certainly a ghost story in its original form, one that the chronicler reinterpreted in demonic terms. Some vestigial traces of its original focus remain. For instance, the protagonist of the tale is specifically characterized as "the living man" in contrast to the others, a qualification that would make little sense unless the others were understood to be dead. Likewise, the group's physical form—dwarfs—is recognizably human, if unusual, and one that (as we shall see in the next chapter) often was associated specifically with the dead.

For Christian chroniclers, the motif of the dead congregation often included some element of retribution or reward as well. Thietmar's contemporary Raoul Glaber, for instance, tells of a monk who witnessed a matins service early one Sunday, conducted by a dead bishop on behalf of some recently killed crusaders en route to paradise.[83] A *vita* of Hraban Maur, abbot of Fulda and archbishop of Mainz, tells how the abbot instructed his cellarer to distribute the food portions of each dead monk to the poor. When the man neglected this duty, a congregation of dead brethren of the monastery beat him senseless, crying out, "after three days you will receive worse, for then you shall be counted among the dead, with us!"[84] And so, of course, it transpired. Finally, a popular exemplum in later popular sermon literature shows us another murderous group of cadavers put in service to Christian

---

82. Stevenson, *Chronicon de Lanercost*, 127–28.
83. Raoul Glaber, *Historiarum sui temporis libri quinque*, in *PL*, 142, cols. 640a–642b.
84. Joannes Trithemius, *B. Rabani Mauri vita altera auctore Trithemio*, in *PL*, 107, col. 92c. The text is late, dating from around 1515, but is based on earlier sources. Hraban Maur's dates are ca. 780–856; this incident is dated to 837.

FIGURE 3.2. The legend of the grateful dead told of a man who assiduously prayed for the dead whenever he passed a churchyard. One day when the man was fleeing from his enemies, the dead rose up from their tombs to defend him in gratitude for his prayers. In this illumination, the dead are also shown pouring from the church itself. Illumination from a Book of Hours, Dutch, fifteenth century. Biblioteca Marciana, Venice; no catalog information available.
Album / Art Resource, NY.

piety. The thirteenth-century monk Caesarius of Heisterbach tells of a man who prayed on behalf of the dead every time he passed the churchyard. One day, the man was chased by enemies along the same route and "behold: all the graves in the cemetery fell open! And all the corpses of the dead were seen to exit them, armed with swords and cudgels."[85] The dead put to flight the man's enemies. Figure 3.2 shows an illumination of this motif: cadavers pour out in force from the church doors, while others rise up from the cemetery to save their pious living friend. All are still clad in shrouds; rather than being armed with swords and cudgels, however, here they carry a variety of agricultural tools: a scythe, pitchfork, shovel, hoe, and threshing flail. Thus dead congregations retained some of their fearful, aggressive aspects, as well as some of their communal, fertile references, even after being subordinated to Christian lessons about the value of prayer. Now the dead attack the living for pious motivations of quite a different kind; we have traveled far from the burnt offering described by Thietmar.

As traditions about the living dead persisted into new social and religious contexts they were updated to reflect contemporary conditions and realities. The most important such shift we have noted is the relocation of the revenant societies from their original location inside mountains to the sacred precincts of the cemetery and the church. While this move worked to Christianize these stories, at a nominal and imperfect level, it also had another, perhaps unintended effect: to enshrine within Christian traditions and texts ideas drawn from pagan culture.

The afterlife of the pagan dead in these tales suggests a trajectory for the afterlife of paganism itself. The purity of religious boundaries seldom remains inviolate in contexts of mixed allegiances and populations; stories that expressed pagan sensibilities were ultimately smuggled into Christianity as the two cultures intermingled, and this process accelerated as more pagans converted and more opportunities for exchange arose. Mutual, bilateral acculturation is thus an inevitable component of cultural or religious transformation. Though conversion to Christianity required a formal renunciation of older practices, rites, and beliefs, the old traditions were not so easy to kill; ancient beliefs persisted as commonsense assumptions about the nature of reality. And at the forefront of this deep cultural persistence were the dead: the ancestors, source of society, cultural meaning, and life itself.

---

85. Caesarius of Heisterbach, *Die Fragmente der Libri VIII Miraculorum des Caesarius von Heisterbach*, ed. Aloys Meister (Rome, 1901), 122–23.

CHAPTER 4

The Ancient Army of the Undead

From Mountains to Marches

In the twelfth century some communities of the dead suddenly poured out from their subterranean mountain redoubts to go wandering.

> In the province of Worms a not inconsiderable multitude of armed knights was seen coming and going for several days. The troop seemed to be having friendly conversations among themselves, now here and now there. At about the ninth hour they would go back into a certain mountain that they earlier had been seen to leave. Finally, one of the local people approached them, though not without great fear of such an enormous company of this kind. Protecting himself with the sign of the cross, in the name of Our Omnipotent Lord he adjured the first person in the company he met to explain the reason why they were appearing.
>
> The man replied by saying, among other things, "We are not, as you think, illusions. . . . Rather, we are the shades of knights who recently were killed. The arms and armor and horses that previously were our tools for sin are now the instruments of our torment. For truly, everything that you see us with is burning, though you cannot see it with your bodily eyes."[1]

---

1. Ekkehardus Uraugiensis, *Chronicon Uraugiensis*, in *PL*, 154, cols. 1051–52.

The above quotation, composed around 1126 by the chronicler Ekkehard of Aura, gestures toward a new phase in the history of the macabre imaginary. A military host of the dead pours out from a mountain stronghold and peregrinates as an armed column; they converse with the living, explaining their (after)lives and "the reason[s] why they were appearing." They stress that they are not illusions, but truly dead men. The previous chapter explored a related motif of revenant congregations as well as some tales centering upon the mountain homes of the dead. Yet other stories describing the dead as a collective society persisted as well—including some that were decidedly more secular than pious in apprehension.

The image of a dead military troop presented by Ekkehard was based upon a Germanic folk motif known variously as the "Ancient Army," the "Wild Chase," the "Furious Horde," "Hellechin's (or Herlequin's) retinue," or simply "the Hellequin."[2] These were names for an unruly mob of marauding shades who had died untimely and violently and who traveled together in the afterlife as a fearsome band of dead warriors. The motif was an ancient one. In traditional Teutonic mythology, such a band of warriors was associated with Odin's *Einherjar*, a dead army that continually battled among itself and then resurrected to fight again. Scholars of the ancient army have identified scattered references to the Germans' mythology of the warlike shades of the dead in classical ethnographies (including Tacitus), but these passages are brief and offer few details. The poem *Eiríksmál* ("Eirik's Poem"), commissioned by an Anglo-Saxon widow for her warrior husband in 954, describes the Einherjar being awakened by Odin and then joyously readying the halls of Valhalla for "the coming of the slain."[3] A fuller reference

---

2. Jacob Grimm, *Teutonic Mythology*, 6 vols. (London, 1883), 3:918–50; Otto Dreisen, *Der Ursprung des Harlekin: ein kulturgeschichtliches Problem* (Berlin, 1904); Gaston Reynaud, *Mélanges de philologie romane* (Paris, 1913), 1–17; Howard Rollin Patch, "Some Elements in Mediaeval Descriptions of the Otherworld," *Publications of the Modern Language Association* 33, no. 4 (1918): 601–43; Hermann Flasdieck, "Harlekin: Germanischer Mythos in romanischer Wandlung," *Anglia* 51 (1937): 225–340; Walter Liungmann, *Traditionswanderungen Euphrat—Rhein: Studien zur Geschichte der Volksbräuche* (Helsinki, 1938); Karl Meisen, *Die Sagen vom Wütenden Heer und Wilder Jäger* (Münster, 1938); W. E. Peuckert, *Deutscher Volksglaube des Spätmittelalters* (Stuttgart, 1942), 86–96; Brian Stock, *The Implications of Literacy: Written Language and Models of Interpretation in the Eleventh and Twelfth Centuries* (Princeton, NJ, 1983), 495–99; Philippe Walter, *Le mythe de la chasse sauvage dans l'Europe médiévale* (Paris, 1997); Jean-Claude Schmitt, *Ghosts in the Middle Ages: The Living and the Dead in Medieval Society* (Chicago, 1998), 93–121; Claude Lecouteux, *Chasses fantastiques et cohortes de la nuit au Moyen Age* (Paris, 1999); C. S. Watkins, "Sin, Penance and Purgatory in the Anglo-Norman Realm: The Evidence of Visions and Ghost Stories," *Past & Present*, no. 175 (2002): 3–33; Carl Watkins, *History and the Supernatural in Medieval England* (Cambridge, 1997), 170–201; Alan Bernstein, "The Ghostly Troop and the Battle over Death: William of Auvergne (d.1249) Connects Christian, Old Norse, and Irish Views," in *Rethinking Ghosts in World Religions*, ed. Mu-Chou Poo (Leiden, 2009), 115–61.

3. Angus Somerville and Andrew McDonald, eds., *The Viking Age: A Reader* (Toronto, 2010), 93–94.

to the ancient army comes to us from the pen of the eleventh-century Cluniac monk Ralph Glaber. This is among the earliest expanded discussions. Ralph tells of a village priest of Tonerre who sighted "as dusk was falling . . . a column of an innumerable multitude of knights ready for battle, coming from the north and traveling west." Unnerved by the sight, the man called for his servants to come see, but the group suddenly vanished into thin air. Glaber comments, "This fact should be committed to memory with the utmost attention: Whenever such clear prodigies are shown to people who are still alive and in the body . . . they do not remain alive for long."[4] Most detailed narratives about the dead army derive from the twelfth and thirteenth centuries, however. They appear in chronicles, exempla collections, courtly literature, and antiheretical treatises. By this time, the army had shed some (though not all) of its pagan associations and become a widespread folk motif, often expressing a kind of popular theology about postmortem penance. The authors who write about this group universally assume that their readers already know of it and recognize the name of its leader Hellequin (or some variant thereof).

The general contours of the belief can easily be sketched. The dead men who made up Hellequin's troop were thought to be the embodied shades of those who had died while still relatively youthful and who had suffered a brutal and traumatic battlefield demise. They would remain restless, wandering until their natural lifespans were fulfilled. For this reason the theologian William of Auvergne called them the *disgladiati*, "men undone by swords."[5] The group also is called the Hellequin, the Herlething, and simply, the Army of the Dead. (In the discussions that follow, I match my vocabulary to the terms used by each author I discuss.) The group was active at night, and most especially at moments of ritual transition into and out from the winter months, when the gates between worlds temporarily fell open.[6] To encounter this army of revenants was a harrowing experience for any living man or woman: true to its warrior ethos, the deadly host could physically harm, and certainly terrorize, the living. Even for those who survived such an encounter, the very fact of having seen the dead group was often a portent of one's own approaching demise. Many of these details duplicate themes found in the earlier tales of the collective dead examined in the previous chapter.

---

4. Rodulfus Glaber, *The Five Books of Histories*, ed. and trans. John France (Oxford, 2002), 222.
5. WA, 1067.
6. Claude Gaignebet and Marie-Claude Florentin, *Le Carnaval: Essai de mythologie populaire* (Paris, 1979), 17–39.

Complementing the male companies of embodied dead warriors who wandered the earth were companies of female spirits who flew through the skies. The latter often were known as the "good things" (*bonae res*). They were led by a feminine deity identified by a wide variety of names, depending upon the author and context of the report. Works penned by authors of a classicizing bent designated this goddess with biblical or classical names such as Diana or Herodias; in other texts the Germanic appellations Holda or Perchtha are found; Abundia or Satia (labels that suggest themes of fertility) were utilized by authors in French regions; while in Italy, the figure was sometimes known as Madonna Oriente.

The classic description of the feminine horde of spirits in the medieval textual tradition is the famed canon *Episcopi*, a tenth-century penitential warning to bishops to uproot from their dioceses a superstitious belief about flying spirits. It was a distinctively feminine cult or belief, described as follows:

> Certain wicked women, turned after Satan and seduced by the fantasies and illusions of demons, believe and assert that they ride on certain beasts at night with Diana, the pagan Goddess, and an innumerable multitude of women, and that in the silence of the dead of night they traverse great distances over the earth. They say they must obey her orders like a mistress and that they are called to serve her on certain nights.[7]

Other clues suggest that at least some regional variants of this female society may have been understood as a means for the living and the dead to interact across the boundary of the grave, preserving connections between worlds. For instance, in an inquisitorial trial held in Milan in 1390 against two women, one defendant confessed that she regularly attended the games of the "good folk" and that "both living and dead people attend, but those who have been decapitated or hung are very shamefaced and do not dare hold up their head in that society."[8] Thus, the company of the good things included both the living—special women possessed of the shamanistic ability to journey in spirit, leaving their bodies behind—and the permanently disembodied spirits of the dead. At such gatherings the living and the dead feasted richly together upon fat oxen that later were resurrected by their leader, Madonna Oriente, with a touch of her wand.[9] Lastly, another set of

---

7. Joseph Hansen, *Quellen und Untersuchingen zur Geschichte des Hexenwahns und der Hexenverfolgung im Mittelalter* (Hildescheim, 1962), 38.

8. Luisa Muraro, Latin text edited as an appendix to *La Signora del gioco: Episodi della caccia alle streghe* (Milan, 1976), 243.

9. Maurizio Bertolotti, "The Ox's Bones and the Ox's Hide: A Popular Myth, Part Hagiography and Part Witchcraft," in *Microhistory and the Lost Peoples of Europe*, ed. Edward Muir and Guido

texts provides clues that the good things were regarded as beneficent agents of fortune, bestowing increase and fertility upon the homes that welcomed them. William of Auvergne scornfully describes the "foolishness of men, and the insanity of little old ladies, such that they leave out, uncovered, flagons of wine and dishes of food" for Lady Abundia, in the expectation that such gifts would be rewarded with fertility and prosperity for the home.[10] Étienne de Bourbon likewise references a peasant belief that a visit from the good things would mean that they would "take one; return one hundred."[11] Fertility in exchange for a token offering of food, then, was key to the veneration of these strange spirits. William considered such acts to be idolatry: expecting fertility from the good things suggested that an agent other than the Creator could provide increase of fortune and goods. He castigated women who clung to the belief and taught other, younger women about it; thus they "preserve and retain the vestiges of idolatry."[12]

The good things' cult and belief in the wandering army of the dead were deeply intertwined in the minds of medieval commentators. For example, when William of Auvergne addresses superstitions pertaining to the dead, his discussion pulses back and forth between attacking the convictions of little old women that they fly by night with the female horde and refuting the popular belief in the embodied apparitions of the army of dead warriors. Other commentators such as Étienne de Bourbon pair them up as well. All the same, it is somewhat difficult, across the distance of centuries, to discern the exact basis of this perceived coherence between the dominantly masculine army and dominantly feminine good things. It seems most likely that these paired motifs both sprang from an original conception of the dead as forming a complete afterlife society among themselves, including all the elements of daily life: feasting, farming, sex, marriage, dancing, and so forth. We have seen portrayals of such societies existing inside mountains in chapter 3. As Ekkehard of Aura's quotation suggests, the army of the dead may be regarded as a mobile, masculine branch of this postmortem society, a column of warlike dead folk that sometimes left their mountain afterlife home in order to wander the countryside. Conversely, the feasts and dances of the good things required living women to journey, in spirit, to the otherworld. Their feasts replicate the light-hearted,

---

Ruggiero (Baltimore, 1991), 42–70; Emma Wilby, "Burchard's *strigae*, the Witches' Sabbath, and Shamanistic Cannibalism in Early Modern Europe," *Magic, Ritual, and Witchcraft* 8, no. 1 (2013): 18–49.

10. WA, 1066.

11. Étienne de Bourbon, *Librum seu tractatum de diversis materiis praedicabilibus . . . secundum dona Spiritus Sancti*, ed. A. Lecoy de la Marche, in *Anecdotes historiques, légendes et apologues tirés du recueil inédit d'Étienne de Bourbon* (Paris, 1877), 324–25.

12. WA, 1066.

celebratory aspect of the afterlife as it was often imagined to exist inside the mountain halls of the dead. On the good things' journeys to or from this feast, they might stop off at homes that had left offerings, tasting the wine and food and blessing the home. Thus the good things' role in fostering abundance functions within a symbolic economy in which the ancestors are the source of all wealth and fertility. In sum, it seems possible to tentatively propose that the two beliefs both descended from a pre-Christian vision of afterlife as a fecund, feasting society arranged much like the society of the living, and that they evolved over time along slightly divergent trajectories, ultimately achieving the distinct forms that are attested in later texts. It is impossible to fully reconstruct the original linkages between these two motifs, however, or their true significance within pagan religions. In any event, our chief interest is the folklorization of these traditions as they persisted within Christian society.

Of the two variants, the army of the dead is of greater significance for my purposes, however. My chief interest is upon instances of the dead wandering into the world of the living, rather than the reverse. Thus the remainder of this chapter is dedicated to analyzing multiple textual rescensions of this grim military column, mobilized for different rhetorical purposes by various authors. I will analyze the good things' cult when it intersects with material on the dead army, however.

Though references to a nighttime procession of revenants may be found in many different areas, the theme had a particularly strong presence in Anglo-Norman regions. This is where we find both the earliest detailed writings about it, as well as the lengthiest descriptions of encounters. Normandy is where the earliest extensive version of the story is set: that of Orderic Vitalis, recounted in his *Ecclesiastical History*. The region was something of a cultural crossroads before the turn of the millennium and the home base for an aggressively expansionist aristocratic regime afterward. Germanic ethnic groups had been settled in northwestern France since the fifth century, where they mingled with the older Gallo-Roman inhabitants; later the area was subject to a second influx of pagan peoples, in the form of the Scandinavian Viking cultures that settled there in the ninth and tenth centuries. In 911, the independent Duchy of Normandy was formed; in 1066, the Normans brought the cultural admixture of their region to Britain by conquest. By the mid-twelfth century, Norman aristocrats were in control of Sicily and portions of southern Italy, thus crafting a far-flung and powerful network of kingdoms and duchies across continental Europe.[13] These are the regions in

---

13. Neil Price, *The Vikings in Brittany* (London, 1989); Johan Callmer, Jean Renaud, and Neil Price, "Scandinavia and the Continent in the Viking Age," in *The Viking World*, ed. Stefan Brink in

which discussion of the dead army was most common, though there are also some important texts that derive from other areas.

The pages to follow present close readings of several different texts about the ancient army of the unquiet dead. In each case, I try to be purposefully provocative in suggesting how these narratives transmit a complex alchemical mixture of ideas that ultimately descend from an anterior cultural and religious system. The twelfth-century writers who discussed the army of the dead did not do so as ethnologues discussing an exotic religion or superstitious holdover, but as literary observers of their own living, contemporary religious culture. Many of them also believed these tales made sense within a Christian worldview. Thus some early literary versions of the army of the dead were reframed as opportunities to teach about the increasingly important notion of purgatory. In the thirteenth century, however, this situation shifted. University-trained theologians reacted against the army of the dead motif, finally condemning it as a demonic illusion rooted in pagan superstition. Thus this chapter also charts a shift from a Gregorian to an Augustinian outlook in regard to the motif of the dead army.

I will not discuss every passing reference to this story, but instead confine myself to a handful of richer treatments. The two earliest narratives are also the most atavistic. I begin with Orderic Vitalis. Here, I give my attention by turns to the author's attempts to appropriate this tale as a purgatorial vision and to those more archaic aspects of the account that remained wholly unassimilable for Christian moralizing. I then move to an account from a secular English author, Walter Map. This author's tale of King Herla imagines a myth of origins for the wandering column of revenants, explicitly linking it to a prior culture and rule displaced by "modernity." In both cases, the stories preserve significant elements of pre-Christian cultures. Next, I move on to analyze two narratives that tame and "modernize" the army of the dead and present it as convergent with the Christian afterlife system. These two texts—an earnest one by the Sardinian bishop Herbert of Clairvaux, and an ironic one by Andreas Capellanus—present the errant revenants as the saved, the purging, and the damned all in a single vagabond column of the dead. The vision from Herbert of Clairvaux sets forth this system straightforwardly; Capellanus's version is satirical, but the terms of its framing suggest that this way of conceiving the group had become a commonsense notion, available for parody. The next section traces the complete reversal of this interpretation. The last pair of texts treats the army as a demonic

---

collaboration with Neil Price (London, 2012), 439–61; Neil Price, "The Vikings in Spain, North Africa, and the Mediterranean," in Brink and Price, *The Viking World*, 462–69.

illusion, not as a true appearance of the dead. William of Auvergne in his thirteenth-century *De universo* wrote of the ancient army as an error in need of correction; he adopted a standard Augustinian ideal in arguing that the dead cannot cross the border of the grave in order to visit the living. William's interpretation changed the ways in which the Hellequin was presented in most subsequent tradition. Finally, with the last text to be considered, we at last meet the leader of the army of the dead face to face. In the vernacular French *Roman de Fauvel*, and accompanying illuminations, Hellequin is both demon and giant, pagan leader of the dead and diabolic inciter of sin.

Walchelin, meet Herlechin

Decades after congregations of the dead were claiming churches and slaughtering priests in Thietmar's corner of Europe, a different type of revenant group appeared by night to yet another terrified cleric. On the night of January 1, 1091, a young priest encountered a wandering company of dead warriors along a moonlit forest road in Brittany. Like the undead described by Thietmar of Merseburg in 1013, the revenants in this story were corporeal, aggressive, and acted as a group. Moreover, just as Thietmar had done many decades previously, the teller of this story, an Anglo-Norman monk named Orderic Vitalis, claimed to have collected it directly from an oral source.

Orderic Vitalis was a Benedictine brother; he had been raised in the foundation of Ouche since being offered to the house as an oblate at the age of ten.[14] He came from Anglo-Norman stock. His father Odelerius of Orléans was a Norman priest in the household of Roger de Montgomerie. The latter participated in the Norman invasion in 1066; after settling in England, he became the first Earl of Shrewsbury. Odelerius accompanied him and acquired both a chapel and a lover in Shrewsbury; there Orderic was born and received his early education.[15] Yet Orderic's father must have preserved significant ties to his homeland, for in 1085 he offered his son to the monastery of Ouche, located in a rather remote and densely forested region of Brittany.

Orderic composed his *Ecclesiastical History* in the 1130s. The text presents the first extensive description of the army of the dead that has come down to us. Much had changed between Thietmar's time and Orderic Vitalis's account of a young cleric encountering a procession of errant revenants

---

14. Amanda Jane Hingst, *The Written World: Past and Place in the Work of Orderic Vitalis* (Notre Dame, 2009), 2.

15. Hingst, *Written World*, xvii.

on a cold New Year's night, however. Orderic's context of twelfth-century Normandy was fully Christian, by contrast with the more ethnically and religiously mixed society of Thietmar. At the same time, however, the popular culture of Orderic's time preserved many beliefs, folk customs, and other traditions that had roots in the pagan cultures that had migrated throughout the region. Indeed, Brittany was known as a bastion of ancient folklore and custom at this time period, providing the setting for many folktales and preternatural tales in the literary tradition. Moreover as I will show, Orderic himself appears to have been aware of the pre-Christian underpinnings of the motif.

The story Orderic recounts is quite lengthy, and the setting of the tale is rife with multiple funerary symbolisms and allusions. On January 1, 1091, Orderic tells us, a young priest named Walchelin, of the diocese of Lisieux, was called abroad by night to visit to a sick person on the outer fringes of his parish. The timing of the story is significant: it was New Year's night, a moment of the calendar that was intimately associated with the return of the dead and the opening of a gap between worlds in traditional northern European paganisms.[16] Moreover, during the dead of winter, nights were long and fearsome; for Walchelin to undertake such a journey after nightfall suggests that the situation was an emergency and that the parishioner was on his deathbed. A priest's presence would have been required to give the last rites. Returning from this doleful mission alone, while far from any human habitation and in the middle of the night, Walchelin heard a "huge clashing sound, like a great army."[17] Trembling, Walchelin feared that the clatter came from the army (*familia*) of the "grasping and cruel" aristocrat Robert of Bellême, which he thought might have been returning home from a military siege.[18] Spying a nearby clump of medlar trees, Walchelin moved to take refuge behind them. The choice of tree has symbolic valences as well: medlars are a winter-bearing fruit that cannot be eaten direct from the living tree, but only after being "bletted"—that is, buried in loose dirt for some time, until they begin to decompose and the flesh becomes soft and brown.[19] Thus medlars symbolized something that reaches fullness only after having become blighted and rotten under the earth. What better fruit to choose as a portent for a tale about the dead, risen from the grave and showing their

---

16. Gaignebet and Florentin, *Le Carnaval*, 17–39.
17. OV, 4:238. All translations from this text are my own.
18. OV, 6:178; Kathleen Thompson, "Orderic Vitalis and Robert of Bellême," *Journal of Medieval History* 20 (1994): 133–41.
19. John R. Baird and John W. Thieret, "The Medlar (*Mespilus germanica, Rosaceae*) from Antiquity to Obscurity," *Economic Botany* 43, no. 3 (1989): 328–72.

power? Like Walchelin's journey to and from a deathbed, and the setting of the tale on New Year's Eve, Orderic's mention of the medlar trees is surely deliberate. Even before the dead army appears, a forebodingly funereal atmosphere has been established.

Walchelin never reached the cover of the medlars, however; he was detained at the roadside by a gigantic figure armed with a mace, who ordered the priest to remain where he was, brandishing his weapon to ensure compliance. Walchelin has just met Herlechin, the leader of the nighttime troop of the dead. The similar structure of these two names is striking: they have the same ending and rhythm to their pronunciation. "Walchelin"—Latinized as *Gualchelinus*—was a typical Norman name: it appears in the genealogy of the de Ferrières family, for example (though our protagonist does not appear to pertain to this particular kin group). At the same time, however, the name Walchelin, particularly when juxtaposed with that of Herlechin, is provocative. This similarity appears to be signaling something to the reader, and it is worth pausing for a moment to explore their etymologies. As it turns out, their meanings cover a similar symbolic terrain. To begin with the giant: the origins of the name Herlechin—and its variants Harlequin or Hellequin—have long been debated, but recent scholarship appears to have coalesced around one theory: Herlechin or Hellequin likely derives from the Old High German *hari* ("troop, army") combined with *thing* (the assembly of arms-bearing free men in Germanic cultures). The name formed thusly would be reduplicative, since the *thing* already comprises all adult, armed men.[20] When we examine the etymology of Walchelin we find a surprising convergence of meaning. The Old High German root *Wal-* means "battlefield, slaughter." This word is related to the Old Norse *valr*, "those slain in battle," to *Valhöll*, "the hall of the battle-slain," and of course to *Valkyrjur*, "the choosers of the slain." Conjoined to this root is a variant of the suffix, *-chelin*, that appears at the end of Herlechin.[21] Conceptually, then, the name Walchelin evokes the battlefield dead, whom Herlechin leads. The unusual resonance between the two names might possibly be coincidence, but more likely suggests that literary considerations influenced Orderic's attribution of

---

20. Alternatively, the name has been regarded as a derivation from *Hel,* the realm of the dead in Germanic mythology, followed by the personifying masculine suffix *-echin* typical of the Germanic tongues. This derivation was proposed by Grimm, *Teutonic Mythology*, 3:942. More generally on the question of the name and its meaning, see Leo Spitzer, "Anglo-French Etymologies," *Studies in Philology* 41, no. 4 (1944): 521–43; Lecouteux, *Chasses fantastiques et cohortes de la nuit*, 104–5; Schmitt, *Ghosts in the Middle Ages*, 100; Bernstein, "Ghostly Troop and the Battle over Death," 134; Flasdieck, "Harlekin," 225–338.

21. Douglas Harper, *Online Etymology Dictionary* (2001–15): http://www.etymonline.com/index.php?l=v&p=1&allowed_in_frame=0.

the narrative to a person of this name. The visionary and the envisioned are mirrors of one another.

As the intimidating giant forced the priest to remain and watch the passing of the column of dead folk, a series of five distinct subgroups appeared in succession. When the troop first came into view, Walchelin discerned a crowd on foot, with each member burdened by animals, clothing, household goods, and other objects. This segment of the column was composed of "pillagers," who in life stole the goods they now carry. The priest recognized some of his recently deceased neighbors, who all lamented "the great sufferings with which they were tormented on account of their crimes [*facinora*]."[22] The second group had two components, one collective and one singular. The main element was a cluster of five hundred funeral biers, each carried by two men and bearing a dwarf. In the midst of this group, however, was one man bound to a large tree, being gleefully tormented by a demon with red-hot spurs. Walchelin recognized the latter as a man who had killed a priest two years earlier, dying impenitent. The third group in the column was a cohort of women mounted sidesaddle on horses and mules. Each saddle was studded with burning nails, and a swirling wind continually lifted each woman and then dropped her down again on her mount. This was a collection of lewd ladies, and again Walchelin made out some former acquaintances. Next came a contingent of clergy and black monks, some of whom had possessed a reputation for high sanctity. Orderic names some specific individuals—a bishop and two abbots—whom living people believed to be among the blessed, but who instead were included among the band of wandering revenants. Though the group of religious men "wept and wailed,"[23] and though some of them begged Walchelin to pray for them, no particular torments are described for this group.

Finally, the rear of the column was brought up by an immense multitude of knights on horseback. (As we will see, the detail of the countless numbers of the dead is one that will recur often; and of course, it is one that emphasizes the universal fate of all humankind.) While watching these thousands of desperate dead men pass by, Walchelin suddenly realized that he was witnessing Herlechin's *familia*. He resolved to steal an unmounted horse from the group in order to prove to skeptics that he had seen the fabled troop, of which he had heard many times. However, the stirrup of the horse was red hot and the reins icy, and four knights in the column immediately accosted him angrily. Next, a dead man approached the priest and asked

---

22. OV, 4:238.
23. OV, 4:240.

him to convey a message to his surviving family, involving the restitution of a mill he stole while alive. Walchelin refused, however, and the enraged dead knight attacked him in a furor, grabbing him by the throat: here the element of violence and anger that are the primary sins of this group come to the fore. The materiality of the horse and its trappings and the detail of the dead knight throttling Walchelin alert the reader to the fact that the army is made up of risen cadavers, rather than of immaterial apparitions. The young priest was saved from his attacker by the timely intervention of another revenant, however—who turned out to be Walchelin's own deceased brother. The latter told Walchelin that he would have been killed for trying to steal the horse but for the fact that he had celebrated mass earlier that day: he was thus protected from harm. In fact Walchelin's masses on behalf of the dead had already assisted his own family: their father was earlier released from torment in the column, graduating from penitential torments to salvation. Walchelin's brother begged him to pray for him too, as he hoped to be released within a year. With that, the brother hastened away after his comrades, for the rest of the group had already moved away down the road. Walchelin fell desperately ill for a week but recovered to live another fifteen years.

Wild Men and Priest Killers

This tale is a typical product of its time in many ways. To begin, the composition of the procession is a rough approximation of twelfth-century social structure. The "three orders"—nobility, clergy and commoners—are all present; the addition of a separate category for women rounds out the portrayal. Orderic includes other "modernizing" elements in his narrative as well: a system of retributive punishments, in which individuals are tormented in ways that refer back to their sins; and individuals who beg Orderic for prayers to alleviate their postmortem torment. Likewise, a reference to "purgatorial fire" shows Orderic's attempts to assimilate the vision to standard Christian theology.[24] Herlequin's army is here confected as a postmortem penitential column upon the earth's surface, its endless motion acting as a purgative cleansing of sin. Orderic stresses that the army's sufferings can be alleviated by suffrages and acts of Christian piety offered by the living. In sum, the army of the dead here functions as a purgatory avant la lettre, before it became it "fixed" as a specific place.[25] Thus, even after the era of

---

24. OV, 4:240, 248.
25. Jacques Le Goff, *The Birth of Purgatory*, trans. Arthur Goldhammer (Chicago, 1984); Isabel Moreira, *Heaven's Purge: Purgatory in Late Antiquity* (Oxford, 2010).

the conversions, ghost stories remained useful as a means to teach the details of Christian doctrine in regard to the afterlife.

Walchelin, as the direct recipient of the vision and purported oral informant for Orderic, serves to certify the reality of the otherworld. The priest is presented as the key to the vision's verisimilitude: a real, living person who encountered some wandering purgatorial dead folk and lived to tell the tale, and who recounted it firsthand to the author. The dead are but two degrees of separation from the reader. Indeed, Orderic anticipated potential skepticism on the part of his audience and addressed it directly in his narrative. As Walchelin watched the final group in the column, the warriors, pass by, he paused to reflect:

> "Doubtless this is Herlechin's retinue! For so long I have heard tales from many people who have seen it, but I was incredulous and ridiculed those who gave such accounts, for I never saw any certain evidence of such things. But now I well and truly see the shades of the dead! And no one will believe me when I give an account of what I have seen, unless I can display a clear proof to living men."[26]

The passage forms part of a long tradition of ghost and revenant stories that pointedly argue for their own veracity in the expectation of incredulity. In this case, Walchelin plays the role of converted skeptic: just as he once ridiculed others who claimed to have seen Herlechin's army, now he himself is placed in the position of needing to convince others of the reliability of his account. He therefore attempts to secure material evidence of his encounter, which leads to his abortive attempt to steal a horse. The narrative addresses its own lack of credibility a second time soon thereafter: when the dead man William of Glos asks Walchelin to convey a message to his heirs about the unjustly held mill, Walchelin retorts, "William of Glos died a long time ago . . . if I dared tell these things to Roger of Glos, his brothers, or his mother, they would ridicule me as a madman."[27] In the end, Walchelin's response garners the only proof he does bring back to the living: a scar around his neck from the burning hands of William of Glos, who tries to throttle him in a rage. Orderic Vitalis dutifully reports having seen the scar. In the end, the best support for Orderic's account is the fact that belief in the army of the dead already was current in the region. As we have seen in the previous chapter, known and believed stories of postmortem encounters were very useful to the pastoral agenda of the church. If such motifs could

---

26. OV, 4:242.
27. OV, 4:244.

be recontextualized to comport with Christian theology, then they could be used to prove contemporary Christian teachings about the afterlife through the vehicle of an already accepted ghostly legend. Orderic tried to accomplish this goal, using the army of the dead in order to teach about postmortem penitence and the value of masses and suffrages for the dead.

And yet, there remain elements within Orderic's narrative that resist Christian contextualization; here we return to a theme from the previous chapter, recurring under different circumstances. These dissonant elements of Orderic's narrative appear to have been reproduced from an originally oral context without significant alteration. For example, the setting of the tale at the New Year clearly frames the story around a major festival of the pagan, but not the Christian, calendar. This was traditionally a time for the dead to wander from their graves and for the living to don animal masks of various kinds perhaps in response to a perceived threat from the dead.[28] Furthermore, the second group within the column is particularly unassimilable to Christian ideology. In this early part of the vision, Walchelin stands rooted to the earth, under threat by the giant Herlechin. He watches as "a crowd of pall-bearers followed, to which the giant mentioned above joined himself. They were carrying about five hundred biers, each one borne by two porters. And sitting upon the biers were little men, like dwarfs, but they had large heads like barrels."[29] The image is puzzling and escapes clear taxonomic categorization; this segment of the procession is cryptic. In the case of every other subgroup, it is clear both who the people were in life and what was the nature of their sin: thieves, lustful women, negligent religious men, rapacious nobles. But the five hundred dwarfs carried upon funeral biers remain a cipher. Moreover, the giant, mace-wielding wild man Herlechin joins this part of the procession. This subgroup would seem to be reserved for marvelous creatures of uncommon height; as Richard Bernheimer has pointed out, gigantism and dwarfism are common in portrayals of medieval wild men, with the former usually appearing as unique figures and the latter in collective groups.[30]

Whatever the contemporary function or symbolism of this group, it remains outside the framework of Christian piety and penance that characterizes the

---

28. The pagan significance of the timing was noted by Bernstein, "Ghostly Troop and the Battle over Death," 131. See also Jean-Claude Schmitt, "Les masques, le diable, les morts," in *Les corps, les rites, les rêves, les temps: Essais d'anthropologie médiévale* (Paris, 2001), 211–37.

29. OV, 4:238.

30. Richard Bernheimer, *Wild Men in the Middle Ages: A Study in Art, Sentiment, and Demonology* (Cambridge, MA, 1952), 22. For a fascinating photographic documentation of the many wild man festivals that still survive in communities throughout Europe, see Charles Fréger, *Wilder Mann: The Image of the Savage* (Heidelberg, 2012).

rest of the narrative. Perhaps for this reason, most historians who have analyzed this vision have failed to comment upon this part of the account: the segment is difficult to understand and therefore easy to ignore. However, there are a few clues in the text that may be triangulated with one another in order to suggest an interpretation.

This section of the army is composed, as we have seen, by five hundred dwarfs on funeral biers, joined by the giant Herlechin. There is also one more unique figure traveling in this part of the procession. Like the dwarfs, this personage is bound upon a conveyance carried by two bearers, but his circumstances are rather different: "An enormous tree-trunk was carried by two Ethiopians, and on the trunk, some wretch was tightly bound. . . . A terrifying demon, seated on the tree-trunk, was goading him violently with red-hot spurs, in the loins and on his bleeding back."[31] This individual is unique in many ways. He is the only sinner in the entire column of shades who is punished singly and uniquely, rather than as part of a collective. Likewise, the above passage contains the sole appearance of a tormenting demon in the whole of the narrative; the other shades are tormented by burning arms, by spiked saddles, or by the army's continual movement, but this is the only diabolic presence in the vision. This would seem to be an indication of the gravity of the person's trespass, for he alone merits a dedicated demon for torment. Likewise, the demon suggests that this section of the group is more "infernal" than the later portions, which allow for the possibility of purgation and release.

The recipient of the vision, Walchelin, recognizes the individual who is thus singled out for torment: he is "the killer of Stephen the priest . . . who had died without performing penance for such a misdeed [*piaculi*]."[32] Modern historians have not been able to identify the individuals or the incident involved in the passage. However, a clue may perhaps be sought in the rather unusual term *piaculum* with which Orderic designates the man's crime. The word has a long history in classical usage, chiefly designating the propitiatory blood-sacrifice offered to a pagan god in expiation of some misdeed. Secondarily and metonymically, the term designates the misdeed that *requires* such a propitiation. Assuming that Orderic selected this word consciously (rather than selecting a more common term such as *homocidium, murtrum, peccatum, scelus, nefas, crimen*, or any number of other, more appropriate ones) we must also acknowledge that the choice is unusual and provocative. The term subtly equates the act of killing the priest with the rite of blood-sacrifice to

---

31. OV, 4:238.
32. OV, 4:238.

the gods, the ritual that, as we have seen, was most widely associated with paganism in medieval Christian writings. Yet we need not go as far as to regard the man as actually a pagan. I believe, rather, that Orderic's language is intended to add a subtle overtone to the nature of his crime, presenting him as someone with an unremitting hostility to the church itself. The priest killer need not be seen as a literal pagan offering the priest in sacrifice (like Thietmar's revenant congregation). Orderic does seem to be suggesting, however, that the man was so impious and so unrepentant, he *may as well* have been completely outside the religious community of the church: a pagan in spirit, if not in fact.

That the priest killer is portrayed among a crowd of dwarfs and a giant now takes on new resonances. Dwarfs, in traditional Germanic cultures, were avatars of the ancestors; scholars have long known that "there are clear parallels between the dead—especially the returning dead [*les revenants*]—and the categories of beings that are more or less subterranean, such as giants [and] dwarfs. . . . Giants have always been held . . . to be the *urtidsfolk* (the peoples coming from originary times, hence the prefix *ur-*) who disappeared long ago."[33] Dwarfs, like the dead, lived under the earth or inside mountains and possessed elemental powers. Thus, it seems plausible to suggest that this segment of the procession represents an atavistic, archaic core of Herlechin's *familia*, or retinue. It is the most unfiltered representation of the traditional elements of the Herlechin motif, of the pagan Germanic cultural past of Brittany, and perhaps, of the ancestors who populated this past. Added into this section of the horde is a locally infamous criminal of more recent memory, who was also regarded as acting in ways that were antithetical to Christianity—not unlike the pagan ancestors of the far past.

Triangulating Orderic's text with some others can help illuminate this aspect of his narrative. For when we turn to the next major discussion of this horde of wandering revenants, we find an important convergence of themes, particularly around the links between dwarfs and the ancestors. Let us then shift our attention to another part of the Anglo-Norman world five decades later: England in 1181–82.

---

33. Régis Boyer, *La mort chez les anciens Scandinaves* (Paris, 1994), 41–42. See also Ármann Jakobsson, "The Hole: Problems in Medieval Dwarfology," *Arv* 61 (2005): 53–76; Bernheimer, *Wild Men in the Middle Ages*; Brian Stock, "*Antiqui* and *Moderni* as 'Giants' and 'Dwarfs': A Reflection of Popular Culture?," *Modern Philology* 76, no. 4 (1979): 370–74; Sidney Johnson, "Medieval German Dwarfs: A Footnote to Gottfried's Melot," in *Gottfried von Strassburg and the Medieval Tristan Legend: Papers from an Anglo-North American Symposium*, ed. Adrian Stevens and Roy Wisbey, Arthurian Studies 23 (Woodbridge, 1990), 209–22; Anne Martineau, *Le nain et le chevalier: Essai sur les nains français du Moyen Âge* (Paris, 2003); Laurent Guyénot, *La mort féerique: Anthropologie du merveilleux XIIe–XVe siècle* (Paris, 2011); Claude Lecouteux, *Les nains et les elfes au Moyen Âge* (Paris, 2013).

In the Hall of the Mountain King: The Origins and Terminus of the Herlething

The hybrid account of the monk Orderic Vitalis raises more questions about Herlechin and his army than can readily be answered, as we have seen. Yet a tale found in *De nugis curialium* (*Courtier's Trifles*), composed by the courtly writer Walter Map around 1181–82, offers a highly revelatory complement to Orderic's account. Map, born on the Welsh marches in 1140,[34] studied at the University of Paris as a young man before returning to England and making a career at the court of King Henry II. Map evidently was unimpressed by court life, opening his work with a provocative comparison between the Angevin curia and hell. He claimed to have composed the book for a friend named Geoffrey, though this may be a literary fiction. The work did, however, remain largely private and did not circulate beyond Map's own circle.[35]

Map writes that "legends transmit to us" a myth of origin for the army of the dead, explaining how they came to be the errant revenants that appear in other narratives such as Orderic's.[36] The symbolism of the story swirls around the theme of regeneration of life through death. The protagonist is a king of the "very ancient Britons"[37]—that is, the ruler of the indigenous people subjugated by first Saxon and then Norman settlers. This British ruler, Herla by name, suddenly was approached one day by another king, though this peer was of rather unusual aspect:

> He looked like a pygmy, his height not reaching even half a man's; it did not exceed that of an ape. As the legend goes, the tiny man was sitting on a great big goat; he was a type of man who could be described as a Pan might be, with a burning face, a huge head, a lush red beard and, covering his chest, a bright skin of a dappled fawn. His belly was covered with hair, and his thighs degenerated into goat paws at the shins and feet. Herla spoke to him face to face.[38]

Map calls the figure a "pygmy" (*pygmaeus*), meaning dwarfed in stature, but more specifically, the king is a Pan or powerful faun. The strange little

---

34. WM, 99.
35. Robert R. Edwards, "Walter Map: Authorship and the Space of Writing," *New Literary History* 38 (2007): 273–92.
36. WM, 14. Cf. Helaine Newstead, "Some Observations on King Herla and the Herlething," in *Medieval Literature and Folklore Studies: Essays in Honor of Francis Lee Utley*, ed. Jerome Mandel and Bruce A. Rosenberg (New Brunswick, NJ, 1970), 105–10. Many commentators have discussed the political dimensions of Map's narrative, which was intended as a sardonic commentary on the vanities of court life under Henry II.
37. WM, 14.
38. WM, 14–15.

being introduced himself to Herla as a very powerful personage who ruled over several princes and countless subjects. He had come, he said, to propose "an eternal pact" between Herla and himself.[39] The Pan explained that he was attracted to Herla because of his greatness and "nearness" to himself; since Herla was his equal, he was worthy to receive the powerful dwarf king at his upcoming wedding celebration. The Pan explained that the king of France had already, unbeknownst to Herla, dispatched envoys to propose an advantageous marital alliance with his daughter. If Herla would invite him and his retinue to his marriage feast, the faun continued, then Herla might attend his own royal wedding the following year. Having proposed this reciprocal exchange, the creature sped away without waiting for a reply.

All came to pass as the Pan foretold: the marriage between Herla and the French princess was arranged and the wedding feast prepared. On the day of the ceremony the pygmy king appeared with an extensive retinue of his people—so many that there were not enough places at the tables Herla had set. But the guests had come prepared: they pitched tents and set tables; their servants brought delicacies to share with all the wedding guests, provided on rich serving dishes of precious manufacture. All of Herla's own servants were idle; his preparations untouched. As the cock began to crow and dawn was imminent, the faun king declared his duty to Herla fulfilled and reminded him of his obligation to attend his own wedding in exactly one year's time.

One year later the Pan came to Herla in order to guide him to his realm. The two came to the opening of a cave set high at the summit of a steep cliff; as they passed underground into darkness, they penetrated deep into the mountain home of the dwarf king and his people. At length they emerged at a rich subterranean mansion, brilliantly lit by lamps. There, Herla and his courtiers attended the pygmy king's wedding celebration, enjoying themselves at the festivities for three days. At Herla's departure, the Pan displayed his customary generosity; he loaded Herla and his cortege with gifts, particularly those relating to the hunt: horses, hounds, falcons, and other trained birds of prey. At the very last, the little faun king brought a bloodhound to the Briton king. He enjoined that none in Herla's group should dismount his horse before this dog jumped to the ground. With that, the two royal friends parted.

---

39. WM, 15.

After journeying back to the surface of the earth Herla and his retinue exited the cavern into the surface sunlight. Spying a shepherd, Herla asked the man for news of his queen. To Herla's astonishment, the man replied thusly,

> Lord, I can scarcely understand your speech, for I am a Saxon and you, a Briton. I have never heard of a queen by that name, except some men tell of a queen of the most ancient Britons with that name. She was the wife of King Herla who, it is said in legend, disappeared on this very ridge with a certain pygmy and never again was seen on earth. But the Saxons have occupied this realm already for two hundred years, after having expelled the original inhabitants.[40]

Herla, who believed he had spent only three days in the underground kingdom, "hardly kept on his horse."[41] Another member of his retinue was not as lucky: forgetting the injunction not to touch the earth before the bloodhound, the courtier dismounted and instantly paid the debt of time, decaying down to dust. Seeing this, Herla repeated the mandate of the Pan, forbidding anyone to descend before the dog—but the dog, according to Map's legendary source, never descended. Thus the army of Herla, returned from the underground abode of the dead, came to be immortals despite themselves. So Herla's column wanders and hunts, "without rest or residence" and were seen by many up to recent times.[42] The group was last spotted on the borders of Wales just as Henry II was crowned, but the contemporary court, Map suggests, has taken the place of the wandering hunt led by Herla.

Map's purpose was to establish a parallel between Herla's *familia* and the court of his contemporary Anglo-Norman sovereign, in which the nobles rushed ceaselessly from one amusement to the next, always on the hunt for something they never could attain. Nor was Map the first to suggest the comparison. A letter of 1175 from Peter of Blois to the Anglo-Norman kings (whom he served as an advisor) criticized the ambitious men conniving at court as "martyrs to the mundane, disciples of dissipation, acolytes of the court: the knights of Herlewin."[43] Peter predicted that such courtiers would go straight to hell after death, unlike the pious true martyrs and disciples who rejected the world in order to attain salvation. The reference shows both that the mythology of the army of the undead was widely known and

---

40. WM, 16–17.
41. WM, 17.
42. WM, 17.
43. Petrus de Blois, *Epistolae* 14, in *PL*, 207, col. 42.

that it generally was regarded as a collection of sinful shades who cared more for secular pursuits than for piety. But Peter's reference is brief; the extended folk legend that Map recounts in order to make the point provides a richer interpretive field.

Let us begin, then, as we did in the case of Orderic's story of Herlechin, with a reflection on the juxtaposition of the two major characters. Though Herla is presented as the king of the Britons, his name is actually of Germanic origin, likely meaning "war leader," someone at the head of the *heer* or army.[44] The relationship to Herlechin is evident. Map's story is set in a hoary past shrouded in legend, and it features the original, indigenous population group of England, the Britons. This population had by the time of Map's writing been doubly displaced: by the Saxons and more recently by the invading Normans, to which group the author belonged. As for the pygmy king, he never is introduced by name, yet certain things are clear about him. First, he is described physically as a faun or satyr. Thus he is associated with a pagan spirit-type that has strong chthonic and fertility symbolisms. At the same time, of course, the figure of the goat-footed, bearded man with a burning face could, in Map's time, also evoke the devil. Yet it would be easy to overexaggerate the significance of the latter association. For one thing, Map explicitly compares the figure to the minor pagan god Pan, which seems to have been the ideal he had in mind; had he wanted to emphasize the demonic connection, he certainly could have done so in preference to the evocation of Pan. More to the point, however: though satyrs could be associated with the devil, they had not yet become a dominant image in this regard. Another Anglo-Norman writer and Map's contemporary, Gervaise of Tilbury, for example, spoke of the French belief in *duses*, a term he translates with two Latin possibilities, both plural: "woodland creatures [*Silvani*] and Pans."[45] Gervaise claims that many people had encountered these beings and made love with them; like Map, he does not suggest that they are demonic. Thus, belief in "Pans" appears to have been a fairly widespread folk tradition; the term referenced a seductive species of creatures that lived in wild places, but that were regarded as closely related to humans and able to mate with them. The image was not yet intrinsically associated with the ancient enemy and king of demons, the devil. Representations of the latter were still in flux and had not settled down into a standard iconography.

---

44. Guyénot, *Le mort féerique*, 93. Earlier scholarship connected the name to the thirteenth-century English "harlot," meaning a wanderer of low life, and from thence specifically back to Harlechin. See Spitzler, "Anglo-French Etymologies."

45. GT, 728.

A more certain reading is that the qualities of the little king's rulership and realm portray him as a sovereign of the dead. He introduces himself as "a king ruling over many rulers and chiefs, set over a countless and infinite population."[46] The focus on the limitless numbers of the Pan's subjects marks him out as king of the deceased. He lives beneath the surface of the earth, inside a mountain, and time moves more slowly in his realm than on the surface of the earth—a common folkloric motif concerning the otherworld. Like the dead, he appears in the world of the living only at night; as the cock crows, he makes a quick departure from Herla's wedding feast. In fact, it appears that the pygmy king is Herla's own ancestor, perhaps even the progenitor of his royal line. This is made clear in a key point in the narrative, when the creature explains why he came to Herla: it is because Herla is "a great man, close to me both by blood and by location."[47] They are close to one another in kind because they share both a bloodline and a realm: Herla rules the land upon the surface of the earth, and the pygmy rules the subterranean realm of the dead beneath the earth. This constitutes another point of alignment with Orderic Vitalis's earlier tale, in which the advance guard of the troop of the dead is a group of dwarfs on biers or litters. In each case, the society of the dead, and the ancient peoples of the region, is associated with small stature. As we already have seen, dwarfs commonly are associated with the ancestors or with bygone generations. While the dwarfs fulfill divergent roles in Orderic Vitalis's and Walter Map's accounts, their presence along with the name of the troop and the notion that it is composed of a band of living dead persons are elements that tie together the two stories. The two tales complement each other, presenting different parts of the history of the same motif.

Map's story also makes an intriguing juxtaposition to a peculiar pavement mosaic in the Cathedral of Otranto, in Norman Italy, from 1170. The image portrays another ancient king of the Britons, Arthur, armed with a large mace, mounted upon a goat, and conveniently labeled "Rex Arturus." As Jean-Claude Schmitt has pointed out, the iconography overlaps both with the Herla story and with the club-wielding Herlechin. As discussed in the previous chapter, Arthur often was encountered as a leader of the dead in Norman regions; he sometimes was imagined to be dwelling in Mount Etna, for instance, and we shall encounter him again ere long. It seems likely that this image represents a visualization of the

---

46. WM, 15.
47. WM, 15.

motif of the king of the dead that so often recurs in the Anglo-Norman cultural sphere.[48]

Returning to Herla's story, once the king enters into the subterranean kingdom in the mountain then he himself is poised between the worlds of the living and the dead. The courtier who crumbles to dust after they reenter the world above demonstrates that the troop's hold on life has become provisional, perhaps even illusory. Moreover, Herla's retinue becomes, according to Map, a depository for more revenants; it is thus fully assimilated to the *familia* of Herlechin described by Orderic. A later passage of *Courtier's Trifles* makes all of this explicit: "The columns or nocturnal troops that are called the Herlething were very famous in England up until the time of Henry II, our present king. It was an army of infinite wandering, of mad rounds, of stunned silences, in which many had appeared as if alive, who were known to have died."[49] Thus Herla was transformed, all unwittingly, into the leader of the Herle-thing, the troop or assembly of noble followers. And once established, the group continued to garner new members within living memory of Map's own time. Since Walter Map was a courtly writer whose purposes were political rather than theological, he made no attempt to Christianize the story of Herla or to make it conform to church teaching about the afterlife. Rather, the army of the dead serves as political critique. Map's Herlething is a cavalcade of an ancient living dead court, restlessly moving through the landscape on a hunt.

Two final elements of the story merit some comment. One of the more puzzling aspects of the story concerns the lopsided generosity of the dwarf king. Some observers have noted that a central motif in the story is the overwhelming wealth and openhandedness of the Pan, first as a guest at Herla's wedding and then later as a host to Herla at his own marriage. On both occasions, the pygmy king loads the living king with gifts. Some have seen Herla's lack of reciprocation as a grave fault that leads to his later punishment, doomed to wander between worlds.[50] Yet, within the symbolic system of the living and the dead, the imbalance makes a great deal of sense. All the wealth the living possess derives from those who came before—that is, from the dead who leave behind the things of this world and thus generously endow the living. Herla's earthly realm, his riches, his power, his very life's blood and body are all transmitted to him from the ancestral dead of his bloodline.

---

48. Schmitt, *Ghosts in the Middle Ages*, 117; Cf. Grazio Gianfreda, *Il Mosaico di Otranto: Biblioteca Mediovale in immagini* (Lecce, 2005).
49. WM, 180.
50. Schmitt, *Ghosts in the Middle Ages*, 112.

The British king's power and abundance are indeed the gifts of his ancestors, here represented by this royal, underworld counterpart. However, the price of such gifts is, ultimately, that one must surrender them in one's own turn. Death gives, and in turn death takes away.

An additional noteworthy detail is the prominence of weddings in the story, as the occasion for the kings' visits with one another. On the one hand, the detail simply provides a setting for two kings to interact in friendship: medieval royalty were most apt to congregate socially upon occasions such as marriages. On the other hand, the detail evokes the symbolism of family, generational change, and rites of passage. Combined with the suggestion that Herla and the Pan are in actuality separate generations of the same family, the marital setting of the story reinforces a theme of continuous familial transmission. Likewise, as we have seen in a previous chapter, the motif of a society of dead folk living inside mountains, feasting, having sex, and concluding marriages was well attested in the Middle Ages. The underlying symbolism concerns regeneration. The ancestors symbolized generational change, not only in terms of the past but also in terms of guaranteeing the fertility of the present and the arrival of the next generation. As the elders pass away, so a new generation comes into being. This was true not only for human reproduction, however; belief in the continuing consciousness and presence of the dead under the ground also linked them to the fertility cycles of the earth. The ancestors were buried underground, just as were the seeds that brought the harvests. Thus the friendly dead might be expected to assist the germination and growth of crops for their descendants from their privileged vantage point under the earth.[51] Death is the dark face of fecundity; what passes away is the precondition for what arises and flourishes.

The Army of the Dead as Triune Afterlife: Heaven, Purgatory, and Hell

In the 1130s, Orderic Vitalis described an encounter with the army of the dead and tried to adapt it to the doctrine of purgatory; some fifty years later, Walter Map's tale of Herla provided both a myth of origin and point of disappearance for the army of the dead. Other writers roughly contemporary to Map, however, were attempting to further extend the theological implications of the army of the dead as a representation of an intermediate afterlife stage. The two writers I discuss next thoroughly reinterpreted the motif

---

51. Elizabeth Barber, *The Dancing Goddesses: Folklore, Archaeology, and the Origins of European Dance* (New York, 2013), 3.

of the army of the dead in order to align it with the increasing Christian focus upon a tripartite afterlife. In service to this goal, they also clarified and streamlined their accounts, eliminating the most atavistic and non-Christian elements. The next author to be examined, Herbert of Clairvaux, was a Cistercian abbot of Mores in Jura, who later was elevated to the archbishopric of Sassaria or Porto Torres on Sardinia.[52] While resident in this Norman area he collected a set of miracle stories, resulting in a three-volume work in 1178. The second writer was, like Walter Map, someone of a literary and satirical bent: Andreas Capellanus, whose *De amore*, composed between 1184 and 1186, incorporates a sardonic vision of an army of the dead comprised solely of women. We know little about Andreas Capallanus; though his moniker means "chaplain," it is unclear whether this was a literal claim to the priesthood or a satirical fiction like the rest of his writing. Though the moral tones and purposes of each tale could hardly be more diametrically opposed, they have in common the assimilation of the army of wandering dead folk to a tripartite afterlife system of reward, punishment, and penitence.

The framing device of Herbert of Clairvaux's story follows a formula not unlike Orderic Vitalis's: an honest priest in a lonely place encounters the wandering horde of the dead and is instructed by them. As Herbert tells the story, the priest served an isolated church. One day while leaning against the wall behind the church and facing east (a direction sometimes associated with entry to the afterlife), he suddenly felt suffused with horror; his heart shrank and his flesh crawled, hair standing on end. Though he desperately desired to flee, some unknown force kept him rooted to the spot, so he squeezed his eyes shut in terror. After a moment, "opening his eyes he saw crowds of innumerable multitudes, mounted and on foot, passing before him with hurrying steps."[53] As always, the text emphasizes that the dead formed a limitless crowd and was diverse, including men and women of all ages and social classes. And as we have come to expect, the visionary priest recognized several individuals among the group, "whom he had known formerly while they were living in the flesh."[54]

The priest began conversing in a friendly way with a deceased acquaintance and asked about the purpose of the wandering crowd of dead folk. "These are souls who have been freed from the flesh who all, for a variety of faults, are given over to diverse torments," the dead man replied. "They thus continuously wend their way wandering near and far, to and fro. Some will

---

52. Bernstein, "Ghostly Troop and the Battle over Death," 138.
53. Herbertus Turrium, *De miraculi libri tres*, 3:31, in *PL*, 185, col. 1375.
54. Ibid.

be liberated more quickly and some more slowly; but the torments of many will remain inescapable."[55] Thus Herbert of Clairvaux presents the army of the dead for the first time as an afterlife system in accord with the Christian theological imagination. The saved, the purging, and the eternally damned are all referenced, though only the latter two are included in the wandering tormented group. In order to emphasize his point, Herbert presents an example of each type. First is Baldwin of Pisa, formerly a Cistercian monk and therefore someone of particular interest to Herbert. When Herbert inquired about him his informant replied, "Know for certain that this man is a saint and a man of exalted merits, and that great is his glory before God."[56] Yet, however perfect Baldwin was, the people of Pisa and Lucca had begun a war during his episcopate, and he would not be permitted to enjoy his "glory before God" until peace was made. His status represents the purgatorial dimension of the group. A second dead man illustrates the presence of the damned. A profiteering crusader was "twisted and impious; he lived with excessive carnality and tyrannously; therefore he is consigned to eternal torments."[57] And finally, Herbert describes the heavenly apotheosis of a shade who completed his process of purgation in the troop. As the priest and his informant were discussing the damned crusader, a column of light suddenly descended upon the group and exalted another one of their number to the stars. The dead man was Constantine, lord of Torres in Sardinia, a judge; he referenced the heavenly dimension of the vision. Though Constantine had lived lavishly he had been a fair judge, liberal to the poor, and scrupulous at confessing his faults. After nine years of torment, he had just been cleared for ascent to heaven. As the tale concludes, the priest's dead friend warned him of his own impending demise: "Know that you undoubtedly are going to die this year, and according to how you have acted, so shall you receive."[58]

Herbert's story is relatively simplistic: an edifying tale dramatizing postmortem fates. What stands out from previous versions is the integrative nature of the afterlife here portrayed, with the focus squarely on postmortem penitence and retribution. Moreover, all mention of dwarves, giants, Pans, underground mountain homes, and other pagan or chthonic elements have dropped out of Herbert's miracle story. Lastly, unlike most iterations of this tale, no leader of the army is portrayed, nor is the group as a collective referred to by any specific term or phrase such as the Herlething. The

---

55. Ibid., cols. 1375–76.
56. Ibid., col. 1376.
57. Ibid.
58. Ibid., col. 1377.

wandering army of the dead was reframed in order to function, as far as possible, within a wholly Christian imaginative field. The only symbolic head of such a theologized penitential column is God himself, watching over the shades from on high.

Herbert's tale forms an interesting comparison with a purely heavenly version of the army of the dead, which appears in an anonymous Cluniac poem titled *Relatio metrica de duobus ducibus* (*The Versified Story of Two Kings*). The eponymous leaders are the cruel Duke Ostorgius from Sicily and the compassionate Eusebius of Sardinia. Eusebius instituted policies of great charity and compassion, centering upon the giving of alms and support for continual prayer for the dead. Ostorgius seized the town that Eusebius had established as the chief center for these good works; when the latter wished to retake his rightful holding, he found himself badly outmatched. Suddenly, a gleaming, bright army of men on shining white horses appeared from the heavens to assist Eusebius. He learned that the army was comprised of dead men who had been released from purgatory as a result of his prayers and offerings. Thus this version of the legend, uniquely, associates the army of the dead with the heavenly afterlife realm.[59] As we shall see, this was not an association that was to persist.

Andreas Capellanus's version of the legend, though highly irreverent and satirical, nonetheless presumes the framework of a tripartite afterlife. His army of the dead was composed of various ladies who in life conducted their amours in ways both praiseworthy and promiscuous. Following Capellanus, the ironic motif of the afterlife of cruel ladies was incorporated into other courtly love literature, including the *Lai du Trot*, the *Conseils d'Amour* of Richard de Fournival, and Gower's *Confessio Amantis*. Andreas's vision is the originator of this style of representation, however. Like Herbert of Clairvaux's vision, the dead are arranged in a triple pattern of retribution.

The vision is recounted in book 1 of *De amore* during a dialogue between a nobleman and a noblewoman. As with all the imagined dialogues in this work, the male interlocutor's goal is to convince the woman to enter into a love affair. As part of his seductions, the nobleman threatens the object of his affections with eternal torments if she does not respond to his overtures. When she asks for an explanation, he recounts a highly unusual version of the motif we have been tracing.

The speaker unlocks a memory. Once, he wandered away from his companions while they were resting from military exercises in a shady bower. He

---

59. Scott Bruce and Christopher Jones, eds. and trans., *The Relatio metrica de duobus ducibus: A Twelfth-Century Cluniac Poem on Prayer for the Dead*. I thank Scott Bruce for sharing with me this work in progress, which is currently under review for publication.

became lost. Suddenly he spied a mounted troop in the distance, and thinking it was his companions, he approached. But it was not a column of his friends, but rather a column of countless women led by a man seated upon a fine horse, wearing a golden crown. The women that followed him traveled in widely divergent circumstances, however:

> In the first place, there was a huge chorus of elegant women, with every one seated upon a beautiful fat horse ambling along placidly. Their clothes were most precious and rare and they were swathed in gold-embroidered cloaks. Knights, similarly attired, accompanied each woman, one to the right and one to the left. A third knight walked before each woman like a servant. . . . Second, there followed another not inconsiderable multitude of women. Various types of men aggressively insisted on offering them obsequies, but the noise of those wishing to serve was so loud, and the crowd of them so noxious, that the women could not make use of their service. . . . In the third place there followed an army of some women who were lowly and destitute. The women themselves were extremely beautiful, but their clothes were of the grossest kind and not appropriate for the weather. . . . As well, they were very dirty and disheveled to an unseemly degree. . . . No one offered any aid to those women; all were destitute of any assistance. Moreover, all the riders and walkers who had gone before them were sending up such a cloud of dust that they could scarcely see each other, for their eyes were irritated by the dust and their lips were clogged.[60]

The nobleman was perplexed by the diversity of the group but still most anxious to find his comrades. He addressed one of the women—a rare beauty seated on a nag—asking her to help him find the way back to his friends. She replied, mysteriously, "I cannot show you the right road until you first will have seen this present militia arrayed in their proper positions on the field. . . . What you see is the army of the dead [*exercitus mortuorum*]."[61]

The lady went on to explain the composition of the army. The crowned leader was the God of Love, who joined in the procession once a week in order to determine the just deserts of new arrivals. According to whether they acted good or ill in their love affairs in life, they would be assigned to one of the three groups in the column. The first group of joyful ladies was comprised of those "most blessed of women who, while they lived, knew

---

60. Andreas Capellanus, *De Amore*, 232–36. Online at The Latin Library, http://thelatinlibrary.com/capellanus.html.
61. Ibid., 239–40.

well how to manage the soldiers of love."[62] These saintly figures received every afterlife reward. The second group was made up of the promiscuous, who in life assented to any proposition from any man. Thus in the afterlife their overabundance of servitors created a chaotic cacophony. As for the third group, these "most miserable women" were those who remained virginally pure and chaste. As the now penitent lady shade informed the lost man, "we suffer deservedly, for we receive our just deserts from the King of Love, by whom the whole world is ruled and without whom nothing good happens on earth."[63]

At the chaste lady's insistence, the nobleman traveled along with this army of the dead until they reached their goal, a field laid out in concentric circles. At the center, the Queen of Love awaited her consort and King; they seated themselves under a luscious fruiting tree sheltering a spring of pure water. The blessed women who loved well arranged themselves in the inner circle, an idyllic garden setting likewise shaded by the fruit tree. The next circle, a muddy marsh, was home to the lascivious women; and the last, outer circle of torment, destined for the chaste refusers of love, was an arid desert. At the very end of the encounter, the King of Love entrusted the observing nobleman with a mission: to provide "salvation" to worthy women by telling them of his vision and, further, instructing them in the Twelve Commandments of Love.

Capellanus's religious satire only works, of course, on account of its simultaneous mimicry and inversion of contemporary religious teachings. The universal rulership of the God and Goddess of Love, the "Twelve Commandments," and not least, the tripartite afterlife of reward and punishment seemingly mock Christian doctrine. Here, hell is reserved for the chaste and virginal; the promiscuous are moderately punished; and the saints who garner postmortem rewards are those who love wisely—including, in the world of this text, loving with their bodies and possibly adulterously. However, the jest only is amusing because Capellanus's army of the dead so deftly parodies what must have been common knowledge. The army of the dead was fairly widely referenced by the end of the twelfth century, and it was sufficiently identified with the Christian afterlife such that Capellanus could skewer it thus and count on the understanding of his audience. Yet the story also gestures, cheekily, toward paganism in its imagining of a postmortem world of retribution and reward judged by the pagan deities of love and sexuality. The self-styled chaplain uses Christian afterlife folklore,

---

62. Ibid., 243.
63. Ibid., 245.

adapted from an originally pagan motif, in order to farcically exalt sensuality while denigrating chastity as a mortal sin. The connections are both perverse and extremely apt.

Demonizing the Dead

Postmortem societies were glimpsed in many different forms. In the far north of the continent, we find reports of a society of cadavers arising in cemeteries and worshipping in empty churches. This likely represents a relocation of the embodied dead from their more ancient traditional home, for they traditionally were imagined feasting under the surface of the earth, inside mountains. There they married and formed families. Beginning in the twelfth century, however, the dead increasingly began to appear in Norman regions as a lengthy column or army of shades, venturing forth from their mountain halls to form a feudal *familia* on the march.

The originary, central tension of this folklore limned the divergent worlds of life and death, fecundity and decay, the passing-away of the ancestors as life continually is regenerated. Literate people who heard stories about revenants as they circulated in oral tradition found them appealing for different reasons. For many writers, the tales could be an end in themselves, dramatic and titillating: then as now a good horror story presented a frisson of fearful pleasure. However, these motifs also were utilized for critiques of secular values: ambitious courtiers and courtly lovers both were satirically targeted through subversive uses of the motif. For religious writers, as I have argued, revenants of all kinds seemed to offer precious, firsthand proof for the central Christian notion of life after death, or more latterly, of postmortem purgation. Thus they were appropriated to theological purposes, with Gregory the Great's tales of the living dead providing a useful precedent. In one case, we even have encountered an exclusively celestial version of the dead army assisting the benefactor who provided them with salvific suffrages.

However, in the thirteenth century a new generation of church writers began to fundamentally shift their perspective on the utility of ghost stories, including the motif of the dead army. With the rise of critically trained university scholars, men who were deeply concerned about the internal consistency and purity of Christian doctrine, these tales suddenly came to be perceived as transgressive and appallingly superstitious. In this spirit, academic evaluations of revenants increasingly correlated with Augustinian attitudes toward postmortem return, in preference to Gregorian interpretations. The contemporaneous rise of medical discourses charted in chapter 2 further promoted the Augustinian preference for death as event over death as long-term process.

The reevaluation of the ancient army was led by William of Auvergne, Master of Theology at the University of Paris and bishop of Paris from 1228 to 1249. The known details of William's life are few. According to one manuscript of his works, he came from Aurillac. He likely was born some time between 1180 and 1190, for he was teaching theology by 1225 and this career was open only to men over the age of thirty-five.[64] Beyond this, little is known of his background or of how he came by his extensive knowledge of the rustic beliefs he discussed in his writings. William's major work, the encyclopedic *De universo*, shows at every turn that he knew a great deal of traditional folklore. William's reports about the army of the dead harmonize in many respects with the stories we have seen before, though he also provides new details. He was the first academic author to discuss these beliefs, and his evaluation of them, informed by his logical university training, was strikingly different from those of earlier writers. Looking forward, William's thorough and innovative treatments were to become highly influential upon subsequent thinkers. Thus it is rewarding to explore his thought at some length.

To begin, William first alludes to the army of the dead in a chapter dedicated to the false imagination and the deceptive visions it may engender through sickness, melancholia, or demonic interference. Amid discussions of persons who believe that they themselves are dead (a syndrome now known as the Cotard delusion) or that they are werewolves,[65] he comes to a discussion of visionaries who believe that they see

> an armed militia, and jousts and fights. I affirm that in some cases this is due to sickness, though truly in many cases these things are painted into their imaginations by an evil spirit. You should know this about the things I have described (the weapons, the armies waging wars, the arms used for evil): the people who appear in these visions usually are there either because they were killed by a sword or they killed themselves with a sword. They appear to those who were dear to them, in a state of intolerable trouble and sadness because of the arms and the fighting in which they appear to be engaged. . . . Not a few people state that they have heard, during such visions . . . that this torment is a form of purgatory for them. Sometimes people who claim to have seen the

---

64. Thomas de Mayo, *The Demonology of William of Auvergne: By Fire and Sword* (Lewiston, NY, 2007), 11–12.
65. WA, 878–79.

army also report that they were told certain things: they say that they reveal many things that will happen to their loved ones; I remember I met one of these people.⁶⁶

William thus gives quite a detailed portrayal of the army of the dead. He suggests that he has discussed this belief with at least one person who claimed to have had a firsthand encounter with the group, and clearly he has heard much discussion of it from other sources as well. The most salient elements are that the dead form an army, that the group is comprised of those who died untimely through force of arms, that the weapons and battles with which they appear inflict suffering and are a form of purgatory, and that some who have seen the army of the dead also claim to have conversed with some of the members of the group, often people formerly close to them, and to have received prophecies and messages. The description closely parallels the texts we have previously examined. These elements seem to be the most widely known, agreed-upon points of belief about this representation of the dead.

However, William also departs from the attitudes of previous reporters on the army significantly. Despite his personal contacts with those who uphold the reality of the dead's return in this form, and despite the theologizing suggestion that the army of the dead might be regarded as a form of purgatory, he argues forcefully that the apparitions are purely illusory. Visions of this kind likely are brought about by evil spirits, "for some evil end, and in order to confect some harmful deception of the recipient of the vision," or alternatively at times by good spirits, "so that they might reveal the pains of purgatory to the good, or even the pains of hell to the evil . . . as a warning to the living."⁶⁷ Whether good or evil, however, the visions are purely spiritual illusions according to the learned bishop.

A bit later in *On the Universe*, William returns to the army of the dead in passing, as part of a discussion of demons who impersonate the gods and goddesses worshipped by pagans. Here, he names the army: "the nocturnal horsemen are called in the French vernacular 'The Hellequin' and in Spanish, 'The Ancient Army.' . . . They are evil spirits; I will discuss them later."⁶⁸ A dozen chapters later, William takes up the question of the nighttime armies in a systematic fashion. He titled the chapter "Concerning what manner of spirit are those that appear in the form of an army; and about the nighttime things that deceive little old ladies; and concerning apparitions of the dead." As

---

66. WA, 879.
67. WA, 879.
68. WA, 1037.

the title indicates, he treats both the armies and the throng of "good things" led by female goddess figures. The Vatican Library's manuscript of *De universo*, Vaticanus Latinus 848, includes the marginal jotting *de familia hellequini*, "On Hellequin's retinue," tying this discussion back to the passage quoted above.[69]

William initiates his analysis of the Hellequin with an argument against one of its core elements. These beings, he announces, are not corporeal: "To begin, then, you must recall to mind that the things that appear in this form are not embodied, nor even physical."[70] William argues that the individual bodies that appear in the army of the dead are purely aerial in character. The word "aerial" is an important clue; with it, William signals the chief influence on his thinking about the dead and about spirits, Augustine of Hippo. The patristic saint was the pioneering theorist of the idea that demons (and angels) possess purely aerial bodies that are invulnerable, insubstantial, and highly labile. The word also, of course, signals where William's discussion is headed: he will argue against the Gregorian suggestion that human beings might return from the dead in embodied form. Rather, William will go on to present a demonological explanation to account for appearances of the Hellequin. No longer are the members of this cortege to be regarded as corporeal dead folk wandering upon the surface of the earth for purposes festive, antagonistic, or penitential. No longer should they be feared as fleshly presences that can touch and harm the living. The deceased, William argues, pass on to another world and do not return. Thus the ancient army is composed of demonic spirits impersonating dead men, and they have purely insubstantial, aerial bodies that are incapable of physical attacks.

The next question concerns the apparently martial purposes of the Hellequin. Why does the cortege appear armed to the teeth and mounted, as if ready for a battle charge? William's line of questioning suggests that many people feared attack from the ancient army. While it is not particularly surprising that visions of the armed and mounted dead should elicit fear, the information has not been attested in the historical record before this. We have seen the dead slay the living in Thietmar's churchyard stories, but not in the accounts of Hellequin's army. Indeed, the revenants in that column have generally been portrayed as mild-natured unless antagonized. Here William adds to our knowledge by allowing that the martial character of the group was taken as an indication of bellicose intentions toward the living.

In line with the exhaustive approach characteristic of an academic treatise, William appraises the idea that these warriors might truly be vengeful dead

---

69. De Mayo, *Demonology of William of Auvergne*, 192–93.
70. WA, 1065. All future references derive from part 2, chapter 24 of the work.

folk, so that he may then logically refute it. If they *were* dead men, William states, and if their purpose *was* to kill the living, then they would seem to be highly incompetent at the task: "If this were a war against men, then in the first and only conflict they would have killed all men and would have destroyed nearly the entire human race. For all men would be vulnerable to the wounds and harms of these dead men, such that they would be unable to evade them."[71] William's language brings to mind an image illustrating the Office of the Dead in the *Tres Riches Heures de Duc de Berry*, which visualizes the terror of an army of living men facing an army of the dead in battle (figure 4.1). The confrontation takes place in a cemetery where graves lie open; led by a pale rider, a cohort of corpses armed with pikes, scythes, and lances grin as they advance upon the living army. The latter drop their weapons and flee in utter panic, unsure of how to prevail against such foes. The artists aptly render the living men's expressions of terror.

But William did not believe the armies of the dead he had heard about in folklore were real. Rather, he asserts, the appearance of warriors ready for battle is simply a demonic *ludus*: that is, a type of sport or play; a trick or an illusion. Indeed, William himself makes a play upon words, juxtaposing *ludus* with *hastiludium* (a joust) as well as with the commonplace *ludificationes daemonum* (the tricks of demons):

> Therefore, the fact that any of them bear arms, or seem to, is a game [*ludus*]. A game, I say, of the kind that commonly is called a joust [*hastiludium*]. It is clear to anyone who has enough understanding that the horses and arms and things of this kind are appearances and visions as well, since they too are invulnerable, immortal, and impervious to harm, just like those who seem to be bearing the arms. But it is impossible for a horse to be immortal and impervious to harm. . . . Therefore everything that appears there or that they seem to do in a vision is either illusive or is only a figment of being and doing. . . . This is one of the ways they appear; for the tricks [*ludificationes*] of demons are not only of this kind, to appear in the likeness of dead men from time to time, but also to appear in terrifying magnitude, along with arms and horses; or they appear even with torches or candles or other forms of fire.[72]

We have seen many of these elements before: mounted, fearsome dead men in an army; men of giant stature; and dead men with torches or candles—a

---

71. WA, 1066.
72. WA, 1066.

FIGURE 4.1. An army of shrouded cadavers confronts an army of the living in this illumination from a luxury Book of Hours. The living stumble over one another in a horrified panic, desperate to flee from the advancing troop of shrouded cadavers. Illumination by the Limbourg Brothers in the *Tres Riches Heures de Duc de Berry*, 1416. MS 65, fol. 90v, Musée Condé, Chantilly, France.
© RMN-Grand Palais / Art Resource, NY.

motif we last saw when spying upon dancing and singing dead men in cemeteries. Yet William consistently argues that these appearances are demons, not the dead, and wholly spiritual in nature, rather than reanimated cadavers. Demons wish to play tricks upon human beings in order to delude them into believing that the next life is similar to this one (as, indeed, pagan imaginings would have it) rather than an entirely separate order of reality based upon God's retributive justice. Rather than finding such tales of the dead useful proofs of the afterlife, William reframes them as harmful deceptions.

William continues in this interpretive mode when he moves on to a lengthy discussion of the women's night ride, led by Abundia and her "good ladies." He attributes the continued vigor of this belief to illiterate little old women, who "disseminate it and maintain it through time, and who fix it in the minds of other women nearly ineradicably."[73] It appears that William construes the nighttime ride of living women in the air, following a goddess, and the nighttime march of the male army of the dead upon the earth as parallel beliefs. After arguing that these appearances, too, are merely a demonic figment, or perhaps a side-effect of feminine melancholia, he then returns again to the question of appearances of the Hellequin.

His next set of questions concerns the precise geographical preferences of the dead armies, as well as the makeup of these groups. He notes that

> some see the army of the nighttime multitude swarming over mountain ranges and valleys. . . . As for the fact that they appear in the likeness of men, that is, of dead men, and particularly those killed by the sword: this might seem to some people to confirm the opinion of Plato, that the time owed by the souls of people who died in this way equals the time that they would have lived if violent death had not expelled them from the world.[74]

Again, William's descriptions reinforce many themes we have already seen: the dead are often reported to move along the public roads at night, but are also known to be seen near mountains and their valleys; the Hellequin is believed to be composed chiefly of slain warriors; those who have encountered these shades say that they conduct postmortem penance for their violence through sufferings related to their arms and armor. Moreover, the persons making up the army of the dead are apt to be those who died untimely, thrust from this world in the midst of life.

---

73. WA, 1066.
74. WA, 1067.

Was William Equivocal in His Interpretation? Rereading a Key Paragraph

As William's text continues, however, he moves into a rather vexing discussion that at first glance appears to reverse course. It is possible to read this section of the text as diametrically opposed to William's earlier assertion that the Hellequin is unreal, an *illusion* of dead men, rather than *actual* revenants returned from beyond the grave. In consequence, some scholars have presented William as muddled and befuddled. One states, "He seems to hesitate between two interpretations";[75] another elaborates, "William's position is not entirely clear, for he voices many possible theories as he seems to proceed haphazardly from argument to argument."[76] I believe these assertions are based upon a misunderstanding of William's language and intent. The following passage has been central to the perception that William was unclear about how to interpret visions of the army of the dead:

> Since the men who appear in these armies are persons who were cut off from life by force of arms, the vulgar call them "the sword-slain." They believe that these men conduct penance through arms because they used to sin with arms. For this reason, these dead men sometimes seek out their dear ones so that the latter might assist them with prayers and other suffrages, and so they may be helped along toward liberation from the torments they suffer, if only they were helped effectively. Thus they instruct their dear ones from the book of Wisdom, "One is tormented via that with which one sins," [a passage] that seems to support this opinion.
>
> According to common talk, these [dead men] who appear in this way often reveal things such as the torments they are undergoing and the reasons for their punishments. Likewise, in regard to the above things, you have learned that it is because purgatory (that is, a place appropriate to the purgation of souls and set aside for this purpose) has an earthly location. And you have heard this reason for it: to wit, that this kind of purgation is a supplement for unfinished penitence, when that penitence could not be completed in this life, and that therefore it is appropriate that it be in the same location.[77]

Technical questions about how to translate William's sophisticated Latin require some elaboration, but the meaning of his text changes radically

---

75. Schmitt, *Ghosts in the Middle Ages*, 119.
76. De Mayo, *Demonology of William of Auvergne*, 195.
77. WA, 1067. This section is followed closely by the passage attached to note 81.

depending on how this section is understood. To begin, the language here is complex; it is easy to miss certain cues that signal when William is reporting others' beliefs, versus when he is presenting his own. In my reading, the quotation above is a bit of ethnographic reportage: William is describing his investigation into popular theology, not disclosing his own opinion. It is worth taking some time to unpack this passage carefully; though the discussion may seem picayune at times, a close reading can help clarify elements of William's thought that have hitherto seemed puzzling.

First, William identifies the conceptual category that the "common people" or *vulgus* attach to those who make up the army of the dead: they are the *disgladiatos* or "sword-slain." This harkens back to his earlier discussion, in book 2, in which he identifies the population of these armies as those killed by the sword, either through their own hand or by another. William next elaborates on the logic of their postmortem fate: the common folk also believe, he notes, that the weapons borne by these dead warriors constitute a postmortem penance. Likewise, he notes that the dead sometimes were said to ask for assistance from relatives. Such an opinion, he allows, seems to be supported by the book of Wisdom: William's language here is grudgingly concessive. He does not wholly endorse these ideas, but he seems to approve of the impulse to link the character of the penitence to the type of sin. Again, all these ideas were referenced earlier, in the chapter on illusive visions in part 2. Both discussions outline the belief in the same way; there is no inconsistency here.

The next sentence likewise sums up some information we already know—the fact that the army of the dead was believed to reveal their sins and penitential burdens—but William again stresses that this belief is "according to common talk" (*prout fama est*). It is the next two sentences that introduce ambiguity. The following sentence begins, "Likewise, in regard to the above things, you have learned" (*In eis quoque, quae praecesserunt, didicisti* . . .); the one after that is prefaced with "And you have heard this reason for it, to wit:" (*Et causam in hoc audivisti hanc, videlicet* . . .). I take these lines as referring back to William's invocation of oral tradition and street chatter just before. In short, I would suggest that William is assuming that his reader is familiar with stories about the Hellequin and its functions, and he invokes this common knowledge with the second-person verbs, "you have learned" and "you have heard." Moreover, if the reader has not learned or heard these things on the street, he will have learned and heard them from William's earlier discussion on false visions, which outlines the exact same commonplace traditions.

Previous commentators appear to have interpreted the Latin as suggesting that this paragraph represents William's *own* opinions about the army of the dead—for example, that it might indeed be a mobile, earthly purgatory.[78] And since, both before and after this above passage, William presents a wholly alternative argument about the army of the dead, this reading inevitably leads to the perception that William was inconsistent. However, it makes far more sense to simply read these lines as a summary of the popular logic of the Hellequin belief that the reader is already expected to have heard or learned, either through personal exposure to it or through William's own précis. In fact, these were exceedingly commonplace ideas about the army of the dead, as we have seen in the versions of it analyzed above. There likewise exists another independent mention of the specific belief referenced in these lines—that the army of the dead purges sins on earth because they must be atoned for in the dimension where they were committed. The book of miracles of Peter the Venerable, abbot of Cluny, recounts a tale set in Spain in which a revenant appears alone but tells his living acquaintance that he was "traveling with a great army . . . so that [they] might be free of the punishment incurred by our sins, in the very place where we committed them."[79] In sum, the ideas presented here certainly are not William's, but those of popular theology. Finally, it is noteworthy that, later in the same chapter, William pairs the same verb—*didicisti*, "you have learned"—with *per me*, "from me."[80] This suggests that when William wanted to acknowledge a particular teaching as his own, he was careful to clarify the point.

Reading the section thusly eliminates inconsistencies that others have perceived in William's text and does not require us to regard the bishop as thoroughly confused about his own arguments. William of Auvergne, though fairly neglected in modern scholarship, was a leading mind of his day. He was an academically trained, logical thinker who valued consistency and seldom presented vague or scattershot explanations for the phenomena he discussed: it hardly is likely that he would contradict himself so completely within the space of a single chapter. Once it becomes clear that the above discussion of the Hellequin as a mobile purgatory is *not* in fact William's own opinion, but a representation of the attitudes of the uneducated masses, then we can anticipate that he will go on to refute these beliefs. And that is, indeed, exactly what he does. The text shows a very clear shift of voice when William begins presenting his own perspective: these opinions are clearly differentiated from what has come before.

---

78. Schmitt, *Ghosts in the Middle Ages*, 119–20; de Mayo, *Demonology of William of Auvergne*, 199–202; Bernstein, "Ghostly Troop and the Battle over Death," 140–43.
79. Petrus Venerabilis, *De miraculis*, in *PL*, 189, cols. 903–8.
80. WA, 1068.

In reality, just as I said before, and for all the reasons discussed above, they are not real horses, nor real arms that appear; nor real jousts, nor real battles, nor a real wandering or riding; but only *signs* of things of this type, which appear as if in a vision to move men's actions and deter them from the above-mentioned evils, as well as to solicit them to offer suffrages for the dead. Indeed, I assert that none of those punishments—of arms, of ghosts, of riding, and of conflicts between warriors and jousters—are imaginable for a disembodied soul. Nor is it possible that they should be punished thusly, given that it would be impossible for them to do these things. It is not possible for a disembodied soul to ride a horse, to bear arms, to train with weapons, or to fight with them.

Therefore it is clear that, since it is not possible that they are suffering torments, and since they cannot suffer without doing those things, these are signs of the torments that certain deeds, accomplished while in the body, would merit. Nor is it necessary that these souls who thus appear should be present in their own essence or person, any more than it is necessary that a thing one seems to see in a dream should be there present in reality.[81]

This section employs language that could not be more distinct from what came before. Here, William consistently makes clear that he is offering his own opinion, and he introduces his ideas with strong, first-person perspectives: *Verum, sicut predixi*, "In reality, just as I said before. . . ." These words signal the shift: now William will tell his reader exactly what they *really* ought to think about these apparitions, and he acknowledges that the ideas he is about to present recapitulate points he made earlier, before his thumbnail sketch of erroneous popular attitudes. He uses the same forceful language in the next sentence: *Dico etiam*, "Indeed, I assert. . . ." The following sentence in the original Latin includes a strongly worded introductory clause as well: *Quapropter, manifestum est*, "Therefore, it is clear that. . . ." Each sentence is introduced in a manner that suggests William is now setting the record straight, so to speak. Moreover, throughout this section there is also an insistent rhetorical repetition of the unreality of these visions: "not real horses, nor real arms that appear; nor real jousts, nor real battles, nor a real wandering or riding." With this rhythmic series of negations, William meticulously rejects the reality of each and every aspect of the army of the dead that he earlier attributed to "common talk." The next sentence presents a similarly

---

81. WA, 1067.

exhaustive list of purported postmortem "punishments" that William thinks are pure bunk: "of arms, of ghosts, of riding, and of conflicts between warriors and jousters." William not only is extremely clear about his opinion, he systematically rebuts the opposing view and makes sure that no detail escapes his condemnation.

Moreover, aside from these linguistic cues there is the fact that William's argument here returns to the exact same ideas he stated at the outset of the chapter: these apparitions are not embodied, and neither are they really the dead people themselves. As he noted earlier, dead folk are unable to do any of the things that they popularly are credited with doing, precisely because, according to William's Augustinian-based logic, the dead are disembodied souls that cannot interact with material objects. When living individuals witness what *appear* to be dead persons existing in this world, speaking to the living and interacting with the material plane—William here cites Gregory the Great's bathhouse attendant as a preeminent example—such apparitions are never really what they appear to be. William tends to believe that such apparitions are the work of demons, but he also supports Saint Augustine's suggestion that good spirits or angels may sometimes send the appearance of the dead as a "sign." These arguments return to the discussion William advanced earlier in his work about illusory visions. Thus, for William, the army of the dead is simply a sign, akin to a waking dream. It is an immaterial vision, perhaps the result of a demonic game or illusion; more rarely, perhaps, a divinely sent warning or gesture. But one thing is certain: the Hellequin should not naively be accepted at face value.

Indeed, far from waffling, the bishop goes on to decisively reject the idea that the Hellequin really is composed of the returned dead. And again, his language could not be more Augustinian in spirit:

> Wherever the dead may be in the next life and the otherworld, it is likely that they either cannot leave their location or do not wish to do so. If indeed they exist in the society of the blessed and sublime spirits, why would they descend from such delights of happiness to engage in these activities? If, however, they are held in the infernal prison or the purgatorial fire, in either case they would seem to be confined and incapable of leaving.[82]

As for the suggestion that these were embodied dead men who simply arose from their graves, "It is certain that the power to re-form human cadavers that are already decayed, and to bring back their souls and stick them inside

---

82. WA, 1069.

again, pertains solely to the omnipotent Creator."[83] Again, William uses clear, declarative language and effective rhetorical devices in order to lend strength to his own thoughts. The dead do not come back from their world to ours; whatever their fate, they are consigned to their place and there they will remain until the Creator re-forms the putrid bodies of the dead at the end of time and reinspires their souls into their shells. The Hellequin, then, must be something other than what it appears: this is William's message throughout the chapter. He is not equivocal, but entirely consistent.

William's viewpoint was to become the standard clerical interpretation of this phenomenon. Earlier reporters on the dead army strived to extricate it from its non-Christian origins, to a greater or lesser degree. Once the motif entered into the lexicon of Christian popular folklore, it was used as evidence of the Christian afterlife system, particularly purgatory. William's own account of popular theology provides evidence that the purgatorial interpretation was beginning to take hold, for people understood the purpose of the army specifically as a postmortem punishment in kind. However William, as the first university-trained scholar to take up the question of the wandering undead army, was also the first to call this opinion into question and to forcefully rebut it. He presented an alternative interpretation of these appearances as simulacra, not reality, the illusions of demons or, perhaps more rarely, signs sent by divine agency for the instruction of men. The dead themselves were translated to an alternate realm of existence, utterly disconnected from the world of the living. Death is an instantaneous severing of body and spirit. In every way, William's viewpoint is thoroughly consistent and wholly uncompromising.

Face to Face with Hellequin

William's new interpretation of the Hellequin not only came to be the standard interpretation of the learned, it also was successfully disseminated down the social scale to other sectors of society. We can trace the acceptance of William's demonizing interpretation quite clearly. Consider, for example, the following preaching exemplum, penned later in the thirteenth century:

> Sometimes devils play at transforming themselves into knights with burning faces who fight one another. People traditionally call them the *arzei*, that is, the burning ones or the flaming ones. Or sometimes they take on the appearance of kings who are hunting or playing, in which case they are called the retinue of Allequin or of Arthur.

---

83. WA, 1070.

I once heard about a certain peasant near Mont du Chat who, while bringing back a bundle of wood by moonlight, spied a countless number of hunting dogs, followed by an infinite multitude of people on foot and mounted. When he asked one of them who they were, he responded that they were the retinue of Arthur, to whose nearby court they both might go, if he wished. It seemed to the peasant that he followed them and entered into a great and very noble palace, where he saw knights and ladies playing and dancing, and eating and drinking fine dishes. At the end of the evening he was told to go to bed, and was led to a room with a richly ornamented bed in which there lay a certain lady who was wonderfully beautiful. After he had gone in and had slept, the next day he woke to find himself lying foully on his face, draped over his firewood as the butt of a joke.

I also heard about another peasant who likewise encountered a similar company of horsemen. One of them turned toward another, and then spun his head all the way around backward. He said, "Is my hood on straight?" And they kept on doing this over and over again. The women glimpsed in dances seem to be of the same kind.[84]

This tale was included in a vast text known either as *De septem donis Spiritus Sancti* (*On the Seven Gifts of the Holy Spirit*) or *Tractatus de diversis materiis praedicabilibus* (*A Treatise on Various Preaching Materials*). The author was a Dominican preacher interested in superstition and heresy, Étienne de Bourbon, who composed it in the years leading up to his death around 1261. The work is chiefly comprised of exempla: short moral stories, occasionally followed by a brief exposition of their meaning. The goal of such a work was to present model materials for preachers to use in sermons—compilations of entertaining stories that might be used to capture the attention of an audience and then instruct them in correct belief and behavior.

Stephen's presentation of the retinue of "Arthur or Allequin" incorporates many of the traditional elements we have seen above. Indeed, with this text we nearly have come full circle: the "flaming ones"—*arzei* in the vernacular—who conduct tournaments, speed by in hunts, or simply march together in military formation are all familiar. Likewise, the notion that the dead continue to feast, dance, flirt, and have sex represents an alternative way of imagining the dead in social groups that exist in parallel to the societies

---

84. Étienne de Bourbon, ed. de la Marche, in *Anecdotes historiques*, 321–22. Very soon after this, he discusses the *bonae res* and the canon *Episcopi* (323).

of the living. Like William of Auvergne, however, Stephen insists that this is a vast demonic illusion or joke. And indeed, we know that Stephen had read William of Auvergne's works; he incorporated several complimentary stories about him into his own writings.[85] Since Stephen studied in Paris around 1220, when William was part of the faculty of Theology at the University of Paris, it is likely that they were personally acquainted. Via Stephen's works, then, William's reappraisal of the Hellequin as a demonic *ludus* entered into the mainstream of common preaching materials. William's demonization of the dead army thus was brought to the attention of a wider audience of readers and sermon hearers, beyond the exclusive ivory tower milieu. For a crowd gathered in a city square or village clearing, such a story would be entertaining and familiar, but they would hear it reinterpreted as a cautionary tale concerning, not a purgatory for dead souls, but a demonic illusion. The detail of the knights pivoting their heads backward, mentioned in the coda to the story, reinforces the notion that these apparitions are demonic in nature: the grotesqueness of this deformation, combined with a cheery inquiry about one's hood, signals an unclean disorder.[86] As for the "women in dances," this is a brief reference to the female "good things" or fairies; we shall encounter them again in the next chapter.

By the thirteenth century, this freshly demonized Hellequin was making his move to the realm of vernacular literature. Now, of course, he appeared in his demonic guise. Hellequin lived on in popular vernacular songs such as,

---

85. Étienne de Bourbon, ed. de la Marche, *Anecdotes*, 383, 387–88, n. 1, 388–89.

86. A parallel case from Gdansk in the fourteenth century seems to provide an additional account of an encounter with a vagrant spirit, perhaps an outlier from the dead army. The repetition of the word *larva*, meaning either mask or ghost, is key: "It happened one time, that during Lent he veiled his face with a mask, which the witness made himself. And, veiled in this way, he left his place of habitation in the town of Gdansk, saying, 'I'm going to go out and commit some sin!' As he was leaving home, he met someone else who was also wearing a mask. He didn't know who it was, and so, not worrying about this person he arrived at a certain confraternity or party for the goldworkers of that town, whose custom was to come together and have a party every so often. And when he got there, he entered into a dance, whereupon all the young girls and women who were dancing fled from the dance, terrified because the witness was masked like that. Then the hosts of the party grasping him said that if he wanted to be at the party, he should take off the mask. And the witness states that when he wanted to take off the mask, his face was turned around backward. Then, taking his head into his hands, he attempted to twist his face back to its prior place, but since he was unable to do so, he lay down on the ground as if dead, destitute of understanding or thought. . . . And the witness added that his friends and the others who were standing there while he was lying prostrate on the earth, all said that his face was exactly similar to the face on the mask that he had been wearing before. . . . And the witness added that he firmly believed, that the masked man, who associated himself with him as he left home, was an evil spirit." The Latin is edited in Richard Stachnik, Anneliese Triller, and Hans Westfall, eds., *Die Akten des Kanonisationsprozesses Dorotheas von Montau von 1394 bis 1521* (Cologne, 1978), 367. I present a longer interpretation of the account in *Discerning Spirits: Divine and Demonic Possession in the Middle Ages* (Ithaca, NY, 2003), 52–53.

for example, *Luque la maudite* (*Luca the Damned*), a popular ditty that portrays demons bringing witches and necromancers to Hellequin in hell:

> Unhappy are those whom they find:
> they make them come where they are led
> And if anyone knows the art of necromancy
> They lead them along in a dance
> before Hellequin, in hell.[87]

Thus the link between Hellequin and the demonic that William of Auvergne had argued for was becoming quite firmly established even in vernacular culture.

At long last, a century later Hellequin finally showed his face. In 1316, he was memorialized in art alongside literature in a series of manuscript miniatures. A passage interpolated into the 1310–14 French vernacular poem *Roman de Fauvel* shows us the giant leader of the horde as a Christian demon, yet bearing the distinct imprint of his funereal and pagan past. Accompanying illuminations allow us to see him for the first time.

The eponymous character in the *Roman de Fauvel*'s moral allegory of virtue and vice is a horse who represents the height of immorality and corruption, but who nevertheless is favored by fortune. Toward the end of the poem Fauvel takes Lady Vainglory in matrimony; the interpolated passage that features Hellequin describes a charivari directed against the couple. Charivaris were popular rituals performed in order to satirize "inappropriate" weddings; they suggested communal disapproval.[88] In the poem, as Fauvel is about to deflower his bride a band of costumed local men arrive on the scene, cross-dressed or adorned with masks; they beat drums, make obscene gestures, and sing lewd songs to the pair. In the midst of this highly sexualized cacophony, funereal and diabolic elements suddenly intrude.

> They carry two biers with them
> and upon them were some who were only too willing
> To sing the devil's song to him.

Thus the bawdy parade of revelers quite unexpectedly transforms into a funereal and diabolic procession. The imagery here clearly harkens back to

---

87. "Trestouz iceus que il trouverent / Firent qu'avec eus amenerent / Qui savoient del'ingromance / Amenerent fesant la dance / Devant Hellequin en enfer." Gaston Raynaud, "*Des avocas, De la jument au deable, De Luque la maudite*: trois dits tirés d'un nouveau manuscrit de fableaux," *Romania* 12 (1883): 226; See also Nigel Wilkins, *La Musique du Diable* (Sprimont, 1999), 21.

88. Jacques Le Goff and Jean-Claude Schmitt, eds., *Le Charivari* (Paris, 1981).

Walchelin's vision of Herlequin's army, which included a series of funeral biers occupied by dwarfs. Not surprisingly, Hellequin himself appears soon thereafter:

> They were led back by a large giant
> Who came along with a great tumult
> He was dressed in his shroud.
> I believe it was Hellequin
> And the whole rest of the army
> that follows him, completely enraged.[89]

The giant Hellequin "leads back" the dead from the grave to the realm of the living. Dressed this time in a shroud, rather than with arms, he nevertheless is portrayed as a war leader. Indeed, the reference to his army being "completely enraged" is a closer approximation of the traditional representations of the Einherjar in Norse mythology than we have seen hitherto. Yet the suggestion that those on the bier "sing the devil's song to him" also explicitly identifies Hellequin with the devil.

An illumination that accompanies the above passage shows the giant Hellequin mounted on a horse, with several masked revelers carrying the two funeral biers or caskets (figure 4.2).[90] Each has three arched niches with three heads peering out from within, "sing[ing] the devil's song." Most of the heads are shrouded, though with their faces visible; one has begun to blacken and decay and looks more like a skull. As for Hellequin, he is bearded, mounted on a horse, and crowned with the "demonic winged headgear" that Ruth Mellinkoff has identified as an iconographic motif used in medieval French manuscripts "to deprecate paganism and its adherents,"[91] while simultaneously suggesting the presence of the diabolic. Though conceived as an illustration for the romance, the way the scene is illumined seems very close to part of the account of Orderic Vitalis: "a crowd of pall-bearers followed, to which the giant mentioned above joined himself. They were carrying about five hundred biers, each one borne by two

---

89. "Avec eus portoient deux bieres / Où il avoit gent trop avable / Pour chanter la chançon au deable.... Il y ravoit un grant jaiant / Qui aloit trop forment braiant / Vestu ert de bon broissequin / Je croi que c'estoit Hellequin / Et tuit li autre sa mesnie / Qui le suivent toute enragie." Margherita Lecco, "Lo charivari del *Roman de Fauvel* e la tradizione della *Mesnie Hellequin*," *Mediaevistik* 13 (2000): 55.

90. A second image on the same leaf shows Hellequin with a cart, described in the poem as an engine of thunderous noise, accompanied by one dwarf in a green hooded robe and another nude and beating a drum.

91. Ruth Mellinkoff, "Demonic Winged Headgear," *Viator* 16 (1985): 369.

FIGURE 4.2. Hellequin appears in the vernacular French poem *Le Roman de Fauvel*: this is our first glimpse of how the leader of the dead army might have been imagined. Hellequin appears at left riding a horse and wearing a winged headdress; he follows two biers or coffins, each with three heads peering out from arched niches. Miniature from *Le Roman de Fauvel*, ca. 1316–20. Bibliothèque Nationale de France, MS Français 146, fol. 34v.
© BnF, Dist. RMN-Grand Palais / Art Resource, NY.

porters. And sitting upon the biers were little men, like dwarfs, but they had large heads like barrels."[92]

A larger image on a later folio (figure 4.3) shows a broader view of the charivari procession. Hellequin is recognizable in the upper register

---

92. OV, 4:238.

FIGURE 4.3. Hellequin and some dead folk participate in a charivari, or popular ritual satirizing an inappropriate marriage. Hellequin is recognizable in the top tier by his winged headdress; he is followed by a figure in a shroud, and he carries a dwarf. Throughout the image are several other figures who likely represent the dead. Miniature from *Le Roman de Fauvel*, ca. 1316–20. Bibliothèque Nationale de France, MS Français 146, fol. 36v.
© BnF, Dist. RMN-Grand Palais / Art Resource, NY.

by his wing-adorned head and scruffy beard. This time he is on foot and appears to be carrying a small person on his back in a basket. On all three levels of the image we see a variety of undersized figures, or figures that appear only from the shoulders up. It is notable that every one of these small-scale figures is transported in some sort of conveyance: either Hellequin's basket at top, in a cart or upon a man's back in the center register, and in a wheelbarrow at the bottom. The figure receiving a piggyback ride in the center area wears an unusual hat emblazoned with a crescent moon; this matches the headgear on one of the dead faces looking out from the funeral caskets in the earlier image (bottom row, center). It seems likely that these small figures who are carried by others also are meant to represent the dead, in and among the living revelers participating in the charivari. As we have seen, the dead often were associated with dwarf stature. In addition, several figures in the image—notably the one just behind Hellequin at top, carrying a drum, and one at the bottom just behind the wheelbarrow—are wrapped in loose white cloths like shrouds. The group thus seems to represent a mix of dead folk, living folk in animal masks and costumes, and perhaps some living folk in ghost costumes.

The appearance of Hellequin and his retinue in this passage has puzzled commentators, who have wondered whether the charivari customarily invoked the army of the dead and/or macabre themes.[93] Indeed, there is much that remains elusive in this account. For our part, we may set aside the history of the charivari (which is not our concern) and focus solely on the representation of Hellequin and his retinue. We see here a series of convergences between elements that originated as dichotomies: between death and fertility (the occasion, after all, is a marriage); between pagan motifs and Christian reframings; and lastly, between the dead and the demonic. What we do *not* see in this passage, however, is any attempt to align the army of the dead with purgatory or to appropriate it to teachings on penitence. Indeed, the framework of the *Roman de Fauvel* is already that of moralizing allegory on sin and virtue: Hellequin is not needed for this precise purpose. Instead, here he is a demon *as well as* a pagan leader of dead warriors, a double figure whose two identities were not incommensurable but, of course, harmonious within Christian thought worlds. Above all, he is a figure of illusion to be shunned. Fauvel suggests Hellequin has nothing to teach us anymore, a conclusion William of Auvergne surely would have approved.

The shifting representations of the motif of the afterlife as a collective society—as a civilization within a mountain, as a feudal army of the dead on the march, as the vagabond revenant remnant of an earlier population, as a retributive afterlife system, and finally, as a demonic illusion—provide an excellent case study of temporary cultural convergence and then divergence. We can trace this motif's movement "up" and then back "down" through

---

93. Carlo Ginzburg, "Charivari, associations juvéniles, chasse sauvage," in LeGoff and Schmitt, *Le Charivari*, 131–40, has argued for such a connection; Nancy Regalado, "Masques réels dans le monde de l'imaginaire: Le rite et l'écrit dans le charivari du *Roman de Fauvel*, Ms B.N. fr.146," in *Masques et déguisements dans la littérature médiévale*, ed. Marie-Louise Ollier (Montréal, 1988), 111–26, against one. See also Schmitt, "Les masques, le diable, les morts."

different levels of culture: learned and oral, elite and popular, religious and secular. The history traced in this chapter shows, above all, that these levels of culture interpenetrated one another and existed in ongoing dialogue, rather than in diametric opposition. The terms "popular" and "elite" simply represent different points on the spectrum of a single culture, one that evolved constantly and reproduced itself through varying mechanisms of interpretation.

Though the motif of the army of the dead had pagan origins, it came to be incorporated into Christian oral folklore in dialogue with the theology of purgatory. At this level of culture, we see oral storytelling from the past coalescing with teachings from religious leaders to craft a unique imagining of Christian teachings on the afterlife. This particular set of meanings was then taken up and endorsed in the twelfth century by various learned writers, who possessed divergent historical and literary goals but who mostly accepted the troop of revenants as a representation of the Christian afterlife. The Gregorian principle of appropriated ghost stories was here utilized in order to disseminate the new doctrine of purgatory. Over time, the story came to be sheared of unassimilable pagan elements and reimagined as a moralizing image of retribution and reward. In the thirteenth century, however, university-trained clerics such as William of Auvergne reversed course. He decisively reinterpreted these reports as veiled demonic simulations. From there we can trace the demonized Hellequin back into vernacular literature, where pagan, Christian, funereal, and demonic elements intertwined freely. The afterlife of the dead moved through different realms of texts and culture, just as they were imagined moving through different landscapes and regions.

CHAPTER 5

Flesh and Bone
The Semiotics of Mortality

When a human being dies . . . the body that gave comfort to many people while it was alive, provokes horror in the same people after death. Hence the saying:

> Human flesh is viler than a sheep's skin.
> When a sheep dies, its remains still have value:
> The skin is stretched and written on, both sides.
> When a human being dies, both flesh and bones die.[1]

As this fourteenth-century preacher placed nib to parchment, he was moved to reflect upon the durability of the words he put down, as contrasted with the destruction of his body to come. His melancholy thoughts were realized, for although the manuscript still exists, the author's name, along with the details of his bodily existence, are lost. This particular writer's musing on the eternity of death is deceptive, however, for the finality of his tone contrasts sharply with the fluid conceptions of death and afterlife that are expressed in many other medieval texts.

Portions of this chapter have appeared as "Wraiths, Revenants and Ritual in Medieval Culture," *Past & Present*, no. 152 (1996): 3–45.

1. Siegfried Wenzel, ed. and trans., *Fasciculus Morum: A Fourteenth-Century Preacher's Handbook* (University Park, PA, 1989), 98.

The previous chapter noted that after the thirteenth century, stories about the revenant dead were reframed by university-trained theologians as demonic deceits. Whereas earlier generations had attempted to assimilate such stories to theological and pastoral purposes, now such stories troubled the Christian imagination. We also see, in this evolution, a shift from Gregorian modes of thought (which accepted the notion that the embodied dead might return) to an Augustinian model (in which such events were implausible and required an alternate form of explanation). The current chapter approaches some of the same themes, but from a different angle and through slightly different evidence. Here I chiefly discuss reports of individual revenants—the "outcast dead"—as opposed to the collective groups of dead folk encountered previously. Moreover, this chapter foregrounds social structure rather than chronology, for even as theologians increasingly turned to theories of demonic interference in order to explain away visions of the returned dead, many laity continued to uphold the idea that certain kinds of dead folk might return of their own accord. This chapter suggests that a more materialist model of life and death persisted within the lay society of northern Europe until the end of the Middle Ages. It continued to compete with the otherworldly, spirit-based model of life and afterlife that emanated from the university milieu and that undergirded medical norms defining death—in both cases, an Augustinian outlook. Furthermore, this materialist model was quite specific and consistent in its cultural logic. As we have seen, the dead who returned were usually those who had perished untimely or through violence. This chapter adds some new patterns to the latter observation. As I will show, the dead were believed to remain active and dangerous specifically until their flesh decayed and nothing but bones remained. Thus the logic of revenancy was constrained by specific factors relating to the manner of death and the condition of the corpse. This model implied that the death of the body was not completed until the destruction of the body through decay; it contrasted sharply with the dominant medical and theological ways of understanding death as a discrete and swift event.

Finally, this chapter moves on from an analysis of paganism to the realm of popular culture. The previous two chapters explored how the church appropriated themes about shades, revenants, and ghosts as a means of proving the existence of the otherworld. One unintended consequence of this process was that originally pagan cultural logics were imported into Christian texts and traditions in these regions. Ultimately, the reproduction of these motifs through time engendered parallel sets of discourses about how to understand reports about the returned dead: interpretations of reports about revenants varied by social strata and educational level. This chapter focuses on the ways in which originally pagan traditions about the unquiet dead functioned within northern European popular culture in a fully Christian context.

Demonically Possessed Corpses

The following quotation can serve as a point of entrée into the themes of this chapter:

> In the town of Nivelles lived a virgin worthy of God. . . . [She] used to rise in the early morning to go to church, observing the stipulated hours [for prayer]. It happened one time that the defunct corpse of a certain dead man was brought to the church in the evening without her knowing about it. Getting up in the middle of the night, the virgin went to church and found the dead man, but she was hardly afraid at all, so she settled down and began her prayers. When the devil saw this he looked upon her with malice, and entering the dead corpse he moved it a little in the coffin. The virgin, seeing this, crossed herself and bravely shouted to the devil, "Lay down! Lay down, you wretch, for you have no power against me!" Suddenly the devil rose up with the corpse and said, "Truly, now I do have power against you, and I will revenge myself for the frequent injuries I have suffered at your hands!" When she saw this, she was thoroughly terrified, so with both hands she grabbed a staff topped with a cross, and bringing it down on the head of the dead man she knocked him to the ground. Through such faithful daring the demon was put to flight.[2]

Some themes are familiar: a deserted church, a living person who arrives at night only to field an attack from an aggressive physical revenant—albeit a single one this time, rather than a group. This tale was written down in the mid-thirteenth century by the Dominican Thomas of Cantimpré in his manual for preachers, *Bonum Universale de Apibus* (*On the Universal Good of Bees*). Thomas probably adapted the tale from gossip he had heard in Nivelles, an area within his sphere of mobility, in order to teach certain points of dogma about unclean spirits and, more importantly, about the death of the human body. Alongside these teachings, however, a delicate reading of the story may reveal much about local ideas that conflicted, even as they coexisted, with ecclesiastical teachings. To explore these other ideas, we must extricate Thomas's interpretation of the incident from the cultural facts that he is reporting.

---

2. Thomas of Cantimpré, *Bonum Universale de Apibus*, ii. 57. 8 (Douai, 1597), 541–42.

Two questions of boundary transgression are at issue here: between the living and the dead, and between flesh and spirit. First Thomas, consistent with contemporary theological trends, emphasizes the fact that the corpse itself does not come to life; it is mere dross moved by the demon. As we have seen, this is a classic teaching that reaches back to Tertullian and Augustine, one that was increasingly endorsed by university thinkers from the early thirteenth century onward and that undergirded contemporary medical discourses as well. The body, according to Thomas, is uncoordinated, stiff, and unnatural. Neither the flesh nor the spirit of the dead man is an active principle as the author repeatedly emphasizes in redundant phrases like, "the defunct corpse of a certain dead man." Thus the body is usable by any spirit, not just the original human spirit of the deceased. In fact, bodies often are referred to as a sort of clothing in hagiographers' descriptions of spiritual dislocation: entering and exiting the body is like "putting on a tunic" or "shedding a garment."[3] This tradition, again, goes back to Saint Augustine, who had likened the body to a piece of clothing or jewelry that was worn in a particularly intimate manner.[4] This conception is linked as well to the notion of the human spirit as the principle of life or vitality. Thus the body, as some sort of envelope or tool, could be "put on" by a demonic spirit and used as a means to interact more directly with the tangible world.

Indeed, Thomas's language emphasizes the demon's manipulation of the body as an object: "[The demon] moved [the body] a little in the coffin . . . suddenly the demon rose up with the corpse." There is a clear subject/object distinction between the unclean spirit as mover and the body as inert matter. Nor was Thomas alone in this particular emphasis; other ecclesiastical authors also interpreted the movement of a corpse after death in precisely the same way. For example, a tale from the anonymous *Life* of Ida of Louvain, another thirteenth-century virgin from the Low Countries, emphasizes the way in which a dead body's limbs may be maneuvered by an unclean spirit:

> One time [she] beheld a bier placed before her . . . and on it . . . the corpse of a certain deceased man. Leaping into it, the skin-changing inventor of all evil stood the body on its feet, and thus moving forward

---

3. See, for example, *Vita Venerabilis Idae Virginis*, in *AASS*, 11 (April 13), 178.

4. Elizabeth A. R. Brown, "Death and the Human Body in the Later Middle Ages: The Legislation of Boniface VIII on the Division of the Corpse," *Viator* 12 (1981): 223. See also Brown, "Authority, the Family, and the Dead in Late Medieval France," *French Historical Studies* 16 (1990): 803–32, for a modification of the earlier essay's conclusions based upon the same evidence; Agostino Paravacini Bagliani, "The Corpse in the Middle Ages: The Problem of the Division of the Body," in *The Medieval World*, ed. Peter Linehan and Janet L. Nelson (London, 2001), 27–41.

inside it and together with it [*sic in ipso simul cum ipso progrediens*], he approached the maidservant of God.[5]

The passage is explicit in describing how the demon enters the body, props it up on its feet, and then makes it take a few steps. One can easily picture it gracelessly shambling forward. Like Thomas of Cantimpré, the author of this story also emphasizes a strong subject/object distinction between unclean spirit and dead body. In so doing, both authors emphasize the point that the only animate force is the possessing spirit, the demon; the man, by contrast, is only a thing, an inert cadaver. In essence, this view of reanimated corpses denies any transgression between the living and the dead and instead makes the central action a transgression between flesh and the demonic spirit. Corpses cannot come back to life, but they may temporarily be inhabited by an unclean spirit that takes the place of the departed human spirit.

This opposition between different ways of reanimating the body was even invoked in an ecclesiastical ritual for consecrating cemeteries, which prayed God to protect the body's safety from demonic misuse or reanimation until the true and final resurrection:

> Grant, distributor of kindnesses, a seat of repose for the bodies of your menservants and womenservants entering into this cemetery, a place fortified against all incursions of evil spirits, so that at the resurrection of their bodies and spirits . . . they may be worthy to receive the eternal blessing.[6]

This blessing conjures up the extraordinary mental picture of medieval demons seeking out cemeteries in order to rob graves of their occupants and juxtaposes it with the true resurrection to be expected at the end of time.

Other macabre tales emphasized the total death of the body in slightly different ways. For example, the mid-thirteenth-century Dominican Jean de Mailly recounts an exemplum of a demon animating the corpse of a beautiful young woman in order to tempt a pious man.[7] On the one hand, the tale is a meditation on the transitory nature of sensual delights, but the fact that the girl's body turns putrid as soon as the demon leaves it also emphasizes the death of the body, as opposed to the illusory life given it by the unclean spirit.

---

5. *Vita Venerabilis Idae Virginis*, 160.

6. "Famulorum famularumque tuarum corporibus in hoc cimiterium intrantibus quietis sedem ab omni incursionem malorum spirituum defensis benigniis largitor tribue ut post animarum corporumque resurrectionem . . . beatitudinem sempiternam percipere mereantur." Vatican City, Biblioteca Apostolica Vaticana, MS Borghes. 35, "Rituale Romanum," fol. 74r–v.

7. Jean de Mailly, *Abrégé des gestes et miracles des saints*, trans. A. Dondaine (Paris, 1947), 338–39.

Caesarius of Heisterbach likewise interprets some such incidents as demonic reanimation of the body: two tales speak of dead bodies "living with an evil spirit in place of the soul."[8] In the second of this pair the departure of the demon prompts the long-dead body to crumble, theatrically, into dust. More explicit on the theme of demonic possession versus the living dead is another tale from Thomas of Cantimpré. This exemplum tells of the animate corpse of a knight who appears to his former servant and asks him to remove from his wound the point of the lance that killed him (as verification of his own materiality) and then gives a lecture on the evils of tournaments.[9] Thomas follows up his lesson against institutionalized violence, however, with an explanation of how the movement of a corpse might come about, utilizing the theological metaphor of the body as garment: "Since the matter of a dead body remains behind like a garment, the devil can enter into the human body as an instrument, and can mold the mouth to voices and words again, and recall the tendons to the movement of its members."[10] Again, it is not the body that moves, but the animating demon. Hildegard of Bingen likewise writes that God revealed to her, "When someone departs from this life whose soul is in the power of the Devil, by [God's] permission he will sometimes perform illusions in the corpse, making it move as if alive."[11] Dante Alighieri utilizes the motif of the demonically possessed corpse in order to place a still-living contemporary in hell. When, in the eighth circle of the inferno, Dante encounters Fra Alberigo he is startled, for he believed him to still be alive in 1300, the date in which the work is set. How, then, was it possible for his soul to be in hell? The answer, Dante learns, is that the souls of those who betray unto death their friends and guests are cast into the abyss immediately, while their bodies are kept animated by demons until the appointed time for their decease.[12] Individuals of this ilk are so evil, Dante implies, that no one even notices the switch when their bodies come to be animated by demons.

The interpretation of revenants as possessed by demons accords with the broader intellectual background of these authors. Their interpretation of animate corpses as demonically possessed was supported by the learned tradition, which after the thirteenth century increasingly turned to Augustinian

---

8. CH, 2:317–18.
9. Thomas of Cantimpré, *Bonum Universale de Apibus*, ii. 49. 6, 446–47.
10. Ibid., ii. 49. 7, 448.
11. Hildegard of Bingen, *Scivias,* trans. Columba Hart and Jane Bishop (Mahwah, NJ, 1990), 503.
12. Dante Alighieri, *The Divine Comedy*, ed. and trans. Charles Singleton, 3 vols. (Princeton, NJ, 1970), *Inferno*, 33:120–23, 129–35 (1:356).

models of vitality and mortality. The basis of human life was the spirit; corporeal matter was inert; death was the separation of body and spirit; and unusual phenomena might always be explained with recourse to the depredations of demons. Even within a didactic book such as Thomas's *Bonum Universale de Apibus*, however, the very terms of the argument reveal the beliefs that the preacher was attempting to eradicate. For example, we see in Thomas's relentless insistence on the absolute nonvitality of the corpse that attacked the virgin ("the defunct corpse of a certain dead man") an argument against the opposite proposition: that the dead *do* have a continuing vitality of their own. If we separate the ecclesiastical interpretations of these events as caused by demons from the basic "cultural facts" that they report, we are left with a different set of ideas: dead men sometimes roam from their graves and attack the living. Underlying these learned authors' arguments for the demonically possessed corpse was a set of long-standing traditions about the inherent vitality of the enfleshed body itself.

The Original Living Corpse: Icelandic *Draugar*

As we have seen, belief in corpses coming back to life is well attested in medieval Europe. The types of stories that interest me in this chapter, involving individual, outcast dead, occur most notably in Icelandic culture. However, we also find such tales in areas where there was extensive Scandinavian raiding, settlement, and influence: England (particularly Yorkshire, the heart of the old Danelaw), the Low Countries, northern France, and parts of Germany. The Icelandic saga literature presents the most extensive portrayal of this set of beliefs and provides some clues as to how they may have functioned within a pagan social context, albeit retrospectively, from the vantage point of the thirteenth century. According to the sagas, the average dead conducted their afterlives in a social fashion, dwelling inside a mountain close to their ancestral holdings. However, in certain instances the dead were outcast from this society, perhaps because they were irascible in life, died too early, or perished in a craven or unworthy manner. In such cases they were believed to remain upon the surface of the earth, preying upon living men.

The importance of revenants within Icelandic culture is attested by the existence of a specific word for the undead in the Icelandic language: *draugr*.[13]

---

13. Aron Gurevich, *Historical Anthropology of the Middle Ages* (Chicago, 1992), 116–21; Àrmann Jakobsson, "Vampires and Watchmen: Categorizing the Mediaeval Icelandic Undead," *Journal of English and Germanic Philology* 110, no. 3 (2011): 281–300.

These creatures were loners who acted in a hostile manner. Most famous, perhaps, is the revenant Glam of *Grettir's Saga*.[14] In life, Glam was a widely disliked shepherd who was killed violently—possibly by another unnamed *draugr*. After Glam's body was buried, he nevertheless wandered from his grave at night, stomping on the rooftops and storehouses and frightening off the local inhabitants. Eventually, Glam's corpse killed two living men. The *draugr* was only put to rest after a terrific battle with Grettir (the saga's protagonist), who beheaded the revenant and reburied it with its head between its legs.[15] The same saga contains another such confrontation, this time between Grettir and the *draugr* Kar, for the sake of a treasure the corpse watches over in his tomb. Kar, too, was subdued by beheading.[16] More peaceable is the revenant of Thorgunna in *Eyrbyggja Saga*, who cooked dinner for those bearing her corpse away for burial. However, Thorgunna's death also brought on what might be called an epidemic of aggressive revenants back at the farm where she had lived. The first to die mysteriously was the farm's shepherd. His *draugr* in turn killed another man named Thorir Wood-leg, and the two of them were seen together at night. Then six more men perished in the vicinity, followed by six who drowned at sea and came back to the farm, dripping seawater. The two bands of revenants had a fight, the sailors against Thorir Wood-leg's troop. Next, a local witch died and was seen strolling about with her dead husband. Finally, all the revenants were banished through a formal legal procedure against them for trespassing.[17] Earlier in *Eyrbyggja Saga* the case of the *draugr* Thorolf is recounted: after expiring from sheer rage his undead corpse killed so many men that the valley he haunted was decimated of the living, though the area was correspondingly well populated with revenants, who wandered about with Thorolf.[18] *Laxdaela Saga* comments upon the aggressive nature of the *draugr* Killer-Hrapp thus: "Difficult as he had been to deal with during his life, he was now very much worse after death, for his corpse would not rest in its grave; people say he murdered most of his servants."[19] Hrapp's body finally was dug up and reburied far from the district. These tales represent only a few of the numerous *draugar* within Icelandic literature.

---

14. G. A. Hight, trans., *The Saga of Grettir the Strong* (London, 1913), 86–100.

15. Ármann Jakobsson, "The Fearless Vampire Killers: A Note about Icelandic Draugr and Demonic Contamination in Grettis Saga," *Folklore* 120, no. 3 (2009): 307–16.

16. Hight, *The Saga of Grettir the Strong*, 42–46.

17. Hermann Pálsson and Paul Edwards, trans., *Eyrbyggja Saga* (London, 1989), 131–41.

18. Ibid., 92–95.

19. Magnus Magnusson and Hermann Pálsson, trans., *Laxdaela Saga* (London, 1969), 78.

CHAPTER 5

Though the Icelandic phenomenon of aggressive living corpses has been widely studied and discussed,[20] its counterpart on the Continent has been largely neglected.[21] In this broad region we find a body of evidence about hostile revenants that is strikingly similar to tales of the Icelandic undead. Numerous "horror" stories of hostile revenants may be found in chronicles and exempla collections from septentrional Europe, beginning in the early eleventh century and flourishing especially in the thirteenth and fourteenth centuries. The tales I just examined about demonically animated revenants are not isolated instances but are part of a larger continuum of stories about reanimated corpses, many of which are told with a high degree of local detail and verisimilitude. In most cases, the dead are presented not in Christianizing terms as possessed by demons, but as coming back to life on their own. Indeed, as I shall demonstrate, many tales of the undead explicitly *reject* a demonic interpretation; the idea of the criminal, hostile revenant persisted, especially in secular culture, through to the end of the Middle Ages.

By contrast, the demonic-possession school of thought about revenants was a viewpoint linked to two circumstances. First, it generally appears in texts penned by authors with a strong religious commitment and education; and second, this interpretation most frequently occurs after the thirteenth

---

20. See Gurevich, *Historical Anthropology of the Middle Ages*; Claude Lecouteux, *Fantômes et revenants au moyen âge* (Paris, 1986); Hilda Ellis Davidson, "The Restless Dead: An Icelandic Ghost Story", in *The Folklore of Ghosts*, ed. Hilda R. Ellis Davidson and W. M. S. Russell (London, 1981), 155–75; Reidar Christiansen, "The Dead and the Living," *Studia Norvegica* 2 (1946): 3–96; N. K. Chadwick, *Norse Ghosts: A Study in the Draugr and the Hangbui* (Cambridge, 1946); Juha Pentikainen, "The Dead without Status," in *Nordic Folklore: Recent Studies*, ed. Reimund Kvideland and Henning K. Sehmsdorf (Bloomington, IN, 1989), 128–34; Kathryn Hume, "From Saga to Romance: The Use of Monsters in Old Norse Literature," *Studies in Philology* 77, no. 1 (1980): 1–25.

21. Lecoutoux, *Fantômes et revenants au moyen âge*; Jean-Claude Schmitt, *Ghosts in the Middle Ages: The Living and the Dead in Medieval Society* (Chicago, 1998); Hughes Neveux, "Les lendemains de la mort dans les croyances occidentales (vers 1250–vers 1300), " *Annales E.S.C.* 34, no. 2 (1979): 245–63; Karl Frölich, "Germanisches Totenrecht und Totenbrauchtum im Spiegel neuerer Forschung," *Hessische Blätter für Volkskunde* 43 (1952): 41–63; Nikolaus Kyll, *Tod, Grab, Begräbnisplatz, Totenfeier: Zur Geschichte ihres Brauchtums im Trierer Lande und in Luxemburg unter besonderer Berücksichtigung des Visitationshandbuches des Regino von Prüm (†915)* (Bonn, 1972); Ronald Finucane, *Appearances of the Dead: A Cultural History of Ghosts* (New York, 1984); Caciola, "Wraiths, Revenants and Ritual"; C. S. Watkins, "Sin, Penance, and Purgatory in the Anglo-Norman Realm: The Evidence of Visions and Ghost Stories," *Past & Present*, no. 175 (2002): 3–33; Jacqueline Simpson, "Repentant Soul or Walking Corpse? Debatable Apparitions in Medieval England," *Folklore* 114, no. 3 (2003): 389–402; G. David Keyworth, "Was the Vampire of the Eighteenth Century a Unique Type of Undead Corpse?," *Folklore* 117, no. 3 (2006): 241–60; John Blair, "The Dangerous Dead in Early Medieval England," in *Early Medieval Studies in Memory of Patrick Wormald*, ed. Stephen Baxter et al. (Burlington, VT, 2009), 539–59. Paul Barber, *Vampires, Burial and Death: Folklore and Reality* (New Haven, CT, 1988), gives a cross-cultural view. For a critique, see Otto Oexle, "Die Gegenwart der Toten," in *Death in the Middle Ages*, ed. Herman Braet and Werner Verbeke (Louvain, 1983), 19–77; and G. Wiegelmann, "Der 'Lebende Leichnam' im Volksbrauch," *Zeitschrift für Volkskunde* 62 (1966): 161–83.

century—though it never succeeded in wholly eclipsing the alternative viewpoint. Texts such as chronicles and histories, which lack a moralizing agenda, tended to reject or ignore the possibility of demonic animation in regard to revenants, even after the thirteenth century. For these more historical authors, the transgression involved in a corpse coming back to life remained that between life and death, rather than between flesh and unclean spirit. In the previous chapter, I focused more closely on broad chronological shifts in the interpretation of the living dead army; in this chapter, I foreground the question of social strata as a factor in the understanding of the individual returned dead. The two analyses should be regarded as complementary and overlapping, though they are framed in different ways.

Outcast and Criminal Revenants

In 1090 the Yorkshire Abbey of Burton was home to a strange episode involving the revenant corpses of some local men. The abbot of this foundation, Geoffrey of Burton, composed *The Life and Miracles of Saint Modwenna* to honor the Irish saint whose bones rested there.[22] In a lengthy miracle story, two wicked peasants from the village of Stapenhill—treacherous runaways and fomenters of discord between the monastery and the local count—were struck by Modwenna's vengeance: they suddenly expired in the midst of their afternoon meal. The next morning the troublemakers were buried in wooden coffins at the churchyard in Stapenhill, the village from which they had fled from their rightful lord. That very evening, as the sun lowered in the sky and the shadows lengthened, the dead pair suddenly appeared in the neighboring village of Drakelow. Each carried on his shoulders his wooden coffin; together they wandered through local fields and the lanes of the village. The story correlates with artistic conventions: images of corpses carrying their coffins appear with some frequency in medieval manuscripts, as shown in figure 5.1.

Like some of the revenants we have examined previously, the Stapenhill undead brought death to their fellows. Indeed, they sought out the living to follow them into death, knocking on the doors of the living and urgently commanding them to come along: *Agite! Agite et venite!* In consequence all but three souls in the village swiftly perished. Finally the terrified survivors requested permission from the bishop to disinter the revenant peasants. The pair was put to rest after drastic physical interventions: their heads were cut

---

22. Geoffrey of Burton, *The Life and Miracles of Saint Modwenna*, ed. and trans. Robert Bartlett (Oxford, 2002), 193–99.

216 CHAPTER 5

FIGURE 5.1. This cadaver has arisen from his grave and is on the move, bringing his coffin along with him. Illumination from the *Hours of Mary of Burgundy*. Flemish, Bruges-Ghent, ca. 1480. Kupferstichkabinett, Staatliche Museen, Berlin, Inv. 78 B 12, fol. 221r.
Photo: bpk, Berlin / Kupferstichkabinett, Staatliche Museen / Jörg P. Anders. / Art Resource, NY.

off and placed between their legs. This detail of the reburial is rather interesting since archaeological excavations of early British cemeteries have uncovered many sets of human remains in precisely this configuration.[23] Beyond this, the pair's hearts were removed and burned.

---

23. Ralph Merrifield, *The Archaeology of Ritual and Magic* (New York, 1987), 71–76; Elizabeth O'Brien, *Post-Roman Britain to Anglo-Saxon England: Burial Practices Reviewed*, British Archaeological Reports 289 (Oxford, 1999); Howard Williams, *Death and Memory in Early Medieval Britain* (Cambridge, 2006); Barber, *Vampires, Burial, and Death*; Andrew Reynolds, *Anglo-Saxon Deviant Burial Customs* (Oxford, 2009).

Four decades later, several entries in Walter Map's English chronicle (home also to the tale of King Herla and the Herlething) likewise tell of the predations of living, not possessed, corpses. The author's tone gives these tales in particular an air of immediacy: for Walter and his contemporaries these were strange, but real, events. One incident concerns a revenant wreaking havoc in its former neighborhood. A local knight, William, complained to the bishop about it:

> Lord, I take refuge with you seeking advice. A certain evil Welshman quite recently died unhappily in my village, and immediately afterwards for each of four nights he walked back to the village at night and will not stop calling out by name each of his neighbors. As soon as they are called they take ill, and within three days they die so that already very few are left.[24]

Interestingly enough, the bishop suggested that the body may in fact be demonically reanimated and advised William to open the tomb and sprinkle the corpse with plenty of holy water. However, this method was a dismal failure: the revenant continued his nightly visits, demonstrating that an indwelling demon was *not* the source of the problem. The corpse moved under its own power. Only when the knight William himself chased the corpse back to its grave and cleaved open its "head down to the neck" did it cease its troublemaking. In conclusion, Map himself explicitly sets aside the demonic viewpoint and opines instead that the cause of the phenomenon is unknowable: "We know about the true circumstances of this event, but we do not know the cause."[25] Another of Map's tales describes the vagabond corpse of a man "who they say died unhappily" that wandered for over a month before being cornered at the town limits by a crowd of local townspeople.[26] Only after the corpse received a proper burial—that is, when a cross was placed to mark his grave—did it cease wandering.

Toward the end of the twelfth century, more revenant tales may be found in William of Newburgh's chronicle *Historia Rerum Anglicarum*.[27] In discussing the case of a wandering corpse in Buckingham in 1196, William notes that "such things often happened in England" and then gives three additional examples of terrifyingly disruptive revenants.[28] The Buckingham case

---

24. WM, 103–4.
25. WM, 104.
26. WM, 104.
27. For background on the Augustinian priory at Newburgh, see Janet Burton, *The Monastic Order in Yorkshire, 1069–1215* (Cambridge, 1999).
28. *HRA*, 475–82.

concerns the corpse of a sinful man that was aggressive toward its remaining family. It crawled into bed with its widow, nearly crushing her with its weight, then attacked other family members when they tried to intervene. Although the locals suggested to the bishop that the corpse must be disinterred and burned to ashes, he convinced them that a letter of absolution for the man's sins, if laid in the tomb, would be just as effective—and it was. It is possible that the bishop was inspired by monastic practice: the *Constitutions of Lanfranc*, an exactly contemporary document drawn up by the archbishop of Canterbury, prescribes that a formula of absolution ought to be read aloud at the gravesite of a deceased brother and then placed on his chest before the actual interment.[29] Newburgh's second case, in Berwick, concerns the cadaver of a wealthy man that wandered abroad at night, terrifying the people and causing the dogs to howl loudly at its malign presence. This time, the expedient of burning the cadaver was undertaken by some local youths, who dug up the offending corpse, dismembered it, and cremated its remains. The third case is that of a too secular chaplain in the vicinity of Melrose Abbey: this man, known in life as the *hundeprest* because of his love of hunting, returned to give his attentions to his former mistress. Terrified, she recruited some young men to watch by the cemetery for her. Upon the corpse's return to its hideout, one of them "killed" the revenant by hitting it with an axe. When the grave was later opened, the gaping wound was clearly visible and appeared as fresh as if the corpse were alive. Despite this incapacitating wound, however, the locals burned the cadaver for good measure. Newburgh's final case is perhaps the most frightening: A wicked and choleric man died suddenly in a fall from his rooftop after he spied his wife in bed with another man. He, too, wandered at night, attacking all he met and leaving them on the point of death, while a pack of dogs followed after him, howling and whining. The locals, in fear of the revenant's malice as much as the possibility of a pestilence from the corruption of the air caused by the rotting corpse, began to leave the district in droves. Finally, two brothers dug up the cadaver and burned it to ashes.

The author of these tales, William of Newburgh, seems to have studied revenants at some length: he explains how he searched in vain for parallel incidences in earlier literature and emphasizes the newness of the phenomenon.[30] Yet he, too, like many of the other authors we have examined, professes perplexity as to the mechanism by which the reanimation of a corpse might come about and hesitates to ascribe it to demonic intervention:

---

29. David Knowles, ed. and trans., *The Monastic Constitutions of Lanfranc* (London, 1951), 130.
30. *HRA*, 477.

> Certainly the fact that a cadaver of a dead person, having gotten out of its grave, should be borne about by I know not what spirit to terrorize or injure the living . . . would not easily be accepted as true if there were not so many examples from our own time, and if the testimony were not so abundant. . . . If I wanted to write about every incident of this sort . . . it would be too complicated and onerous.[31]

Despite the frequency William ascribes to these events, he remains puzzled by them. The explanation that demons possess dead bodies and move them does not satisfy him entirely, as indicated by his use of the phrase "borne about by I know not what spirit." Ultimately William, like Walter Map and Caesarius of Heisterbach, fails to assign a cause to the corpses' wanderings.

William of Auvergne, who discusses the armies of the dead, also writes of individual revenants. He references the popular tales he had heard, "many times, about certain dead men who kill other men from among the living."[32] As we have seen, William was an innovator in the interpretation of the armies of the dead; he also, however, was aware of the popular belief in individual dead men returning from their graves and discusses them in the same section of his *On the Universe*. The examples discussed thus far would all fit nicely within William's definition of this phenomenon: dead men who move, who act, and who kill. The learned bishop might equally well have had in mind incidents like the one recounted in the thirteenth-century *Historiae Memorabiles*, a text from Colmar by the Dominican Rudolf von Schlettstadt. A tale headlined "On Henry, who was Seriously Wounded by Dead Men" tells of a man traveling near a river who suddenly was attacked by three dead men mounted on horseback, whom he recognized and later named. One was a recently murdered knight. After beating him savagely, the revenants left Henry for dead, but he survived.[33] These bloodcurdling dead men certainly tried their best to kill Henry, yet despite their malicious nature, they are not associated with demonic possession or illusion in any way. Similarly, the thirteenth-century Cistercian Caesarius of Heisterbach provides an illuminating glimpse into the dominant themes of local revenant belief, for his *Dialogue on Miracles* discusses many revenants. Caesarius, however, evinces a rather sanguine attitude toward the undead; they appear in the world of the living with no explanation other than their own volition. Consider the following narrative: A servant was supervising her master's children during a call of

---

31. *HRA*, 477.
32. WA, 1069.
33. Rudolf von Schlettstadt, *Historiae Memorabiles: Zur Dominikanerliteratur und Kulturgeschichte des 13. Jahrhunderts*, ed. E. Kleinschmidt (Cologne, 1974), 110–11.

nature at dusk. Suddenly she noticed a "monster" in the form of a woman with pallid face and tattered clothing emerge from a cemetery, stare at her over the fence, then enter the household next door. The apparition soon reentered its grave, but the entire family of neighbors perished soon thereafter.[34] In Caesarius's next tale, the emergence from a tomb of another dead "monster" in human form is a portent of impending death for the living as well: two canons who witnessed the event died soon thereafter.[35] More detail is given in a later exemplum that discusses the corporeal, but invulnerable, revenant of a wicked knight named Henry.

> After he had died . . . he used to appear to many people wearing the sheepskin that he wore when he was alive, and he especially frequented the home of his daughter. . . . He often was felled with a sword, but could not be wounded: he emitted a sound as if a soft bed were being hit.[36]

The terrified girl eventually rid her home of the revenant through an aspersion of holy water. Similarly, another dead man, this time a usurer, pounded on the door of his son, who wisely refused him entry; the corpse then hung on the door some snakes and toads—universally considered venomous within medieval thought—as proof of his evil intention.[37] In these examples, there is no indication of demonic intervention: the dead simply come back to life on their own and interact with the tangible world. Like the Icelandic *draugar*, they have three dimensions and material capabilities. Most importantly, they are presented as ill-intentioned from their own desires or instinct—not as animated by the devil for the downfall of the human race.

Revenants were known in Scotland as well. An anecdote from the thirteenth-century Scottish *Chronicle of Lanercost*, which has been attributed to an Augustinian monk,[38] also leaves aside the possibility of demonic animation of the corpse. Again, the protagonist is a man of the church who did not live up to his calling:

> There was a certain fellow wearing the garments of holy religion who lived wickedly and died most wretchedly, being bound by sentence of excommunication. . . . Long after his body had been buried it vexed many in the same monastery by appearing plainly in the shade of night.

---

34. CH, 2:313–14. The previous tale identifies this apparition as "Mors": Death embodied.
35. CH, 2:314.
36. CH, 2:327.
37. CH, 2:328.
38. James Wilson, "Authorship of the Chronicle of Lanercost," *Scottish Historical Review* 10 (1913): 138–55.

This child of darkness proceeded to the house of [a] knight in order to . . . terrify [the family] by molesting them in broad daylight. . . . Having then assumed a bodily shape (whether natural or aerial is uncertain, but it was hideous, gross, and tangible) he used to appear at noon-day in the dress of a black monk and settle on the highest parts of the dwellings or store houses. . . . He so savagely felled and battered those who attempted to struggle with him as well-nigh to shatter all their joints. . . . One evening . . . this malignant creature came into their midst, throwing them into confusion with missiles and blows.[39]

The revenant succeeded in killing the family's heir on this occasion, underlining its brutal and vengeful nature. Although the unknown chronicler does not inform the reader whether the creature was ever disposed of, it is plainly a corporeal revenant, with its "hideous, gross, and tangible" body. Moreover, the guiding force of the "malignant creature" is its own internal will. The author specifies that the corpse was permitted to wander by God, but there is no question of demonic possession or reanimation by anything other than the creature's own residual life-force.

Tales of revenants sometimes were compiled into groups, as in a Yorkshire collection of twelve revenant stories carefully assembled by a Cistercian monk of the Abbey of Byland and dating from about 1400.[40] These tales were written onto some empty folios of a manuscript of Cicero. The style is rather crude and at times obscure, and certain details of these stories are unique, without parallel attestations in other sources. Although the scribe used the Latin word *spiritus* ("spirit") to refer to the beings in his tales, they all plainly involve tangible bodies. In one anecdote, for example, a woman "caught" a spirit and unaccountably decided to carry it home on her back. An observer notes that "the woman's hands were sinking deeply into the spirit's flesh, as if the flesh of the spirit were putrid and not solid, but illusory."[41] This is an interesting contradiction: on the one hand, the being is a "spirit" and "illusory"; on the other, it can be caught and carried home, and it has flesh (for which two different words are used: *carne* and *caro*) that can become putrid. A case with parallels to William of Newburgh's *hundeprest* has the rector of Kerby leaving his grave at night and molesting his former

---

39. Joseph Stevenson, ed., *Chronicon de Lanercost MCCI – MCCCXLVI e codice Cottoniano nunc primum typis mandatum* (Edinburgh, 1839), 163–64.

40. The Latin text is edited in M. R. James, "Twelve Medieval Ghost-Stories," *English Historical Review* 37 (1922): 418. Jacqueline Simpson, "'The Rules of Folklore' in the Ghost Stories of M. R. James," *Folklore* 108 (1997): 9–18. On the foundation at Byland, see Burton, *Monastic Order in Yorkshire*.

41. James, "Twelve Medieval Ghost-Stories," 418.

concubine, until his corpse was disinterred and thrown, along with its coffin, into a local body of water.[42] One tale builds to a dramatic conclusion:

> Concerning the spirit of Robert, the son of Robert de Boltebo of Killebourne, who was caught in the cemetery: Robert junior died and was buried in the cemetery, but he used to go out from his grave at night and terrify and disturb the townspeople, and the dogs of the town used to follow him and howl mightily. Finally, some young men . . . decided to catch him somehow if they could, and they met at the cemetery. But when he appeared, they all fled except one named Robert Foxton, who grabbed him as he was going out from the cemetery and put him on the church-stile, while another shouted bravely, "Hold him until I can get there!" But the other answered, "Go quickly to the parish priest so that he can be conjured!" . . . Having been conjured in this way, he answered from the depths of his entrails; not with his tongue but as if from an empty jar, and he confessed various trespasses.[43]

There are several parallels here to earlier tales, especially those of William of Newburgh. Like William's first story, absolution of sins puts the revenant to rest; like some of William's other tales, the inquietude of the local dogs is a sign of the thing's malign nature. An interesting and unusual detail, however, is the discussion of the corpse's voice: although clearly endowed with a body that can be grasped and held, the revenant speaks, eerily, from its depths. Again, it is worth noting here that no outside agency, spiritual or otherwise, is posited as the cause of the corpse's wanderings: the dead man is sentient and comes back to life of his own fierce volition.

The Yorkshire region also is notable for the prominence of shape-shifting revenants among its returned dead. Many of the dead in these tales possess the capacity to turn into animal and even vegetable forms, in addition to their own human appearance. Such stories are relatively uncommon: they are found in Scandinavian culture but are not widespread on the Continent. Several tales in the collection of twelve mentioned above include elements of shape-shifting; the range of animals—and even of inanimate objects—represented is quite broad. In the first story, the deceased appeared at first in the form of a rearing horse, which quite terrified the wage laborer who encountered it on the road. The living man conjured the horse, in the name of Jesus Christ, not to harm him, whereupon the beast walked along peaceably by his side. After some time, however, the spirit changed form into a

---

42. Ibid.
43. Ibid.

haystack with a light shining from its middle. Only at the very end of the tale did the spirit take on the shape of a tangible man.[44] A later tale likewise features a dead man who appeared as a "pale horse," later changing into some form of fabric that twists and puffs.[45] Another case, dated to the reign of King Richard II (1377–99), includes quite a dizzying number of form shifts. The story's protagonist was a good-hearted tailor who goes by the charming name of Snowball. Snowball encountered a dead person who first took the form of an aggressive raven with sparks shooting from its wings. The bird was strong enough to knock the tailor from his horse, and Snowball was forced to defend himself with his sword. Later the dead man reappeared, this time as a dog with a collar or chain on its neck. Snowball, realizing that the raven and the dog were avatars of the same dead soul, conjured the animal to reveal its name and trespasses. Thus enjoined to speak, the dead man revealed that he had died excommunicate. At this point, though the text is unclear, it seems that the revenant had altered form again to appear as a glowing man, for the text notes that "he looked like a flame" and that Snowball could "see his insides through his mouth."[46] The deceased also mentioned that there were two other souls in the general vicinity, both very dangerous: one was in the form of either a fire or a thorn bush, while the other preferred to take the form of a hunter. At a subsequent meeting between Snowball and the dead man (after Snowball had helped alleviate his eternal condition), the revenant chose to appear first as a she-goat and then as an emaciated man. Again, during this conversation the dead man referred to other spirits that lingered nearby. A dead man who had killed a pregnant woman would wander the earth without recourse until Judgment Day as "a little ox, with no mouth and no eyes and no ears."[47] Another appeared as a hunter, continually blasting his horn. Similarly, the pair of peasant revenants from *The Miracles of Saint Modwenna*, mentioned above, often appeared as men, but sometimes "they bore the likeness now of bears, now of dogs, and likewise, now of other animals."[48]

The only other geographical area in which revenants were described as shape-shifters in the Middle Ages was the Icelandic and Scandinavian realms. *Eyrbyggja Saga*, to use only one example, describes the return of a dead soul as a seal that mysteriously rose through the packed-earth floor of a house. It threw the household into a panic until it was finally pounded back into

---

44. Ibid., 414.
45. Ibid., 419.
46. Ibid., 416.
47. Ibid., 417.
48. Geoffrey of Burton, *Life and Miracles of Saint Modwenna*, 194.

the earth by the young hero Kjartan, armed with a sledgehammer.[49] Later in the same work, Thorolf Twist-foot, after a long and troublesome career as a human-form *draugr*, returned yet again in the form of a bull that impregnated one of his farm's cows, which gave birth to a monstrous calf.[50] It is likely that the Yorkshire ghost material preserved, into late medieval popular culture, a belief that was imported into England centuries earlier via Viking culture, since Yorkshire had been the center of the Danelaw. What is more surprising, perhaps, is that the shape-shifting theme persisted from some of the earliest texts (the eleventh-century *Life and Miracles of Saint Modwenna*) to the latest (the collection of twelve ghost stories).

Portraying Revenants

Horror at the potential life of the corpse is also supported by a variety of nontextual evidence endemic to northern Europe. Two unusual illuminations from religious manuscripts are worthy of notice. First, sometime between 1325 and 1340 an eccentric illuminator working on a luxury Psalter for a wealthy family decided to portray a revenant vignette in the margins of the manuscript he was decorating. This unique image (figure 5.2), which appears on folio 108 recto of the *Lutrell Psalter*,[51] includes several details that are difficult to interpret.

The main portion of the image portrays a kneeling, nude revenant about to be decapitated by a living man wielding a broadsword. The living man places his left hand on the corpse's head to steady it and lifts the sword over his shoulder to gain more power for the coming stroke. The corpse is submissive and retains some personality and consciousness: it kneels, hands joined in prayer, and accepts the coming, second death. Unlike the living man, the revenant's skin is brown with degeneration, its eyes are blank and lack pupils, and its lips have decayed away to show the teeth. However, the cadaver is fresh enough that its skin is intact, and blood trickles from its toe- and fingernails, ears, and nostrils.

Thus far, the scene would appear to be a fairly straightforward portrayal of a revenant being immobilized by a living person: decapitation, as we have seen, was a standard technique for dealing with revenants. Yet there are some odd elements to the image that complicate this reading. First, and most

---

49. Hermann Pálsson and Edwards, *Eyrbyggja Saga*, 137.
50. Ibid., 156–60.
51. Michael Camille, *Mirror in Parchment: The Luttrell Psalter and the Making of Medieval England* (Chicago, 1998).

FIGURE 5.2. This puzzling marginal image appears to show a living man about to behead a kneeling revenant corpse. Beheading was a common way of dealing with the revenant dead. However, certain details—such as the revenant's halo and the figures in the clouds at right—are difficult to interpret. From the *Lutrell Psalter*, ca. 1325–40. British Library, London, MS Add. 42130, fol. 108r. Courtesy of the British Library Board.

unusually, the revenant has a halo, a detail that aligns it with the saints. It is possible that the halo here is (mis)used to convey a sense of the revenant's postmortem power: perhaps the illuminator perceived the halo as a means of emphasizing the consciousness and abilities of the corpse. Revenants, like relics, were powerful cadavers, a point to which I will return below. Second, to the right of the main pair of figures, a winged angel emerges from a cloud, carrying a small figure or human soul in a blue cloth. It is unclear whether this small personage is meant to portray the soul of the cadaver, though it seems noteworthy that its prayerful position mirrors that of the bodily revenant. It is likewise unclear whether the two sets of figures are meant to be read simultaneously (in which case the angel and the soul are witnesses to the death of the revenant) or sequentially (in which case, the angel may be whisking away a soul that has just been released from entrapment in an unquiet corpse). Lacking further information, the image cannot fully be decoded; it seems likely that it is based upon a specific story or anecdote that has not survived. The iconography does not wholly conform to any written account.

A later, 1533 illumination from the *Hours of Antoine le Bon*, Duke of Lorraine, shows a more typically aggressive revenant attacking a living man (figure 5.3). Like the image from the *Lutrell Psalter*, this image from across the channel presents difficulties of interpretation. The scene occupies a wide marginal border on the page that begins the Office of Vigils for the Dead; the central

FIGURE 5.3. This image appears in the margins of an illumination of the crucifixion. It shows a peasant carrying a corpse in a backpack-basket. However, the cadaver has become a revenant and appears to be vampirically sucking the life from the living man. The peasant's legs have begun to shrivel like those of a corpse. From the *Hours of Antoine le Bon*, 1533. Bibliothèque nationale de France, Paris, MS NAL 302, fol. 58r.
Courtesy of the Bibliothèque nationale de France.

image is of the crucifixion and redemption of sinners from hell. In the margin, amid blue, red, and gold foliate motifs, a peasant carries a corpse seated in a basket on his back, its lower legs hanging over the side. A large curlicue of foliage tickles the rustic's crotch, drawing attention to his sexuality and perhaps suggesting that he is a sinner. The peasant has been surprised by the sudden reanimation of the carcass he is transporting for unknown reasons (is he an undertaker? a grave robber?). The ribcage and upper body of the corpse stretch up over the man's right shoulder; its hands seize the man's head, twisting his face away from the viewer and pulling him in for a violent kiss. The peasant shrinks back in horror, shoulders and arms torqued left, away from the cadaver's embrace. But it is too late: already the peasant's legs have become shrunken and mummified. The image conveys the sense that the corpse literally is sucking the life out of the man, a vampiric exsufflation of his vitality from the toes upward. The peasant's desiccated lower half already has been emptied of life as he begins to mirror the corpse wrapped around himself; only his upper body remains full and muscular. Meanwhile, above, a large magpie picks at the remaining flesh of the cadaver's head. These birds, especially when seen singly rather than in groups, were considered evil omens in the Middle Ages, harbingers of death or misfortune. This perhaps stemmed from their "demonic" mimicry of human speech, a point that is emphasized in the bestiary tradition. Some legends of indeterminate age claim that the magpie was cursed because it was the only bird not to grieve the passing of Jesus on the cross.[52] Corvids of all kinds were associated with death and often are represented scavenging bodies in medieval art.

In addition to these two portrayals of individual revenants, paintings of groups of returned corpses were once abundant in the decor of cemeteries and churches in the north of Europe. I am referring here to the dance of death motif, the late medieval iconography in which grinning, half-decomposed corpses frenetically lead away a procession of human victims from all walks of life, and to the related theme of the three living and the three dead.[53]

---

52. I am indebted to Leigh Ann Craig, Annie Murphy, David Winter, and Susan Amussen for a productive online brainstorming session about this image.
53. On the dance of death motif, see Philippe Ariès, *The Hour of Our Death*, trans. Helen Weaver (New York, 1981); Emile Mâle, *Religious Art in France: The Late Middle Ages* (Princeton, NJ, 1986); Helmut Rosenfeld, *Der Mittelalterliche Totentanz: Entstehung-Entwicklung-Bedeutung*, 2nd ed. (Cologne, 1968); Wolfgang Stammler, *Die Totentänze des Mittelalters* (Münich, 1922); James Clark, *The Dance of Death in the Middle Ages and in the Renaissance* (Glasgow, 1950); Karl Künstle, *Die Legende der Drei Lebenden und der Drei Toten und der Totentanz nebst einem Exkurs über die Jakobslegende* (Freiburg im Breisgau, 1908); Leonard Kurtz, *The Dance of Death and the Macabre Spirit in European Literature* (Geneva, 1975); Florence Whyte, *The Dance of Death in Spain and Catalonia* (Baltimore, 1931); Ann Tukey Harrison, ed. *The Danse Macabre of Women: MS. fr. 995 of the Bibliothèque nationale* (Kent, OH,

FIGURE 5.4. The motif of the three living and the three dead was a common one in the later Middle Ages. The three cadavers shown here viscerally illustrate for the living their coming fate. Illumination from the *De Lisle Psalter*, ca. 1310. British Library, London, MS Arundel 83 II, fol. 127.
Courtesy of the British Library.

The latter theme made its way into French literature in the thirteenth century, and from thence spread into the realm of iconography during the fourteenth century.[54] The tale describes a pleasure party of three young persons who suddenly find themselves in a cemetery. There they are confronted by a group of three decaying corpses: the revenant dead are upright and animate, with their emaciated limbs showing through their tattered shrouds. The famous lines "What you are, we once were; what we are, you will become" derive from this tale, which was popular in vernacular and in Latin literature. Sometimes, it was accompanied by illuminations such as that in the *De Lisle Psalter*, ca. 1310 (figure 5.4), which is accompanied by a middle French poem describing an encounter between the living and the dead. By the fifteenth century, the story had been appropriated by clerical writers, who disseminated the tale as a meditative exemplum on the brevity of this life.[55]

1994); Jean Batany, "Une image en négatif du functionnalisme social: Les Danses Macabré," in *Dies Illa: Death in the Middle Ages*, ed. Jane Taylor (Liverpool, 1984), 15–28; Peter Walther, *Der Berliner Totentanz zu St. Marien* (Berlin, 1997); Elina Gertsman, *The Dance of Death in the Middle Ages: Image, Text, Performance* (Turnhout, 2010).

    54. Mâle, *Religious Art in France*, 324.
    55. Ibid., 328.

Although the *danse macabre* has sometimes been interpreted as derivative from the three living / three dead theme,[56] Emile Mâle sees its origins in literature reaching back earlier, in germinal form, to the twelfth-century work of the poet Hélinand.[57] Whatever its precise origins, by the opening of the fourteenth century the *danse macabre* existed in the form of a morality play, to be publicly performed with actors playing dead men in their winding sheets and taking the hands of the living from all walks of life.[58] Although debate exists about the earliest pictorial depictions of the dance of death,[59] the earliest fresco that can definitively be dated was painted in the Holy Innocents Cemetery in Paris in 1424, and indeed, the theme very commonly graced churchyards.[60] The theme rapidly spread throughout the whole of Europe. It is important to note that the *danse macabre* and three living / three dead motifs usually depict emaciated corpses, midway through the process of decay. This is especially the case in northern European art; in meridional regions, by contrast, one sometimes finds such depictions featuring "dry" skeletons, rather than enfleshed cadavers (see figure 5.7, below). Typically, in the north of Europe the artists portrayed skin stretched tautly over the bones of the figures' limbs but burst open over the entrails—an area of the body subject to early decomposition.[61]

A very clear example is figure 5.5, a portrayal of death personified, wrapped in a rotted shroud and looming over an enclosed graveyard with ossuary walls. The inscription on the image, from the *Hours of Marguerite de Coetivy*, reminds the viewer that all humanity must die and one's beloved body decay. The fleshliness of these images is a vital detail, for the dance of death and the three living / three dead motifs are iconographic counterpoints to revenant stories, intimately related to the same set of mental attitudes. Indeed, one tale from the group of twelve Yorkshire tales specifically notes that the revenant's appearance was "horrible and emaciated, along the lines of one of the paintings of the dead kings."[62] Just as recipients of miraculous healings often described dreaming of a saint and recognizing him because he looked just like his portrait on the walls of the local church, so too, those who met revenants mediated their experiences through public art. And, moving in

---

56. See Künstle, *Legende der Drei Lebenden*; Kurtz, *The Dance of Death and the Macabre Spirit*.
57. Mâle, *Religious Art in France*, 329; Batany, "Une image en négatif du functionnalisme social" discusses the poetic origins of the theme.
58. Mâle, *Religious Art in France*, 329–30.
59. Compare, for example, Clark, *Dance of Death*; Rosenfeld, *Der Mittelalterliche Totentanz*; and Mâle, *Religious Art in France*, for various chronologies and geographical emphases.
60. Mâle, *Religious Art in France*, 331.
61. Barber, *Vampires, Burial and Death*, 90.
62. James, "Twelve Medieval Ghost-Stories," 417.

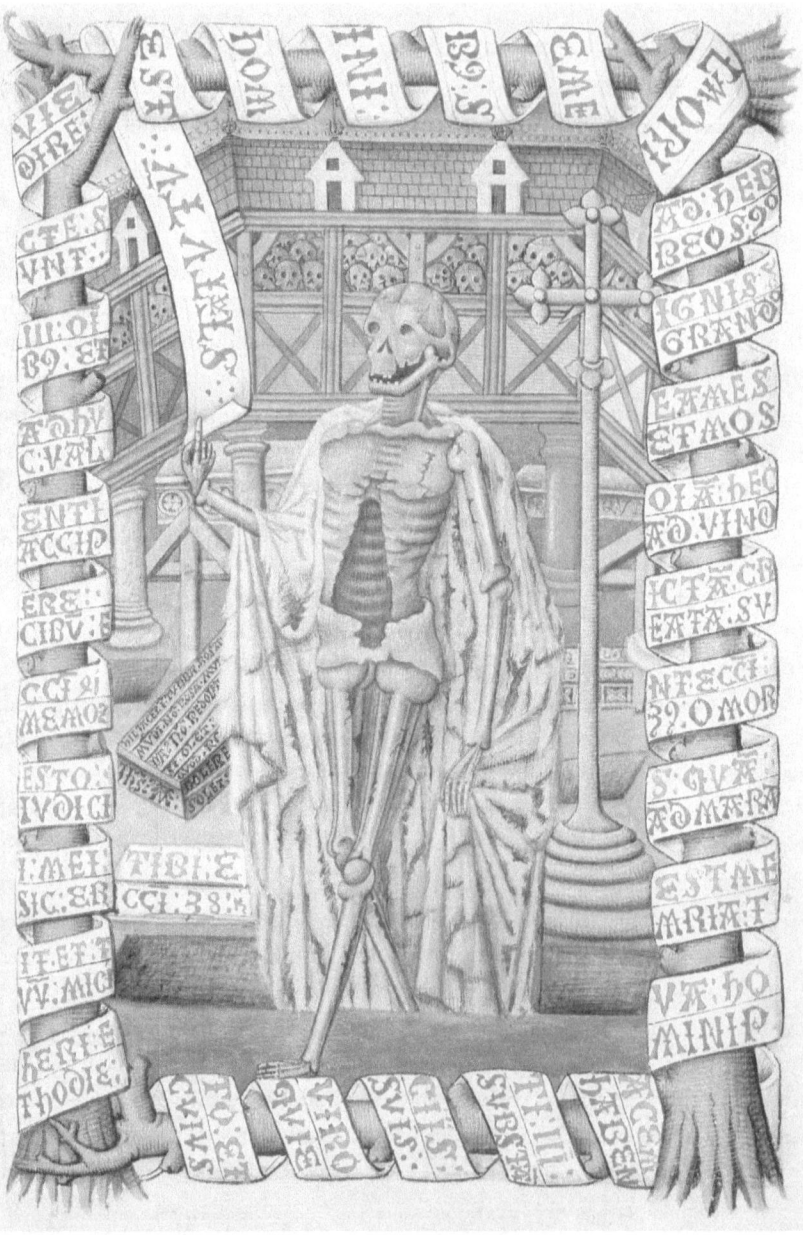

FIGURE 5.5. This cheery revenant stands at the forefront of an ossuary: the walls behind him are filled with skulls. The scrolls on the border of the image explain that it is the fate of all men to die, but only once. As was typical of medieval portrayals of the dead in northern Europe, the figure is enfleshed, rather than a skeleton. Illumination from the *Hours of Marguerite de Coetivy*, fifteenth century. Musée Condé, Chantilly, France, MS 74/1088, fol. 90.
Photo: Erich Lessing / Art Resource, NY.

the other direction, just as tales of the undead were reinterpreted by certain churchmen as useful proofs of the otherworld, the iconography of the dead, too, was appropriated by the church in order to convey a message of worldly transience and memento mori. Regardless of how these various representations were used and interpreted within ecclesiastical circles, however, the geographic coincidence of fleshly macabre iconography and tales about corpses coming back to life is striking. I shall return to this theme below.

Bad Deaths

These stories about singular revenants, though scattered chronologically from the mid-twelfth through the fifteenth centuries, geographically across the north of Europe, and textually throughout disparate authors and genres, nevertheless display a basic unity of form. William of Auvergne's reportage on the popular belief provides a useful starting place for deeper analysis: he claims to have heard "many times, about certain dead men who kill other men from among the living."[63] This brief comment may serve as the basis for teasing out some fundamental similarities among revenant tales.

First, William notes that he had heard of such events "many times." He was not alone in his observation. Although some authors classify such events as *prodigia* or *mirabilia*—terminology that suggests the extraordinary—others discuss the wanderings of the dead in a matter-of-fact, naturalistic way: "Robert junior died and was buried in the cemetery, but he used to go out from his grave at night";[64] "A certain man, whom they say died unhappily, used to wander about publicly in his hairshirt."[65] Although such appearances were terrifying to the populace, the writers' laconic tone suggests that revenants were not unique or unknown. Furthermore, several texts testify to the frequency, even the normalcy, of such events. As William of Newburgh writes,

> [These stories] would not easily be accepted as true if there were not so many examples from our own time, and if the testimony were not so abundant. . . . If I wanted to write about every incident of this sort . . . it would be too complicated and onerous.[66]

William of Malmesbury likewise suggests that belief in revenant dead was widespread among his contemporaries: "This nonsense and the like (it is

---

63. WA, 1069.
64. James, "Twelve Medieval Ghost-Stories," 418.
65. WM, 104.
66. *HRA*, 477.

believed, for example, that the corpse of a wicked man after death is possessed by a demon and walks) wins credit among the English from a sort of inborn credulity."[67] Clearly, belief in the return of certain dead people was widespread across northern Europe, a form of popular belief that descended from anterior pagan traditions about the wandering, corporeally embodied dead. These older traditions persisted into the medieval Christian world, shifting meaning over time to become a set of horror stories about the unruly, aggressive dead.

A corollary to this point, however, is the fact that not all the dead were believed to wander. Only "certain dead men," again to borrow William of Auvergne's formulation, left their tombs. How and why was a corpse believed to become a revenant?

There seem to be two related answers to this question: the manner of the individual's life and the manner of the individual's death. Indeed, these two factors can scarcely be extricated from one another. Caesarius of Heisterbach, for example, enumerates four different kinds of death: those who live well and die well, those who live well and die badly, those who live badly but die well, and those who both live and die badly.[68] Indeed, though not always explicitly articulated, the distinction between a "good" and a "bad" death was widespread throughout medieval society (as it is cross-culturally) and was thought to provide a vital clue to the soteriological fate of the deceased. Caesarius's fourfold set of categories, of course, is rooted in an antecedent we already have encountered: Isidore of Seville's *Etymologies*, with its discussions of bitter, untimely, and natural forms of death. The "good" death was the "tame" death:[69] it is ritualized, foreseeable, even welcomed. The concept also is alluded to in the proliferation, after the twelfth century, of liturgical images dedicated to Notre-Dame de la Bonne Mort in France, testifying to a cult of pious prayer for a good death, and it reached its fullest expression in the late medieval ritual *artes moriendi* manuals for "dying well."[70] By contrast, the "bad" death, as Caesarius explains, is sudden or violent; those who die badly are ripped too soon from this world and unprepared for the next.[71] While such persons still could be buried in the consecrated ground

---

67. William of Malmesbury, *Gesta Regum Anglorum*, ed. and trans. R. A. B. Mynors, R. M. Thomson, and M. Winterbottom, 2 vols. (Oxford, 1998–99), 1:196–97.
68. CH, 2:266.
69. Ariès, *The Hour of Our Death*, 5–92.
70. Roger Chartier, "Les arts de mourir, 1450–1600," *Annales E. S. C.* 31, no. 1 (1976): 51–75. Still valuable is Alberto Tenenti, *Il senso della morte e l'amore della vita nel Rinascimento (Francia e Italia)* (Turin, 1957).
71. CH, 2:267.

of a Christian cemetery if they had lived a righteous life, their corpses could not be taken into the church for the funerary service. William Durandus, in his *Rationale divinorum officium*, writes that the cadavers of those who died by violence could not be brought into the building, lest their blood drip down and pollute the space.[72] The cultural category of *mors improvisa*—a death that is sudden and unprepared-for—was intimately linked to survivors' fears of the dead's return. An untimely death was a bad death.

The significance of the individual's manner of life and death underpins nearly all medieval revenant tales. To wit, the undead most often are presented as having lived an evil life leading up to a bad end. To begin with the manner of life, from Caesarius we have the cases of a usurer and of a violent and dissolute man prone to every kind of criminal behavior. Map's dead Welshman is "evil." William of Newburgh discusses a wealthy man and a choleric and jealous husband, and both William of Newburgh and the anonymous Yorkshire collection of revenant tales include restless dead men who find repose through absolution of sins. The two revenant peasants described in *The Life and Miracles of Saint Modwenna* were runaways and troublemakers; so serious were their trespasses, in fact, that the image of Saint Modwenna herself was ritually humiliated as a result of dissensions that they had fostered. She struck them with sudden death soon thereafter.[73] Likewise, the Icelandic evidence emphasizes the unpleasant nature, in life, of those who become *draugar*, such as the surly and irreligious Glam or the violent Killer-Hrapp. Especially prone to revenancy in England and Scotland were secularized men of the church: William of Newburgh's *hundeprest* is a prime example, to which may be added the *Chronicle of Lanercost*'s "fellow wearing the garments of holy religion who lived most wickedly"[74] and the rector of Kerby mentioned in the Yorkshire collection of revenant stories. Such men of religion abdicated their sacred duties and became embroiled in pursuits that were properly the preserve of the laity: sex and violence.

Equally as important as these details of a sinful life, however, is the precise manner of the individual's death. Many stories specify the bad death of those who later become the undead: Walter Map explicitly notes in each of his cases that those involved died "unhappily." Similarly, both Thomas of Cantimpré and Rudolf of Schlettstadt give examples of killed or murdered men

---

72. *The Rationale divonorum officiorum of William Durand of Mende: A New Translation of the Prologue and Book One*, trans. Timothy M. Thibodeau (New York, 2007), 58.

73. Geoffrey of Burton, *Life and Miracles of Saint Modwenna*, 194. Patrick J. Geary, "Humiliation of Saints," in *Living with the Dead in the Middle Ages* (Ithaca, NY, 1994), 95–115.

74. Stevenson, *Chronicon de Lanercost*, 163.

as revenants. Such sudden deaths imply that the life force was cut off in midstream, before one's house was in order, so to speak. William of Newburgh tells of a jealous husband who, spying from the rafters upon his wife in bed with another man, became so enraged he fell to his death and later wandered from his grave. The revenant in the *Chronicle of Lanercost* not only lived wickedly but "died most wretchedly, being bound by sentence of excommunication." Similarly, those revenants whom we are told were put to rest through absolution of sins must not only have led improper moral lives, but apparently also died without proper confession. Related to the manner of death is the question of proper burial: it will be recalled that one of Walter Map's revenants was put to rest after a cross was placed to mark its grave. Within the Icelandic context, being lost at sea appears to have been considered an especially unfortunate death, as was death at the hands of a *draugr*: both these forms of dying commonly resulted in revenancy.

The underlying logic of the revenant belief, then, is that of a remaining life-force in the bodies of those who projected strong ill will or who died too suddenly, leaving "energy still unexpended," in Lester Little's felicitous phrase.[75] The bad death of a malicious person gave cause for fear that his cantankerous vitality might live on within the corpse itself: hence William of Auvergne's observation about popular belief that revenants "kill other men from among the living." This, as I have emphasized, was a common aspect of tales of the undead. Nearly all the singular revenants are represented as dangerous, terrorizing villages and bringing others to their own untimely demise. A death before the span of one's natural lifetime leads to aggression against the places and people of one's life. These revenants beat and smother the living, at times succeeding in killing them, or else they call the living to come and join them in the world of the dead. They are particularly apt to attack those with whom they had some sort of connection: family members, mistresses, denizens of the town in which they lived. The unruly packs of dogs that follow them about, howling, testify to their malign nature. This kind of motif made its way into artistic representations, which quite frequently portray the undead in acts of aggression against the living. We have already seen several such portrayals in earlier chapters; figure 5.6 provides yet another example. Here, a group of three blackened cadavers attacks some living folk out for a ride in the country, while dogs scurry underfoot.

Given this logic, it is not surprising that preventive measures against potential revenants may be discerned in some medieval practices related to

---

75. Lester Little, *Benedictine Maledictions: Liturgical Cursing in Romanesque France* (Ithaca, NY, 1994), 151.

FIGURE 5.6. Revenants often were portrayed as aggressive, as in this image of a revenant attack on three living people. The detail of the dogs underfoot also correlates with a common textual motif in stories about revenants. Illumination from the *Hours of Mary of Burgundy*. Flemish, Bruges-Ghent, ca. 1480. Kupferstichkabinett, Staatliche Museen, Berlin, Inv. 78 B 12, fol. 220v.
Photo: bpk, Berlin / Kupferstichkabinett, Staatliche Museen / Jörg P. Anders / Art Resource, NY.

disposal of the dead. Indeed, evidence for such apotropaic burial practices antedates many of the tales of revenants related above. The early eleventh-century penitential composed by Burchard of Worms, known as the *Corrector* and incorporated into the latter's *Decretum*, discusses many contemporary "superstitions," among them the course of action to be followed in the case of an untimely death. One entry describes the disposal of a baby that dies without baptism. The body of such a child was to be buried in an out-of-the-way place and transfixed through to the ground with a stake, or else "the little infant would rise up and injure many."[76] The subsequent section prescribes penance for those who bury stillborn infants and women who die in childbirth in like manner.[77] In such cases of bad or premature death, the body is disposed of in a location that places it outside the normal activities of the living. Moreover, the corpse is firmly held down by a stake placed through the body and into the earth, thus preventing it from wandering. Likewise, archaeologists of early Europe (especially Britain) have interpreted burials of decapitated men and women as likely aimed at the prevention of revenancy.[78] The suggestion of these scholars is that the wanderings of the dead were thought to be prevented when the connection between their senses (the head) and the source of their mobility (the torso) was severed. Another penitential, that of Bartholomew Iscanus, bishop of Exeter (1161–84), proscribes apotropaic rituals carried out upon a corpse or its clothing, "lest the dead take vengeance."[79] Such burial customs, though attested from pre-Christian times in the archaeological record, persisted into the late fifteenth century in some regions of northern Europe. The *Malleus Maleficarum* (*Hammer of Witches*) recounts a tale about a village so struck by sudden deaths it was in danger of total depopulation. A rumor began to circulate that the pestilence was due to a certain dead woman who was consuming her shroud in her tomb. After a consultation among the leading men of the town, her body was uncovered, and it was observed that she was, indeed, eating her winding sheet. The horrified mayor removed her head and threw it out from the grave, and the plague ceased.[80]

---

76. Burchard of Worms, *Decretum*, in *PL*, 140, col. 974.

77. Ibid., cols. 974–75.

78. An exhaustive recent study is Reynolds, *Anglo-Saxon Deviant Burial Customs*. See also Merrifield, *Archaology of Ritual and Magic*, 71–76; O'Brien, *Post-Roman Britain to Anglo-Saxon England*, 7–8, 54–55, 173–74; Williams, *Death and Memory in Early Medieval Britain*; Roberta Gilchrist, "Magic for the Dead? The Archaeology of Magic in Later Medieval Burials," *Medieval Archaeology* 52 (2008): 119–53.

79. John McNeill and Helena Gamer, trans., *Medieval Handbooks of Penance: A Translation of the Principal Libri Poenitentiales* (New York, 1990), 350.

80. Heinrich Kramer, *The Hammer of Witches: A Complete Translation of the Malleus Maleficarum*, I, q. 15, trans. Christopher MacKay (Cambridge, 2009), 237.

We know of alternative means of depriving the dangerous dead of local mobility as well. Suicides, for example, commonly were disposed of in rivers in the Middle Ages.[81] Denied burial in the common cemetery of the community, the bodies of these unfortunates instead were banished to parts unknown so that their corpses might not become revenants.[82] Nevertheless, a protective charm likely of tenth-century provenance includes a formula for safeguarding specifically against the returns of suicides and the unquiet dead: "expel every shade, every Satan, and all the diabolical plots of unclean spirits, whether of damned suicides or of wanderers."[83] Water not only was used to prevent the return of suicides, however, it seems to have been considered an important barrier within medieval thought about the dead more generally: rivers often are presented as liminal spaces between spiritual realms in visions of the afterlife and its denizens.[84] In one revenant tale, at least, the attack of the dead took place next to a river: the story of the knight Henry in the *Historiae Memorabiles*. Similarly, in the Yorkshire collection, the corpse of one revenant was disposed of in water, while another revenant that walked with a living man at night refused to continue when they came to a river.[85] Fear of revenants and their disposal in watery places may also help to explain the bog burials uncovered by archaeologists in northern Europe: these bodies were discovered pinned into peat bogs with thorns and stakes.[86] The treatment of such remains may be juxtaposed with the observation of the first-century Roman historian Tacitus that according to the justice system of the German tribes, "the coward, the shirker and the unnaturally vicious are drowned in miry swamps under a cover of wattled hurdles":[87] a special means of execution and bodily disposal for those convicted of living an evil life. In the twelfth century, such practices persisted. William of Malmesbury tells us that the unruly corpse of a certain Brihtwald was weighted down into a bog in order to prevent it from its frequent wandering.[88] The prime importance

---

81. Jean-Claude Schmitt, "Le suicide au Moyen Age," *Annales E.S.C.* 31, no. 1 (1976): 3–28.

82. The related issue of water as a barrier between the living and the dead cannot be discussed at length here. Perhaps related to this belief is the section in Burchard's *Corrector* that describes the practice of pouring water under the departing bier of a dead man: the water, even after its evaporation, forms a symbolic barrier preventing the corpse's return. Burchard of Worms, *Decretum*, cols. 964–65.

83. Auctor incertus, *Benedictio salis et aquae*, in *PL*, 138, col. 148b–c.

84. See Eileen Gardiner, ed., *Visions of Heaven and Hell before Dante* (New York, 1989); Peter Dinzelbacher, "Il ponte come luogo sacro nella realtà e nell'immaginario," in *Luoghi sacri e spazi della santità*, ed. Sofia Boesch Gajano and Lucetta Scaraffia (Turin, 1990), 51–60.

85. James, "Twelve Medieval Ghost-Stories," 413.

86. P. V. Glob, *The Bog People: Iron-Age Man Preserved*, trans. R. Bruce-Mitford (New York, 1969).

87. Tacitus, *Germania*, trans. H. Mattingly (Baltimore, 1954), 110.

88. *Willelmi Malmesbiriensis monachi de Gestis Pontificum Anglorum Libri Quinque*, ed. N. E. S. A. Hamilton, Rolls Series (London, 1870), 411–12.

of physically constraining the undead is provided in the following case from Caesarius of Heisterbach, wherein a corpse's transformation into a revenant is interrupted *in processu*:

> Concerning the Knight Everhard who sat up on his Bier: At that time in the same province died another knight named Everhard, and he was a wicked man. . . . In the middle of the night his corpse sat up on the bier and struck terror into all who were present. . . . After tying up the body, they buried it before mass.[89]

By hindering the body with bonds, the physical activities of a potential revenant (once again, a wicked man) are minimized. The corpse is then buried as soon as possible—even before the morning mass.

Flesh and Bone

The dangerous dead, then, usually were truculent folk who perished under violent circumstances. Moreover, a close reading of the sources suggests that the source of these corpses' vitality inheres specifically within the conjunction of flesh over bone. The fresher the cadaver, the more dangerous it is. This set of symbolic associations differs sharply from the concurrently emerging medical discourses discussed in chapter 2, which construed mortality as a singular event rather than as a long-term process. According to the medical view, the flesh was inherently inert in the absence of the animating spirit. This definition of life and death eventually came to be broadly disseminated, but the process was gradual. The worlds of the intelligentsia and of the common people only slowly converged toward the end of the medieval period.

A focus on fleshliness is found in many of the accounts of revenants. William of Newburgh, for example, places great emphasis upon the intactness of the cadavers that become revenants. In his tales, the bodies in question are all recently deceased, and they gush forth blood when wounded.[90] Moreover, the preferred remedy for revenants that William presents is cremation, a form of complete destruction of the vital flesh. (Presumably it would be difficult to re-kill a dead man by any means other than total bodily destruction.) In all William's cases, burning is the immediate solution suggested by the frightened townspeople.[91] Similarly, Thomas of Cantimpré in another

---

89. CH, 2:324.
90. This is not usually attributed to bloodsucking, although William of Newburgh refers to his last corpse as *sanguisuga*: HRA, 482.
91. HRA, 482.

passage from *Bonum Universale de Apibus* explicitly links the possibility of reanimation to the intactness of the corpse itself (though again with his characteristic demonic interpretation): "[The animation of a dead body by a demon] cannot be done for long, for the body is fluid by nature, and cannot be preserved in the necessary vigor without an enlivening spirit. The body corrupts swiftly when its humor slows down."[92] Here Thomas suggests that the body is dangerously potent, and apt to become reanimated, until the flesh is fully corrupted and destroyed. It must have "the necessary vigor," which is eliminated by putrefaction. Yet alongside his demonic interpretation may be discerned a basic connection between flesh and vitality. If we separate Thomas's interpretation of revenants as demonically possessed from the "cultural facts" he is reporting, we are left with the belief that cadavers are only in danger of becoming revenants before they "corrupt" and are reduced to bones. Similarly, William of Auvergne also stresses the importance of remaining flesh even as he refutes belief in revenants. His description of the revenant belief continues, "the bodies of those dead men, at the time when they seem to be doing this thing, either are lying *intact* in their graves, or at the very least their bones and the rest of their bodies, *which decay has not yet been able to consume*, are there."[93] Like Thomas, William implies that once the decomposition of a body was complete, it would no longer have been considered a potential revenant by those who held such beliefs. The question of a reanimated skeleton is moot: there must be flesh upon the bone.

The importance of the remaining flesh in iconographic representations of the living dead now takes on greater resonance: the revenants in the *danse macabre* and three living / three dead motifs are within the fleshly danger zone during which the undead may wander. If the flesh itself is vital, then the representation of these revenants as in the process of decay takes on an added significance. As we saw in chapter 2, putrefaction is, in fact, the sole irrefutable proof of physical death; all other signs of mortality are uncertain. The logic of popular belief extends this notion to an extreme conclusion: until putrefaction takes hold, there is a liminal period in which the death of the personality is absolute, but the death of the flesh is not complete. Psychic death and physical death do not coincide. It is only when the body has passed through its "wet" enfleshed stage and become "dry" bones (to borrow categories from anthropological studies of death)[94] that it is fully

---

92. Thomas of Cantimpré, *Bonum Universale de Apibus*, ii. 49. 7, 448.
93. WA, 1069. Emphasis added.
94. Maurice Bloch and Jonathan Parry, eds., *Death and the Regeneration of Life* (Cambridge, 1982). The related issue of secondary burial is discussed in Robert Hertz, "Contribution à une étude sur la

CHAPTER 5

defunct. Dichotomies between flesh and spirit, as well as between living and dead, are broken down.

Aside from burial practices specifically aimed at preventing revenants, other traditions surrounding disposal of the dead body also are characterized by a desire to avoid the flesh of the corpse as much as possible. This hints at a more general mental outlook of dismay at the freshly dead. From the twelfth century onward common funeral practice in the north of Europe insisted upon sewing the body into a shroud, then nailing it into a wooden coffin masked with cloth. If the identity of the deceased were to be revealed, it was through a wooden or wax effigy placed atop the coffin; the flesh itself must remain boxed up and concealed.[95] This practice has the double effect of constraining the flesh as much as possible and of replacing the "empty" physical identity of the corpse with the more acceptable neutrality of an artistic representation. Once the body were interred, it might well have a handful of the so-called flesh-eating soil of the Holy Innocents Cemetery in Paris added to the grave. This earth was highly prized for its supposed capacity to reduce a body to bare bones in nine days.[96] Finally, the institutionalization of secondary burial practices, through the use of ossuaries, was once widespread in northern Europe. The custom of disinterring the dead, after earth and time had consumed the flesh and left behind only a skeleton, and of then placing the anonymous bones on display, en masse, as a memento mori for the community is first attested in the 1100s in Western Europe. In the following century, synods at Münster and Cologne prescribed the construction of ossuaries for German churches, to serve as receptacles for bones that were disinterred from the small plots of consecrated earth in order to make way for new remains.[97] There, the disarticulated bones of the faithful patiently awaited the moment of their reintegration and resurrection. Time has left behind relatively few medieval examples.[98] One of the oldest medieval ossuaries that has been preserved to the modern day is located in Schorbach, Lorraine. The existence of a charnel house there is attested as early as 1136; its use continued until 1789. The current building is a small structure with

---

représentation collective de la mort," *Année Sociologique* 10 (1907): 48–137. For a study of the practice in a rather different context, see Katherine Verdery, *The Political Lives of Dead Bodies: Reburial and Postsocialist Change* (New York, 1999).

95. Ariès, *Hour of Our Death*, 127, 168–70.

96. Ibid., 58.

97. Caroline Walker Bynum, *The Resurrection of the Body in Western Christendom, 200–1330* (New York, 1995), 203–4.

98. Paul Koudounaris, *The Empire of Death: A Cultural History of Ossuaries and Charnel Houses* (London, 2011).

a narrow walkway behind an arcade of columns and arches; inside are heaps of bones piled high, now behind wire fencing.

Among the highest levels of the nobility a different, but equally interesting, set of new funeral practices also made their appearance around this time, as Elizabeth A. R. Brown and Agostino Paravacini Bagliani have shown.[99] The habit of immediately boiling or dismembering the body in order to extract the bones may likewise be seen within the context of desiring to pass the body through its dangerous fleshy stage as quickly as possible. The custom is best known in cases where an individual died overseas and the remains had to be transported back home for burial. So, for example, when King Henry I of England expired while overseas in Normandy in December 1135, his entrails, brains, and eyes were extracted and buried locally, while the remainder of his cadaver was cut up, salted, and wrapped in bulls' hides for transport back to England. Chroniclers describing this process comment on the sad pass to which the mortal remains of even the most exalted must arrive.[100] Yet the habit of separating the body into its constituent parts is widely attested in England, France, Germany, and the Low Countries even in cases where the person died in bed. Philip the Fair referred to the habit of dismembering the body for plural burial as "the practice of his ancestors."[101] Likewise, Boncompagno referred to boiling and dismemberment as the "German custom" for disposal of the body, while Saba Malaspina spoke of cleaning the bones as "ancestral custom in France."[102] Within European culture, such practices have been interpreted as a means of multiplying prayers for the dead by multiplying its places of burial, for it was customary for visitors to a religious establishment to offer a general prayer on behalf of all those buried there. However, boiling and dismembering might also be seen as the attempt to hasten the dissolution of the body, as a means to deprive the corpse of its individuality and so submerge it within the ancestral group, and also as a way of scattering the limbs so as to prevent the possibility of revenants. The total destruction of the flesh was the key to combating the potency of the dead body. Whether by natural decay or by human intervention, the flesh must be dissolved before the corpse would be perceived as truly defunct. By the end of the fifteenth

---

99. See Brown, "Death and the Human Body in the Later Middle Ages," for a discussion of these practices.

100. Henry Riley, trans., *The Annals of Roger of Hoveden, Comprising the History of England and of Other Countries of Europe from A.D. 732 to A.D. 1201*, 2 vols. (London, 1853), 1:226. A similar account also appears in William of Newburgh.

101. Brown, "Death and the Human Body in the Later Middle Ages," 254.

102. Cited ibid., 227 (Germany), 232 (France).

century, however, practices aimed at dissolving the body increasingly were being replaced by attempts to embalm and preserve it.[103]

Fragments of folklore also can help elaborate the notion of vitality as inherent in the material components of the body. Emphasis on the flesh that remains upon the bones as the source of life invites comparison with the mythic motif of the animal that is reenfleshed after having been eaten.[104] Here, too, themes of the dead coming back to life are linked to flesh and bone. The tale exists throughout Europe in both a saintly and a sinister version. It is told in a ninth-century hagiography of Saint Germanus, where the hero resurrected a calf after having eaten it by folding the bones into the skin and praying over it.[105] A variant of this type may also be found in Thomas of Cantimpré's *Bonum Universale de Apibus*, where an ox was killed in order to cure an ailing pregnant woman, and the abbot of a monastery secretly resurrected it.[106] In Snorri Sturluson's *Edda*, dating from the second half of the thirteenth century, the tale is told of Thor.[107] After eating two goats for dinner, Thor asked that the bones be collected and placed in the skins. However one legbone was damaged, for the marrow was eaten. When Thor hit the skins with his hammer, the animals received flesh and came back to life—but one limped. Interestingly, the identical topos is also present in some Italian witchcraft confessions of the fourteenth through early sixteenth centuries.[108] The beliefs described at the trial relate to the tradition of the "good things," the feminine branch of folklore that often was paired with the masculine ancient army motif. The witnesses explained to their interlocutors that they occasionally attended feasts in spirit, after which the bones of one of the oxen slain for dinner were placed in its skin and revivified by the lady, Madonna Oriente, who presided over the festivities. She used a magic twig to touch them and bring them back to life. If a bone were lost or broken, it could be replaced by a little piece of wood, which would serve

---

103. Patrice Georges, "Mourir c'est pourrir un peau . . . Techniques contre la corruption des cadavres à la fin du Moyen Age," in *Il Cadavere / The Corpse*, Micrologus 7 (Turnhout, 1999), 359–82.

104. Maurizio Bertolotti, "Le ossa e la pelle dei buoi: Un mito popolare tra agiografia e stregoneria," *Quaderni Storici* 14, no. 41 (1979): 470–99; Gábor Klaniczay, *The Uses of Supernatural Power: The Transformation of Popular Religion in Medieval and Early-Modern Europe* (Princeton, NJ, 1990), 129–50; Carlo Ginzburg, *Ecstacies: Deciphering the Witches' Sabbath* (New York, 1991).

105. The earliest hagiography does not mention the incident. See M. Bertolotti, "Le ossa e la pelle dei buoi," 478. The anecdote also is retold of Germanus in Jacobus de Voragine, *The Golden Legend*, trans. W. Ryan, 2 vols. (Princeton, NJ, 1993), 2:29.

106. Thomas of Cantimpré, *Bonum Universale de Apibus*, ii. 25. 5, 246–47.

107. The relevant passage is quoted, in Italian translation, in Bertolotti, "Le ossa e la pelle dei buoi," 480.

108. See Bertolotti, "Le ossa e la pelle dei buoi"; Ginzburg, *Ecstacies*; Klaniczay, *Uses of Supernatural Power*, 129–50.

just as well. Finally, one version of the tale involves a person rather than an animal. Burchard of Worms's *Corrector* censures the belief of some women that they can kill human beings, eat their flesh, and then place straw or wood under the skin and bring the person back to life.[109] The common substratum of these tales points to a long-standing, popular definition of animal vitality as located within the conjunction of flesh and bone (or their substitutive equivalents). The skeletal structure, overlaid with the material flesh, together form an animate body.

Similarly, a tension between two different definitions of life—material and spiritual—also is manifest in the medieval devotion to relics. Despite the protests of theologians that relics themselves were not animate or sentient— being mere matter left behind in the world while the soul of the saint dwelt in heaven—the widespread imputation of a powerful *virtus* to saints' relics parallels revenant beliefs rather closely.[110] In both cases, the local community's evaluation of the individual's manner of life and death is central to the definition of their bodies as powerful after death. Saints, like revenants, were likely to die before their time, through persecution or simple austerity, thus leaving energy still unexpended in their physical remains.[111] As is well known, the cult of the saints originated around veneration of the memories, and the corpses, of the martyrs, those with the power to endure fatal suffering in testimony to their faith. Occurring within the context of expectation of imminent Parousia prevalent within the primitive church, these deaths were regarded as charged with power, their relics as suffused with lingering life-force. Their triumph over death was not simply a triumph of suffering but literally of overcoming the inertia—both psychic and physical—of mortality. Indeed, throughout the medieval period, relics were kept in containers intended to highlight and exhibit the intactness of the body parts they contained. Thus, whole body relics were exposed to the faithful laid out on biers under iron grates; later, partial relics sometimes were placed under crystals

---

109. Burchard of Worms, *Decretum*, col. 973. Cf. Emma Wilby, "Burchard's *strigae*, the Witches' Sabbath, and Shamanistic Cannibalism in Early Modern Europe," *Magic, Ritual and Witchcraft* 8, no. 1 (2013): 18–49.

110. See Peter Brown, *Cult of the Saints: Its Rise and Function in Latin Christianity* (Chicago, 1981); André Vauchez, *Sainthood in the Later Middle Ages*, trans. Jean Birrell (Cambridge, 1997); Patrick Geary, *Furta Sacra: Thefts of Relics in the Central Middle Ages* (Princeton, NJ, 1990); Geary, *Living with the Dead in the Middle Ages*; Joan M. Petersen, "Dead or Alive? The Holy Man as Healer in East and West in the Late Sixth Century," *Journal of Medieval History* 9 (1983): 91–98; Robert Bartlett, *Why Can the Dead Do Such Great Things? Saints and Worshippers from the Martyrs to the Reformation* (Princeton, NJ, 2013).

111. Miri Rubin, "Choosing Death? Experiences of Martyrdom in Late Medieval Europe," in *Martyrs and Martyrologies*, ed. D. Wood (Oxford, 1993), 153–83.

surrounded by costly and elaborate gold-work. These methods guaranteed visual access to the powerful, undecayed cadaver that was the object of a devotee's veneration and pleas for healing. Canonization processes investigated claims of saintly incorruptibility, inquiring closely into the condition of the cadavers of potential candidates for sainthood. Preservation of the body could be a powerful indicator of postmortem power of a holy, as well as of a sinister, type. This persistent emphasis upon describing, displaying, and venerating relics' lack of decomposition suggests, yet again, a definition of vitality as connected to the flesh upon the bone. Relics thus may be seen as a special category of revenant: the blessed, rather than the damned and dangerous, undead. As noted above, this kind of parallelism may possibly explain the presence of a halo around the head of the revenant portrayed in the *Lutrell Psalter* (figure 5.2). Though this point is admittedly speculative, it may be that the detail was meant to express, in a visual shorthand, the continuing power of the corpse. Remaining flesh was an index of postmortem vitality for revenants and relics alike.[112]

These fragmentary bits of belief and custom may at first glance seem highly impressionistic. Yet they cohere around a core definition of the body itself as possessing vitality as long as the flesh remains intact. This material definition of life contrasts sharply with the medical-theological tradition, which defined the numinous element of the spirit-soul as the main element in the definition of life. In the local traditions of northern Europe, the life force was thought to be literally embodied, held within the flesh and bone, while in ecclesiastical doctrine the life force may be either embodied or not—depending upon whether it is in the "garment" of the flesh or awaiting the final resurrection. These differing viewpoints led to differing interpretations of reports of wandering corpses, as either the living dead or as possessed by demons.

The Dancing Dead: Fairies

Not every revenant was aggressive. Female revenants form an important exceptional group to these patterns. Apparitions of the individual, outcast dead overlap geographically with another macabre motif endemic to northern Europe: reports of the dead glimpsed dancing. Such tales are likewise

---

112. A process of discerning among the good and bad dead is suggested by the eighth-century *Indiculus Superstitionum et Paganiorum*, which notes the error, "They pretend to themselves that the dead of any kind are saints." *Capitularia Regum Francorum*, ed. Alfred Boretius and Viktor Krause, 2 vols., Monumenta Germaniae Historica (Hannover, 1883–97), 1:223, #25.

found in the British Isles and the northern parts of the Continent, in a similar pattern of dissemination. Rather than preying on the living, the dancing dead transfer their energies to a new community of fairies (or elves) dancing together in fairy rings.[113] There also is a gendered dimension to this differentiation: the dancing dead were usually (though not always) female. An anonymous English Franciscan of the fourteenth century described belief in such women thusly: "What shall we say of those superstitious and wretched men who say that, at night, they see the most beautiful queens and other girls dancing in time with Lady Diana, the goddess of the Pagans, leading them in a circle dance—women who in our vernacular are called 'elves'?"[114] Walter Map mentions such incidents twice in his *De nugis curialium*. In the first, a man buried his wife only to see her dancing in a ring shortly thereafter:

> A certain knight reverently buried his dead wife, then snatched her back from a ring dance. Afterward he had children and grandchildren with her, and the family survives to this day. Those who trace their origin to her have become a large group, and everyone calls them "children of the dead woman."[115]

Map's tone suggests an utter lack of surprise at someone finding a dead woman dancing in this way. The fact that the woman dies and that her husband then snatches her back from a fairy ring is presented as an entirely logical set of circumstances in no need of further explanation. Similarly Map's second tale also concerns intermarriage between the living and the dead. Here, we are told of a nobleman who "snatched the most beautiful of a group of women dancing at night," wed her, and had a son.[116] The end

---

113. Lewis Spence, *British Fairy Origins* (Wellingborough, 1981), especially 65–84; Claude Lecouteux, *Fées, sorcières et loups-garous au Moyen Âge: Histoire du double* (Paris, 1992); Emma Wilby, "The Witch's Familiar and the Fairy in Early Modern England and Scotland," *Folklore* 111, no. 2 (2000): 283–305; Éva Pócs, *Fairies and Witches at the Boundary of South-Eastern and Central Europe*, Folklore Fellows Communications 243 (Helsinki, 1989); Éva Pócs, *Between the Living and the Dead: A Perspective on Witches and Seers in the Early Modern Age* (Budapest, 1999); Elizabeth Barber, *The Dancing Goddesses: Folklore, Archaeology, and the Origins of European Dance* (New York, 2000); Emma Wilby, *Cunning Folk and Familiar Spirits: Shamanistic Visionary Traditions in Early Modern British Witchcraft and Magic* (Brighton, 2005); Alaric Hall, "Getting Shot of Elves: Healing, Witchcraft, and Fairies in the Scottish Witchcraft Trials," *Folklore* 116, no. 1 (2005): 19–36; Alan Bernstein, "The Ghostly Troop and the Battle over Death: William of Auvergne (d. 1249) Connects Christian, Old Norse, and Irish Views," in *Rethinking Ghosts in World Religions*, ed. Mu-Chou Poo (Leiden, 2009), 115–61; Laurent Guyénot, *La mort féerique: Anthropologie du merveilleux XIIe–XVe siècle* (Paris, 2011). A fascinating discussion of a modern case of fairy belief in Ireland is Angela Bourke, *The Burning of Bridget Cleary: A True Story* (New York, 1999).
114. Wenzel, *Fasciculus Morum*, 478–79.
115. WM, 8.
116. WM, 170.

of the anecdote explicitly notes that she had been abducted from among the dead, who were quite annoyed at his temerity. Female revenants, though rare among the individual, hostile variety of the undead, seem to have been common as fairy dancers. This may be related to women's relatively tenuous connections with violence: women did not lead the kinds of lives, nor die the kinds of death, associated with the evil undead.

It is unclear precisely how or why the transformation from dead woman to fairy was believed to come about, but a linkage between these two categories of being certainly is indicated by Map's descriptions. In Celtic tradition, the fairies or *sídh* (plural *sídhe*) were females with supernatural qualities who possessed an intricate, yet indirect, set of linkages with the dead.[117] As Map suggests, these fairies sometimes were identified with particular dead women; yet they also could rejoin the living and even give birth. Otherwise, they dwelt under the earth inside hills or mounds, which also were known as *sídhe* and which were culturally identified with ancient burial locations.[118] Belief in the fairy-dead also is attested in the English marvel writer Gervaise of Tilbury's *Otia Imperialia*, which likewise is a compilation of natural and human history, odd wonders, and offbeat anecdotes intended for courtly consumption. In a chapter titled "On Lamias and Nocturnal Larvas," Gervaise notes that "some men have become lovers of larvas of this kind, which they call fays. And when they have transferred their loyalties toward marriage with other women, they die."[119] The term "larva," of course, was a common word for a ghost or supernatural dead being, while "fay" is related to the modern "fairy" or "fée" in French.

Dead men also danced upon occasion, though more rarely. Thomas of Cantimpré mentions a dance of "demons" dressed as monks sighted near Cologne in 1258. Yet these figures could equally well have been interpreted as a group of the dead. As I have demonstrated above, the demonization of revenants is a characteristic trait of Thomas's *Bonum Universale de Apibus*.

> In the present year 1258 near the city of Cologne . . . a huge ring dance of demons in the garments of white monks was seen in the open part of the fields. With their voices lifted on high, they were dancing in time and joyously leaping. The people of the village gathered there along with the priest, but when they wanted to approach the dance, the demons edged toward a river the same distance that

---

117. Bernstein, "Ghostly Troop and the Battle over Death," 153.
118. Ibid.
119. GT, 730–31.

the men approached, until the whole malignant crowd disappeared into the river.[120]

The demonic explanation seems to be Thomas's refuge of first resort, but this tale was in all likelihood based upon a local belief in a sighting of revenants. Since Thomas did not give credence to the undead, he interpreted the boisterous dancers as demonic. For those who believed in the dead's return, however, there would be no reason to interpret these human figures in human dress as anything other than revenants: once again, the cultural facts of the tale differ from the collector's interpretation. There is nothing demonic in these dancers' aspect, and the fact that they escape the approach of the living by entering a river is suggestive. As I have noted above, rivers often were seen as boundaries between the realms of the living and the dead.

To these textual references on the dances of the dead must be added the *danse macabre* iconographic motif, wherein the bodies of the dead lead away the living in a dance. Figure 5.7 pairs the dance of death with the triumph of Death. Above, a personified and crowned Death triumphantly prevails over a heap of bodies filling a large sepulcher. Two decayed minions to his right and left shoot down more victims. A collection of great men kneels before him, offering their riches and power (symbolized by their crowns) if only they can be spared. Of more direct interest to the current topic of the dancing dead, however, is the frieze just below this tableau, which shows a series of dead figures emerging from a charnel house in order to lead off living folk from a variety of backgrounds. The latter group includes a beautiful lady, a penitent or flagellant in white, a young man with a mace, a farmer with a watering can, a jongleur with poulaines and a bagpipe, a merchant with a large purse, and a scholar with a book. The dead and the living are interspersed; all hold hands or interlink their arms. The coexistence of the living and the dead in one dance suggests some interesting connections, for not only did the dead dance in churchyards, but so too did the living dance, both in cemeteries and at vigils, wakes, or commemorations for the dead.[121] Indeed, such practices

---

120. Thomas of Cantimpré, *Bonum Universale de Apibus*, ii. 57. 42, 568. According to Frederic Tubach, *Index Exemplorum: A Handbook of Medieval Religious Tales* (Helsinki, 1969), the tale also appears in J. A. Herbert, ed., *Catalogue of Romances in the Department of Manuscripts in the British Museum*, 3 vols. (London, 1910), 575.

121. Louis Gougaud, "La danse dans les églises," *Revue d'Histoire Ecclésiastique* 15 (1914): 5–22, 229–43; Louis Backman, *Religious Dances in the Christian Church and in Popular Medicine* (London, 1952); Barber, *Dancing Goddesses*; Gertsman, *Dance of Death in the Middle Ages*, 51–75. A more popular treatment of ecstatic dance is Barbara Ehrenreich, *Dancing in the Streets: A History of Collective Joy* (New York, 2006).

FIGURE 5.7. This outdoor fresco combines two macabre motifs: the triumph of Death, above, and the dance of death, along the lower edge. At the top, a personified Death is shown as a crowned corpse flanked by two minions who shoot down the living; along the bottom, a series of personified Death figures leads away a variety of different kinds of living people. External wall of the Oratori dei Disciplini, Clusone, Italy. Fifteenth century.
Scala / Art Resource, NY.

have long genealogies. As early as the fourth century, Basil of Caesarea complained of women who "execute ring-dances in the churches of the martyrs and at their graves."[122] In the ninth century Hincmar of Rheims discussed the traditional one-year anniversary rites for the dead, which included feasting and *convivia* in which the dead were represented among the living by masked individuals.[123] Burchard of Worms in the early eleventh century instructed confessors to inquire, "Have you attended the vigils over the cadavers of the dead, wherein the bodies of Christians are guarded by a pagan ritual, and have you sung diabolical songs there and participated in dances?"[124] Thomas of Cantimpré mentioned identical practices in the thirteenth century, censuring the customary "games" played at vigils over the biers of the dead.[125]

---

122. Quoted in Backman, *Religious Dances*, 25.
123. "Quomodo in conviviis defunctorum aliarumve collectarum gerere se debeant." Hincmar of Rheims, *Capitularia Presbyteris Data*, xiv, in *PL*, 125, cols. 776–77. For more on masks and the dead, see Jean-Claude Schmitt, *Religione, folklore, e società nell'Occidente medievale* (Bari, 1988), 206–38.
124. Burchard of Worms, *Decretum*, col. 964.
125. Thomas of Cantimpré, *Bonum Universale de Apibus*, ii. 49. 23, 457–48.

By far the most detailed medieval description of the traditional ring dances held in cemeteries derives from the twelfth-century work of Gerald of Wales, whose *Journey through Wales* reads much like the diary of an anthropological expedition. Gerald describes the ecstatic dances he witnessed in the local cemetery thus:

> Here you may see men or girls, either in the church, in the cemetery, or in the ring dance that winds through the cemetery with songs, suddenly fall to the ground. At first they are led into an ecstasy and are subdued; then suddenly, as if swept into frenzy, they leap up. Then they mime, with hands and feet, in front of everyone, whatever actions they are accustomed to engage in improperly during feast days. You might see this one put his hand to the plough; another as if goading oxen. Each of them, as if to ease their work, emits traditional cries in a barbarous tone. You might see this one imitate a cobbler, that one, a tanner; or a girl, as if she were carrying a distaff, now pulling out the thread at length with her hands and arms, and then, when it is out, winding it back onto the spindle. One, as she walks, seems to work fiber to the loom; another sits as if all is ready and tosses a shuttle from side to side, from hand to hand, and with flourishes and rhythm, she seems to weave.[126]

This account is remarkable for its detail and sympathetic presentation. Gerald's description of miming, or theatrical elements, as central to the celebration also may be compared to Burchard of Worms's censure of dances held on feast days in front of the church (meaning, perhaps, in the cemetery?) that involved cross-dressing.[127] A century after Gerald, the Dominican Étienne de Bourbon was unable to contain his repugnance for dances in cemeteries, which scandalized him utterly. The dances appear often in his collection of exempla, along with appropriately scathing remarks and exhortations to abandon the custom. One tale tells of a church struck by lightning after a group of local young people "led ring dances the whole night long in the cemetery."[128]

Though clearly not all dances in cemeteries were directly concerned with the dead—cemeteries, as centrally located open spaces, would have been a natural ground for dances, as well as for games of all kinds—it is

---

126. Giraldus Cambrensis, *Itinerarium Kambriae*, ed. J. Dimock (London, 1868), 32–33.
127. Burchard, *Decretum*, col. 839.
128. Étienne de Bourbon, ed. A. Lecoy de la Marche, in *Anecdotes historiques, légendes et apologues tirés du recueil inédit d'Étienne de Bourbon* (Paris, 1877), 169.

likely that at least some such dances served as a ritual means of interacting with the dead.[129] Indeed, certain ring dances—most notably a "bridge" or "arch" dance, in which the circle of dancers threads itself under the clasped hands of one link—were closely associated with funerary rites or fertility cycles for precisely this reason: by dancing so, one symbolically crossed the border between life and death, guaranteeing fecundity for the living and harmony with the dead.[130] The connection between ring dancing, death, and renewal or fertility is certainly applicable to the following description of a ring dance from the thirteenth-century Scottish *Chronicle of Lanercost*:

> About this time, in Easter week, the parish priest of Inverkeithing, John, was preparing the profane rites of Priapus. Gathering together young girls from the village, he made them dance in circles in honor of Father Bacchus. When he had these females in a troop, then he himself, led by wantonness, headed up the dancers while holding aloft on a pole a representation of the human organs of reproduction at the head of the procession. Thus he was dancing to the beat and dancing like an acrobat while everyone looked on.[131]

To be sure, the entry is puzzling, and the strong disapproval of the narrator makes it difficult to discern the accuracy of the account or the motivations of the actors. Certainly the use of a phallic image, first at the head of the dancing group and later in the center of the ring the girls formed, clearly marks this dance as concerned with sexuality. Yet at the same time, the timing of the dance during Easter week is highly significant, indicating a symbolic concern with death—or, more precisely, with the *overcoming* of death or resurrection. Death and its transcendence through faith and fertility thus seem likely to have been the basis for the Inverkeithing dance. Here we may follow the intriguing suggestion of Penelope Doob, who has argued that ring dances were a traditional Easter week festivity in medieval France, often being performed by clergy and regular canons as a liturgical celebration of

---

129. Ibid., 168–69, 229–30, 398–99. See also J. T. Welter, ed., *La Tabula exemplorum secundum ordinem alphabeti: Recueil d'exempla compilé en France à la fin du XIIIe siècle* (Paris, 1926), 11; Wenzel, *Fasciculus Morum*, 444–45. For a close reading of one of these episodes, see Schmitt, *Religione, folklore, e società nell'Occidente medievale*, 98–123. On dances as ritual interaction with the dead, see Curt Sachs, *World History of the Dance* (New York, 1937), 251–53, 257–58; Gertsman, *Dance of Death in the Middle Ages*, 77–99.

130. Sachs, *World History of the Dance*, 162–63; Barber, *Dancing Goddesses*, makes this argument more broadly.

131. Stevenson, *Chronicle of Lanercost*, 177.

the Harrowing of Hell during this time of the year.[132] Doob notes that some cathedrals, such as Reims and Auxerre, are known to have scheduled such dances during the paschal season, using the labyrinths embedded in their pavements as a sort of map for the dancing ring. These events specifically celebrated Christ's triumph over death and retrieval of the just dead from the maw of hell.

Yet ring dances need not have been led by a priest holding aloft a phallic symbol in order to excite the ire of more sober-minded clerics. As the Middle Ages wore on, church councils continuously inveighed against dances on sacred burial precincts. In 1206, the Synod of Cahors declared dancing in churches or in the churchyard worthy of excommunication. Two years later, in 1208, Eudes de Sully, archbishop of Paris, forbade dances especially in three places: churches, processions, and cemeteries. In 1212 or 1213, the Council of Paris adopted this prohibition, singling out ring dances of women in churchyards. The year 1227 saw the Council of Trier forbid ring dancing and step dancing in the churchyard.[133] The Council of Rouen in 1231 forbade dances to be held in the cemetery, as did a 1279 council in Buda, Hungary, the Council of Wurzburg in 1298, and the Statutes of Tréguier in the late thirteenth or early fourteenth century.[134] The Rouen prohibition reappears in 1405.[135] In 1435, the Council of Basel referred to the "Feast of Fools, or of Innocents, or of Children" and the dances that were held on this occasion without shame "even in the cemetery."[136] These repeated condemnations suggest that ring dancing in cemeteries was a very widespread and deeply rooted custom indeed.

Thus there exist three bodies of evidence with thematic similarities: reports of dances of the dead; the dances of the living in cemeteries or in other funereal contexts; and the *danse macabre* motif, which includes both living and dead. Certain connections, though tenuous, may be made among them. The iconographic motif may represent in pictorial form the perceived coexistence of seen and unseen worlds. When the living held dances in cemeteries, might they have believed themselves to be dancing with the dead among them, as shown in the frescoes? A ring dance of the living upon a ring dance of the dead?

---

132. Penelope Doob, *The Idea of the Labyrinth: From Classical Antiquity through the Middle Ages* (Ithaca, NY, 1990), 123–28.
133. Backman, *Religious Dances*, 51.
134. For the foregoing, see Gougaud, "La danse dans les églises," 12–13; Backman, *Religious Dances*, 51.
135. Ariès, *Hour of Our Death*, 69.
136. Carol du Plessis d'Argentre, *Collectio Judiciorum*, 3 vols. (Paris, 1724), 1:231, 243–47.

There is some evidence to this effect. At Montserrat, for example, according to Florence Whyte, the local dances in the cemetery led directly to the painting of a dance of death fresco in the church. Monks at the Abbey of Montserrat patronized the *danse macabre* theme because of what they saw as its somber memento mori associations.[137] But mindfulness of mortality may mean different things within different semantic systems. The dance of the living with the dead, which was to the monks an indicator of the brevity of this life, may have been to others in Montserrat a celebration of the continuity of the living and the dead as one circular community. The ritual dance relates to the iconography in different ways when seen from different perspectives. Similarly, Elina Gertsman, in her exhaustive study of the dance of death motif, emphasizes its performative origins. Early literary works on the theme originate within the theatrical genre: there survive several dramatic scripts for such performances, in which the living would dance the dance of death.[138] Likewise, some of the painted versions of the motif seem to present scripts as well, in the form of text or scrolls accompanying the images, which imagine Death and his living victims conversing. Furthermore, there also is evidence of actual theatrical stagings of the motif. In 1393, the *danse macabre* was performed in Caudebec;[139] in 1449, the Franciscans of Besançon had such a dance performed in the Church of St. Jean. Gerald of Wales's description of the Welsh cemetery dance might also be interpreted as such an event: perhaps the activities mimed by the dancers among the graves represented the different professions and daily activities in which one might be engaged when death comes, just as the later *danse macabre* iconography pictorially represents this theme. Even though the *danse macabre* acquired a history and a meaning of its own within ecclesiastical traditions, it appears to have been based upon performative dramas, which in turn were appropriated from traditional dances with ritual overtones.

Thus traditional beliefs, ritual, and iconography overlap and trace upon one another a cultural map of the common activities of both living and dead. Some cemetery dances may well have served the apotropaic purpose of fixing revenants within their own social sphere lest they prowl among the living: dancing revenants do not appear to have been violent. By ritually transgressing the border of life and death, such practices might have been perceived as a

---

137. Whyte, *Dance of Death in Spain and Catalonia*, 45.

138. Gertsman, *Dance of Death in the Middle Ages*, 90–93; see also Mâle, *Religious Art in France*, 329–30.

139. Elina Gertsman, "Pleyinge and Peyntinge: Performing the Dance of Death," *Studies in Iconography* 27 (2006): 1.

way of strengthening the border itself. This would make dances of the living a form of sympathetic magic by which the dead were encouraged to remain within their own realm.[140] At the same time, they celebrate communal linkages between living and dead.

This chapter sought to unveil the inner logic of revenant beliefs as they persisted in the popular culture of a Christianized northern Europe. Such stories continued to circulate as tales about the returned dead, rather than as tales of demonic delusion, long after theologians and other intellectuals had begun to adopt the latter explanation. Rather, popular versions of these stories assumed that those who died a "bad death" would continue to retain some vitality in their corpses and that this vitality would remain there until the flesh decayed and the body was reduced to dry bone. Though on the one hand, this logic was in continuity with the pagan past, it may also have been reinforced by the cult of relics, which likewise were venerated as powerful, incorrupt cadavers. Such notions remained widespread in northern Europe until the very end of the Middle Ages, functioning within a wholly Christian culture and no longer perceived as formations with roots in a pagan past. The latter was but a vestigial trace, preserved in the genealogy of these tales but no longer expressed as such. In the early modern period, such concepts eventually fused with central European traditions in order to form the notion of the blood-sucking vampire, who maintains postmortem vitality by draining the life force of others. The living dead continued to be preserved in European culture, even as the precise form and meaning of the motif shifted over time.

---

140. Rosenfeld, *Der Mittlealterliche Totentanz*, pp. 298–99, interprets the dance of death iconography as serving the apotropaic purpose of warding off plague.

❦ Part Three

The Disembodied Dead

Part 3 turns to the south of Europe, examining regional cultures in the meridional sphere. This area tended to envision the returned dead as disembodied shades, rather than as corporeal revenants. Geographically, the two chapters that follow are centered on the southern part of France, from the Pyrenees to the Alps, and on the Italian peninsula and Portugal. Some motifs found in this section overlap with traditions we already have encountered for northern Europe, yet we also will detect some significant divergences and new elements. Like northern European revenants, the unquiet dead of the Mediterranean usually were those who died untimely. However, here the dead were presumed to be purely spiritual presences that moved invisibly and anonymously among the living, revealing themselves only to a privileged few. Like revenants, these ghosts sometimes haunted churches, but they also frequented the bedchambers of their loved ones, awakening them at night in order to ask for boons and to relay accounts of the afterlife. Lastly, like revenants, the ghosts of the south could be harmful and aggressive, but their attacks were spiritual rather than physical in nature. In particular, they were feared as spirits that might possess the bodies of the living.

These differences in the collective representation of the dead should not be surprising, for the cultural history of this region was distinct from that of northern Europe in important ways. The ancient histories of Italy, southern France, and Portugal were marked by the strong influence of Roman paganism, yet all were Christianized relatively early in the process of church expansion. Rome and the Italian peninsula had small pockets of Christian converts very soon after the death of Jesus, as documented by the historian Tacitus. As for southern France and Portugal, between the second and the first century BCE both areas fell under Roman control and became provinces of the empire: Gallia Narbonensis (current-day southern France) and Lusitania (modern-day Portugal). This political situation led to the importation of classical Roman paganism to these regions; the indigenous, druidic religion of the Celts (about which we know very little) slowly disappeared. As Christianity grew within the Roman Empire in succeeding centuries, it too was exported across the Alps to the provinces through Roman networks of trade, administration, and settlement. In the fourth and fifth centuries CE, Germanic tribal peoples migrated through France and Iberia in large numbers, bringing with them Teutonic pagan forms and setting up independent kingdoms of their own.

As a result of this cultural intermingling, regional attitudes toward the dead were complex and sometimes contradictory. The dead tended to be conceived as invisible presences detectable only by a select few, a tradition that has continuities with Roman pagan modes of thought; yet at the same time they were also described as having some material capabilities, an element that may be due to Germanic influence. It is not my goal to suggest a specific genealogy for each and every element in the regional imagining of the dead, however; only a few such connections may reliably be traced. Rather, the two chapters that follow simply strive to show two different faces of the dead's interactions with the living in the twelfth through the fourteenth centuries in southern Europe. Chapter 6, "Psychopomps, Oracles, and Spirit Mediums," focuses chiefly on southern France, analyzing several spiritist cults that formed around individuals who claimed to be in regular contact with the dead. These spirit mediums, though at first taken aback when the dead began to appear to them, ultimately learned to control their interactions with the latter. They became voluntary oracles who opened up the world of the afterlife to crowds of other people, and they acted as psychopomps for the dead, helping them to find rest in the afterlife. Clerics, of course, also evaluated local popular beliefs according to their own religious values, sometimes condemning mediums as heretics, at other times arrogating oracular roles to themselves. The seventh and last chapter, "Spectral Possession," focuses upon a more involuntary and hostile form of interaction with shades of the dead: spirit possession. In Italy and Portugal dead human spirits sometimes were suspected of seizing the bodies of the living for themselves. Belief in ghostly possession was an ancient idea, one that may confidently be traced to classical

Roman paganism. In the form in which it is encountered in Italy and Portugal, however, it appears to have coexisted with the Christian teaching that demons possessed the dead. Thus Christian notions of spirit possession did not replace, but were merely added to, earlier ideas. The possessing shades of the dead use the bodies they seize to articulate their own postmortem needs. By setting aright business left unfinished in life, they are enabled to find peace in the otherworld.

The two chapters present complementary cultural forms in many ways. In both cases, the disembodied dead use the living to assert their own needs and to reveal information about the next world. In southern France, however, interactions with the dead were regarded as predominantly amicable and controllable, whereas in Italy and Portugal, the dead aggressively stole the bodies of others and in consequence were perceived as hostile forces. As a pair, these chapters unveil a regional way of thinking about the dead that was distinct from the imaginative formations of northern Europe.

Chapter 6

Psychopomps, Oracles, and Spirit Mediums

Cluny and the Mountain of the Dead

Let us begin with a myth of origins, one that returns us to the early eleventh century. As Thietmar of Merseburg was writing of resurrection and revenants in the northeastern marches of Germany, farther south, in the Auvergne region of France, the dead were at the top of the agenda of the monastery of Cluny. A charismatic abbot, Odilo, had become head of the foundation in 998, and it was he who brought the dead to the forefront of the institution's prayers and thoughts. By 1030, under his abbacy, Cluny had introduced wholly new ways of thinking about relationships between the living and the dead. This story is the ratifying text for Cluny's arrogation of control over the afterlife; the speaker is a Sicilian hermit and his audience a group of shipwrecked monks:

> I beg you: Remember what you are about to hear!
> There are places nearby that by the manifest will of God spew forth scorching flames most violently. There, the souls of sinners undergo sufferings for varying periods of time. A multitude of demons is assigned to renew their torments continually, day after day. . . .
> The souls of these condemned ones often are freed from torment, through God's mercy, because of the prayers of the religious and the alms that are given to the poor in holy places. Know that in their great

laments, the dead mention in particular the monastery of Cluny and its abbot among other things. For this reason, by God I beg you . . . let this congregation know everything you have heard from me, and exhort them to multiply their prayers, their vigils, and their alms, for the release [of these souls] as much as they can.[1]

The story returns us yet again to a familiar theme: that of the mountain inhabited by the dead. In this instance, however, the mountain is filled neither with feasting warriors, as in the Icelandic sagas, nor with men and women marrying and having families, as reported by the ghost Reyneke. There is no society of fauns celebrating a wedding, as Walter Map's King Herla experienced, nor is it the location for King Arthur's court, as Caesarius of Heisterbach imagined the interior of the very same mountain. The volcano is not a Christian hell, as Gregory the Great described Etna centuries earlier. Rather, this time the mountain is purgatory avant la lettre: an afterlife destination for sinners in torment, but who may yet be saved by offerings of Cluniac prayers.[2] Though many earlier sources testify to the long-term development of interest in a third, intermediate afterlife place, this story appears to be the earliest one to syncretize the monastic impulse concerned with the alleviation of postmortem torment via suffrages with the motif of mountains as afterlife places from which the dead attempt to reach the living.

Thus, an originally pagan motif about the dead living inside mountains here becomes a visionary warrant for the latest Christian innovations in thanatological doctrine. This new paradigm taught that the condition of one's deceased ancestors could most productively be improved by formal religious specialists, that the means of assisting the dead functioned like an economy, with regular rules of exchange and benefit, and that the best means of guaranteeing postmortem assistance for oneself or one's family was to be inscribed in a monastic necrology, most particularly that of Cluny. In return for economic support for the foundation, one's ancestors could be included in the great, commemorative list of departed souls for whom Cluny's monks prayed.[3] Other monasteries swiftly followed suit as Cluny spearheaded an

---

1. Jotsald, *Vita Sancti Odilonis*, in *PL*, 142, cols. 926–27. Cf. Johannes Staub, ed., *Studien zu Iotsalds Vita des Abtes Odilo von Cluny* (Hannover, 1999).
2. Jacques Le Goff, *The Birth of Purgatory*, trans. Arthur Goldhammer (Chicago, 1984); Jean-Claude Schmitt, *Ghosts in the Middle Ages: The Living and the Dead in Medieval Society* (Chicago, 1998), ch. 3; Megan McLaughlin, *Consorting with Saints: Prayer for the Dead in Early Medieval France* (Ithaca, NY, 1994); Michael E. Hoenicke Moore, "Demons and the Battle for Souls at Cluny," *Studies in Religion / Sciences Religieuses* 32, no. 4 (2003): 485–97; Isabel Moreira, *Heaven's Purge: Purgatory in Late Antiquity* (Oxford, 2010).
3. Dominique Iogna-Prat, "The Dead in the Celestial Bookkeeping of the Cluniac Monks around the Year 1000," in *Debating the Middle Ages: Issues and Readings*, ed. Lester Little and Barbara

important new feast day and liturgical remembrance for the Christian world: the feast of All Souls' Day on November 2. In sum, the tale of the hermit gesturing to the fires of Mount Etna is, in essence, an apologia for Cluny's institution of a formal monastic cult of the dead. Yet as we shall see, this appropriation of control over the dead was not without controversy.

The notion that monks should take charge of the dead and merit economic support from the living for so doing was a sharp departure from earlier norms. The Cluniac system of tariffed spiritual profits, or "celestial bookkeeping,"[4] was far more formalized than private offerings of alms or lay prayer on behalf of the dead. Both of these had long been customary.[5] At the same time, the "third place"—the afterlife destination that would come to be named purgatory—was evolving into an increasingly bureaucratized antecedent to paradise. Intercessions and inscriptions into necrologies were being transformed from spontaneous acts of piety to an expected and necessary charity for the dead, underwritten by their survivors.

Cluny and her abbots assiduously cultivated a reputation as specialists with regard to the dead.[6] A century after Odilo another activist abbot, Peter the Venerable, continued to align Cluny's interests with the postmortem world throughout his abbacy from 1122 to 1156. Peter's *Two Books of Miracles*, a compilation of edifying tales, contains many examples of the dead appearing to the living in order to request masses and other suffrages, then returning at a later time to demonstrate their relief. Indeed, Peter writes that visions of the dead were *the* characteristic miracle of his time.[7] The effectiveness

---

Rosenwein (Oxford, 1998), 340–62; Frederick Paxton, with the collaboration of Isabelle Cochelin, *The Death Ritual at Cluny in the Central Middle Ages / Le ritual de la mort à Cluny au moyen âge central* (Turnhout, 2013). See also Dominique Iogna-Prat, *Order and Exclusion: Cluny and Christendom Face Heresy, Judaism and Islam (1000–1150)* (Ithaca, NY, 2003); Georges Duby, *La société aux XIe et XIIe siècles dans la région mâconnaise* (Paris, 1971); Jacques Chiffoleau, *La comptabilité de l'au-delà: Les hommes, la mort, et la région d'Avignon à la fin du Moyen Âge (vers 1320 – vers 1480)* (Rome, 1980); Barbara Rosenwein, *To Be the Neighbor of Saint Peter: The Social Meaning of Cluny's Property, 909–1049* (Ithaca, NY, 1989). On monastic commemoration, see Pierre-Marie Gy, "La liturgie de la mort," Jean-Loup Lemaitre, "La commemoration des défunts à Saint-Pons de Thomières," and Daniel Picard, "Les suffrages prescrits pour les défunts par les chapitres provinciaux des dominicains du Midi," all in *La mort et l'au-delà en France méridionale (XIIe–XVe siècle)*, Cahiers de Fanjeaux 33 (Toulouse, 1998), 65–75, 77–102, and 103–120 respectively; Michel Lauwers, *La mémoire des ancêtres, le souci des morts: Morts, rites, et société au Moyen Âge (Diocese de Liège, XIe–XIIIe siècles)* (Paris, 1996); Scott Bruce and Christopher Jones, eds. and trans., *The Relatio metrica de duobus ducibus: A Twelfth-Century Cluniac Poem on Prayer for the Dead*. I thank Dr. Bruce for sharing with me this work in progress, which is currently under review for publication.

4. The phrase is borrowed from Iogna-Prat, "The Dead in Celestial Bookkeeping."
5. Peter Brown, *The Ransom of the Soul: Afterlife and Wealth in Early Christianity* (Cambridge, MA, 2015).
6. Iogna-Prat, *Order and Exclusion*, 219–52.
7. Petrus Venerabilis, *De miraculis libri duo*, in *PL*, 189, col. 871.

of monastic prayers and suffrages in these tales is one of the chief messages of Peter's collection. As was typically the case with medieval exempla stories and miracle accounts, Peter drew from many sources for his tales. One inspiration, of course, was prior tradition: the *Dialogues* of Gregory the Great provided an obvious precedent for Peter's form and content. As well, Peter looked to locally sourced oral accounts for his stories, taking gossip he had heard about ghosts and shaping it to the moral lessons he wished to convey.

Peter's miracle stories simultaneously exalt Cluny, promote the tripartite afterlife structure that was then making its way toward Christian doctrine, and posit the singular role of monks' intercessory prayers within the penitential system that linked this world and the next. Thus in one tale the deceased abbot of a different monastic foundation appeared to the monks of Cluny in order to beg for their highly effective masses;[8] in another, a rapacious local noble who had terrorized Cluny's lands in life returned by special dispensation in order to ask the abbot of Cluny to forgive his sins and offer suffrages for his soul.[9] There are tales of dead monks holding a postmortem chapter meeting in the cemetery of Cluny,[10] and another that involves the ancient army of the dead, with a deceased knight begging for prayers from the Cluniac brothers.[11]

However, the monasteries' new role as mediators for the dead was not uniformly endorsed. Those who hesitated to accept the new teachings were categorized as heretics by monks and clergy and accused of promulgating new and unheard-of ideas. And yet, as R. I. Moore persuasively has argued, such accusations often inverted the true character of ongoing cultural shifts: the "crime" of many dissenters was in fact to fail to keep pace with novelties that were pioneered by church institutions, rather than the reverse.

> While the heretic was always accused of innovation, the greatest source of religious novelty in this period was the Church itself.... Those who denied the necessity of infant baptism, or the sanctification of matrimony, or intercession for souls in Purgatory ... were not rebelling against the ancestral patterns of faith and practice.... These were innovations in the daily life of the faithful.[12]

Rejection of monastic necrologies and suffrages was actually continuity with ancient custom, which traditionally left intervention on behalf of the dead

---

8. Ibid., cols. 873–74.
9. Ibid., cols. 874–75.
10. Ibid., cols. 941–43.
11. Ibid., cols. 891–94.
12. R. I. Moore, *The Formation of a Persecuting Society: Power and Deviance in Western Europe, 950–1250* (Oxford, 1987), 71.

to surviving family, to be dealt with in a secular manner. Peter the Venerable seems to acknowledge this, albeit indirectly, when he complains in a letter about good Catholics—people who were otherwise faithful in all respects—who erred solely by rejecting the need for monastic suffrages on behalf of the departed.[13]

The Cluniac-led shift in the conceptualization of mediation for the dead provides a useful point of entry into an exploration of the regional context for this chapter, which chiefly is centered in southern France. The debate about death and afterlife was quite vigorous here in the central and late Middle Ages. Indeed, it is noteworthy that many local dissenting religious movements—the teachings of Peter of Bruys and Henri of Lausanne, for example, as well as those attributed to Cathar *parfaits*, Waldensians, Passagians, Spiritual Franciscans, and Beguines—specifically fostered skepticism toward the latest church teachings about death and afterlife.[14] In Moore's terms, however, they might simply be seen as clinging to more traditional models of the afterlife, which rendered them skeptical about the existence of purgatory, the effectiveness of postmortem suffrages, and the need for cash endowments to monasteries on behalf of the dead. Dissent ranged on a spectrum. Some believed almsgiving and other acts of charity on behalf of the dead could be equally as helpful to the departed as masses, thus subtly undermining the pre-eminence of monastic suffrages. Others suggested that nothing could help the dead at all: if condemned to a punishment, the status of the dead could not be alleviated by the actions of the living.

We encounter these and other skeptical attitudes with great frequency in a series of inquisitorial trials held in the Midi of southern France in the fourteenth century. At one point in the questioning of a certain Raymond of Saint-Foy, for example, the following exchange occurs:

> He was asked: "Are the masses, prayers, and alms that are given on behalf of the dead profitable in any way?"—"I believe that if the person is in paradise, then they don't help at all; and it's the same thing if the person is in hell. So, they do not profit anyone, whether they are in heaven or in hell. I think they only are useful for the living. . . . I don't know of any passage of scripture that mentions purgatory. I want to

---

13. Petrus Venerabilis, *Contra Petrobrusianos Hereticos Epistola*, nos. 146–47, ed. J. Fearns, Corpus Christianorum, Continuatio Mediaevalis 10 (Turnhout, 1968).

14. Huguette Taviani-Carozzi, "La mort et l'hérésie: Des hérétiques de l'An Mil à Pierre de Bruis et à Henri, dit de Lausanne," and Jacques Paul, "Des fins dernièrs dans les doctrines cathares," both in *La mort et l'au-delà en France méridionale*, 121–58 and 159–96, respectively; J. N. Garvin and J. A. Corbett, eds., *Summa contra Haereticos: Ascribed to Praepositinus of Cremona* (Notre Dame, IN, 1958), 185–212.

know how the soul could do any useful penitence in the next world, without being united to a body!"[15]

Raymond ultimately was convicted of being a Waldensian, but it seems that his reasons for doubt stem from his own thoughtful considerations of what actions a disembodied soul might be able to accomplish. Indeed, he sounds rather Augustinian! Likewise, a defendant named Guillaume Fort, who was convicted of having Cathar sympathies, rejected the doctrine of resurrection on starkly empiricist grounds:

> He was asked whether he believed in the resurrection of human bodies after death? He answered that, even though he had heard this preached in church, nevertheless he never was able to believe it. For he had seen for himself how the human body decayed and returned to the earth. Therefore he couldn't believe then, nor does he believe now, that a body that had decayed like that could ever rise up again.[16]

Such testimony not only provides evidence of materialism and skepticism, it also gives rare glimpses into the thought processes and rationales behind individuals' rejection of certain doctrines. In nearly all cases, the witnesses held considered opinions, arrived at after weighing the evidence of sensory experience against the teachings of the church. They did not blindly accept the doctrines of preachers, whether orthodox or heretical; rather, they engaged with the content of these teachings and tested them against their own observations and logic. In some cases, this skeptical spirit led to outright denial of the soul and afterlife. A peasant woman named Guillemette Benet fits this pattern. A neighbor testified that once, when she was chatting with Guillemette,

> they began to talk about the dead and about the souls of dead people, and Guillemette said, *Arma—arma! Yeu no veg reissyr dels homes ni de las femmes can se moro! Que si yeu ne vis ysshir s'alma o cal que altra causa, yeu sabrera que aquelo fos anima. Mays ara non veg reisshir et per aquo nom se que ses aquela anima.* [Soul, Shmoul! I don't see anything come out of men or women when they die! If I saw the soul or something else issue forth then I would know that there was a soul. But so far, I have never seen anything come out, so I do not know what this "soul" is.][17]

---

15. JF, 1:42.
16. JF, 1:447.
17. JF, 1:261.

In an unusual move, the notary preserved the witness's report of Guillemette's speech in the original vernacular Occitan, perhaps indicating a particular sense of interest, shock, or puzzlement at this committed expression of skepticism. Again, Guillemette arrived at her disdainful conclusion entirely on her own: like the others, she does not invoke any authorities other than the evidence of her senses and her own logical deductions. If the soul were truly the basis of life and afterlife, then it should be visible leaving the body at death; since Guillemette had never observed this, she deduced that the soul must not exist. (Interestingly, her argument about looking for the soul to exit the body precisely replicates that of the skeptical Peter in Gregory the Great's *Dialogue on Miracles*.) Aside from illiterate peasant women, however, even some literate folk could have doubts about the afterlife. Amiel de Rieux, vicar of Unac, confessed that he had believed that the souls of the dead would not resurrect to regain their bodies for all eternity, based on his pondering of 1 Corinthians 15:50: "This I say to you, brothers: just as flesh and blood cannot inhabit the Kingdom of God, so corruption will not inhabit incorruption."[18]

In antiheretical literature such opinions are reduced to stark statements of belief or disbelief and uniformly regarded as indications of affiliation with sects or organized groups rather than as individualistic ideas. The *Summa contra haereticos*, for example, includes chapters with titles that strive to correlate specific beliefs with distinct sects: "Cathars: On the equality of the punishments [of the damned] and the rewards [of the blessed]"; "Pasagians: That there is no one in hell or in paradise until the Day of Judgment"; or "Pasagians: One should not pray for the dead."[19] Yet the evidence of the Inquisition register suggests that dissenting beliefs about death and afterlife were equally likely to arise from individual reflection. If there is a soul, then why is it not visible leaving the body at death? Since the body decays to earth, how can it ever be recomposed and brought to life again? If the postmortem soul persists in a disembodied state, how could it undergo suffering and thereby accomplish penitence? How could the actions of one person assist someone else who was dead? These were not thoughts that could only arise from the teachings of determined heresiarchs; rather, they are based upon everyday observation and curiosity. Neither are they particularly exceptional, but indeed rather banal. As such, we must presume that many others in this world, whether adherents of organized dissident groups or not, must also have considered similar chains of reasoning.[20]

---

18. JF, 3:7–11.
19. Garvin and Corbett, *Summa contra Haereticos*, 185, 200, 210.
20. See Walter Wakefield, *Heresy, Crusade, and Inquisition in Southern France, 1100–1250* (Berkeley, 1974); John Edwards, "Religious Faith and Doubt in Late Medieval Spain: Soria circa 1450–1500," *Past & Present*, no. 120 (1988): 3–25.

Spirit Mediums and Cults in Regional Culture

Many laypeople also sustained an old tradition of envisioning the recent dead as moving, invisibly, among the living for some time before they reached a fixed place of rest. The culture of this region recognized a special type of lay seer, psychopomps who could assist the dead in finding rest and who could inform the living of the fate of their departed relatives. These abilities brought prestige to the visionaries; sometimes they even became the centers of informal spiritist cults, presiding over regular séances during which they mediated conversations between living people and the ghost whom only they could see and hear. According to this mode of imagining mortality, immediately after death the dead transited through a period of displacement between worlds lasting from three to five days. This period seems to have been conceived as the minimum time for the spirit or soul to detach fully from the body. Death was a long-term process, and this was the first phase. After this interim, the shades of the recently departed underwent a variable period of restlessness on the surface of the earth. During this time, which usually persisted for an interim of several months or even a few years after death, the dead haunted their old homes, neighborhoods, and churches, often in groups. No longer alive, they had not yet fully reached their final afterlife status, either. Eventually these shades would undergo something like a second death, finding eternal rest at last—what some called the "place of repose." The transient nature of the intermediate stage of wandering the earth, combined with the fact that the dead attained a restful state afterward, meant that such ghosts could readily be identified with denizens of purgatory by the learned. Indeed, purgatory gave a sort of license for many of the ghost stories that continued to circulate through medieval culture. Tales of the immanent dead were no longer needed for purposes of Christian conversion, but they were useful for other purposes: namely, vivid illustration of the latest church doctrines about the postmortem world.

However, by contrast with the church teaching of purgatory as a place of postmortem retributive justice, popular accounts of the newly dead haunting local churches and homes envisioned their situation as relatively free from torment. Their postmortem existence was not fulfilling, but neither was it terribly uncomfortable, merely restless and unsettled. Most importantly, however, as long as the dead remained in this status they could still communicate with the living—or at least, with certain living persons. The recently dead could appear either to those who were gifted with second sight, specialists who had a unique ability to communicate with spirits, or to someone with whom they had shared an especially intense bond before their deaths.

In the latter instance, it is possible that such spirit-possession scenarios may have originated as a form of informal divination, a consultation with the family ancestors, who might be expected to take a continuing interest in the affairs of their relatives and descendants. Those who were visited by shades of the dead assumed the function of spirit mediums and psychopomps: they transmitted messages from beyond the grave, relaying the words of dead folk whom only they could perceive; and they helped the shades ease their way to the place of repose. We know that experiences of hearing voices (and, presumably, of seeing things) that others do not sense is subject to culturally conditioned understandings.[21] That is to say, where one society may take such events as evidence of madness, another group sees sanctity, possession, shamanism, or divination. In fact, as we shall see, the social role of spirit medium was a recognized taxonomic category in the culture of this region.

The surviving evidence about these individuals is cohesive, yet sparse. Examples of well-documented mediums are relatively few in number: there are detailed dossiers of evidence about five different individuals, plus a number of ancillary references to others whose careers remain more obscure. At the same time, however, the data is uncommonly rich: the sources are in most cases lengthy accounts based upon firsthand observation; they include extensive background detail about the individual mediums and the responses of others to them; and in two cases they incorporate transcriptions of purported dialogues with the dead. These latter elements, though highly literary, offer unique insight into the ways in which a this-worldly postmortem existence was imagined. Thus we can attain considerable richness in our understanding of the culture of spirit mediums and oracles in this region. Not surprisingly, we also readily discern tension with clerical authority figures. Such tensions played out differently in each case, sometimes in an overtly adversarial way, sometimes more subtly.

Briefly, the best-documented cases of medieval mediums, ordered from the most direct to the most mediated accounts, are as follows.

The first case is that of Arnaud Gélis of Pamiers, whose own direct speech is preserved in the register of inquisitorial activity conducted in southern France between 1318 and 1325 by Bishop Jacques Fournier. While the register is most famous for the light it casts upon purported Cathar sympathizers in the region, it also includes abundant information about many other local traditions and beliefs, including spirit mediumship. Most

---

21. Tanya Luhrmann et al., "Differences in Voice-Hearing Experiences of People with Psychosis in the USA, India and Ghana: Interview-Based Study," *British Journal of Psychiatry* 206, no. 1 (2015): 41–44. I thank Dr. Luhrman for sharing this article with me.

MAP 6.1. Southern France. The region shown here, stretching from the Pyrénées to the Alps, was home to beliefs about spirit mediums. The surviving stories are all attested in this fairly circumscribed area. This map also shows the monastery of Cluny and the papal city of Avignon, important centers of religious influence in the later Middle Ages.

importantly, the nature of the document, which directly recorded the speech of the witnesses—albeit in translation from Occitan to Latin—is far more immediate than the other cases. The Fournier register allows us to "hear" the words of common people directly through these transcriptions of their words. Carlo Ginzburg has, as a deliberate provocation, suggested parallels between the inquisitor and the anthropologist;[22] though the comparison ultimately falls short, it does highlight the degree to which inquisitions documented the practices and beliefs of people who would otherwise be lost to

---

22. Carlo Ginzburg, "The Inquisitor as Anthropologist," in *Clues, Myths, and the Historical Method* (Baltimore, 1992), 156–64.

history. The Fournier register, which freely records individuals' own detailed self-descriptions and memories, is invaluable despite being produced under conditions of compulsion and, implicitly, the threat of punishment. With its dense, first-person descriptions of Arnaud's encounters with the dead, this source provides our most unmediated glimpse into regional beliefs about the lingering dead, their stages of separation from this world, and the living folk who could see and speak with them. Arnaud and others also mention a few other mediums working in the area, though the details of their careers are less well documented.

A second instance of a well-documented spirit medium is chronologically anterior to the interrogation of Arnaud Gélis. The source is not a direct interview, though the author was a direct witness to many of the events he recounts. In 1211, a young virgin in the town of Beaucaire claimed to be haunted by the shade of her cousin. The young man had died violently, the victim of a family feud. The name of the eleven-year-old girl medium remains unknown to us, but we possess a detailed report about her by Gervaise of Tilbury, who dedicated one of the longest chapters of his *Otia Imperialia* (*Emperor's Diversions*), to describing the case. Gervaise is a sympathetic and engaged narrator. Though his erudite text is carefully constructed and edited, his account nevertheless remains valuable, particularly since he was directly familiar with much of what he describes. Gervaise's report provides a clear window into the dynamic formation of a local spiritist cult, as the local villagers' curiosity about the world beyond the grave led them to cluster around the girl and to pepper her with questions for her dead cousin. As the virgin of Beaucaire began to gain a measure of local fame and authority, however, a cleric of Gervaise's acquaintance attempted to arrogate to himself the role of medium. In an echo of broader clerical appropriations of the dead, this individual cleric aimed to replace the girl as the primary interlocutor of the ghost. This man thus becomes a second medium described in Gervaise's text. Unsurprisingly, in line with the changed character of the medium who interposes himself between the dead and the living, this section of Gervaise's work becomes correspondingly more orthodox and doctrinal in tone. At the same time, however, it appears that the girl's meetings with her dead cousin continued, suggesting a kind of competition among the two. This dynamic is rather intriguing: though the girl's relationship with her cousin's ghost may be seen as a spontaneous expression of the local culture and belief system, the cleric's claims to be a medium are appropriative expressions of his patriarchal clerical power.

Another well-known instance of extended dialogue with a deceased relative took place in the town of Alès, quite near Beaucaire. The event occurred in 1323, thus roughly contemporaneously with the Fournier register. In this case, a widow began to be haunted by the shade of her late husband, a knight named Gui de Corvo. The ghost of Gui continued to frequent the bedchamber the couple had shared; the wife seems to have been the lodestone of his attraction to the world of the living, which otherwise was lost to him. After about a week, the prior of the local Dominican convent, Jean Gobi, was called in for assistance. He generated the first documentation of the haunting, a transcript of a theological dialogue between himself and the dead Gui. Though the source is somewhat obscure about certain details, there appear to be clear parallels to the case in Beaucaire: the hauntings of this spirit also attracted large crowds of interested spectators, who formed themselves into a regularly meeting group wishing to learn more about the otherworld directly from the source, with meetings over the course of several months. Also in parallel with the Beaucaire ghost, the role of mouthpiece for the dead was appropriated by a clerical authority figure, the Dominican prior who became the central interlocutor of the ghost. The dialogue between the prior and the dead man became rather celebrated, circulating in Latin, French, and English versions. The text also was rewritten several times, became the focus of correspondence emanating from Gobi's fellow Dominicans at the papal court at Avignon, was illuminated, and ultimately gave rise to a formal treatise on purgatory. However, even the earliest version of the story, the one crafted by Jean Gobi himself, is a highly literary and theological product.

Our final detailed documentation of a medium concerns a man who was active in Bern, Switzerland in the first part of the fifteenth century. Johannes Nider in his book *Formicarius* (*The Ant Hill*) relates the case of a "fraticello"—a pejorative term meaning a dubious sort of friar or religious personage—who became a minor sensation in the city by claiming that his chamber was frequented by the dead and by transmitting their messages. Like the others before him, the unnamed fraticello became the center of a small cult group, which seems to have visited him regularly for séances and conversations with spirits. Nider's evidence about this medium, unlike that of the other sources, is both distant and hostile. He was not a firsthand observer of these events, and he is dismissive of the fraticello's claims. In fact, Nider uses the story to reflect upon the evils of frauds and charlatans who exploit the gullibility of the common herd. Upholding a strictly Augustinian view of the impossibility of postmortem return, Nider rejects out of hand the notion that the dead might visit the living. However, by triangulating Nider's story with the others and reading it against the grain, we may discern clear continuities with the earlier accounts. It also bears remembering that there existed another famous spirit mediumship belief in the Alps: that of the funereal *benandante*, documented by Carlo Ginzburg.

As previously noted, all the evidence for belief in spirit mediums in contact with the dead falls into a relatively discrete geographical zone: an arc embracing the French Mediterranean and stretching east and up into the Alps.[23] Indeed, the culture of this region recognized spirit mediums as a particular category of person, and therefore possessed linguistic terms for them in various vernacular languages. In the Occitan tongue of the Midi, mediums were known as *armariés*;[24] in Alpine Italy, by contrast, those who saw and conversed with the dead were called *benandante*; in Switzerland we know a sixteenth-century case of one such seer with the title *Seelenmutter*, "Mother of Souls."[25] Within this rather broad category, however, there was some variation. While some mediums claimed to see many recently dead persons and specialized in carrying messages back and forth between the dead and their living family members, others developed a relationship with a single ghost, usually someone with whom they were close in life. In some cases, the mediums alone could hear the dead; in others, the dead were heard by all, but seemed bound to a particular space and its inhabitant. Despite these divergent details, however, these oracles of souls universally became the focal point of local community curiosity about the next world, its rules, and its inhabitants. Establishing a reputation as a known spirit medium could garner one a certain social standing as neighbors, friends, and relatives flocked to attend séances and hear more about the otherworld. They acted as psychopomps, assisting the dead in finding peace by conveying messages to their survivors. As we shall see, mediums were regarded as noteworthy people with a special gift and something to teach; they were consulted by people around them seeking information, advice, and solace. Indeed, the spiritist cults that developed around these figures were somewhat similar to unauthorized popular saints' cults.

Before we examine the evidence on the ground, however, it is instructive to pause in order to examine church teachings in regard to spirit mediums. Scripture includes a single example of a such a medium, in 1 Samuel. The

---

23. See Élisabeth Schulze-Busacker, "La complainte des morts dans la literature occitane," in *Le Sentiment de la mort au Moyen Âge: Études présentées au cinquième colloque de l'Institut d'études médiévales de l'Université de Montréal*, ed. Claude Sutto (Montreal, 1979), 229–48; Marie-Anne Polo de Beaulieu, "De Beaucaire (1211) à Alès (1323): Les revenants et leurs révélations dsur l'au-delà," in *La mort et l'au-delà en France méridionale*, 319–32.

24. René Nelli, *La vie quotidienne des Cathares de Languedoc au XIIIe siècle* (Paris, 1969), 199.

25. Carlo Ginzburg, *The Night Battles: Witchcraft and Agrarian Cults in the Sixteenth and Seventeenth Centuries* (New York, 1983), 33–39 (*benandante*) and 52 (*Seelenmutter*). See also Carlo Ginzburg, *Ecstacies: Deciphering the Witches' Sabbath* (New York, 1991).

interpretation of this passage provided guidance, at least for educated clerical observers, as to how they ought to regard contemporary reports of such phenomena.

The Medium of Endor and Medieval Theology

As with all questions pertaining to the return of the dead, church doctrine was complex and multistranded in relation to the issue of spirit mediums. While many medieval theologians denied that mediums could directly channel the spirits of the deceased, other individual clerics did accept that such events could occur, because (as always) they found them useful devices for teaching about the otherworld. In this arena, as in all matters pertaining to the return of the dead to this plane of existence, formal Catholic doctrine was silent. Thus, the question of mediumship was open for interpretation, and the dominant viewpoint about it shifted over time.

The first book of Samuel, chapter 28, recounts the story of the medium of Endor (often called the "witch" of Endor in older scholarship). King Saul, faced with an intimidating army of Philistines, wished for inspired dreams and prophecies, but none came to him from God. He became desperate to gain prophetic insight into the coming battle with this superior force. Though Saul had outlawed all mediums and divination, now he wished to consult precisely such a specialist. He asked his servants to locate a reliable spirit medium or "pythoness," and then he and a few attendants disguised themselves and set out to visit the woman. The medium was at first reluctant to admit her gifts since practicing them was now illegal, but Saul promised no harm would come to her. Once the medium agreed to work with Saul, he requested her to summon the spirit of Samuel. The medium saw the shade of Samuel rise up from the earth and described his appearance in detail to Saul, who could not see him. Saul, satisfied that the shade was indeed Samuel's, took counsel of him about the Philistine war. The shade conveyed a true prediction that Saul would lose both the coming battle and his life.

Medieval theologians' interpretations of the passage were varied.[26] While some held that the entity calling itself the shade of Samuel was actually a demonic imposture, others accepted the attribution of the spirit's identity as truly Samuel's ghost. Even Augustine, usually so deft and sure, was

---

26. K. A. D. Smelik, "The Witch of Endor: I Samuel 28 in Rabbinic and Christian Exegesis till 800 A.D.," *Vigiliae Christianae* 33, no. 2 (1979): 160–79; Jean-Claude Schmitt, "Le spectre de Samuel et la sorcière d'En Dor: Avatars historiques d'un récit biblique: I 'Rois' 28," in *Le retour des morts*, special issue, *Études rurales*, nos. 105–6 (1987): 37–64.

flummoxed by this tale and changed his mind about its significance, shifting from the demonic to a more accepting interpretation of the event over the course of years.[27] On the one hand, the biblical text itself implies that necromancy involves some form of unclean power—witness Saul's initial indictment of the practice, in fulfillment of the Deuteronomic prohibition of all forms of soothsaying and mediumship (Deut. 18:11). Moreover, the consultation of any form of spirit specialist seemed, to many patristic authors, unsettlingly close to the public cults of the ancestors and the spiritual oracles that were common to various paganisms of the classical world. On the other hand, the spirit explicitly was identified as Samuel in the sacred text, and his shade rendered a true prophesy to Saul; thus it seemed difficult to doubt its veracity entirely.[28] The interpretation of this incident, like so much else pertaining to return from the dead, shifted according to authorial agenda. Some authors saw stories about mediums as useful for doctrinal purposes like the promulgation of purgatory. At the same time, however, contemporary tales of mediums often involved the troubling spectacle of laypersons teaching about weighty matters of death, the otherworld, and salvation. Ventriloquizing the dead was rightly seen as an act of power and prestige, one that most clerics felt should properly be the preserve of those specifically charged with pastoral duties. From this perspective, then, it would be reasonable to conclude that uneducated lay mediums were well-intentioned dupes of demons. Regardless of the divergent clerical interpretations of these events, those in authority clearly were responding in uncoordinated ways to what appears to have been a fairly stable, long-term regional belief on the ground.

The *Armariés* of the Midi

Let us begin with a spirit medium's own self-description of his gifts and his experiences. In February 1320, Arnaud Gélis from Pamiers was called before the inquisitorial court of Jacques Fournier, on suspicion of holding a novel opinion about the universal salvation of all humanity. In a fit of misplaced enthusiasm, Arnaud spontaneously volunteered abundant details about his career as an *armarié*: "He habitually asserted that he saw the souls

---

27. In *De diversis quaestionibus ad Simplicianum*, composed 396, Augustine inclined toward the demonic school of interpretation, but by the time he composed *De cura pro mortuis gerenda*, in 421, he had changed his mind and admitted that the vision truly was Samuel. However, he maintained that this was an exceptional case of postmortem return permitted by God, rather than a usual or expected event.
28. Schmitt, "Le spectre de Samuel et la sorcière d'En Dor," 45–48.

of the dead and spoke to them, and that he reported their words to their former friends."[29]

Arnaud explained that his initiation into an oracular career had begun eight or nine years earlier. At that time the canon Hughes of Durfort, for whom Arnaud had worked as a domestic servant, died and was buried in the churchyard. Five days after Hughes's death, as Arnaud was sleeping at night in bed, the canon woke him up. Arnaud made out the figure of a man dressed in a surplice, with the hood up on his head. Arnaud noted that he saw all this by the light of the flames glowing in the hearth, even though he had snuffed the fire before going to bed.

Seeing this hooded figure, Arnaud grew frightened and asked him who he was and why he had come into the house. The visitor replied that he was Hughes of Durfort. At that, Arnaud told Hughes he was dead and asked him not to touch him and to go away. The canon told him to have no fear, for he would never do him any harm, but that at the following dusk Arnaud should come meet him in the cloister of Saint-Antonin, because he wanted to talk with him there. Arnaud responded, somewhat stubbornly, that he didn't know how he would find him given that he was dead. Hughes answered that he would find him in the cloister. Having said this, Hughes left.[30]

When Arnaud arrived at the cloister the next night, he was greeted by the shade of Hughes. The latter requested that he relay a message to his sister Brunissende, a married woman of Pamiers who still was living. If Brunissende were to endow two or three masses in Hughes's name, then he would be released from this plane of existence and transition onward to the place of repose. Arnaud transmitted the message, and for a time afterward he continued to see Hughes occasionally in the cloister of Saint-Antonin. Once the endowed masses had been completed, however, Hughes ceased appearing to Arnaud, so he presumed that the canon had indeed moved to the place of repose. Arnaud thus acted as an indirect psychopomp, assisting the dead toward their final destination of rest.

Shortly thereafter, Arnaud encountered another shade, that of Hughes of Rous. This Hughes had died long before Hughes of Durfort, yet he still had not been released to the place of repose. He told Arnaud that he believed he

---

29. JF, 1:128. For context and background, see Nelli, *La vie quotidienne des Cathares de Languedoc*; Emmanuel Le Roy Ladurie, *Montaillou: Promised Land of Error* (New York, 1979); James Given, *Inquisition and Medieval Society: Power, Discipline and Resistance in Languedoc* (Ithaca, NY, 2001); James Given, *Inquisition and Power: Catharism and the Confessing Subject in Medieval Languedoc* (Philadelphia, 2001); Mark Pegg, *The Corruption of Angels: The Great Inquisition of 1245–45* (Princeton, NJ, 2005); R. I. Moore, *The War on Heresy* (Cambridge, MA, 2012).

30. JF, 1:128–29.

would make the transition soon but did not request any masses or other favors. After that, Arnaud's visionary gift disappeared for about five years until suddenly he saw the shade of another canon, Athon of Uzent, likewise in the same cloister of Saint-Antonin. This time, the ghost greeted Arnaud by his nickname "Botheler" (the moniker appears to be something akin to "Tippler"), suggesting that Arnaud's status as an *armarié* was known to the dead.

> "Are you Botheler?"—"Yes. May God grant you paradise!"—Athon answered, "Yes, soon: for me and for all the other dead. Also all of you who are still living will attain paradise, God pleasing." And he said as well that no man's soul will be damned before the Day of Judgment, but they will not be damned afterward either, for Christ made them in his image and redeemed them with his blood. He said that neither he nor anyone else should fear damnation.[31]

After this third encounter, Arnaud began seeing the dead more and more often. He spied them wandering about the towns, churches, and plazas; he saw them singly and in groups; and he conversed with them regularly. As Arnaud spent more time in the company of the dead his grasp of the structure of the afterlife became clearer.

Arnaud explained to his interlocutors that the dead spend all their nights in churches: here we detect resonances with Thietmar of Merseburg's congregations of the dead. Each night, they moved to a different church, especially rural foundations, though each shade held a particular attachment to the foundation that had served as their parish church while alive, and most particularly to the church in which his or her body was interred.[32] Like the saints, who gazed down from heaven toward their physical remains, encased in costly reliquaries, these dead folk paid particular attention to the location of their corpses. Their afterlife involved penitence, though according to Arnaud, it merely was unceasing movement and activity—faster for the more sinful, more leisurely for those with lighter burdens to purge.[33] No other punishment awaited those who move on to the next life according to Arnaud; the afterlife is neither worse nor better than the life known to the living, merely restless.[34] As day broke, the dead would each move on to their next location. Arnaud Gélis offhandedly told the inquisitors, "in the mornings, they come out of the churches where they were keeping vigil,

---

31. JF, 1:129–30.
32. JF, 1:134.
33. JF, 1:533. Sundays were days of rest.
34. JF, 1:545.

and especially when the weather is fine they go and run around through the streets."[35] There could be thick crowds of ghosts: as Arnaud added in a later interrogation, "people who move their arms and hands from their sides when they walk do great harm . . . for by moving their arms in this way they knock many souls of the dead to the ground."[36] The shades of the dead, though invisible to most people, still enjoyed the warmth of the sunshine and were able to be struck, pushed, and injured corporeally by the heedless living. Likewise, they were sensitive to cold, for on frosty days, Arnaud explained, they tended to stay indoors and warm themselves by the hearths of homes.[37] They particularly haunted the houses of their relatives or their own former domiciles. Dead mothers would visit their children, tenderly yet invisibly caressing them; dead children would softly kiss their parents' cheeks to help soothe them to sleep restfully.[38] As night fell, the dead must needs hurry to the church designated for that evening's vigil. Arnaud, then, described a doubled afterlife system divided along a temporal axis: at night, the dead wandered through churches in collective penitence, hurrying more or less according to the severity of their sins; during the day, they visited their survivors, individually frequenting familiar places, homes, and locales. They seem to have had bodies, for they could use their senses; yet they were invisible to everyone but the *armariés*.

Their existence was sociable: the dead formed friendships among themselves, or spent time with other dead family members, dead husbands with their dead wives and so forth. Here the motif of postmortem society, which we have seen so often above, reappears. In appearance, the dead looked the same as they had while alive, so the dead could recognize one another in the afterlife. Deceased teenagers mingled with others of their own age, raising a tumult; and the Jewish dead, while visible to Arnaud, tended to stay apart in groups of their own.[39] Arnaud also suggested that the dead fervently wished that all the living were dead as well, perhaps because then all family groups would be fully reunited.[40] Yet even this afterlife was merely a transitional stage that eventually would rupture the family unit. For at length, the dead abandoned their nighttime vigils in churches and their daytime hauntings in order to move on to the place of repose, which remained somewhat

---

35. JF, 1:134.
36. JF, 1:544–45.
37. JF, 1:537.
38. JF, 1:135, 545.
39. JF, 1:173 (friendships), 547 (two young men together), 134 (husband and wife), 135–36 (Jews).
40. JF, 1:135.

mysterious. Arnaud stated that "he did not know, nor had he ever learned from any of those dead people, what kind of place it was or where it was located. However, he believed it was on the surface of the earth."[41] This transition was highly desired and could be hastened by the provision of prayers and masses by the living, as suggested by Arnaud's encounters with Hughes of Durfort (among others), or by the donation of oil for church lamps.[42] Indeed, so anxious were the dead for these assistances from the living, they would beat Arnaud harshly if he failed to deliver messages to their survivors relaying their needs.[43]

Baptized children under the age of seven went to a "dark place, in which there is neither evil nor good" immediately after death.[44] However the older and less innocent awaited the completion of their penitence and a form of second death, a postmortem mortality that marked their graduation to the place of repose. This death from death, though joyful for the individual, would be mourned by their dead community just as the first death, the death from life, was mourned: "When the soul of anyone is ready to enter the place of repose, the souls of the others that were traveling with it through the churches make just as great a wail, and mourn just as do the living when they mourn and wail when their friends die."[45] Once transitioned to the place of repose, the individual soul would there await the Day of Judgment when, Arnaud repeatedly averred, *everyone* who had ever lived would be saved. "God will call them to the Heavenly Kingdom," he insisted.[46] "All unbaptized children, and in general all rational creatures, will be saved on account of the great compassion of Jesus Christ; none shall perish!"[47] Other witnesses recall Arnaud stating that the Blessed Virgin Mary would save all Christians and Jews, and that even those who converted to Islam, away from Christianity, would likewise find their way to heaven.[48] Such assertions about the afterlife puzzled the inquisitors. If none are damned, then of what use was hell, they asked?

> In hell there are demons. Since Christ first raised the souls of the saints, no human soul has entered into hell, nor will any enter there in the future. Only demons will be tormented in hell, for I do not believe that

---

41. JF, 1:135.
42. JF, 1:135.
43. JF, 1:136.
44. JF, 1:134.
45. JF, 1:544.
46. JF, 1:135.
47. JF, 1:134.
48. JF, 1:534–35 (Virgin's intercession), 544 (converts to Islam).

any man of Christian faith and holy baptism will be damned. Even Jews, Muslims, and heretics, if only they beg for mercy from God, God will have pity on them and will give them paradise.[49]

Arnaud's unwillingness to believe that God would be so cruel as to damn anyone is somewhat touching, but also clearly was of great concern to his interrogators.

Likely in response to a question now lost, Arnaud noted that his second cousin Raymonde also possessed the ability to see the dead.[50] It is possible that this discussion was prompted by the inquiry, typically asked at inquisitional courts, of who had taught Arnaud his unusual ideas. Cousin Raymonde, who lived near Fanjeaux, frequently told Arnaud of her experiences seeing and speaking to the dead. According to Arnaud, she sometimes would be absent from her father's home for days at a time, returning in a despondent state. Once—presumably before Arnaud's own gifts as a medium began to manifest—she told him that she had seen his recently deceased mother, Rousse, who was poorly dressed in the afterlife for lack of a proper veil. Likewise Arnaud's father, according to Raymonde, was held back from the place of repose because he had died while still owing three measures of wheat. Once Arnaud gave a new veil to a pauper and distributed three measures of wheat to some needy folk, his parents were more comfortable, according to Raymonde's next report.

At various points throughout Arnaud's testimony we see how mediums for the dead could attain a special standing in their communities. They served important mnemonic functions, bringing the dead back into the consciousness of the living and providing means for survivors to solace themselves with the knowledge that they had alleviated the suffering of their loved ones in their new state. While Raymonde seems to have volunteered her information about Arnaud's parents to him, others actively sought out spirit mediums in order to consult with them about their dead. Thus, a witness named Guillelmette described how, about a year after she lost her adult daughter Fabrissa, a woman named Mengarde mentioned to her that there was a man in Mas-Saint-Antonin who could see and speak to the dead and report on their condition. The man, of course, was Arnaud Gélis. Mengarde knew about Arnaud's gifts because she, too, had lost a daughter, and the seer had consoled her about her status; she recommended that Guillelmette should find him and enquire about Fabrissa.[51] Mengarde appears to have been a great

---

49. JF, 1:136.
50. JF, 1:136.
51. JF, 1:537.

promoter of Arnaud's gifts: another witness named Raymonde was likewise persuaded by Mengarde to visit Arnaud's home in order to inquire about her mother.[52] Arnaud consoled each one with assurances that their dead relatives were content, and he explained about the nighttime vigils in churches and the daytime visits to families. He likewise consistently emphasized that no one would be damned, but all saved, on the Day of Judgment. To Raymonde, he explained that her mother had gone to repose on the feast of All Saints' (not, significantly, the neighboring monastic feast of All Souls').[53] This information apparently was highly valuable to Raymonde, for she, too, began to promote Arnaud's gifts to other women of her acquaintance. She told a widow named Navarre about Arnaud, so the next time she encountered him she asked about her dead family members. Navarre appears to have lost many relatives: she inquired about her dead mother, husband, son, and later her brother and received similar replies as the others. In these testimonies, we can track the growth of gossip cells[54] that bruited about the news of Arnaud's unusual abilities: one woman told another, who met with Arnaud and was impressed; she in turn would spread the word to others. It is easy to detect the widespread concern about the fates of dead family members, the appeal of Arnaud's answers (which usually were reassuring and emphasized the lack of postmortem punishment and eventual salvation of all), and the growth of his reputation as the person to consult about the fate of dead loved ones.

Arnaud's career as an *armarié* is the best-attested one in the Fournier register, but a few other individuals with similar abilities appear in passing. There was, as we have seen, Arnaud's second cousin Raymonde. Moreover, two years later, in the course of the same inquisition, we hear of two other spirit mediums. Witness Guillaume Fort told the inquisitors that he knew a woman named Arnalda Riba from Beaucaire and that she "went with the souls of dead men and dead women."[55] Her vision of the afterlife was somewhat harsher than Arnaud's: she saw demons torment the dead by throwing them down on the rocky mountain landscape. Guillaume was inclined to believe Arnalda because her information was confirmed by the testimony of

---

52. JF, 1:546.
53. JF, 1:547.
54. Max Gluckman, "Gossip and Scandal," *Current Anthropology* 4, no. 3 (1963): 308; Robert Paine, "What Is Gossip About? An Alternative Hypothesis," *Man*, n.s. 2, no. 2 (1967): 278–85; Sally Merry, "Rethinking Gossip and Scandal," in *Toward a General Theory of Social Control*, vol. 1: *Fundamentals*, ed. Donald Black (Orlando, 1984), 271–302; Jörg Bergmann, *Discreet Indiscretions: The Social Organization of Gossip* (New York, 1993); Patricia Meyer Spacks, *Gossip* (New York, 1985); Pamela J. Stewart and Andrew Strathern, *Witchcraft, Sorcery, Rumors and Gossip*, New Departures in Anthropology (Cambridge, 2007).
55. JF, 1:448.

yet another spirit medium, also from Beaucaire. Once, Guillaume recounted, the local rector was rebuking Arnalda for saying that she saw the dead thusly when a craftsman named Bernard de Alazaic piped up in her defense. Bernard explained that he, too, could see groups of dead souls, and likewise that he saw them being cast down by demons.[56] This independent, confirming testimony convinced Guillaume that the visions were true.

It is interesting that these two individuals both lived in the town of Beaucaire, for that location was home to one of the very best-attested spirit mediums of the Middle Ages. In order to explore this case, however, we must move back in time a little more than a century, to 1211. That year, a significant spiritist cult developed in Beaucaire, centered upon the person of an eleven-year-old girl.

The Ghost and the Virgin

"The Dead Man Who Appeared to a Virgin and Spoke, Explaining Wondrous Things" is one of the lengthiest chapters of *Otia Imperialia*, a compilation of natural history and preternatural wonders. This book circulated widely in the Middle Ages: the Latin survives in some thirty manuscripts, and the text was twice translated into French.[57] The author of this tour de force, Gervaise of Tilbury, was a well-traveled Englishman who had settled in Arles, near Beaucaire. He had received legal training in both civil and canon law in Bologna and later lived in Sicily for some time before moving to Provence and acting as a judge attached to the curia of the archbishop of Arles, Imbert d'Aiguières.[58] Gervaise later married a relative of Imbert's, an heiress who brought him both wealth and status within Provençal society.

Gervaise had firsthand knowledge of the events he describes, and he believed in the truth of the virgin's contacts with the dead man. In this, he differed from the clerics who would later interrogate Arnaud Gélis: the inquisitorial judges believed Arnaud had fallen into an error perpetrated by duplicitous demons. Gervaise, far from questioning the idea of spirit mediumship, seems rather to have found the incident to be highly instructive:

> Many people say . . . that what we teach about the otherworld is nonsense: they suggest we made it up! . . . They will not believe what they read in scripture unless they hear it either from someone who

---

56. JF, 1:448.
57. De Beaulieu, "De Beaucaire (1211) à Alès (1323)," 322.
58. Banks and Binns, "Introduction," to GT, xxvii–xxx.

resurrected from the dead, or else from a dead person who appears to the living postmortem. For how can anyone know about something they have neither seen nor experienced? . . . In order to satisfy those incredulous people who deny, as some sort of impossibility, that one could return here after death . . . I shall describe a novel thing that has recently been made known among us. Let hearts be filled with wonder, let minds be perplexed, and let limbs tremble at this strange event![59]

The circumstances of the "strange event" may quickly be summarized. In July 1211 a young man, still beardless, but old enough to have engaged in certain unnamed "excesses," was exiled from his hometown of Apt. The impression Gervaise conveys about the young man is that he was good-natured, handsome, and generally well intentioned, but reckless in the way of young men. His trespass may have been sexual in nature, since Gervaise refers to the crime as *lubrice*, a term that usually denotes lewdness. The young man set out to spend his exile in Beaucaire, likely planning to stay with his uncle's family there until the situation in Apt cooled. En route, however, the youth was ambushed and mortally wounded by his enemies.[60] Though being cut down by sudden violence was of course a bad death, in this case the badness of the youth's demise was somewhat diminished by the fact that he survived long enough to confess his sins, receive the sacrament and last rites from a priest, and piously forgive his killers.

As the family sat in vigil, waiting for the young man to pass, his eleven-year-old cousin and favorite kinswoman arrived from Beaucaire. "Amid the sufferings of a sad parting, she forcefully made him swear to a pact that if it were possible for him to return to her in any way, he would enlighten her about his state."[61] And so, "three or five" nights after his burial, the dead man came back as the girl was praying by lamplight at night. Though the girl had asked him to return, still she was fearful, "for it is naturally implanted in the hearts of those who will die, that they abhor those who have died."[62] The youthful ghost reassured the girl that he could not harm her and then explained the goal of his visit: "It is permitted to me to speak with you alone, and to transmit my answers to others through you."[63] As if to confirm this statement the girl's parents, overhearing her conversing with someone in her room, entered at this juncture and asked with whom she was speaking. She

---

59. GT, 758–60.
60. GT, 760, 780.
61. GT, 770.
62. GT, 760.
63. GT, 760–62.

responded, "Don't you see my freshly dead kinsman William standing there and speaking to me?"[64] But the parents could neither see nor hear the dead man at all. This detail thus confirms that the girl was the exclusive "voice" for the shade of the young man. The story likewise suggests that the ghost would remain present on this plane of existence for some time and indicates that it would be natural for other people to wish to pose questions to him, through the intermediation of his cousin.

The girl—whose name never is mentioned—may be regarded as actively constructing a scenario of access to the otherworld, with herself situated in a privileged position between the world of the living and that of the dead. Certain details of her claims bear significant similarities to the ways in which Arnaud would later describe the early stages of his career as a medium, suggesting that they both drew upon a common store of regional traditions. The wait of between three and five days after death for the shade to appear; the appearance to someone with whom the dead person was close; the initial fear of the living and reassurance from the dead; the fact that others do *not* see the deceased; and lastly, the sense that this appearance portends initiation into an ongoing contact with the dead: all these details are common to both accounts. An important point of divergence, however, is the fact that whereas Arnaud claimed to be able to see many of the local dead, the virgin was in contact only with her cousin. While it is unclear how long the series of revelations from beyond the grave lasted, we know the cousin's postmortem visits persisted for at least two to three months: the killing took place in July, and Gervaise later mentions that one of the dead man's visits was cut short by his attendance at solemnities in honor of Saint Michael, which was celebrated on September 29. During this time, the young girl's home became the epicenter of what can only be described as a spiritist cult. Though the end of the episode is not described in Gervaise's text, at one point the dead youth promises to remain in contact with the living for as long as his cousin remains a virgin.[65] Thus her charismatic gift as a spirit medium is explicitly linked to her spiritual and corporeal purity.

The first people to learn of the haunting were the virgin's parents, the night of the dead youth's first appearance. Gervaise tells us little about the family's social status, other than that they were upright and faithful citizens of Beaucaire. Combined with the description that they were "industrious" and that their home contained at least two separate bedchambers,[66] this suggests

---

64. GT, 762.
65. GT, 768.
66. GT, 762.

that the family was a bourgeois one of middling status but having some financial resources. We cannot know how these good citizens responded to their daughter's assertion that she was being visited by the ghost of her cousin, but we do know that soon thereafter they took action to assist him in the hereafter. About a week later they set off for the Benedictine monastery of Saint-Michel de Frigolet, a few miles away on the road between Tarascon and Avignon,[67] in order to pray for their nephew's soul and to endow masses and prayers in his name. Perhaps they hoped not only to speed his salvation, but also to stave off any further apparitions to their child. However, in their absence the ghost made a second visit to the girl while she was alone in the family home, relating that he was much refreshed by her parents' attentions.[68] By now, other people had begun to learn of the ghost's visits. As Gervaise tells the tale, "within the space of a few days, the news spread through the vicinity, and people from the area, impelled by amazement and by the strangeness of it, came to visit the virgin."[69]

The chief subject of curiosity, of course, was the experience of death itself. When asked about this, however, the dead man flinched: "As soon as he heard the term 'dead,' he was taken aback and groaned. It was as if he had been taken unawares and wounded by the word 'dead.' He said, 'O, Sweetest Girl, never let this word pass your lips! For the nature of death is so bitter beyond compare that someone who has once tasted death for himself cannot bear even the mention of the word.'"[70] The youth went on to describe death as an unbearable harshness (*asperitas*). The restless, haunting dead, it seemed, mourned their lost lives for some time and found it difficult to come to terms with their cruel exile from embodiment. In a later conversation, some "literate men" in attendance at a larger séance asked the ghost what term was preferable to the word "death," since the dead man detested the word so fiercely. His preferred euphemism was "passing from the world [*migracio a seculo*]."[71]

A broad cross-section of local society was intrigued by the virgin's contact with her dead cousin. People kept flocking to the girl's home to learn more about death and afterlife from a purportedly firsthand source. Even some skeptics were convinced: a reputable knight, a friend of Gervaise, visited the girl with a view toward testing her gifts. After putting many questions

---

67. GT, 762, n. 6.
68. GT, 762.
69. GT, 764.
70. GT, 762.
71. GT, 768.

to her, he avowed himself convinced by the girl's answers, particularly a test of the shade's occult knowledge. Aside from laypeople of various social classes, clerics, monks, and intellectuals also eventually became interested in the ongoing series of revelations from beyond the grave. Like the knight, these men initially were skeptics but open to persuasion. First, the head of the Benedictine priory of Tarascon arrived, perhaps after having heard rumors of the returned dead man from his foundation's brother house of Saint-Michel de Frigolet, which had a relationship with the girl's family. Gervaise states that the prior had come to "test the truth of the things he had heard about." He is portrayed as having a challenging, even aggressive demeanor, yet the eleven-year-old girl evidently refused to be intimidated by him. According to Gervaise's account, the prior opened his visit by firing off a series of curt questions to the girl. She, however, remained implacable: "The prior demanded, 'Where is he? What is he doing? Where did he come from? Did he bring anyone?' In reply, the girl told the prior to move aside, for he had nearly stepped on [the dead man's] foot."[72] Like the villagers of Pamiers, who knocked down the dead by swinging their arms, here the prior is warned against trodding on the foot of a dead person whom he himself cannot see. This would seem to suggest that the dead had a material existence of some sort, though in a later statement, the shade averred that the lightest straw would be an unbearable burden to a disembodied one such as himself.[73] The assertive prior stayed for some time, making inquiries about the dead man's postmortem situation and weighing his answers for veracity and theological orthodoxy. After a thorough examination he departed, seemingly without having found any basis for censure. Perhaps the most revelatory aspect of this encounter, however, is how Gervaise portrays the girl's calm attitude, by contrast with the prior's querulous, even challenging stance. A growing local reputation as a medium appears to have endowed this eleven-year-old girl with an unflappable air of authority and confidence. Her role as a "spiritual celebrity" may fruitfully be compared with that of the local, lay female saints who likewise populated the thirteenth-century cityscapes of Europe. In each case, a youthful virgin lay claim to privileged contact with the supernatural world and thereby became the center of a cult of devotion outside the normal power channels of the institutional church, yet within the boundaries of theological orthodoxy. Her spiritual gifts and ability to see into the afterlife were linked to her virginal purity. The girl was not far off from the contemporary phenomenon of female "living saints."[74]

---

72. GT, 764.
73. GT, 768.
74. Gabriella Zarri, *Le sante vive: Profezie di corte e devozione femminile tra '400 e '500* (Turin, 1990).

At this point, the tale shifts to a more established phase of the cult. After an initial stage in which Gervaise focuses on challenges to the virgin's authority as a genuine medium, she appears to have entered into a more secure position. It is already clear, from the narrative, that the girl's home had swiftly become a site for regular gatherings of a group of devotees, anxious to learn more about the hereafter. At the close of each meeting of this group, the girl would announce the time and day of the ghost's next intended visit, for "he came at agreed and pre-fixed times," and the living would congregate at the scheduled time in order to hear fresh revelations.[75] These gatherings included an assembly of mixed background, including family and neighbors, laity and religious, literate and illiterate. This section of Gervaise's text is particularly interesting insofar as most of the questions posed, and the answers offered, are quite simple and spontaneous in tone. The information that was most ardently sought by the group seems to have been rather worldly in scope, however: "Many times, he was asked about events that were occurring in the world, and about the future."[76] The dead man steadfastly refused to answer such queries: while he willingly set forth some points about the geographical and eschatological dimensions of the life to come, he resolutely refused to discuss the future of this world. For her part, the girl medium or interrogator enacted a sophisticated performative role during the recurring séances she hosted, patiently relaying answers from her cousin that were conventional enough to satisfy expectations, yet sufficiently fresh and vivid to keep the crowd interested and alert. The group thus formed itself into a "textual community,"[77] oriented around the unscrolling "text" of the ghost's revelations, transmitted by the words of the living seer, yet ultimately subject to the interpretations and debates of the crowd. The portrait of the afterlife that emerges from these dialogues had to possess a certain plausibility and verisimilitude in order for the cult to succeed.

How, then, was the fate of the recently dead imagined within this regularly meeting group of people, this spiritist cult led by a youthful virgin? The youthful ghost had much to say about the system of the afterlife through his living mouthpiece. As we have seen, he suggested that he was unable to describe the process of dying because it was too upsetting to recall. He did, however, state that death was not an immediate transition but a slow process: "sometimes, those transiting from the world do not reach their destined

---

75. GT, 764.
76. GT, 768.
77. Brian Stock, *The Implications of Literacy: Written Language and Models of Interpretation in the Eleventh and Twelfth Centuries* (Princeton, NJ, 1987).

place until the third or fourth day."⁷⁸ Thus death is a slow extraction from this life and emplacement in the next. This delay corresponds to the time interval between death and the first postmortem appearance of the ghost, in this case as well as in Arnaud Gélis's reports from Pamiers. Thus it appears that the dead must first be fully fixed in their new state before they may visit the living. The dead man's own postmortem state, he explained, was purgatory, which he insisted over and over again was "in the air."⁷⁹ He now made his "home in the air among the spirits, undergoing the pains of purgatorial fire."⁸⁰ In response to this declaration, some people in attendance inquired about the location of Gehenna. The ghost responded that hell is a horrible place beneath the surface of the earth but that it lay empty, for no one would go there until the Day of Judgment. Likewise, according to the ghost heaven currently was empty and would remain so until the end: the souls of the purged and of the just alike await their reward in the bosom of Abraham.⁸¹ This portrayal of otherworldly geography was more conventional than the ways in which the afterlife was imagined by the *armariés* of the Fournier register: there are no churches filled with dead congregations, or rocky mountain passes where the shades of the dead were thrown down by tormenting demons. But if the geography of the afterlife described in this text was largely consonant with contemporary church teachings, the assertion that Gehenna and heaven would both remain devoid of souls until the Last Judgment clearly deviated from doctrine.

Gervaise's intervention into this spiritist cult went beyond mere observation, however. Midway through the tale of the ghost and his youthful mouthpiece, Gervaise and a priest of his acquaintance staged a coup. They appropriated the girl's oracular abilities to themselves, forming a splinter group or rival spiritist cult of two.

Appropriating the Ghost

> So far, so good [*Hec hactenus*]. Now I turn to the more arcane secrets of divine things. There was a priest, a man learned in literature as well as good, pious, and God-fearing. When these visions first began he considered the things that were being said to be frivolous, so he went to the virgin and addressed the dead man through her. He asked the

---

78. GT, 766–68.
79. GT, 764.
80. GT, 762.
81. GT, 768.

virgin to find out, when he appeared, whether it could be arranged for him to speak to the priest directly, so that the water of salvation might not be transmitted to the garden via a channel (as it had been so far), but in such a way that the priest might receive responses himself, without any intermediary.[82]

In sum, the role of medium was adopted by the priest, and Gervaise became at once the audience, the interlocutor, and the amanuensis for the new oracle. We later learn that the girl likewise continued to relay messages from her dead cousin as well. Gervaise was very pleased with the new situation: "since he is a very dear and intimate friend to us, we posed our questions to him so that he could resolve them. As the Divine Name is my witness, I have written down the things he said in the words direct from his mouth."[83] In conceiving this appropriation the priest, in collusion with his amanuensis Gervaise, arrogated to himself a source of prestige that hitherto had been outside his control. The water of salvation, as Gervaise suggested, no longer required the girl as a "channel" but instead flowed directly to a clerical authority figure. Yet the terms of interaction with the deceased remained stable: one person alone was the medium, while others (in this case, Gervaise) posed inquiries and received answers through that individual.

After this change of interlocutors, the tone of the text shifts radically. The priest's purported conversation with the shade takes rather a different cast than the spontaneous discussions at the girl's home. To begin, whereas previously the ghost had been reticent to claim knowledge of divine things and is never reported to have solicited attention from any particular party, under the priest's mediumship these things changed. Now, the shade of the young man felt comfortable revealing God's opinions in detail. He likewise discussed the structure of the afterlife in greater depth, prompting Gervaise to confess that he believed the ghost's revelations even above the writings of the most learned theologians. In his view, the dead man was "more experienced" in death and therefore more authoritative.[84] Moreover, the form of discourse also changed. The text from this point forward is constituted as an *inquisitio*, the characteristic form used by inquisitors and canonization inquirers alike. Thus there follows a rather formulaic set of exchanges punctuated by "interrogatus ... respondit" ("he was asked ... he answered"). The tone echoes the juridical forms of the day. Lastly, once the priest became a channel for the ghost's revelations, there was a

---

82. GT, 770.
83. GT, 770.
84. GT, 774.

discernable shift of attention toward publicizing the cult to powerful potential patrons. For instance, soon after the priest began conversing with the shade, the latter admitted his great desire to meet William, bishop of Orange.[85] When the bishop was contacted he proved unable to visit in person; he did, however, send a set of questions for the ghost in writing. Next, the enterprising young ghost took it upon himself to dictate to Gervaise, via the priest, a set of counsels intended for Emperor Otto IV. As Gervaise later wrote to his patron, "I am sending to you, most serene prince, a secret document recording the ways in which you are pleasing to God, and the ways in which, by contrast, you displease God, just as I received it from [the dead man]."[86] Thus the priest and Gervaise attempted to cultivate a celebrity cult for the priest as a medium with a higher level of cultural gravitas and sophistication.

Here we discern a new angle to the essentially ventriloquistic element of these cults: the priest suddenly channels a heretofore unknown interest, on the part of the dead man, in gaining the ears of a bishop and even the emperor. Clearly, the situation fostered certain unique opportunities (or perhaps more accurately, hopes) for a medium to gain access to the powerful. For the girl, by contrast, the chief benefit of gaining a reputation as a spiritual channel was being regarded as a powerful figure locally, someone set apart from the ordinary herd. She was a virgin saint, a seer, and/or an *armarié* for others; for herself, perhaps, she gained a sense of continuing closeness to the departed young cousin whom she had loved. It also is possible that the girl hoped her status as a medium might delay any marriage plans on her behalf, for the ghost promised that he would leave her once she lost her virginity. Once the priest began claiming contact with the dead youth, however, we detect interest in a more far-reaching fame and the attempt to garner interest from wealthy and powerful patrons. Not content with the local dimensions of the cult, the priest cast his aspirations farther afield.

Consistent with this attempt to garner attention from a higher and more educated social class, the priest steered his conversations with the ghost into theological territory. His prime question was, again, what was it like to die? As we saw above, the ghost told his young female cousin that he could not bear to speak on this painful subject. For the priest, however, he willingly elaborated:

> When asked, he answered that at the moment when he exited this life he was exceedingly horrified, beyond any compare. Then there

---

85. GT, 778.

86. GT, 780. He writes that he sent these queries, along with their answers, to Otto under a private seal, but such a text has never been found.

appeared to him good angels as well as evil ones, but the good angels prevailed and led him to purgatory. He added that every known suffering is incomparable and unequal to the suffering of death, and that the tiniest pain of purgatory is harsher than any physical pain.[87]

The language and imagery is traditional within the learned, written tradition of afterlife journeys. The appearance of good and bad angels, the terror and suffering that surpass all words: these elements may be found in visions of heaven and hell reaching centuries into the past.

The revelations of the youthful shade to the priest were grouped around several themes. He began with a series of queries about the arrangement of the afterlife, the conditions of its populations, and its geography. The ghost addressed the places of the next world (the saints go to heaven, the saved but flawed to purgatory like himself, and the damned remain homeless, wandering in the air until they enter hell at the Last Judgment); whether souls can recognize one another while disembodied (yes, though he himself can only see the purging and the damned);[88] where Purgatory is situated with reference to Beaucaire (it is on the surface of the earth but eastward, near Jerusalem); and whether the saints have attained full glory yet or must await the Final Judgment (the saints are somewhat glorified, but have not yet attained the fullest state of it).[89] A second phase of questioning centered specifically on conditions in purgatory: whether there is any rest there (yes, on Sundays);[90] whether the alms of the living help (yes); whether he has a guardian angel on whom to rely for assistance (yes, Saint Michael); whether he can see angels and demons (yes, and also everyone's guardian angels); what the ghost's body is like and how it suffers (he is a disembodied spirit and cannot bear any weight, yet his spiritual body can still suffer torments); and whether there is night in purgatory (yes, but it is less dark than the nighttime of this world).[91] Finally, the last several questions and answers hopped from subject to subject, as if the two collaborators had satisfied their chief agenda and now were posing queries as they occurred. What is the highest good (avoiding dishonesty);[92] did John the Baptist doubt Christ (no);[93] does

---

87. GT, 770–72.
88. Both GT, 772. Gervaise comments that this differs from Gregory the Great's teaching, but he (Gervaise) is more inclined to believe the ghost because of his firsthand experience.
89. Both GT, 774.
90. GT, 774–76.
91. All the foregoing, GT, 776.
92. GT, 776.
93. GT, 776–78.

God approve of slaughtering Cathars (oh, yes!);[94] and does Saint Michael act as the guardian angel for all people (Michael is the name of an office—guardian—rather than an individual angel).[95] All in all, the curate of Beaucaire's interviews reveal interests that are precisely what we should expect of an ambitious cleric in a midsized town. He poses traditional questions about the afterlife, the role of almsgiving, and the conditions in purgatory. The answers he proffers on behalf of the ghost are a mix of mainstream theology and uncontroversial opinion.

Yet though initially Gervaise made it seem as if that the priest had orchestrated a complete takeover of the role of spirit medium, later in the narrative it becomes clear that this was not in fact the case. The séance sessions continued unabated at the girl's home, and the two mediums remained aware of each other's activities. For example, the text notes that once, when the priest was late for a rendezvous, the spirit appeared to the girl to complain about his tardiness.[96] And though Gervaise ceased reporting on the séances at the virgin's home, he did include a sort of epilogue concerning her branch of the spirit cult. The ghost, he reported, warned his cousin of an ambush being prepared by the long-term enemies of their family, the other kindred with whom they had been feuding. Having been forewarned by this oracular pronouncement, the girl's male relatives were able to avoid duplicating the fate of the young kinsman who now haunted and protected their home. The ghost's relationship with his family remained loyal beyond the grave. Thus, this regional culture of interaction with the dead, an idiom in which deceased kin return in order to advise and assist their survivors in ways both practical and spiritual, was reproduced and sustained by the provision of this useful occult knowledge. And in the end, this appears to have been a key element in the success of the girl's claims. Though the ghost was claimed by both mediums simultaneously, the girl's séances garnered a level of attention and success that eluded the priest and Gervaise in their attempt to appropriate the cult and transform it to appeal to a more elite and sophisticated audience. Their communications with the dead man seem to have remained a private, small-scale affair between the two of them, in contrast to the crowds that were drawn to the girl. Belief in mediums could not be translated to the upper echelons of society—or at least not yet. We do not know what became of the virgin and her devoted ghost, as Gervaise does not tell us.

---

94. GT, 778.
95. GT, 778–80.
96. GT, 782.

The Widow, the Prior, and the Ghost

A century after the events in Beaucaire yet another spiritist cult formed in the nearby town of Alès. This one began in December 1323 and continued through Easter of the following year, occurring in the household of a widow. The ghost was the woman's recently departed spouse, Gui de Corvo. By contrast with the other cases we have examined, Gui never appeared visibly; only his voice was heard. The story recapitulates much of the same basic structure as the incident in the *Otia Imperialia*: a male ghost visits the home of a female relative, whom he identifies as his most beloved on earth. In this instance, however, the wife did not become the medium. Instead, the oracular figure was a person of institutional authority: the Dominican prior of the local convent. This cult never was under lay or feminine control, but immediately was taken in hand by a clerical figure. The Dominican friar in question, Jean Gobi, posed a series of questions to the dead man, supposedly in the sight and hearing of over one hundred other people whom he had gathered as witnesses and assistants. Perhaps one of these observers kept notes of the conversation between Gobi and de Corvo; in any event, a transcribed version of their exchanges circulated in the later Middle Ages, even making its way to the papal court in Avignon where it was presented to Pope John XXII.[97] The text of their dialogue is relatively brief. It chiefly discusses why the ghost has returned and why he appeared specifically to his wife, followed by a brief discussion of his postmortem condition.

The dead man was returning, we are told, on account of an unexpiated sin that had occurred in the bedchamber, which we may infer was sexual in nature.

> I asked him who he was, and he answered that he was a spirit who was undergoing his purgatory. I asked him why in this place rather than elsewhere; he answered that it was because he had committed a sin in this place. . . . I asked if he was enduring suffering in a common or an individual purgatory; he answered that it was an individual one,

---

97. A French translation of the dialogue and other related texts is Jean Gobi, *Dialogue avec un fantôme*, trans. Marie-Anne Polo de Beaulieu (Paris, 1994). An abbreviated Latin version appears in Gustav Schleich, ed., *The Gast of Gy: Eine englische Dichtung des 14 Jahrhunderts nebst ihrer lateinischen Quelle "De Spiritu Guidonis"* (Berlin, 1898). My discussion in this chapter is based on the longer document presented by De Beaulieu; where possible, I have provided cross-references to the Latin edition in Schleich. See also de Beaulieu, "De Beaucaire (1211) à Alès De (1323)." The phenomenon of hallucinations among bereaved spouses is commonplace. See W. Dewi Rees, "The Hallucinations of Widowhood," *British Medical Journal* 4, no. 5778 (October 2, 1971): 37–41; A. Grimby, "Bereavement among Elderly People: Grief Reactions, Post-Bereavement Hallucinations and Quality of Life," *Acta Psychiatrica Scandinavia* 87 (1993): 72–80. I thank Tanya Luhrmann for this last group of references.

that is, this house, in which he would have to remain for two years, on account of a sin he committed here, unless good deeds and suffrages aided him.[98]

Thus, the ghost's answer privileged a singular purgatory, conducted on the face of the earth, in a familiar location linked to the life of the individual sinner. Evidently this answer was not satisfying for Jean Gobi, for he posed the question again, in slightly different terms, during his second visit. This time, the reference to a "common purgatory" was forthcoming:

> I said to him, "You told me that you were conducting your purgatory here; do you have some other penalty, apart from what you suffer in this house?" He answered yes. I then asked, as before, where or in what place he was undergoing this other penalty. He answered, "In the common purgatory." I was astonished that he could be punished at the same time and even the same moment in two places that were so far apart, so I asked how this could be possible, since we knew exactly when he had arrived at this house. He answered, "I am punished during the day in the common purgatory, and at night in this individual purgatory."[99]

Thus, Gui de Corvo suffers both an "individual" purgatory that is terrestrial and a "common" purgatory that is otherwordly. This latter is described in terms consonant with contemporary church teachings: it is a place of torment with legions of demons inflicting penances upon an innumerable multitude of disembodied souls.

The ghost's answer recalls Arnaud Gélis's avowal that the dead filled up the local churches at night, purging sins in common, but that at daybreak they dispersed to their own business. The temporal dimension is inverted, but the idea that postmortem penitence was divided between periods of communality and individualism is similar. The haunting in Alès was legitimated by the Dominican narrator as expiation of a specific sin in situ, but the effect is to retain the local and the earthly dimensions of postmortem existence that were traditional to the culture of the area. Such an imagining of the afterlife found a clear antecedent in the *Dialogues* of Gregory the Great, which likewise had portrayed shades of the dead conducting postmortem penance in the locations of their sins. Moreover, Dominican theologians in particular

---

98. Gobi, *Dialogue avec un fantôme*, 53–54; cf. Schleich, *Gast of Gy*, lvii.
99. Gobi, *Dialogue avec un fantôme*, 60. This section of the dialogue does not appear in Schleich's abbreviated Latin edition.

had earlier attempted to harmonize the doctrine of a general purgatory with the stories recounted by Gregory the Great, in very similar terms. Gobi may have been influenced by a text known as the *Supplementum*, falsely ascribed to Thomas Aquinas. This treatise, while generally focusing upon a singular, otherworldly purgatory, also attempts to explain the frequency of ghost sightings by positing that some few shades spent time conducting penance on the surface of the earth. Yet by the 1320s, such ideas were, dogmatically speaking, well out of date. The Second Council of Lyons had, in 1274, affirmed a singular purgatorial place.

The text ends rather abruptly after recounting only two visits with the ghost. Nonetheless, this brief dialogue was circulated and copied: it is extant in manuscripts currently held in London, Barcelona, and Paris. Uniquely, the ghost of Gui de Corvo became a cause célèbre of the later Middle Ages. However, the original text's popularity was soon to be eclipsed by a different, longer version of encounter with the ghost of Gui de Corvo. This new textual redaction came about after a transcription of Gobi's interviews with the ghost was sent to the court of Pope John XXII, then located in the southern French city of Avignon, very close to Alès. There it was read out in consistory to the pope and cardinals. Thus, in the fourteenth century, a tale about a medium was able to gain the attention of powerful, interested parties more readily than in the early thirteenth century; this was a second factor favoring the success of the Alès cult over the one in Beaucaire. And indeed, Gobi's text elicited a strong response in Avignon: John XXII swiftly ordered an inquiry into the ghost's visits, advising that the situation should be tested for fraud.[100] We also possess a lively correspondence about the ghost of Alès begun by a well-known member of the papal curia, Bernard de Ribéra. According to the latter, likely writing some time in February 1324, several months after the first manifestation of Gui de Corvo, "this voice continues still; and if it is asked questions by foreigners—Englishmen, Scots, or Germans—it responds to each in his own tongue."[101] Another of Ribéra's letters described the papal inquiry briefly. We learn that the *inquisitio* was led by one Jean, a doctor of law. The papal emissaries posed additional tests and questions to the shade of Gui de Corvo. It is clear, then, that many people were now visiting the de Corvo household and asking questions of its deceased owner. Ribéra further notes that the results of the formal investigation were presented to the pope; no document fulfilling these particulars is known to modern scholarship, however.

---

100. Ibid., 63–67.
101. Ibid., 64.

A final text significantly reframes our understanding of the incident. A second, expanded version of the original interviews conducted by Jean Gobi eventually was crafted, a more sophisticated literary and theological reworking of Gobi's initial version. This text elaborates on the introductory matter and the setting, adds in many more questions and answers with the dead man, and draws explicit conclusions about the theological implications of the ghost's revelations. This time, the prior Jean Gobi is portrayed as more aggressive in his interrogation of the spirit.[102] The tone of this text is skeptical and probing, though in the end the imagining of the postmortem world is similar. Whereas the original document is relatively disorganized, wandering from one topic to another in the manner of a spontaneous conversation, the later version employs the conceit of an interrogation of the dead man as the basis for elaborating a more complex treatise on postmortem penance, the value of clerical and monastic suffrages, and the communion of all the faithful. A long section on the process of dying reads like a forerunner to the fifteenth-century *Ars moriendi* genre.

While no certain date can be assigned to this redaction, it probably derives from the last decade of the fourteenth century.[103] Likewise the later text, though based around Gobi's original core, is likely the product of two hands, with a second author, possibly Italian, adding the amplifying material.[104] This version of the text became extraordinarily popular in the late Middle Ages, being translated into several vernacular languages (including French, German, English, Catalan, and Swedish), as well as being widely copied in the Latin, and published in an incunabula edition in Delft in 1486.[105] The Getty museum in Los Angeles possesses an elaborate copy of the dialogue in French; an illumination portrays the widow, Jean Gobi, and his attendants addressing the "ghost" in an empty space in their midst (figure 6.1).

While it is tempting to wonder whether this more sophisticated and theologically oriented text is a product of the inquiry ordered by John XXII, that does not appear to be the case. The papal investigators would have been unlikely to maintain the format established by Gobi, however enhanced, but would instead have adopted the highly formal, legal language typical of the papal curia. Moreover, the text appears to be of a later provenance than the inquiry itself. It is not impossible, however, that this text

---

102. Ibid., 81.
103. De Beaulieu, "De Beaucaire (1211) à Alès (1323)," 325.
104. Gobi, *Dialogue avec un fantôme*, 15.
105. Ibid., 10; for the Middle English version, see the edition in Schleich, *Gast of Gy*, 1–119.

FIGURE 6.1. In regions where the dead were conceived as invisible and disembodied, it was difficult to paint them. In this illumination that accompanies the text of the *Vision of Guy of Thurno*, the living are shown standing in a circle, conversing with an empty space where the dead man is presumed to be. Illumination attributed to Simon Marmion from the *Vision of Gui*, Flemish, 1475. Getty Museum, Los Angeles, MS 31.
Courtesy of the Getty Library. Digital image courtesy of the Getty's Open Content Program.

meshes Gobi's original framework, setting, and dialogue with some of the conclusions of the papal investigation, thus presenting theological verities in a vivid exemplary form.

In sum, in this case the regional idiom of interaction with the dead—spirits lingering postmortem, appearing to their loved ones and aiding them in their spiritual or material endeavors, while asking for suffrages in return—was appropriated and endorsed by the highest ecclesiastical authorities. Local belief in the dead appearing to their loved ones may have originated as a kind of informal oracular consultation with the protective ancestors of the family, who of course maintained an interest in the affairs of their descendants. Here, however, the dead are transformed into mouthpieces for ecclesiastical doctrine (though in the case of Gui's ghost, the doctrine was somewhat outdated). As always, the imagining of the postmortem world was a site for struggle over meanings, and yet still a space in which stories could function within two separate semantic systems: the regional culture and the abstruse teachings of the church. In short, as official teachings about the otherworld shifted to include new doctrines such as the immediate, individual judgment of the soul after death,[106] purgatory, and the value of monastic suffrages for the dead, preachers and theologians found the direct testimony of the dead to be pedagogically invaluable in promoting this new vision. Just as Thietmar of Merseburg, centuries earlier, had hoped that tales of revenant communities might aid in teaching the resurrection to the still pagan Slavs, late medieval Christian teachers likewise saw opportunity when they heard of spirits haunting homes and speaking through mediums—through special divine dispensation, of course. This time, however, the agenda was to add experiential scaffolding to the promulgation of new doctrines about the afterlife to an already Christianized populace. Indeed, the two most elaborate dossiers of evidence we have for spirit mediums—the girl of Beaucaire and the widow of Gui de Corvo—exist precisely because they became targets for clerical appropriation. This is the tattered afterlife of an antecedent cultural system that envisioned the dead on the margins of the world of the living, but largely invisible. Our view into cults for spirit mediums is filtered through many sieves: of language, of level of religious commitment, of culture and education, and of narrow dogmatic precision versus syncretistic acceptance of older ways of thought.

The Séances in Bern and the *Benandante*

Finally we come to a late, hostile description of a spiritist cult. The passage below describes the formation of a group of devotees centering upon a medium for spirits of the dead in early fifteenth-century Bern:

> There was a fraticello in the city of Bern . . . who got up at night in his house, and using stones and wood, he pretended that some spirit was present. Thus to the admiration of many each night in that place he asserted (and many believed him) that either some divine revelation must be forthcoming, or a ghost was abroad, or an evil spirit. Not infrequently, he changed his voice and in wailing accents like the ghost of some dead man who had been well known in the city, he responded to people who posed questions, saying that he was the ghost of a certain recently deceased person (both people known to him and strangers) whose name he would give. He persuaded them that he would perform a pilgrimage to particular saints' shrines on [the souls'] behalf . . .

---

106. Jérôme Baschet, "Jugement de l'ame, jugement dernier: Contradiction, complémentarité, chevauchement?," *Révue Mabillon* 67 (1995): 159–203.

and while journeying to these saints' shrines for the abovementioned souls, he acquired . . . not a little money.[107]

Johannes Nider incorporated this tale into his *Formicarius* without further explanation, doubtless assuming that his readers would perceive why the man was a fraud. Indeed, from Nider's particular cultural perspective—that of a learned Dominican inquisitor writing between 1435 and 1437—there were excellent reasons to dismiss the fraticello's assertion out of hand. As far as Nider was concerned, it was a self-evident truth that living human beings could not possibly channel the shades of the restless dead, nor speak in their voices and answer questions. Indeed, Nider included the tale of the soul-possessed fraticello in his collection of anecdotes precisely so that it might serve as a negative illustration of a superstitious error in need of correction. Nider's view of ghost stories was thus the classic Augustinian stance: what appear to be shades of the dead are more likely demons. This Dominican, unlike his forbear Jean Gobi, had no sympathy for such nonsense.

If all this was entirely clear to Nider, however, it still was not so to all of his contemporaries and peers. For those who were attracted to the cult, the unnamed fraticello's abilities as a medium presented a peerless opportunity to gaze beyond the veil of the grave. The fraticello's home appears to have swiftly become the setting for a regular evening séance, as groups of admiring devotees arrived each night in order to witness the latest revelations, debate the character of the spirit, hear news of the otherworld from recently deceased ghosts, and perhaps even pose questions of their own. These local folk accepted the fraticello's claims at face value, and Nider conveys a sense of mounting excitement on their part, culminating in their economic support for his journey to shrines. For the fraticello's Bernese supporters, the man was providing an important spiritual service, one worthy of respect and support. In this way, his role was identical to that of the southern French *armariés* like Arnaud Gélis, who likewise interacted with a wide variety of shades of the dead and mediated their needs to their survivors. The passage is too brief to offer many new details about this set of beliefs, other than to show that such ideas penetrated into the Alpine region and persisted into the fifteenth century despite a clear turn toward disavowal by church authorities. Indeed, there is evidence that extends the complex of such beliefs in the Alpine region even later: the cult of the *benandante* famously uncovered by Carlo Ginzburg.[108] While the best-documented aspect of the latter fertility cult

---

107. Ioannis Nider, *Formicarium Ioannis Nider S. theologiae doctoris et ecclesiasticae praestantissimi in quinque libros*, 3:8 (Douai, 1602), 229–35, 181–82.

108. Ginzburg, *Night Battles*.

centered upon the spirit journeys of its male adherents, who believed they fought in spirit for the fertility of the fields four times per year, a female-dominated arm of the *benandante* was characterized by an ability to see and converse with the dead. The picture that emerges from the inquisitorial inquiry against these individuals, in the sixteenth- and seventeenth-century region of the Fruili, was that *benandante* were born into their special status, being brought into the world swathed in the caul, or amniotic membrane. At maturity, male *benandante* would assume duties as shamanistic protectors of the crops, while their female counterparts would attain reputations as seers of the dead. As one witness, Lucia Peltrara, described a woman she knew named Anna La Rossa, "she . . . goes about saying that the rest of us cannot see the dead, but she can, because she was born under that sign."[109] A woman known as Aquilina considered this "gift" a curse, telling friends, "that she could see the dead but she did not want to see them."[110] Likewise, a woman in the canton of Schwyz, locally known as *Seelenmutter* or "Mother of Souls," was prosecuted in 1573 for her claims to provide information about the postmortem fate of various people, in exchange for small sums of money from their descendants.[111] And in 1586, a shepherd known as Chonrad Stoeckhlin similarly claimed to see the dead regularly, beginning with an apparition of his friend Jacob eight days after his death.[112] *Armariés, benandante, Seelenmutter*: all appear traditionally to have been titles of respect, designating a class of people regarded as special for their ability to see the dead and comfort the living. I will avoid entering into an extended discussion of these later cases of seers and mediums for the dead, since they occur beyond the medieval period and have in any case been extensively treated in previous scholarship. However, these later cases certainly testify to the deep roots these beliefs had within the region: only after they were assimilated to diabolic witchcraft, by generations of inquisitors working in these regions, did they begin to falter.

Having closely examined these individual cases of spirit mediums, it is time now to step back and explore the broader question of the mortal imagination in this region. What were these dead folk doing lingering in the streets and churches, or haunting the bedchambers of their surviving loved ones? To what purpose, this attachment of the dead to the world of the living?

---

109. Ibid., 34.
110. Ibid., 38.
111. Ibid., 52.
112. Wolfgang Behringer, *The Shaman of Oberstdorf: Conrad Stoeckhlin and the Phantoms of the Night* (Charlottesville, 1998).

According to our mediums, the answer to this question was simple: they were living immanent afterlives, close to the places in which they had lived and in communion with the people who were important to them. They were the most ancient age class of a vertical community of many ages, embracing both the living and the dead. This is a thanatology of integration, in which the dead pass into their new status but remain part of the community—much as an adolescent assumes the trappings of adulthood but retains the social bonds and background of youth.

It is possible to trace the basic terms of this thanatology rather clearly, for the sources—whether found in a courtly chronicle, an inquisitorial dossier, or exemplary collections—agree with one another to a surprising degree. By triangulating the sources it is possible to present a richer portrait of this belief system than any single account permits. In all cases, these accounts imagine the dead as leading postmortem existences in this world, rather than being translated to an otherworld beyond the access of the living. But the dead not only remained upon the earth, they had an appointed place, a location that awaited each one and that was suited to his or her status and sins. "Sometimes, people leaving this world do not reach their appointed place until the third or fourth day after death,"[113] explained William, the young ghost of Beaucaire. Depending on the circumstances, it seems, the dying may take some time to be emplaced in their new afterlife status. William did not appear to his cousin until "three or five" days after his passing, presumably the time of his transit;[114] the *armarié* Arnaud Gélis likewise testified that the first time he ever saw a ghost, it was his late employer returning on the fifth night after his passing.[115] The shade of Gui de Corvo, by contrast, returned immediately: "for all seven days after his death, a voice was heard."[116]

It is relatively easy to discern that an atavistic notion of the dead lingering on this plane of existence, as postmortem elders, has here been moralized in new ways. The wandering dead, perhaps once regarded as similar in character to Hellequin's army, have here been reconfigured as moving between a series of churches or across rocky ridges and envisaged as conducting postmortem penitence through these errant wanderings. Moreover, the dead not only linger nearby postmortem, they are sometimes described as material, albeit invisible, entities: they have bodies, and they take up space. Recall Arnaud Gélis complaining that those who walk around with their arms swinging

---

113. GT, 766–68.
114. GT, 760.
115. JF, 1:128.
116. Gobi, *Dialogue avec un fantôme*, 51. Schleich, *Gast of Gy*, lv, gives the figure of eight days.

might knock over the dead. Likewise, the girl medium of Beaucaire scolded the visiting prior of Tarascon for crowding her dead cousin William and nearly stepping on his foot. Yet, despite the explicit materialism of the girl's warning to the prior, the ghost also insisted that he was "suffering purgatory in the air," and he repeats the association between purgatory and the air several times.[117] It appears, then, that the shade of William existed both suspended in the air and with his ghostly feet on the ground: his purgatory is both aerial and terrestrial, spiritual and material. Only the late, theologically appropriated spirit of Gui de Corvo affirms the wholly spiritual nature of his existence. When asked to make the sign of the cross, "he responded that he had no hand." Jean Gobi, intrigued, next asked whether he could hear; having received an answer in the affirmative, he then inquired, "how can you hear me if you do not have ears?"[118] The ghost gave the only answer he could: that it was possible through the power of God.

As for the social dimensions of these beliefs, perhaps their most striking element is the large crowds they attracted, often comprising informal spiritist cults. Communication with a ghost was something unusual and noteworthy, yet also something people believed was plausible. In all the cases for which we have detailed descriptions, it is clear that a gossip chain formed very swiftly, bringing news of contact with a ghost out to a broader public, which soon arrived to see for itself. While it seems likely that only a small subset of a given town would make the effort to come out for such an event, in every case the sources convey crowded rooms of people eagerly pressing forward and coming back again and again to hear the latest. As a corollary to this observation, it seems safe to suggest that the mediums themselves achieved recognition and informal social status as a result of these occurrences. The young girl of Beaucaire was, at eleven years of age, the epicenter of a group of adults who met to ask her to convey questions to her dead cousin and who then listened respectfully to her replies; the widow of Alès, while not a direct and exclusive channel of communication with her husband, nevertheless was the hostess for the gatherings of people, some of exalted status, who met to hear him speak about the next life; the fraticello in Bern gained economic support and "admiration" from his public; *armariés* like Arnaud Gélis, *benandante* like Anna La Rossa, and the Swiss medium known only as *Seelenmutter* were sought out by anxious parents and children, seeking news of their dead loved ones' postmortem status.

---

117. GT, 764, 766.
118. Gobi, *Dialogue avec un fantôme*, 60. I do not find a correlating passage in Schleich, *Gast of Gy*.

Furthermore, the social regard for mediums persisted over time. The cults of Beaucaire, Alès, and apparently Bern lasted for months, with regular meetings of informal devotees every few days. They sometimes attracted prominent members of the local elite: the girl of Beaucaire, for instance, was visited by both nobility and clergy. Thus mediums for the dead occupied a role of informal spiritual leadership outside the formal structures of religious authority that normally exerted hegemony over the religious lives of believers. Yet their claims sprang from the local cultural categories of the region, rather than from the ideals of the church universal, and their authority was ratified by personal charisma rather than through the power of office. Much like the "living saints" who garnered informal local cults and exercised spiritual leadership within their communities, the role of medium was a means for those of lower social standing—laity and women—to gain spiritual authority outside the pathways of the dominant culture. Acting as pyschopomps for the dead and oracular visionaries of the otherworld for the living, their careers as mediums could be ambitious in scope.

CHAPTER 7

Spectral Possession

Demons and Ghosts

Sometimes . . . demons invade the bodies of living men and women. Then they lie and say that they are the spirits of the dead, whom they often even name, in order to defame the souls of those dead people.[1]

Displaced, unclean human spirits of either sex sometimes enter into the bodies of living human beings as dwelling places. . . . Such a spirit will confess its sex; it will confess the time and place when it entered; it will confess its proper name and its manner of death. . . . We especially worry about those who died through some violence. . . . You say, "Demons feign these things." . . . But why would they adopt feigned names when their confessions are true in all other ways?[2]

These two testimonies appear to be in dialogue. The first quotation, authored by Giovanni Matteoti, seems to be directly addressed and refuted by the second, penned by Zeno of Verona. Yet the effect is purely an illusion: in fact,

---

Portions of this chapter have appeared as "Spirits Seeking Bodies: Death, Possession, and Communal Memory in the Middle Ages," in *The Place of the Dead: Death and Remembrance in Medieval and Early Modern Europe*, ed. Bruce Gordon and Peter Marshall (Cambridge, 2000), 66–86.

1. *Vita Francescae Romanae*, *AASS*, 8 (March 9), 175.
2. Zeno of Verona, *De resurrectione*, 1:16, in *PL*, 11, cols. 373–76.

Zeno of Verona lived more than a millennium *before* Giovanni Matteoti. Zeno was a fourth-century bishop of the city whose name he bears, likely born circa 300 and died around 371; Matteoti lived in the fifteenth century and composed a lengthy hagiography for the lay penitent Francesca Romana, in which the above quotation appears. Yet across the span of centuries their words seem to engage with one another directly, as though partaking of a unified debate.

In this chapter I address a distinctively southern European belief that the dead might return in disembodied form, as specters, and that these displaced wandering spirits might also, if the opportunity presented itself, attempt to seize new bodies for themselves from among the living, via spirit possession. Unlike the ambivalent, semimaterial, semispiritual dead folk who appeared in the previous chapter, these shades were conceived of as wholly spiritual entities and consistently were discussed as such. Belief in ghostly spirit possession is best attested in the Italian peninsula but also is found in medieval Portugal. Like the northern European belief in corporeal revenants, the belief in spirit possession by ghosts remained in place over the course of many centuries. As with all such seemingly stable formations, however, its emotional content shifted over time. Likewise, the alternative interpretation, that possession was the work of demons that merely impersonated the dead, endured as well. According to church doctrine, the identity of possessing spirits was always demonic, though they might occasionally masquerade as shades of the dead in order to lead astray the faithful.[3] Thus though the two authors above are separated by a vast gap of time, in some senses it is accurate to state that both were responding to the same cultural phenomenon.

This imaginative structure is related to the southern French belief in spirit mediums: though ghostly possession is more intimate than oracular relationships with the deceased, both imply privileged relationships between the dead and the living, with the latter being used as mouthpieces and communicators. Likewise, both beliefs could center on relationships between relatives across the separation of the grave. Spirit mediumship might even be regarded as a more controlled version of spirit possession. As Ioan Lewis pointed out in his classic anthropological study of spirit possession, the chief distinction between the two states is the role of the will. The possessed person is attacked, involuntarily deprived of bodily autonomy and control, whereas the spirit medium becomes familiar with his or her spirits, communicating with them at will and controlling their ventriloquistic pronouncements.[4] Indeed,

---

3. Caciola, "Spirits Seeking Bodies."
4. I. M. Lewis, *Ecstatic Religion: An Anthropological Study of Shamanism and Spirit Possession* (New York, 1971). I discuss various cultural theories of spirit possession in *Discerning Spirits: Divine and*

in some cultures, the two states are aligned on a continuum: relationships with spirits that begin as involuntary can be transformed into willing collaborations that unveil the secrets of the spirit world. The similarities between the return of the dead as possessors, in Italy and Portugal, and as oracles, in southern France and the Alpine regions, evidently must be understood as forming some type of cultural continuum, with more similarities than variance. Thus this chapter and the previous one are conceptually paired.

The pages that follow first sketch out the terms of debate, showing how patristic authors bequeathed a set of arguments about possessing spirits to later generations, who continually repeated them through subsequent centuries. As I will show, many people were strongly attached to the traditional belief in ghostly possession and actively resisted the imposition of another model. Their skepticism that spirit possessions were exclusively due to demonic agency is readily traceable in the sources, particularly those that record the opinions of the common people. As the texts demonstrate, this was an active, contemporary belief that was widespread in medieval Italy, and not simply a "straw man" kept alive by reverence for, and continual rereading of, patristic authors. The chapter next shifts to a discussion of some of the social implications of this view that the dead might return to possess the bodies of the living. While the possessed person clearly was regarded as victimized and in need of healing, accounts of such events also often suggest a sense of compassion for the untimely dead soul, ripped too soon from life, often through violence. The return of the dead shade to a physical body—even one stolen from another—permitted them temporarily to rejoin the community of the living, thus reweaving a ruptured social fabric. This vision of the dead had, then, a fundamentally social underpinning in a way that the competing, theological model of demonic possession—involving amoral and inhuman spirits—did not. As such, questions of community memory and interconnectedness were central to the ways in which local communities dealt with cases of the returned dead in this general region.

Contested Identities: Spectral versus Demonic Possession

The belief that spirit possession was the work of dead human spirits held a respected pedigree in the ancient world. Indeed, we see echoes of it even in the Gospels: the episode of the Gerasene demoniac has clear overtones of ghostly possession.

Demonic Possession in the Middle Ages (Ithaca, NY, 2003), 80–87; and in "Exorcism," in *Encyclopedia of Religion*, 2nd ed., editor-in-chief Lindsay Jones, 15 vols. (Farmington Hills, 2005), 5:2927–38.

> They came to the other side of the sea, to the country of the Gerasenes. And when he had come out of the boat, there met him out of the tombs a man with an unclean spirit, who lived among the tombs; and no one could bind him any more, even with a chain; for he had often been bound with fetters and chains, but the chains he wrenched apart, and the fetters he broke in pieces, and no one had the strength to subdue him. Night and day among the tombs and on the mountains he was always crying out, and bruising himself with stones. (Mark 5:1–5)

As the first generations of Christians spread their "Good News" throughout the Mediterranean, they brought with them a new teaching about the nature of *daimones*. Within classical pagan cultures this term denoted a highly diverse group of spirits considered more powerful than human beings, but less mighty than the pantheon of high gods. *Daimones* were this-worldly beings, subtle presences that populated the earth densely but invisibly, alongside the perceptible realms of nature. In classical Hellenistic thought *daimones* were broadly sorted into two subgroups: beneficent *eudaimones*, which brought happiness and good fortune to those they favored, and *kakodaimones*, unclean spirits responsible for disease and disorder. Subsumed within these two general categories was a vast array of different supernatural entities, however: the *lares* and *penates* that protected each household; air, water, flame, and earth spirits; familiars, the muses, and personal guardians; euhemeristic heroes and local demigods. Finally, of course, shades of the ancestral dead were comprised within this category. The *daimonic* realm encompassed a chaotic blend of disembodied powers and essences, whose attentions could affect human life on an intimate, day-to-day basis.

Christian teachers, however, grouped all these diverse entities into a single category: all were fallen angels in the army of Satan, who provided such perfect literary foils to Jesus and the apostles. It was a taxonomy constructed and wielded to dramatize the triumphant, even apocalyptic, heroism of Christian holy men.[5] Thus the complex and multiform category of *daimones* was assimilated to a singular model of cosmic evil.

The spirits of the dead, which pagans believed lingered on earth near their tombs in order to receive libations and offerings from their descendants, were included in this process of redefinition. It seems likely that a pagan hearing the story of the Gerasene demoniac would instantly have made a

---

5. David Frankfurter, "Where the Spirits Dwell: Possession, Christianization, and Saints' Shrines in Late Antiquity," *Harvard Theological Review* 103, no. 1 (2010): 28. See also Jonathan Z. Smith, "Towards Interpreting Demonic Powers in Hellenistic and Roman Antiquity," *Aufstieg und Niedergang der Römischen Welt* 2, no. 16.1 (1978): 425–39.

mental connection between the location of the man's abode—among the tombs, a detail that is mentioned repeatedly—and the identity of the spirits that had seized him. What Mark calls "unclean spirits," and Matthew and Luke, "demons," would surely have been conceived as the *daimonic* shades of the dead that lingered amid the graves and monuments of ancient cemeteries. The dead also wandered farther afield, however. Ghosts of the untimely dead—suicides or the violently killed, for example—were especially feared as possessing spirits who might seize the unwary. Shades of the departed also were known to haunt their own households, and sometimes could become personal oracles or familiars to human mediums or necromancers who invoked the dead. While classical pagan cultures greatly feared and avoided cadavers, keeping funerary structures well outside their ancient cities, they sought to maintain a respectful détente with the shades or spirits of the departed. *Daimonic* ancestors could be protective or destructive in turn.

This set of interlinked beliefs about the intimacy, even the banality, of daily relationships between the living and the spirits of the dead proved extremely resistant to change. With some exceptions, the weight of patristic Christian thought was firmly against the possibility that the dead might play so prominent a role in human life. Early theologians instead ascribed phenomena such as possessions and hauntings to demonic agencies, just as the Gospels did in the case of the Gerasene demoniac. As *daimones* became demons, so ghosts came to be seen as diabolic agencies in disguise.

The third-century church father Tertullian, for example, writes in his *Book on the Soul* (a work we last examined in chapter 1),

> Some say that those who are cut off by an early death wander about hither and yon until they complete the number of years they would have lived, had they not died untimely. . . . But it is demons that operate under the fiction of being these souls. . . . Sometimes an evil spirit disguises itself as the shade [*persona*] of a dead person . . . as when in exorcisms the spirit sometimes affirms that it is one of the person's relatives, or else a gladiator or a fighter of beasts, sometimes even a god.[6]

Tertullian exemplifies the Christian reinterpretation of spiritual entities: he describes the common sense of his day as a foolish misapprehension of the nature of reality. Augustine agrees:

> Someone says that demons are the souls of men and that . . . they become spooks [*lemures*] or ghosts [*larvae*] if they are evil. . . . Therefore

---

6. *LA*, cols. 746–48.

he says ghosts are harmful demons transmuted from men . . . whereas the blessed may be called in Greek *eudaimonia*, that is "good demons," because they formerly were good souls. Thus he asserts human souls to be demons.[7]

Augustine's presentation of an extensive pagan vocabulary about the shades of the dead and their postmortem transformations is couched in rhetoric designed to sound comical to a Christian audience. The closing proposition that souls were demons is intended as the punch line to a ridiculous joke. Rather, according to Augustine, human spirits were of an entirely separate order of being from demons. Ontologically speaking, demons and the dead had nothing to do with one another; the boundary between these two categories was firm and unyielding. Even the most evil dead person could not be transmuted into a fallen angel, just as the saved could not become celestial angels; the blessed and the damned were always and forever human. While damned souls might be condemned to share an infernal home with demons, they were definitively not of the same essence as demons.

Augustine's positions rapidly became the standard teaching of the church. Theologians, pastoral clergy, preachers, and hagiographers were all in fundamental agreement with the bishop of Hippo that shades of the dead could not invade the bodies of the living. Yet this belief had a vigorous afterlife among the laity. For example, let us return to Giovanni Matteoti's brief comments, from a much later date—the fifteenth century. As quoted at the outset of this chapter, Matteoti makes two points that are worthy of a close reading against the grain. First, Matteoti claims that the spirits that invade human bodies in order to possess them are demons, but that they often pretend to be the spirits of the dead. Once they have possessed someone they explain, through their victim's mouth, that they are displaced dead souls. They even claim the names of recently dead people, increasing their verisimilitude. Second, they enact this charade with a specific goal in mind: in order to "defame the souls of those dead people." Thus Matteoti's statement suggests that popular attitudes toward possessing ghosts were negative: the dead spirits that lingered about on the surface of the earth seeking a body to possess were believed to do so because of a moral defect of some kind. We may assume, further, that the names usually offered by possessing spirits were known to the witnesses and participants in this drama, else the question of "defamation" would have no relevance. This demonic stratagem would be meaningless if the name were

---

7. Aurelius Augustinus [St. Augustine of Hippo], *The City of God against the Pagans*, 7 vols., Loeb Classical Library 411–17 (Cambridge, 1966), 3:188–90.

not familiar to the crowd. Naming was thus a central component of what might be called the ritual drama of a possession episode, as performatively enacted by a community. This drama—often public, often spectacular—was a site of emergent definition and meaning-making for local communities, which made sense of possessions, as well as of recent memorable deaths, through the conversations surrounding cases of possession.[8]

Exactly what is at stake in what Matteoti terms the "defamation" of the dead may be discerned in another, even later quotation about ghostly possession. This one derives from a sixteenth-century exorcists' manual written by a Franciscan friar named Buonaventura Farinerio, published in Venice in 1567: "When demons enter human bodies, they almost always appear to the person first in the form of a man who died an evil death, or sometimes they show themselves as one of the person's relatives."[9] The defamation of the dead noted by Matteoti clearly is linked with Farinerio's observation that specifies two groups from among the dead who were deemed most likely to become spirits seeking bodies: those who "died an evil death," or else relatives of the possessed victim. Presumably the "defamation" of the deceased is connected with the expectation that possessing ghosts frequently are shades of those who died an evil death. The question of "bad" or "evil" death was, as we have seen, a conceptual category of some significance throughout the Middle Ages. This conception may certainly be observed at work in the medieval Italian belief in the depredations of dead spirits seeking bodies. It is likely what Alessandra Strozzi had in mind when, in a 1459 letter to her son Filippo on the occasion of his brother's death, she mused that "whoever dies suddenly or is murdered . . . loses both body and soul."[10] The body is lost through the fact of death; the soul, through the tragedy of a *bad* death. To be torn too suddenly from life leads to restless wanderings, a death without place.

As we shall see, possessed persons in medieval Italy frequently did identify their indwelling spirits as the shades of those who were recently, violently killed. The ancient belief repudiated by Tertullian and Augustine lived on a millennium (and more) later. Those who died by murder or mayhem not only perished in particularly terrible ways, they also presumably led somewhat

---

8. Caciola, *Discerning Spirits*, 225–73.

9. Buonaventura Farinerio, *Exorcismo Mirabile da Disfare Ogni Sorte de Malefici et da Cacciare i Demoni* (Venice, 1567), 360ᵛ.

10. Gene Brucker, ed., *The Society of Renaissance Florence: A Documentary Study* (New York, 1971), 48.

MAP 7.1. The Italian Peninsula. Medieval Italians believed that spirit possession was attributable to ghosts as well as demons. The belief goes back to the classical paganism of the region. Many of the important towns and villages mentioned in this chapter are marked. On the island of Sicily, the volcano of Etna is shown; it is mentioned in several other places in this book.

reprobate lives, in order to end up falling prey to such deaths. There were deep conceptual linkages between those who were cruel and vicious in life and those who perished in sudden and violent ways: in both cases, these individuals were believed likely to be unquiet, aggressive spirits, and thus likely to become postmortem predators. However, some possessing spirits were not criminals but the ghosts of one's own relatives, returning to their familiar home and seizing the bodies of their descendants. This is, as noted above, an alternate version of spiritual return to the haunting ghosts and spirit mediums described in the last chapter. This group of the possessing dead has in common with the criminal dead their undue attachment to this world, rather than acceptance of their transition into the next. Those who died through violence remained attached because their lives were stolen from them; yet the shades of deceased relatives who haunted their own descendants were, likewise, expressing a strenuous sense of attachment to their kin group, the importance of their lineage and, of course, their living family members. In so doing, they unduly mourned their own deaths and failed to accept God's will. Though an informal, nonexhaustive survey suggests that possessions by dead relatives were far outnumbered by those attributed to the violently killed, together these two groups provided the usual suspects for identification as indwelling spirits. This fact itself suggests that the deaths that provoked the most intense emotions (whether of love or of fear), and that lingered in the memories of survivors, provided a mental gallery of potential culprits when local communities sought to identify possessing spirits. Katharine Park has stated that "Italians envisaged physical death as a quick and radical separation of body and soul, [while] northern Europeans saw it as an extended and gradual process, corresponding to the slow decomposition of the corpse."[11] While this is broadly true in terms of the separation of body and soul, in Italy the shades of the dead often still lingered nearby their bodies for some time, seeking an opportunity to seize another living person.

A final quotation about ghostly possession rounds out this broad sketch of the contours of the belief. It comes from an anonymous Dominican bishop, who around 1420 composed a hagiographical work about the thirteenth-century recluse Verdiana of Castelfiorentino. He states that the holy *cellana* Verdiana's "power of expelling from human bodies the worst demons—which the common folk ignorantly consider to be souls divided from their bodies—could be proved by as many witnesses as there were and are men in that province."[12] Like Matteoti and Farinerio, the anonymous preacher likewise assumed that spirit possession was the work of demons masquerading as the dead in order to lead astray the less sophisticated members of the faithful. The fragment of information he adds has to do with the popularity (in both senses) of the belief. He attributes belief in ghostly possession broadly to "the common people," who "ignorantly" hold to this

---

11. Katharine Park, "The Life of the Corpse: Division and Dissection in Late Medieval Europe," *Journal of the History of Medicine and Allied Sciences* 50 (1995): 115.
12. *Vita Viridianae Virgine*, in *AASS*, 4 (February 1), 265.

explanation for possession. His words accord well with the other learned testimonies we have encountered, which describe this belief even as they attempt to refute it.

The chapter thus far has unpacked the cultural logic of several quotations about ghostly possession that derive from learned treatises: two hagiographies and an exorcism manual. Such texts represent a particular standpoint; even as they document the prevalence of the contemporary belief in ghostly possession, they simultaneously refute it, insisting upon a demonic explanation for spirit possession instead. They can be read against the grain of their own ideology. When we turn away from hostile sources, however, and seek other discussions of ghostly possession, we readily find more references to the belief. Such references are occasional, rather than systematic, in tone. That is, rather than describing the belief in general terms, they simply deploy the belief as a heuristic device when discussing specific instances of possession. Thus we move from the level of abstract debate to the level of social application: general observations by elites about the contours of popular belief may be supplemented by specific anecdotes about ghostly possession, where we see the belief in action.

The comments made by learned authors about "demons who lie and say that they are spirits of the dead" correspond closely to some specific case histories of spirit possession recorded in medieval miracle accounts. At times, possession stories are merely evocative of the belief in possession by the spirits of the dead, without being precise. For example, the apparent spirit possession of a little boy described in the *Vita* of Columba of Rieti occurs after he "found a dead cat on the public street. And when, with childish curiosity, he lifted up the head by the ears, and uncovering the eyes, looked into them, he was struck numb . . . and made mindless and mute."[13] This tale seems to preserve, in vestigial form, a connection between possession and death, although it is nonspecific and the dead being is an animal. Similarly, the *Vita* of Zita of Lucca recounts two cases of possession in which the spirits, when interrogated, confess their former human names. One identifies himself as Pintello de Controne; in the other case, a woman is possessed by two spirits who identify themselves as Napoleone and Solidario.[14] These seem more likely to be designations of local dead people than of infernal spirits. In both cases, the victims are freed through the intervention of Zita.

A less laconic case may be found in the hagiography of Bernardino of Siena. This fifteenth-century work explains in some detail how possession

---

13. *Vita B. Columbanae Reatinae*, in *AASS*, 18 (May 20), 190.
14. *Vita S. Zitae Virgine Lucae*, in *AASS*, 12 (April 27), 85, 66.

by the dead was thought to occur, though it simultaneously argues that possession is the work of demons:

> It happened not far from the town that a certain mountain man came to the term of his life. Three days after he was buried, the voice of an unclean spirit was heard outside the house simulating the spirit of the dead man. . . . The rebellious and envious spirits . . . succeed more easily in [their goals] if they can slip into the minds of careless people through any weakness.[15]

A state of depression—mourning—is apt to make one particularly vulnerable to spirit possession. Longing for the presence of the lost loved one may allow a possessing spirit to "slip into the minds of careless people through any weakness." The period directly after burial seems to be targeted in particular in this passage, noting that the attempted possession takes place within three days of the funeral. The timeline for the return of the dead precisely echoes that of the previous chapter, in which haunting ghosts most often were said to appear to their survivors within three to five days.

It seems worth noting in this context that medieval artistic portrayals of death present striking parallels with portrayals of exorcism. In both cases, the spirit is shown exiting through the mouth. Though medieval theologians likely would have understood these two motifs as representing different operations—the human spirit is exhaled out from the heart with the last, dying breath, whereas the demon is forced to exit from its dwelling places inside the open spaces and cavities of the physical body[16]—such niceties are wholly elided in the two parallel iconographies. Given the similarities, it is likely that most casual observers might have conceived the role of demon and human spirit in identical terms. Such representations could, then, work in tandem with oral traditions to perpetuate belief in ghostly possession as a form of cultural common sense. Figure 7.1, for instance, shows the spirit of a newly dead man being led off on a chain by a demon.[17] Though winged, the demon walks along the ground. As for the soul, however, the artist has portrayed a true, weightless ghost. It floats in the air as the demon trails it behind him exactly like a helium balloon. Once it is freed from the flesh, gravity has no pull upon it.[18] It is not difficult, in

---

15. *Analecta S. Bernardino Senensis*, in *AASS*, 18 (May 20), 140.
16. Caciola, *Discerning Spirits*, 176–207.
17. See also Matre Ermengau, *Breviari d'amor*, Occitania, fourteenth century, Paris, Bibliothèque Nationale de France, MS Français 857, fol. 197v.
18. Cf. Mary Edwards, "Altichiero, Giotto, Dante and the Metaphorical Use of Gravity," in *Gravity in Art: Essays on Weight and Weightlessness in Painting, Sculture, and Photography*, ed. Mary

FIGURE 7.1. Medieval people envisioned the soul as exiting from the mouth of the body at the moment of death. Here, the contorted soul of a sinner is being led off by a demon. The soul, as an immaterial essence, is not subject to gravity and so floats in the air behind the demon. Illumination from the *Breviary of Love* by Ermengol de Béziers, late thirteenth – early fourteenth century. Real Biblioteca de lo Escorial, Madrid. Provençal codex, fol. 215v (detail).
Gianni Dagli Orti / The Art Archive at Art Resource, NY.

contemplating this image, to conceive of the idea that such a disembodied soul might wish to enter into another body. Indeed, the ghost's posture is contorted, as if it is uncomfortable in its freshly disembodied state.

In seeking more elaborate textual descriptions of ghostly possession than the scattered allusions discussed thus far, three texts stand out as particularly valuable. All are miracle compilations. Two derive from the central Italian peninsula: the 1325 canonization testimonies for Saint Nicholas of Tolentino;[19] and, moving west to Florence, the fifteenth-century *Miracles of John Gualbert*, appended to his *Vita* and incorporating vivid descriptions of spirit possessions undoubtedly gleaned from interviews with witnesses.[20] In addition, a collection of miracles from 1342–43, attributed to the

---

Edwards and Elizabeth Bailey (Jefferson, NC, 2012), 72–85. I thank Jack M. Greenstein for this reference.

19. The text has been studied in depth by Sari Katajala-Peltomaa, *Gender, Miracles and Daily Life: The Evidence of Fourteenth-Century Canonization Processes* (Turnhout, 2009). See also Alain Boureau, "Saints et démons dans les procès de canonisation," in *Procès de canonisation au Moyen Âge, aspects juridiques et religieux / Medieval Canonization Processes, Legal and Religious Aspects*, ed. Gábor Klaniczay (Rome, 2004), 199–221.

20. See Pierre Sigal, "La possession démoniaque dans la région de Florence au XVe siècle d'après les Miracles de Saint Jean Gualbert," in *Histoire et Société: Mélanges Offerts à Georges Duby*, 3 vols. (Aix-en-Provence, 1992), 3:101–12; Caciola, "Spirits Seeking Bodies."

Virgin Mary and collected at a shrine dedicated to her under the name of "Our Lady of the Olive Tree" in Guimarães, Portugal, describes several spectral possessions.[21] The two texts originating in Italy are both purely in Latin. The Guimarães text, by contrast, preserves detailed descriptions of exorcistic miracles, including dialogues with the possessing spooks, in medieval Portuguese. The miracles of the Virgin of the Olive Tree were recorded by a notary, who was retained by the shrine specifically in order to record these healings. Thus, this last text is not connected to a saint or a canonization inquiry; in fact, Portugal lacked any medieval canonization processes for its holy men and women, the earliest such inquiries being early modern.[22]

A particular virtue of all three texts is that they not only provide abundant examples of spirit possessions, but they record complex sets of viewpoints about the identities of the invading spirits. They thus present multivocal dossiers of evidence, providing an excellent opening to witness the kinds of discussions local communities engaged in when trying to name the spirits that possessed friends and neighbors. We see the possessed identify their invading spirits as the shades of the recently dead; we hear their friends and neighbors excitedly recall their lives and deaths; and at times we encounter local clerics who either dispute these identifications and try to correct the understanding of the less learned or, alternatively, endorse popular ideas. (Priests, after all, shared the same social background as their flock.) Thus these three works provide the bulk of my evidence, though they are supplemented by more scattered references to spirit possession drawn from other sources as well.

---

21. The original text has been published in two editions: Mário Martins, "O Livro de Milagres de Nossa Senhora da Oliveira de Alfonso Peres," *Revista de Guimarães* 63 (1953): 83–132; and Cristina Célia de Oliveira Fernandes, "O livro dos milagres de Nª Sª da Oliveira de Guimarães," *Revista de Guimarães* 109 (1999): 217–97. The two editions are based upon different manuscripts. I generally have followed Oliveira Fernandes but give information on both editions under the title "O livro de milagres de Nossa Senhora da Oliveira." Studies include Cristina Célia de Oliveira Fernandes, "O livro dos milagres de Nossa Senhora de Guimarães," *Lusitania Sacra*, 2nd series, 13–14 (2001–2): 597–607; and the wonderful study of María de Lurdes Rosa, "As andanças dos demónios – uma leitura dos casos de possessão do *Livro de Milagres de Nossa Senhora da Oliveira* (1342–43)," in *Santos e demónios no Portugal medieval* (Porto, 2010), 107–58. Some discussion of the text also appears in Iona McCleery, "'Christ More Powerful than Galen'? The Relationship between Medicine and Miracles," in *Contextualizing Miracles in the Christian West, 1100–1500: New Historical Approaches*, ed. Matthew M. Mesley and Louise E. Wilson (Oxford, 2014), 127–54. I would like to thank Dr. McCleery for kindly sharing with me a version of this paper before its publication.

22. Rosa, "As andanças dos demónios."

Criminal Ghosts: The Miracles of Nicholas of Tolentino

Let us begin with the canonization dossier of Saint Nicholas of Tolentino. Nicholas, an Augustinian friar and hermit born in 1245, swiftly developed a cult of veneration after his death in 1305. His fame reached the papacy in Avignon, and John XXII ordered a canonization inquiry *in partibus* in 1325. Testimony about Nicholas's qualities in life, and about the 301 miracles attributed to him after death, was taken in the summer of that year. Between July and September, in Tolentino and other sites, 365 witnesses were heard and their testimony carefully transcribed in Latin translation.[23] Though the legates presented their findings to John XXII in 1328, the politics of the Great Schism caused a delay in Nicholas's canonization until 1446. In that year, the friar finally received his halo.

What is perhaps most striking about the way in which spirit possession was described in these interviews is that witnesses charged *both* shades of the dead *and* demons as perpetrators. It appears that the witnesses were aware of the church dogma that demons were possessors, but that they perceived this teaching as a complement to, rather than as a replacement for, ancient regional assumptions about the shades of the dead as possessors. Featuring prominently among the miracles attributed to the saintly hermit were the healings of three women possessed both by "devils" and by "spirits of the damned." These cases were described at length, by multiple witnesses, providing an in-depth look at beliefs about spirit possession in Italy in the first quarter of the fourteenth century. The victims included a married woman from Cammoro, Zola, wife of Massio; an unmarried laywoman, Salimbena Vissanuci from Visso; and a Cistercian nun from the convent of Santa Lucia in Pian di Pieca, Sister Philippucia. All three women exhibited classic possessed behaviors: seizures, eye rolling, tongue wagging, foaming at the mouth, and occasional acrobatic feats and contortions. They likewise were notable for their frequent shouting, cursing, and hurling of verbal abuse, along with much immodest behavior.[24] Zola, Salimbena, and Sister Philippucia were each conducted to the saint's tomb in the years leading up to the inquiry into Nicholas's case for canonization in 1325. Once there, they practiced the ancient custom of incubation, spending the night in the Church of Saint Augustine, keeping vigil before the spot where Nicholas's relics lay entombed. All three were healed after one night, and they all later provided firsthand testimonies about their experiences of possession, which were

---

23. *PCNT*, ix–xii.
24. Caciola, *Discerning Spirits*, 36–78.

transcribed by the papal commissioners charged with investigating Nicholas's case *in partibus*. Friends and family who knew the victims also offered their versions of the events, describing the victim's behaviors during the possession episodes as well as testifying about their healing. It is illuminating to examine each of their cases in turn.

In 1322 the Cistercian nun Sister Philippucia began acting strangely. As the other nuns in her convent recollected, Philippucia suddenly became buffoonish and abusive. She took every opportunity to hurl insults at the other sisters, to shout foul curse words, to make grotesque faces with her tongue and eyes, and to run, dance, shout, and sing. As if this weren't bad enough, "she used to walk on her hands and raise up her feet on high" exposing herself through this acrobatic feat.[25] Philippucia was self-aware throughout her possession, however, and she later offered first-person testimony about the experience:

> She stated that while she was living in the monastery . . . she had been invaded so forcefully that she used to roll her eyes back into her head, she twisted her mouth, danced in time, and would say many injurious and nasty things to the nuns of that monastery. Many visions appeared to her, or at least it used to seem to her that they appeared. Day and night she seemed to see mice in infinite numbers, and images of various men of the foulest kind, and many beasts.[26]

The visions of "men of the foulest kind" whose images haunted Philippucia's mind were visions of the dead men whose shades had possessed her. Several of the other nuns who witnessed Philippucia's illness recollected that Philippucia cried out, seemingly in panic, that Lord Johannes, Lord Vivibene de Esculo, and Lord Raynaldo de Burunforte were leading an attack against her.[27] All the witnesses agreed on the same three names, a concurrence that suggests both that Philippucia repeated these shrieks often and that the names were familiar to the nuns. Indeed, Philippucia's interior visionary experience of the process of being possessed was vividly dramatized to others via her own narration of internalized scenes: "Behold! . . . They are coming against me, attacking me along with many knights!"[28] In fact, though the three named men were the "leaders" of the possession of Philippucia, many of the witnesses noted that other, unnamed shades were also involved.

---

25. *PCNT*, 327.
26. *PCNT*, 137.
27. *PCNT*, 140 (Sister Franciscucia), 324 (Sister Francesca).
28. *PCNT*, 140. The testimony on p. 324 is quite similar.

Why were Johannes, Vivibene, and Raynaldo recalled so vividly, and why were they considered to be the chief spectral possessors of Sister Philippucia? The testimony tells us only a little about them, but the facts that are included are significant. The men were clearly members of the nobility given that each is referred to as "Lord," that they have formal surnames such as "de Burunforte," and that Philippucia describes them as leading bands of knights in her possession visions. Beyond this, we know from the nuns' testimonies that by the time of Philippucia's possession in 1322, all three were dead; this excludes the possibility that Philippucia was describing a real encounter with living men, and instead comports with a scenario of possession, in which the ghosts of the dead men lead a spiritual assault against her that she experiences as one of her visions. The interviews with the nuns also reveal that these three men led lives of tyranny and cruelty. As sister Andrea Johannis testified, they were "dead men who were tyrants while on earth, and who had committed many evils during their lifetimes."[29] The testimony of Sister Johanuccia Servidei was slightly more specific, both about the possession of Philippucia and about the men's crimes: "[Philippucia] announced that she *was* the dead men Lord Johannes, Lord Vivibene de Esculo, and Lord Raynaldo de Burunforte; and also many other dead men who, during their lives, committed many crimes, homicides, thefts, and evil deeds."[30] While we do not know how the men died, it seems clear that their evil reputations stirred fears that their strenuous natures might lead their spirits to wander the earth, with "energy still unexpended," in Lester K. Little's phrase.[31] It is a likely inference (though not one that is verified by the testimony) that the three died badly. Perhaps they perished while still young or unexpectedly, a common end among those who engaged in feuds, quarrels, and crimes of violence.

This pattern certainly was present in the other cases of spectral possession in Nicholas's canonization dossier. The two other victims had similar experiences with the shades of violent criminals and tyrants. (In all cases, the possessing ghosts identified in the canonization proceeding were males.) As was the case with Philippucia, the transgressors always were identified by witnesses through the shouts of their victims; the local idiom of spirit possession, as it emerges from these testimonies, required the victim to label her possessing ghosts or demons through continual shouts of their names. Thus the laywoman Salimbena struck others as possessed precisely because

---

29. *PCNT*, 330.
30. *PCNT*, 328.
31. Lester Little, *Benedictine Maledictions: Liturgical Cursing in Romanesque France* (Ithaca, NY, 1994), 151.

she continually yelled out names of a certain group of dead men. As the witness Mattiola, who was present the evening of her cure at the shrine of Saint Nicholas, testified, "There was a certain woman by the name of Salimbena Vissanuci de Visso, who was tempted and invaded by several spirits so intensely that day and night she would scream out, *Scambio Raynaldo! Salvo de Podio! Nicoleta de Paterno!* along with [the names of] several other men."[32] As with Sister Philippucia, the process of naming—part ritual, part dramatic chaos—was a central element of the enactment of possession. Shouting out the names of local dead persons for all to hear was a way of announcing their victimization of the possessed woman. As was the case for the Cistercian nun Philippucia, the laywoman Salimbena's continual shrieking of the dead men's names was an obsessive and consistent behavior. Everyone later remembered it in their interviews, and everyone independently recalled the same names and similar details. Typical is the testimony of Gentile Nugarelli, who offered some information about the dead men's characters and histories:

> She said that Salimbena de Visso was tempted and invaded by devils and by spirits of the damned: to wit, by Scambio Raynaldo, Vecte Salvo de Podio Vallis, Nicoleta de Paterno, and two others whose names she could not remember. Salimbena used to explain that when they were alive these men had been of evil reputation, condition, and life. They were robbers and wicked men. And she said that they had been burned for their crimes, their evildoings and their deeds. And this Salimbena was so stricken and so invaded by these same men's ghosts, she used to shout out their names. Also she often used to say very dirty words.[33]

Similarly, Brother Francisco de Nursia, of the Order of Saint Augustine, recollected how Salimbena cried out the names of these men during her incubation night at Nicholas's tomb: "for the greater part of the night she was calling out in a loud voice certain names of men and demons, for it was said that she was invaded and tempted by devils and by spirits of the damned."[34] She kept this up until she was freed from the possession. Like Sister Philippucia's possessing spirits, Salimbena's ghosts also were wicked men, but likely of lower social status, since they were not described as "Lord." Perhaps because they were less powerful, they had been seized for their crimes and publicly executed by fire. Interestingly, according to Salimbena's own sworn testimony, she was invaded by five ghosts in total: these three and also

---

32. *PCNT*, 453.
33. *PCNT*, 452.
34. *PCNT*, 455.

"two others whom she didn't recognize."[35] These shadowy figures, akin to the troops of knights accompanying the leading possessors in Philippucia's visions, rounded out the scenario of possession as a complicated affair involving many different spiritual entities: there were both devils and the damned, named and unknown.

Though all the women claimed to be possessed by demons as well as by ghosts, the testimonies chiefly focus upon the dead and show only minimal interest in diabolic spirits. And if both types of possessors were mentioned in the interviews, it seems as if the inclusion of demons was in most cases pro forma. The category of demons was treated as largely self-evident, and therefore uninteresting, by the witnesses. For example, only one diabolic name—Belial—appears in the testimonies, in the case of Philippucia; no further elucidation of these entities' nature was presented. By contrast, the shades of the dead who seized living bodies inspired elaborate discussion in the register of the canonization inquiry; their identities are fleshed out including their full names and titles, the nature of their lives and crimes, and the manner of their deaths. Indeed, the final victim of possession, a married woman named Zola, makes this element of obsessive, traumatic memory quite clear.

> A long time ago [Zola] was continually tempted and molested by certain damned spirits from the village of Cammoro named Lardo and Traverso, who had been wicked men. They committed many wicked crimes during their lives; and because of their political sympathies they had been summarily burned, without sentencing or trial. The witness often used to see them in the form of dogs, and it seemed to her that these burnt men were always before her eyes to see. They would say to her, "You will see us every time you go through the streets!" and they used to shout at her.[36]

Clearly these men were known to Zola in life, as they came from the same village. Indeed, it seems likely that the possessed usually were seized by ghosts of similar social standing to themselves. The victims of possession were most likely to identify, as the culprits behind their states, recently deceased individuals who were known to them. The names of Zola's ghosts, which translate roughly to "Porky" and "Twisty," seem like nicknames, perhaps of the kind that remain popular even now in criminal organizations or gangs.

In sum, naming the shades of spiritual aggressors was a crucial component of the public performance of a possession episode in medieval Italy, at least.

---

35. *PCNT*, 445.
36. *PCNT*, 303.

This was a necessary formality prior to healing the victim. Identifying the possessing ghosts by name; recounting the evil deeds of their lives; shuddering over the horrific circumstances of their bad deaths: these acts of collective memory and narrativization were key to resolving the disturbances of possession. The possessing entity's acknowledgement of his name, his crimes, and the details of his death, ventriloquized through the disordered shouts of the possessed person, was thought to be a key veridical point in establishing the basis for exorcism. The fact that so many witnesses independently testified to the same names and biographical details about the possessing entities in these cases suggests that this information was highly resonant with the witnessing community.

Indeed, despite the deep revulsion elicited by some of these criminal ghosts and the memories of their deaths, the high level of public interest in possession events also testifies to a broad social interest in temporary communion with the dead. The fact that possessing ghosts almost always were identified as the shades of those who were torn from life before their time, and by violence, has implications not only for the individual ghost but for the broader social group as well. For the exorcism of a ghost is, of necessity, a different sort of emotional operation than the exorcism of a demon. The model of spectral possession found in these sources opens up the possibility of compassion for both the victim *and* the perpetrator of possession (albeit perhaps unequally). The exorcism of a ghost is an inherently social operation, in a way that the exorcism of a fallen angel is not: demons were never part of the social fabric. A ghost, however, was until recently a local community member: someone's son, someone's husband or lover, someone's father, very likely someone's enemy or oppressor—but a person occupying a particular social identity defined by a unique set of social bonds, both positive and negative. The untimely death of such a person not only snapped his own tenuous life-thread, it ruptured the web of social bonds that connected him to others. Moreover, since in many cases it appears that these individuals died horrific public deaths, such as execution by burning, it seems possible that even enemies might have some compassion for them. Such a person's reemergence among the living, via the possession of a living body, accomplished the temporary mending of a rent social fabric. It likewise provided an opportunity for reconciliation and acceptance of a violent death on the part of the broader community. Thus exorcizing possessing shades of the dead could function as a way of domesticating their troubling memories. The level of interest that bystanders expressed in hearing these ghosts recount their stories suggests both a capacity to empathize with their postmortem confusion and sufferings, as well as intense curiosity about the world beyond the grave. The ultimate act of expulsion, of course, most often occurred at the tomb of a saint, an opposition of the exemplary "good dead" against the "bad dead." After all the details of the possessing specter's past were known and shared among the crowd, the cathartic end of the episode would be a celebration of the pure and blessed power emanating from the holy dead. A saintly dead body could exorcize the evil dead from a living body, in a triangulation of life, death, and corporeity that benefited both the victim of possession and its perpetrator.

The ghosts who possessed the living were named, they were known, and they often were remembered with a piquant admixture of horror and fear. No wonder they were considered appropriate companions to demons, with whom they shared the possessed body conjointly in these testimonies. In these testimonies, the suffering bodies of the possessed are symbolically coterminous with hell: the possessed body is the infernal territory in which shades of the evil dead and unclean spirits dwell together. Thus, the understanding of possession expressed by these witnesses was not impervious to change, not a mere survival without evolution. To the contrary, the culture of the region held ideas about possession that were accumulative, absorptive of sequential influences borne by Christianization alongside older ideas. Demons were given their due and incorporated into the system along with the more elaborately described and recognized local ghosts. The regional system at work here accepted the universalizing Christian epistemology of demons as possessors, yet still upheld a flourishing ancient tradition of ghostly possession that invoked local memories and community knowledge systems. The two were not seen as opposed, but as mutually sustaining, syncretic constructs that literally shared space within the possessed body.

Debating the Spirits

If the Nicholas of Tolentino dossier unveils the porous and accumulative qualities of the regional popular culture, in other texts we encounter the limits of this flexibility. The *Miracles of John Gualbert* is a fifteenth-century compilation of saintly healings attributed to a Vallambrosan monk who died in 1073 and was canonized two decades later in 1093. The author of this text was a Florentine monk associated with Gualbert's order, Jerome de Raggiolo; by the time he wrote in the fifteenth century Gualbert's relics, particularly his arm, enjoyed a reputation for outstanding exorcistic virtue. The possessed were brought to his shrine in large numbers, and it is their testimony, that of their family members, and that of the monks performing the exorcisms with the help of Gualbert's relics that is abstracted in Raggiolo's text. Some tales give quite a bit of circumstantial background to the process of the possession, including information about the identity of the spirit, what the victim was doing just prior to the possession, and how the spirit gained power over the individual. In several cases the spirit either explicitly identifies itself as the shade of a dead person, or else the circumstances of the possession and exorcism clearly imply that the spirit was understood as such by the victim and onlookers. Jerome de Raggiolo, however, aggressively contests this identification and considers the troublesome spirits to be demons. This does not prevent him from having a sense of humor about the situation, however. In one instance he jokes about spectral possession, describing a man possessed by a "comedic demon" whose primary amusement is to sing psalms and hymns in such hilarious parody that he moves even somber religious men to irrepressible laughter. So intent was this spirit upon its liturgical songs "that you would think," remarks Jerome, "it was the shade of some priest!"[37]

Yet despite Raggiolo's light-hearted jest about possession by clerical ghosts, he firmly believed that such a scenario was impossible. Indeed, this text describes a rather unique and fascinating set of disputatious encounters between local folk and learned clerics. These debates about the identities of possessing spirits are vividly presented. Local folk, and the possessed themselves, were apt to identify the possessors as ghosts of the dead; in response the local priest (whose viewpoint is sustained by Raggiolo himself) contested this identification, arguing that spirit possession was always the work of demons. In some instances, this difference of opinion inspired rather lengthy arguments or disputes that are reproduced in the text. It is an excellent example of different levels of culture, popular and elite, in debate over the meanings of contemporary events.

The first detailed example of possession by a ghost in this text conforms closely to the pattern elucidated in the canonization inquiry for Nicholas of Tolentino: the possession was perpetrated by the displaced spirit of an executed criminal. A young man was conducted to the shrine of John Gualbert for a healing. He was in a frenzy, Jerome de Raggiolo reports, as if inhabited by several demons. Jerome's description is suitably lurid:

> He did not want to confess his sins to a priest, nor ask for forgiveness, but renounced even the compassion of Jesus. . . . To these evils he added blasphemies against Jesus and his most pious mother Mary. . . . How many times he commended himself to the Devil! Alas, how many times did he twist his eyes away from an image or picture of the Lord

---

37. *MJG*, 388.

Jesus Christ!! At intervals between his ravings, with what curses did he threaten the knights and others who had gathered there out of pity and in order to witness the wretched spectacle![38]

In random moments of lucidity, the young man tearfully told his story. The whole thing started when the girl he loved best was married to another man. In his melancholy and lovesickness, one day he listlessly wandered the streets, inattentive to his path. At length, he found himself at the edge of town, where the city gallows was located. The corpse of a local criminal hung upon the scaffold; the decaying body had been permitted to remain there as a warning to other potential malefactors. It was there that the possession occurred:

> While the cadaver was still hanging there, tied to the gibbet with a chain, this man, driven insane by love, just happened to take the road next to the scaffold. As is human nature, he raised his eyes to the frightful corpse: it was grisly and putrid, gnawed by worms and by the other insects that are generated from decay. He was repulsed. . . . Then (as he himself told the story), he heard a hissing sound from above. . . . This much is clear: a demon entered into him while he was in this state of fear, and it began to dominate him and to use him as a dwelling-place.[39]

The hissing sound was understood by the victim and his family to be the sound made by the spirit of the executed criminal as it left the carcass hanging on the scaffold and slipped into his own body. Immediately afterward he was possessed and began to rave. The character of the possessing spirit conforms to the pattern we have observed. Criminal execution is, of course, the very worst kind of death, indicating an evil life leading to a violent end. Moreover, like the cases of the burned criminals who always were before the eyes of one of the possessed women in the Nicholas of Tolentino miracles, visual trauma played a part in this young man's case: the sight of the partially decayed corpse is conveyed with a vividness that evokes the fear and horror of the youth, who immediately thereafter became possessed. Lastly, the tale indicates that the low mood of the victim also was regarded as a contributing factor in his possession: the combination of his lovesickness with the shock and terror he experienced at the sight of the scaffold made him more vulnerable to spiritual invasion. Interestingly, the image of the desolated young man at the gallows, rendered ill by the invading vital spirit of the criminal hanging

---

38. *MJG*, 391.
39. *MJG*, 391.

there, is the mirror image of contemporary practices of healing, which also might involve the bodies of executed criminals.[40] Taking a blessing from the hand of a hanged man, or ingesting the blood of one executed by the sword, was thought to transfer healing vitality to the recipient. With proper controls and dosages, the unexpended vitality of the prematurely dead could be harnessed for healing the living; but lacking proper precautions, that same vitality could harm.

Jerome de Raggiolo introduces several more cases of possessed persons whose invading spirits identify themselves as ghosts. However, unlike the testimony in the Nicholas of Tolentino canonization inquiry, in which the interviewers allowed such identifications to stand without challenge, the author of this miracle collection was anxious to correct any misrecognition of demons for the dead. In consequence, his account includes descriptions of some fascinating public debates between himself and crowds of laity over the nature of possessing spirits. The crowds, assembled to view a live exorcism, accepted the identification of the possessors with specific dead men; Jerome de Raggiolo in turn disdains this belief and counters it with theological teachings about human bodies, human spirits, and how they may be conjoined or severed from one another. These sections of the text are rich and rewarding to read:

> Another woman came to us from the town of Pontenano . . . and the demon that had invaded her averred (as many of them are accustomed to do) that it was the shade of a certain Ligurian named Beltramo.
>
> It ought to be pointed out that this is an impudent lie that must be restrained by the authority of Holy Mother Church, so that the average common man might perceive that such a thing is scarcely possible and thus be instructed in true religion. . . . This fact is proved, first of all, by the authority of the prophet who says, "the spirit goes and does not return" (Ps. 77:39). Nothing tells us *where* it goes: either it flies through the air purging itself; or it dwells in an earthly place that is deserted and

---

40. Mabel Peacock, "Executed Criminals and Folk-Medicine," *Folklore* 7, no. 3 (1896): 268–83; Wayland Hand, "Hangmen, the Gallows, and the Dead Man's Hand in American Folk Medicine," in *Magical Medicine: The Folkloric Component of Medicine in the Folk Belief, Custom, and Ritual of the Peoples of Europe and America* (Berkeley, 1980), 69–80; P. Kenneth Himmelman, "The Medicinal Body: An Analysis of Medicinal Cannibalism in Europe, 1300–1700," *Dialectical Anthropology* 22, no. 2 (1997): 183–203; Charles Zika, "Cannibalism and Witchcraft in Early Modern Europe: Reading the Visual Images," *History Workshop Journal*, no. 44 (1997): 77–105; Michael Camille, "The Corpse in the Garden: *Mumia* in Medieval Herbal Illustrations," in *Il Cadavere / The Corpse*, Micrologus 7 (Turnhout, 1999), 297–318; Richard Sugg, *Mummies, Cannibals, and Vampires: The History of Corpse Medicine from the Renaissance to the Victorians* (London, 2011); Louise Noble, *Medicinal Cannibalism in Early Modern English Literature and Culture* (New York, 2011).

uncultivated, or else not deserted; or it goes to a place that is inaccessible to us, which we call purgatory. But to believe that a dead soul should go back into a human body again we consider, and hereby declare, to be a wicked sin [*nefas*]. Moreover, it has never been read among any people that two souls of the same type and nature might occupy the same body and have various experiences together. I was able to cite other pronouncements, at times from the holy gospels at times from other divine scripture, as proofs. However, lest it should seem that I am presenting a sermon rather than a history, it is enough to know that devils are proven liars on this matter. Though in truth, if they request anything useful for souls of the dead—either offices, or Gregorian masses, or alms—once it is asked for then, God willing, we do it. Now I return to my story.[41]

Several aspects of this incident are worthy of comment. First, there is Raggiolo's comment that "many [spirits] are accustomed" to identify themselves as shades of the dead, testifying to how common the belief was in fifteenth-century Italy. Thus the link between the unquiet dead and possessing spirits is again reinforced. Second, there is some discussion of the possibility that souls might linger on earth after their death, though in isolated places rather than inside human bodies. This would seem to admit to the possibility of haunting, but not possessing, as a power of the dead. In fact, the notion that a departed spirit "flies through the air purging itself" seems to echo a belief discussed in the previous chapter that some souls purged their sins through an aerial existence on this plane of reality. Third, there are the intriguing series of arguments against the belief in spectral possession, including both biblical authority as well as a physiological argument that two human souls cannot share the experiences of one body. Jerome de Raggiolo, like other churchmen of his day, accepted the possibility that dead spirits might linger in this world, but not invade living bodies.

We know from the subsequent anecdote, however, that clerical arguments against ghostly possession were largely unsuccessful with crowds of laity. In this tale, the exorcism of another individual possessed by a spirit claiming to be one of the displaced dead led to a spontaneous public debate on the nature of possessing spirits. The priest in charge (this time not Raggiolo) contested the spirit's identity, but to no avail:

> The demon that had invaded her asserted that it was the soul of a certain man [named] Mazzanto, who was murdered with a dagger by a certain scoundrel over a game of dice. Everyone who was witnessing

---

41. *MJG*, 416.

this pressed forward to affirm that it was true. However the priest argued with them, bringing forth . . . many opinions of men outstanding in virtue and learning, through which he demonstrated that when the souls of men first leave their bodies they go to the place they have merited. That is, they find a sweet place; or they find a harsh land for purging or else for eternal torment. They do not find another body to enter. As for those others [i.e., possessing spirits], they are evil spirits who from the cradle are given to human beings for bringing various temptations. . . . It is no wonder, then, if they give out men's names, and if they relate the virtues and vices of those with whom they have had familiarity and awareness from their earliest days!

[But] the priest scarcely could convince them this was true. It is typical of rustic people that the less they understand of what is being said, the more they wonder, and it is only with the greatest difficulty that they can be turned away from any idea that already has caught their ears. This is particularly true because they are stiff-necked and barely capable of reason. . . . Finally, through the virtue of the most blessed John Gualbert, [the possessing spirit] broke forth in these words, "I will make my way elsewhere if prayers and orations are made on behalf of the soul of this Mazzanto." . . . The girl happily went back home with her family, having offered some money right away in order that, as promised, Gregorian masses might be celebrated in the monastery on behalf of Mazzanto's soul.[42]

The belief that possessing spirits were the evil dead seems to have been too deeply rooted in the community to be uprooted by the mere theological disquisitions of a priest. In this particular example, the crowd was particularly impressed by the specificity of the spirit's knowledge. The account of the precise circumstances of Mazzanto's bad death provoked a stirring response among the bystanders, who pressed forward excitedly to hear and corroborate the story. In such a case, community memory had priority over the priest's abstract theological argument about the afterlife and the different kinds of supernatural spirits. Moreover, since the promise of masses on behalf of the soul of the dead man healed the girl, there was little impulse to think that the indwelling spirit was anything *other* than Mazzanto. Here the unseen world reflected the seen world: the supernatural was populated by the "natural" spirits of the local dead rather than by cosmic beings like fallen angels.

---

42. *MJG*, 417.

In addition to tales involving the "bad dead," some cases in the *Miracles of John Gualbert* involve another common category of possessing ghosts: relatives. In one instance a girl was possessed after encountering "an old woman lying on her bed, holding her right hand between her cheek and the pillow."[43] The girl did not recognize the old lady, but the description is vivid, giving a sense of real speech. When the spirit was later conjured, it told the priest it would leave, "if you make sure to have Gregorian masses with the offerings for the dead celebrated on my behalf." The shade ultimately was identified as the girl's great-grandmother. The primary witness whose testimony is preserved was the girl's father; he noted that the spirit was that of "the recently deceased mother of my father."[44] The old lady thus returned to the comfort of her family by first haunting, then possessing, her descendant. Other, similar anecdotes appear in Raggiolo's text, cases in which possessing spirits refuse to leave the bodies they have taken unless masses for the dead are sung for specific, recently dead individuals—that is, presumably, on their own behalf. For example, the spirit inside another woman, when ordered to leave by an exorcist, replied that it would only do so under one condition: Gregorian masses must be said on behalf of the woman's uncle. If the monks were to renege on this bargain and fail to "compensate" the spirit properly, he would forthwith return.[45] Thus, the shades who possess these individuals identify themselves with souls in purgatory, since these are the only shades that might benefit from masses for the dead. Though the popular theology of possession by ghosts was unacceptable to priests like Jerome de Raggiolo, the laity's understanding of postmortem alleviation was impeccable.

There thus seems to be a relatively short interval in which shades of the dead were believed to cling to life, seeking a new living body to possess after an interval of haunting. It is always the recent local dead who seek new bodies from among the living in their community. They are displaced shades who long for a new corporeal emplacement. The communities that gather to interrogate them try to construe their identities and understand their motivations by discovering their names, finding out where they were from, hearing the times and manners of their deaths, and identifying their families. These were thought to be key points in establishing the nature of the dead spirit, its place within the community when it was a living person, and the best way to lay it to rest by placing it within its new community of the dead. Yet at the same time, the high level of public interest in these events testifies to a

---

43. *MJG*, 440.
44. *MJG*, 441.
45. *MJG*, 421.

broad social interest in temporary communion with the deceased. Jerome de Raggiolo communicates an intense sense of excitement when he describes responses to ghostly possession: in one case, "everyone pressed forward to affirm that [the manner of the spirit's death] was true"; in another, we hear from the victim of possession, "as he himself was accustomed to tell it"—indicating that this was a tale much in demand. The opportunity to interview the dead, while it did not obviate the desire to heal the possessed victim, was greeted with great enthusiasm.

Perhaps the ultimate case of this sort of social reintegration and rectification occurred in the case of a spirit named Beltramo, however. This long account of spiritual encounter and exorcism portrays Beltramo as a ghost who is anxious to set right some unfinished business of his lifetime—the classic need of the unquiet dead. Thus Beltramo actually dictates his last will and testament from within the living body he possesses, utilizing it to enunciate his preferences for the disposition of his property. Jerome de Raggiolo adds his characteristic demonic interpretation, but it is easy to discern how the local community would have understood this tale.

> After the demon had, in the guise of this other man, battled both the cross and prayers for a long time, it was afflicted with bitter torments. Finally, persisting in its impersonation, it broke forth into these words: "I will go to my repose if these people, after having diligently investigated and looked into my estate, will make sure to stand up to my children. For if the latter are led by their usual perversity, they would prefer to do anything rather than make things right. If this happens then even though I am now forced to depart for another place, I will come back, bringing many of my colleagues with me, and I will inflict even worse torments upon them!" Hearing this those wretched men, fearing for their own sakes, said, "Give us a way of undertaking this task, if you can, and we will diligently strive to fulfill your request."
>
> "I request that these things should be done," said the demon, "and you must fulfill what I say to the letter. I desire to make a disposition of my possessions through a public testament, in accordance with popular custom." A scribe was brought in, who happened by chance to be in the monastery on some business with the abbot. Then the demon, under oath and upholding his best judgment of the truth of the matter, enumerated his possessions, interests, works, appointments, creditors and debtors; which things should be bequeathed to his children, which things to the church, and which things to other people; while the scribe

put it down in writing as a record. With these things having been diligently fulfilled, the demon then vanished in the form of smoke.[46]

It is easy to see the functionalist dimensions of ghostly spirit possession in this discussion. By permitting the unquiet dead to set his affairs in order, as he was not able to do in life, the surviving community is unburdened of any sense of unease about the fate of the man's property. Everything is done properly and legally, put down in writing as a formal inventory and testament. The formal drafting of a will was, of course, an integral component of the requirements for a "good death" as set forth in the contemporary late medieval *ars moriendi*, treatises for dying "properly." Thus, this possession permits community reconstitution and reconciliation. For his part, Beltramo suggests that fulfilling these tasks will allow him to go to "repose," a clear echo of the place of repose that ghosts mentioned often to the medium Arnaud Gélis, discussed in the previous chapter.

Even more poignantly in this regard, as the text continues Beltramo also confessed to an unsolved crime. Thus another bit of unfinished business is put right through the device of spirit possession and the communication it enables from beyond the grave. Beltramo confessed to a murder and disclosed the location of the victim:

> It does not seem inappropriate to set forth in a few words, a murder that was perpetrated by the abovementioned Beltramo. We believe the true facts of the matter are more and more clear. This man . . . knew of a certain person who was an architect by training, who earned a not insubstantial sum of money for himself and his associates during the summer. Observing this, certain wicked men from the city of Pontenano were seized with greed for that money. They diligently mapped out the streets and routes he took, with this in mind: that they would kill him. One day the plotters, determined in their treachery, slaughtered him in a rather remote area of a horrible, dark wood not far from Pontenano. Having stolen his money they buried him (lest there be any evidence of their deed) and left him there. The demon, while he was here and, as you heard, afflicting with torment a woman from the same family, by divine will told the whole story.[47]

As with the act of dictating a will, thus making his own good death, Beltramo also retroactively made possible a good death for his victim. The

---

46. *MJG*, 416.
47. *MJG*, 417.

performance of proper funerary rites was, of course, of signal importance in completing the transition of the individual from this life to the next. Though the author paints Beltramo as impenitent for his deed—in Raggiolo's view, the revelations come from a demon compelled by God—from the perspective of the local community, this event would represent a significant expression of remorse and an attempt at rectification from beyond the grave. Once the shade's affairs were placed in order—his property bequeathed, masses commissioned for his soul, a murder and a burial place disclosed—he could transition to the place of repose, secure in the hope of eventual salvation. Though Beltramo's crimes were severe, possession permitted him to initiate a penitential process, atoning for his crimes, disposing of his ill-gotten property, and garnering masses to ease his postmortem state.

The Living and the Dead in Guimarães

Turning our gaze now across the Mediterranean Sea and skimming over the Iberian peninsula, we reach medieval Portugal. The small northern town of Guimarães housed a small church dedicated to the Savior and Our Lady; it was originally the chapel of a double monastery founded in the mid-tenth century by a widow named Mumadona Dias.[48] On October 8, 1324, an ancient, moribund olive tree there suddenly revived and came back into leaf, after the arrival of a cross from the church. The miracle was ascribed to the Virgin, and the sanctuary became known as the Church of Our Lady of the Olive Tree. The miracle was duly recorded in writing, and the canons of the church became alert to the possibility of more miracles that might spread the fame of their foundation and encourage a flow of pilgrims. Thus from January 4 until March 27, 1343, a series of miracles or *milagros* were carefully collected at the shrine in order to establish a new cult for Our Lady of the Olive Tree of Guimarães. A notary was kept on call to record the miracles, and exorcists—all laymen, rather than clergy—also seem to have been ready to attend to the possessed when needed. Forty-five miracles ultimately were gathered, of which eleven recount the healings of individuals suffering from "doença de demonjho," or "an illness from a demon."

Yet the possessing spirits in the Guimarães cases were hardly demonic in nature; they were chiefly displaced human spirits. Though not every possessing entity agreed to identify itself, those that did present a motley assortment

---

48. Mário Cardozo, "A propósito do Centenário da 'cidade' de Guimarães e do Milenário da sua existência histórica," *Revista de Guimarães* 63 (1953): 10–11.

MAP 7.2. Portugal. Several cases of ghostly possession also come to us from a vernacular source from the northern Portuguese town of Guimarães. This map shows important cities and the river Douro.

of personae. The possessing entities included the spirits of a notary, a judge, an abbot, a priest, and a pig. Some of the possessions were collective affairs, involving *companhairos*, or colleagues who acted together; in all cases, the possessors were male, while the majority of the victims were female. Some families suffered from multiple possessions of different children, and some spirits were recidivists, appearing more than once inside different people. Under interrogation from exorcists at the shrine, a spirit would often give his full name and those of his colleagues, if any, discuss his background a little, identify his hometown, and explain why he possessed his victim. In addition, many spirits revealed an exact time when they would leave the body they possessed and specified an intended earthly destination once they left. While the text has some overlap with the Italian texts, the tone and emphasis of this particular dossier seems even closer to popular culture than the other sources discussed above. Many of the presuppositions of these *milagros* are culturally atavistic, demonstrating a relatively thin degree of doctrinal sophistication and a high tolerance for internal contradiction.

While the first few spirit possessions in the dossier are relatively spare, they soon become more elaborate. Specifically, the possessing spirits are more densely situated within their social context. In the case of milagro 17, for example, the possessing specter revealed a great deal about himself and his situation—his former life, his reasons for possessing his victim, and his status in the afterlife.

> Item: after this, on Saturday the first day of February Santa Maria of the Olives performed a miracle for a young girl named Maria, identified as the daughter of Martim Miguéis and Maria Frutuosa, a resident of the freguesia of Santa Marinha de Zêzere on the bank of the river Douro in the bishopric of Porto, who had an illness of a demon. She was taken to the foot of the cross and they tried to make [the demon] speak: *Who was he? Why had he possessed the girl? And what would make him leave?*
>
> He said that he possessed her because she was given to him by her mother, for the girl did not want to marry the man who was her mother's choice. And he said that his name was Estêvão Domingues, a resident of Paços de Baião, and that he had been a notary there. He said that he would depart through the power of Santa Maria of the Olives and that he would leave a sign of this on the riverbank of the Douro—the demon boasted that this was near where he saw the girl and possessed her. He said he would leave her forever through the power of Santa Maria of the Olives and that as a sign of this he would make a new coin come up her gullet right away.

And he said that he came to this sinful state because of an inheritance that he seized from the heirs of his neighbors, making it seem like his own land by stealing the boundary markers. And he said that his children should give back what he had stolen to the [rightful] heirs and that his children should have thirty masses said for him upon the altar of Santa Marinha of Paços. That is where [his body] lies buried, but it cannot be consumed by the earth as he wishes it would be. And [his heirs should] give two and a half soldos to each cleric who said a mass for him, so that these clerics could eat and drink after they said the mass, and they should say these thirty masses half in honor of Santa Maria of the Olives and half in honor of Santa Marinha of Paços, in order to alleviate the pain he suffered.[49]

Relatively little information is recorded about the victim of the possession: her name, parentage, residence, and the fact that she was of marriageable age but refused to accept her mother's choice of husband. This detail places the victim, Maria, squarely within a widespread pattern, noted by historians and anthropologists alike,[50] in which reluctant girls on the brink of sexual initiation become victims of possession states. An unusual twist, however, is added by the fact that Maria's mother "gave" her to Estêvão Domingues for possession, though precisely how this was accomplished is unclear. Did Maria Frutuosa, in a moment of frustration over the failing marriage negotiations, angrily curse her daughter? Such a scenario is attested in other sources as an opening for demonic possession. Ultimately, however, the text chiefly focuses its attention on the possessor, the shade of Estêvão Domingues, rather than on Maria, his victim. His speech is certainly based upon an emergent dialogue between the exorcist and the conjoint figure of Maria/Estêvão: medieval exorcisms recommended that the possessed be closely interrogated, in order to obtain as much information about their indwelling spirits as possible.[51] However Afonso Perez, the notary compiling the document, prefers to list the exorcists' questions all at once in the beginning and then to compile the ghost's answers into a single monologue. The result is a rich set of narratives

---

49. "O livro de milagres de Nossa Senhora da Oliveira," ed. Oliveira Fernandes, milagro 17, p. 250; ed. Martins, milagro 18, pp. 113–14. I am indebted to Ana Grinberg and Miriam Shadis for help with translating the medieval Portuguese.

50. Michel de Certeau, "Language Altered: The Sorcerer's Speech," in *The Writing of History*, trans. Tom Conley (New York, 1988), 244–68; Moshe Sluhovsky, *Believe Not Every Spirit: Possession, Mysticism, and Discernment in Early Modern Catholicism* (Chicago, 2007); Lewis, *Ecstatic Religion*; Isabelle Nabokov, "Expel the Lover, Recover the Wife: Symbolic Analysis of a South Indian Exorcism," *Journal of the Royal Anthropological Institute* 3, no. 2 (1997): 297–316.

51. Caciola, *Discerning Spirits*, 225–73.

that read like detailed confessions of souls from the afterlife, reflecting upon their sins in life and their postmortem fates.

The picture of ghostly possession that emerges from this text is quite complex. To begin, the above account suggests that for the community around Guimarães, a sinful human soul in torment would actually come to be transformed into a demon after death. While it is clear that the spirit that possessed Maria is a specific human shade, he is also referred to as a demon—hence the name of the pathology that is cured always is "illness of a demon." (Indeed, as we shall see in some other healings, sometimes the possessed person also is referred to as a demon, their identity wholly subsumed by the possessing entity within.) When Estêvão states that he "came to this sinful state" by defrauding his neighbors, the underlying suggestion appears to be that he was transformed into a demon after death on account of his crimes. This is precisely the idea that Saint Augustine had repudiated nearly a millennium earlier. At the same time, however, it appears that Estêvão was a dead person in a state of postmortem penance, though the term "purgatory" never is used. His concern to rectify the injustices of his life, and to have masses celebrated on his behalf, suggests that his status as a "demon" can be altered. There are some obvious similarities to the case of Beltramo, the Italian thief and murderer who needed to confess his crimes and dispose of his material possessions properly from beyond the grave.

One of the more startling details of the monologue is Estêvão's assertion that his body, though interred in the churchyard of Santa Marinha of Paços, is unable to decompose back to earth. What holds it back? Why will the ground not consume Estêvão's flesh? It appears that his cadaver's involuntary incorruption is a materialist analogue of his spirit's involuntary attachment to life: Estêvão's soul cannot rest, and is functionally a demon, until his sin is put right. As a physical component of this mechanism, his body stubbornly refuses to release its vital energy, forcibly keeping him tied to this world though he should rightfully be displaced from it. He cannot fully move into the next world, the regenerative realm of the ancestors, and yet he cannot find rest and be released from his vaguely purgatorial postmortem state. In fact, it appears that this lack of corporeal corruption is, in itself, a source of suffering for Estêvão. The notary's spirit remains a wandering dead/demonic presence in search of embodiment, his own body remains incorrupt, and he experiences penitential suffering until his crime can be redeemed and appropriate masses are performed. Thus Estêvão is both a demon and a ghost, a suppliant penitent and yet a continued victimizer of the innocent, an incorruptible cadaver and an unclean spirit. There exist some subtle similarities, here, to the northern European precondition for revenancy: in that case, too, as long as the corpse remains intact it is dangerous and may wander from its grave. In Guimarães, however, it is the spirit that wanders and presents a menace, while the body remains undecayed, but in the ground. Lastly, of course, the obvious parallel with sanctity is likewise intriguing: the powerful dead, whether beneficent or malign, are active in this world when their remains persist intact. In Estêvão's case, the fact that his flesh cannot be consumed by earth until his unfinished business is rectified constitutes a sort of inverted antimiracle or form of bodily *virtus*. Corporeity indexes the ability of the dead to be conscious actors.

Maria must eventually have vomited up the coin Estêvão promised, for by the end of the milagro she was considered healed. The vomiting of a coin as a token of the invasive spirit's departure is an unusual element that recurs in many of these miracle accounts. It often is specified that the coin will be brand-new or recently minted, seeming to suggest that the possessing ghosts in these cases still have access to the most up-to-date material items. It remains unclear how the logic of this plays out: How can a man dead for some time have a very new thing? How can a spirit grasp a coin? How does the coin get inside the victim's body? Likewise puzzling is the detail that the shade of Estêvão was wandering, disembodied, near the banks of the river Douro when he saw and seized Maria, who already was especially open to possession because her mother had "given" her to the spirit world. The peculiar imaginative vista opened up by these details is that after his death, the shade of Estêvão dwelt near this riverway, in a disembodied state but somehow acquiring new coins, before taking up residence inside the vulnerable girl.

This was not to be the last we hear of Estêvão Domingues, however. For the same Estêvão later participated in a group possession of Maria's younger sister, "Little Maria." Apparently Estêvão was a recidivist possessor with a particular affinity for this family, and apparently the mother of this clan, Maria Frutuosa, had a particular predilection for "giving" her children over to spirits, since in the case of Little Maria this same detail is mentioned. Indeed, the historian María de Lurdes Rosa, who has published an incisive study of this text, raises the possibility that this milagro may simply be an amplification of the earlier one since they share so many elements in common.[52] However, the two accounts also present some noteworthy divergences, as we will see, and it also would not have been uncommon for two daughters in one Portuguese family both to bear the name Maria. Ultimately Rosa concludes that it makes the most sense to treat them as separate incidents, and I concur.

---

52. Rosa, "As andanças dos demónios," 113.

CHAPTER 7

According to our source, then, the next month, on March 24, Little Maria arrived at the sanctuary of Our Lady of the Olives for a healing. Like her older sister, Little Maria had been given over to spirit possession by her mother, though in this case we do not know why. The possession had been ongoing for eight years, so apparently Little Maria had angered her mother at a relatively young age.[53] The milagro recounts how Maria was taken to the foot of the cross, and then,

> Diago, son of Gil Domingues of Guimarães, laid a stole around her neck and asked her the following questions: *Who were you? Why did you possess her? Will anything make you leave her, apart from Santa Maria of the Olive Tree?* And he ordered the demon to bring himself to a point inside the girl's body where he could speak through her ear, and to tell him the answers through her ear.[54]

The spirit that dutifully spoke to Diago through Little Maria's ear identified himself as the spirit of one André Domingues, a *living* man. André explained that he had seven friends with him, all of whom were still alive except for "Estêvão Domingues from Paços, who formerly was a notary at Baião." The others were all identified as people from the general region, many of them prominent individuals. The list also includes some interesting surprises: Estêvão Pires from Santa Marinha; Geraldo de Paços, "who used to be a lawyer in Santa Marinha, but was now a judge in Carvalho"; Rodrigo Aires, abbot of the monastery of Sedelios; Father Martim Afonso, priest of Santa Maria de Sedelios; another notary, Domingos Gonçalves from Mesão Frio; and finally, the spirit of a particular pig who belonged to one Estêvão Pedro.[55]

The account raises some fascinating but ultimately unanswerable questions. Aside from eccentric details such as the spirit speaking through the girl's ear, there are a number of other astonishing circumstances in this possession, beginning with the fact that a living abbot and a priest were among the invading spirits. The presence of these religious figures adds an element of authoritativeness to the milagro accounts: though mainstream Christian doctrine would hardly endorse the beliefs contained in this miracle account,

---

53. Since the older Maria was involved in marriage negotiations, she was likely in her midteens. The younger Maria must have been at least one year younger and had been possessed for eight years. This places the onset of her possession sometime in childhood.
54. This quote and others pertaining to this milagro, "O livro de milagres de Nossa Senhora da Oliveira," ed. Oliveira Fernandes, milagro 41, p. 282; ed. Martins, milagro 42, pp. 127–28.
55. Here I follow the lead of María de Lurdes Rosa, who suggests a reading of *cochom de Stv pedro* ("Estêvão Pedro's pig") rather than the more mystifying *cochom de São Pedro* ("Saint Peter's pig"). See "As andanças dos demónios," 126 and 143, n. 108.

within the world of the text these religious leaders lend authority to the events that are described. Popular concepts are subtly given the imprimatur of clerical participation through this claim about Little Maria's indwelling spirits. Indeed, this hardly should be surprising: in a location like Guimarães, there seems to have been little cultural difference between laity and clergy of the kind seen in Jerome de Raggiolo's text from the sophisticated city of Florence. For instance, the exorcists in this text are all laymen, some of the possessors are clergy, and the monks and canons dedicated to Santa Maria of the Olive Tree never "correct" the milagro narratives for theological content.

Furthermore, a fascinating set of conventions is presumed here about the ways in which bodies and spirits may combine with one another. How did the spirits of living people dislocate themselves from their own corporeal homes, in order to take up residence inside the body of another? Can a single spirit be in two bodies or two places at one time? And what was Estêvão's role in the group of "companion" possessing spirits in this account—most of whom were still alive? María de Lurdes Rosa raises the fascinating possibility that this detail may indicate the presence of a group of magical practitioners in the region, perhaps led by the priest in the group as a member of the clerical, necromantic underworld.[56] The presence of living clergy supports the interpretation since, as Richard Kieckhefer has shown, necromancy was the province of a clerical underworld in the Middle Ages.[57] Though these questions unfortunately cannot be resolved, the incident opens up a fascinating tableau on the perceived similarities between the living and the dead. Human spirits are able to do the same sorts of things before death as after: the experienced practitioner of spiritual journeys can move through different bodies at will during life as well as after death, in a sort of magical metempsychosis. We might perhaps conceive of this operation as something akin to a shamanistic spirit-journey: just as the living *armariés* and the *benandate* were able to travel, in spirit, to meet the dead, so perhaps these individuals were able to travel, in spirit, to possess the living.[58] Though my study focuses upon the dead, this case brings up a fascinating set of parallels with other shamanistic cultural formations in medieval Europe.[59]

---

56. Rosa, "As andanças dos demónios," 126–28.
57. Richard Kieckhefer, *Forbidden Rites: A Necromancer's Manual of the Fifteenth Century* (University Park, PA, 1998).
58. Rosa, "As andanças dos demónios," 127.
59. Carlo Ginzburg, *The Night Battles: Witchcraft and Agrarian Cults in the Sixteenth and Seventeenth Centuries* (New York, 1983); Carlo Ginzburg, *Ecstasies: Deciphering the Witches' Sabbath* (New York, 1991); Claude Lecouteux, *Fées, sorcières et loups-garous au Moyen Âge: Histoire du double* (Paris, 1992); Wolfgang Behringer, *Shaman of Oberstdorf: Chonrad Stoekhlin and the Phantoms of the Night* (Charlottesville, VA, 1998); Éva Pócs, *Between the Living and the Dead: A Perspective on Witches and Seers in the*

CHAPTER 7

The material suggests a certain ease for the living to wander into the world of the dead, just as the dead can enter into the bodies of the living.

Tempting though it is linger over this unusual coda to the career of Estêvão Domingues, let us turn to another milagro that features the dead more than the living and that is thus more in keeping with the theme at hand. Milagro 33 describes the healing of a young shoemaker named Viçente. In this case a dense family history, involving close ties and betrayals between Viçente's family and that of his possessing shade, forms the social background of the case:

> Santa Maria of the Olive Tree performed a miracle for a young man by the name of Viçente Estevez Chães, a cobbler residing in the town of Tomar, who had an illness of the demon. He said that he had had this illness for eighteen years. The demon was taken to the feet of the cross and questions were put to him: *Who was he? Why did he possess him? What would make him come out?* Speaking through the young man the demon said that his name was Afonso Garcia, a priest, and that he would leave through the power of Santa Maria of the Olive Tree. And he said that he would give a signal beforehand and that he would go to Rua Nova in Lisbon, to the home of the merchant João Martinez, who would give him space, and that he would bring him a newly minted coin. And João would give him space for today and so he would go be with him.
>
> And he said that he had been spiritual coparents with Estevez Chães, being godfather for his son, the young man Viçente; and Estevez Chães was godfather for him four times, for his, Afonso Garcia's, children. And he said he came to this state because he had been with the daughter of his coparent, the girl named Domiga Estevez Chães, whom he kept in his power, having his way with her. And also because he performed other evil deeds. And he said that today he would give a signal of his departure to Diago, who would see it this very day.
>
> The demon was taken to the foot of the cross again and Diago Gil, son of Gil Domingues, told him on behalf of God and of Santa Maria of the Olive Tree to give the signal and that he should leave this young man forever. Speaking through the latter, the demon said that he would leave and that he would give the signal right away by making him vomit a newly minted coin up the gullet.[60]

Early Modern Age (Budapest, 1999); Neil Price, ed., *The Archaeology of Shamanism* (New York, 2001); Emma Wilby, *Cunning Folk and Familiar Spirits: Shamanistic Visionary Traditions in Early Modern British Witchcraft and Magic* (Brighton, 2005). *Magic, Ritual and Witchcraft* 1, no. 2 (Winter 2006) is dedicated to the shamanism/witchcraft connection.

60. "O livro de milagres de Nossa Senhora da Oliveira," ed. Oliveira Fernandes, milagro 33, p. 269; ed. Martins, milagro 34, p. 122.

In the cases of the two Marias it is unclear whether there existed a prior relationship between possessor and possessed. Presumably the victims either knew Estêvão and the other indwelling spirits personally or at least knew of him, since they produced his name when pressed for the identity of their possessor. In the case of Viçente Estevez Chães and Afonso Garcia, by contrast, the bonds between possessor and possessed were both dense and intimate. Indeed, one aspect of this episode that is particularly poignant is the continual betrayal of trust that appears to have occurred in the relationship between the two families.

The possessing spirit identifies himself as the shade of a priest, though clearly quite a sinful one. Afonso reveals a great deal about himself and his serious crimes. To begin, Afonso had four children despite being in orders. In itself, however, this need not necessarily be regarded as a terribly damning detail: village priests were often sexually active without any judgment from their communities; in the later Middle Ages, celibacy was only truly expected from the higher clergy.[61] He might also have conceived these children before entering orders. Yet even if we set aside this detail, Pai Afonso still emerges from this source as a louche. Despite close ties of spiritual kinship with Estevez Chães, formed by standing as godfathers for one another's children over the course of many years, he nevertheless betrayed this bond by beginning a sexual relationship with his coparent's daughter Domiga. Moreover the language of the text suggests that this relationship was fraught with violence: "he had been with the daughter of his coparent, the girl named Domiga Estevez Chães, whom he kept in his power, having his way with her." The wording implies rape and/or abduction. If, in addition, Domiga was one of the children whom he had raised from the font at baptism, then by canon law her violation would have been regarded as a form of incest as serious as intercourse with a blood daughter.[62] Similarly, though Afonso had been godfather to Viçente, he nevertheless violated this young man's physical and emotional integrity by penetrating into his body and possessing him. Certainly, spirit possession often involves erotic undertones, and in this case it is a particularly piquant element. Afonso violated both siblings, penetrating into their private spaces and seizing their bodies for his own uses. Moreover, in possessing Viçente, Afonso symbolically transforms the latter into a demon like himself, as suggested by the phrasing, "The demon was taken to the feet of the cross."

Afonso was wholly unrepentant for his sins. Unlike Estêvão Domingues, this shade did not express remorse, request any alleviating actions, or seek

---

61. Jacques Rossiaud, *Les sexualités au Moyen Âge* (Paris, 2012).
62. Joseph Lynch, *Godparents and Kinship in Early Medieval Europe* (Princeton, NJ, 1986).

restitution or masses. It seems that Pai Afonso was not seeking to move on fully to the otherworld; rather, he embraced his role as a demon. Rather than spiritual rest, Afonso's chief concern appears to be finding a welcoming "space" to retreat into after his expulsion from the body of Viçente. In line with the peculiar presumptions about the dead expressed in this text, this requirement is conceived in very specific terms: "he would go to Rua Nova in Lisbon, to the home of the merchant João Martinez, who would give him space."[63] Afonso even indicates his willingness to pay "rent," for he suggests that he will give his new host a coin. It remains somewhat unclear precisely how this retreat to Lisbon is envisaged: Will he possess João's body, with the latter's consent? Lodge in João's home in Rua Nova? The situation resonates with the image of Estêvão Domingues living as a spirit on the banks of the river Douro and collecting coins. These spirits needed to be conceded a particular space to live, and they maintained connections to the worldly economy.

In this chapter it has been possible, more so than in some of the previous ones, to correlate medieval beliefs with pre-Christian beliefs and traditions. There are well-attested ancient pedigrees for the expectation that the evil dead may enviously seek to possess the living, or even become permanently transformed into demons after death. Indeed, it is easy to trace lines of affiliation between medieval Christian popular culture and anterior paganism in the context of the rich literary traditions of the Mediterranean, as opposed to Slavic, Germanic, or Celtic regions, since the latter cultures were less reliant on the written word.

In this context, it becomes particularly important to recall the lesson of João de Pina-Cabral, that the reproduction of cultural traditions over the *longue durée* should be regarded not merely as ossified, empty "survivals" that persist through inertia, but as actively chosen elements of invariance that continue to be vested with meaning, even though that meaning likely shifts over time.[64] Thus, in medieval cases of possession by ghosts, the shades of the dead are characterized as sinners within a Christian moral frame, their postmortem status is often reckoned as a form of purgatory, and the alleviation of their status often involved requests for masses as a form of spiritual alms. Thus this ancient pattern of understanding was no longer so ancient in terms of its cultural expressions and meanings in a later time frame. The basic pattern persists; the elements of its interpretation do not.

---

63. The question of space is central to the analysis of Rosa, "As andanças dos demónios."
64. João de Pina-Cabral, "The Gods of the Gentiles Are Demons: The Problem of Pagan Survivals in European Culture," in *Other Histories*, ed. Kirsten Hastrup (London, 1992), 49.

All the same, the equation of spirit possessors with shades of the evil dead, rather than with fallen angels or demons, constitutes a divergence from church dogma that rewards closer interrogation. For "the supernatural," writes Peter Brown, "becomes the depository of the objectified values of the group."[65] This chapter has elaborated two fundamentally different conceptualizations of the supernatural world of possessing spirits. On the one hand is the model of the universe advanced by ecclesiastical authors. These men identified possessing spirits with fallen angels and argued that dead spirits cross over into a new realm, another world of reward and punishment that is disconnected from our present existence. On the other hand, it is clear that within certain local communities around the Mediterranean, shades of the bad dead, or of relatives, were believed to linger among the living. In the previous chapter, we have seen them interact with the living through a voluntary rapport of spirit mediumship; in this chapter, we saw them seize the opportunity to regain a human body through the intrinsically violent, and violating, tactic of spirit possession.

Can we, according to Brown's dictum, extrapolate social values from different constructions of the supernatural world? In the remaining pages of this chapter, I would like to explore the social-historical dimensions of these divergent mental constructs. For the process of collectively constructing the spirit's nature and meaning is fundamentally a social act, deeply expressive of community priorities and interests. I would suggest that theologians, in line with their desire to prove the existence of the next world and the persistence of the soul, utilized stories about spirit possession and spirit mediums as a means to explore questions of individual soteriology and universal eschatology. Local communities, however, regarded these same events as opportunities to ritually reconstruct community boundaries and definitions, to place themselves amid the memories of local history and of their ancestors.

A religion both transcendent and soteriological, medieval Catholicism developed an anthropology that was based upon a perception of congruence between the microcosm of an individual and the macrocosm of the universe. And in turn, the cosmos imagined by medieval theologians may be described as the material backdrop—almost a material analogue—to a vast eschatological conflict between God and the devil, the ancient enemy of the human race. Microcosmic choices toward sin or righteousness reflect a macrocosmic, elemental tension that pervades the whole of creation and history. After death, a soul's assignment to hell, or to purgatory and/or heaven, positions it eternally on the side of evil or of good. One leaves behind the body

---

65. Peter Brown, *Society and the Holy in Late Antiquity* (Berkeley, 1982), 318.

to exist among the sinful or the righteous, the fallen or the blessed, demons or angels, for all eternity. Dead spirits do not seek new bodies; they already are emplaced within a new spiritual realm, from whence there is no return. As an anonymous encyclopedist phrased it, "after death there is no means of gaining merit.... Afterward, there is no possibility of returning to the body or to the world."[66] This gap between worlds could only be crossed by the living to join the dead; never by the dead seeking to return.

Within this system, the spirit possession of a material human body by a fallen angel inevitably was bound up with moral questions of sin and retribution. Demons thus play a retributive role within the universal scheme of divine providence, and possession signals a negative soteriological state: only fallen Christians attract fallen angels. Moreover, demonic spirits and human spirits are entirely different and separate orders of creation: ghosts do not become demons. From this perspective, then, possession by a demonic agency is necessarily violent and painful, a hybrid, wrenching violation of immense power brought to bear upon fragile flesh. At this moment, the human body not only reflects but actually incarnates the tensions of the macrocosm. A possessed individual is not him- or herself, but Other: the person's voice, actions, and consciousness are all that of the demon whose personality is dominant. Finally, as a reflection of this unique state of alterity, possession also places the victim in a socially liminal position. The demon-possessed body is placed beyond the bounds of human society because it no longer retains a human identity: it is in thrall to the demon inside. In short, one's individual spiritual state, soteriological status, and the broader social order are all tightly interwoven within this rationalist system, in which human events and choices reflect broader cosmic and moral conflicts.

By contrast, in turning to the supernatural world constructed by local communities, we see a universe that is far more intimate in its structure, though less systematic in its meanings. The building blocks of the supernatural are presumed to be natural in themselves; it is their unwonted combination that produces a miraculous effect. Indeed, in many communities it was the human dead that dominated the local supernatural, rather than beings of an entirely different essence, such as angels and demons. Or, in the world of the *Milagros de Nossa Senhora da Oliveira da Guimarães*, the evil spirits of the sinful were actually transmuted into the unclean spirits of the demonic hosts after their deaths. This is a more "humanistic" view of the unseen world, one in which the activities of transcendent beings are remote and ineffable,

---

66. Vincent of Beauvais, *Speculum morale* (Duaci, 1624; repr. Graz, 1964), II, I: IV, 710–11. Though attributed to Vincent of Beauvais, this is the work of an anonymous author.

while the memories, experiences, and local common sense of the community form a vivid cultural basis for constructing the supernatural. The possessing shades were identified as local malefactors, whose crimes and biographies were known to the possessed and to their surrounding community. Furthermore, the cure for possession—visiting a saint—involves the invocation of yet another category of the human dead: those heroic dead whose sufferings merited them a participation in the reserves of divine supernatural power. In viewing the human body as a possible repository for displaced human souls, these communities constructed for themselves a supernatural that was more knowable because smaller in scale. If, in some cases, the spirits were conceived as having material capabilities and needs, this apparent contradiction likewise gestures toward the familiarity and intimacy of this system of imagining the postmortem state.

For its part, the procedure of identifying the possessing spirit—of gradually attaching a social identity to the invading entity—is an act of collective memory. In the creative process of construing meaning, we see local knowledge, memories, and idioms interwoven to express the evolving self-definitions of the group as well as its collective anxieties. Rather than an automatic placement according to merits that theologians endorsed, these local communities felt that certain souls among the dead needed to be placed in their new status in a more active way. The defining boundaries of the entire community—including both living and dead—were at stake. With good deaths, community boundaries were effortlessly fractured and immediately reconstituted as the dead left the community of the living and entered into their new status. These shades were believed to be ready to accept their new place. In cases of bad death, however, the process of placing the dead was more complex and gradual. Death could become a drawn-out process, not an event. Not only did these individuals have to make their initial entry among the dead too suddenly, while still desperately attached to life, but those left behind likely experienced a heady mixture of horror, titillation, and guilt in recalling the terrible ends of murder victims or executed criminals. Collective memories of such deaths would linger as a mental apparition that could become vividly present—particularly in cases of highly traumatic deaths, such as executions. In other cases, memory of bad deaths might be not only a mental image, but literally a public presence: the bodies of criminals commonly remained in their place of death for some time in the Middle Ages.[67] We have seen an example above, where a lovesick youth was possessed by

---

67. Robert Mills, *Suspended Animation: Pain, Pleasure and Punishment in Medieval Culture* (London, 2006).

the spirit of an executed criminal, whose fetid corpse remained upon the public scaffold. Such sights provided a constant reminder of the person, their crimes, and their final sufferings.

A similar, though less sinister, process could be said to occur in the case of relatives. In these cases, significantly, it is always the family that makes the identification of the possessing ghost, not the broader community as a whole. The recent deaths of family members haunted the imaginations of survivors, as the bad dead haunted the thoughts of a town more generally, providing a group of usual suspects in the event that someone were possessed. Such local memories were considered probative and irrefutable by the group, as demonstrated by the skeptical reactions Jerome de Raggiolo attributed to a crowd of bystanders when a priest attempted to dispute with them about the nature of a possessing spirit. When the hapless ecclesiastic explained the theology of spirits and bodies, demons and the dead, the local folk remained unimpressed. After all, the possessing ghost had given his name, Mazzanto, and had specified in minute detail the known and remembered circumstances of his bad death. Experience was firmly credited over authority.

Furthermore, within these local communities the moral valences of possession were the inverse of theological belief. Victims might be rendered vulnerable through trauma, mourning, or other forms of depression; in the Portuguese cases, they sometimes were cursed or "given" to the spirits—but the victims were not understood as sinful. In this system, evil is displaced from the living and projected instead onto the ghost who takes possession. By specifying that possessing spirits are the shades of those who died a bad death, sin and violence are linked to the dead shade, not the living victim. In consequence, the social aspects of the possession drama tend to be conceived in rather a different way from theologians' representations of demonic intervention. When viewed theologically, possession engenders an absolute alterity: the demoniac incarnates an ancient and hostile supernatural being dedicated to nothing less than the downfall of the human race. The possessed person is socially, morally, and mentally dis-integrated for the duration of the possession. As viewed through the lens of the regional popular cultures of Italy and Portugal, however, possession may become a temporary means to social reintegration beyond the threshold of death. A former member of the community seeks to possess one of the living both to reexperience embodiment and to reconnect with the community of the living. The living, moreover, evidently felt some sympathy for such spirits: taken too soon from the body, such spirits had not yet come to terms with the fact of their own death. They thus desperately attempted to regain life by obtaining another body, wrested from among the living. Although the possession was seen as disruptive for the possessed individual, the motives of the possessing spirit were perfectly understandable. The conversations and interviews conducted with such possessing ghosts—often asking who they were, and how to help put them to rest—signal the reconstitution of a community that temporarily includes the dead individual once again. This positive social aspect of possession thus both mediates group memories and restores past circles of community. In the case of the bad dead, finally laying such a ghost to rest exorcises collective anxiety and guilt about the individual's violent end. Once fully placed among the dead, the collective memory of the individual's violent end can be allowed to fall into obscurity.

Ultimately, the entire scenario of possession and exorcism lays the errant spirits of the dead to rest in the imagination of the community. Whether relatives or sinners, possessing ghosts must complete the process of death by abandoning the new body they have taken. The community or family places itself under the protection of a local saint, or good shade, and thus lays to rest the unquiet shade that has tried to force its way back among the living. It is a reconstitutive ritual that redefines the community at its center—the living—and at its peripheries: the dead. Ultimately, such episodes place the living even as they place the dead, repositioning both within new social groupings as the population of a given town constantly passes away and renews itself.

Conclusion

The jacket of this book features the image of a tarot card from the most complete surviving medieval deck. Dating from about 1451, this particular deck was made for Francesco Sforza and his wife Bianca, the illegitimate daughter of Duke Filippo Maria Visconti. Today the deck is held by the Pierpont Morgan Library in New York.[1] The Viscontis were the ruling family of the city of Milan, and some cards in this commissioned deck reflect Bianca's family history. Her ancestors and relatives, for example, appear among the characters of the trump cards.[2] Aside from this pleasing mnemonic and memorializing function, however, the chief purpose of the deck was entertainment. In the fifteenth century tarot was used not for divination, but for a light amusement or parlor game called *tarocco*. While it is not entirely clear how tarocco was played at this time, we do know that there were multiple players and that each card was assigned a value that could trump other cards lower in the scale.[3] In the Visconti deck's rendering, Death is personified as a coyly grinning corpse holding a longbow in his left hand and an arrow pointed at the earth in his right. A shred of fabric wrapped around his head flutters in the air around him. Though emaciated, the figure's

---

1. Helen Farley, *A Cultural History of Tarot: From Entertainment to Esotericism* (London, 2009), 38.
2. Ibid., 55–58.
3. Ibid., 35–37.

skin is intact everywhere except his abdomen, where the viewer may peer into his body cavity in order to inspect his spinal column. The corpse stands in a rather graceful contraposto pose on a grassy cliff that falls away at the lower edge of the card. At the far horizon looms a mountain range. A close ridge of three dark blue peaks curves slightly toward the viewer at the right of the card; behind them two more, paler peaks rise up. The sky is replaced with a stamped, geometric gold background that matches that of the other cards in the deck, just as the mountains match the background of the other trumps that are set outdoors. Two subtle golden flowers blossom from the earth at Death's feet.

The fact that such an image should appear in a set of cards designed as a leisurely entertainment for the most powerful members of society is telling. In a random dealing of the deck, any player at a card party might suddenly be confronted with the figure of Death staring out from his or her hand. Tarocco brought into diversionary time, and into domestic space, an image more often seen in settings reserved for pious contemplation. Pages of the Office of the Dead in prayer books often featured macabre art of course; the triumph of Death and dance of death loomed over cemeteries and church naves; passion plays and performative spectacles had long dramatized Death's indiscriminate nature. Now, Death even was infiltrating the realm of social leisure.

One theory about the iconography of the trump cards in the early tarot decks is that they were partly or wholly inspired by public performative dramas including the dance of death. Additional dramatic sources would have included passion plays and other pious theater.[4] Certainly, many of the figures in the tarot trumps are related to the medieval *danse macabre*, including cards such as Death, the Emperor and Empress, the Pope, the Hermit, the Fool, the Lover(s), and the Bachelor or Magician. All these characters sometimes appear in the dance of death iconography, being led away by his or her own personified Death figure. Likewise, dramatic characters such as the allegorical virtues (Fortitude, Justice, Temperance), Fortune, and the Devil had a long prior history in the performance traditions of the public sphere. While we lack a direct chain of evidence linking the tarot trump cards with popular theater, a connection of some sort seems very likely.

The tarocco deck shows us mortality as a subject of ubiquitous engagement and meditation. Indeed, for Bianca Sforza the whole deck was rife with symbolisms related to death, since many images on the cards represent

---

4. Paul Huson, *Mystical Origins of the Tarot: From Ancient Roots to Modern Usage* (Rochester, VT, 2004), 32–39.

CONCLUSION

her specific ancestors. The Popess card, for instance, represents a famous relative of Bianca's from the previous century, the heresiarch Maifreda de Pirovano. Maifreda was dedicated to the memory of a pious dead woman named Guglielma, whom she identified as the female Holy Spirit; she taught that she herself would become the first female pontiff after Guglielma's resurrection and second coming.[5] The Lovers card may represent the marriage of Bianca's father Filippo Maria Visconti to Maria of Savoy, and other cards appear to relate to the family's history as well.[6] Thus the experience of playing with this deck of cards seems to have been intended as a combination of fun, nostalgia, and melancholy. The images suggest the relentless march of the dance of death of Bianca's own family line, and thereby suggest her own place in the chain of generations and mortality. Her family was an exalted one, yet Death takes each of them in turn. Indeed, even the figure of Death as portrayed on the card seems almost to bear the Visconti symbol: the lateral segmentation of his bow makes it superficially resemble a snake, recalling the Visconti family symbol of a *biscione* or serpent.[7] It is likewise significant, however, that Death was not the highest card in the hierarchy of assigned values in the deck. Rather, it was close to the middle; other cards such as the Star, the Moon, and the Sun were ranked higher, suggesting that human death is but a small part of the vast cosmic stage. The highest two cards in the trump sequence of the tarot deck are Angel (today known as Judgment) and The World. These two represent resurrection and the postapocalyptic renewal of the earth at the end of times. The trump cards thus not only tell the story of the Visconti family, they tell the human story of transcendence of death and attainment of eternal life.

Contemporary tarot readers who employ the cards for divination (a distinctively modern usage of the deck) usually interpret the Death card in positive terms despite its funereal theme. The card signifies an ending, but it also suggests a period of fertility and creativity that is enabled by this termination: death makes room for new life. In this, the modern tarot meaning unintentionally echoes medieval sensibilities surrounding death. Older scholarly traditions sometimes portrayed late medieval culture as paralyzed by its dismal obsession with the macabre,[8] yet this outlook misses the regenera-

---

5. Barbara Newman, "The Heretic Saint: Guglielma of Bohemia, Milan, and Brunate," *Church History* 74, no. 1 (2005): 1–38.
6. Farley, *Cultural History of Tarot*, 58–59.
7. I am indebted to Leigh Ann Craig for directing me toward this connection.
8. Johan Huizinga, *The Waning of the Middle Ages* (New York, 2013); Millard Meiss, *Painting in Florence and Siena after the Black Death: The Arts, Religion, and Society in the Mid-Fourteenth Century* (Princeton, NJ, 1979).

tive qualities associated with mortality in the period. Medieval musings about death, I have found, almost always offer a broad reflection on the perdurance of life. Like the delicate golden flowers springing up beneath Death's feet in the Visconti-Sforza card, mortality constantly gestures toward vitality in the medieval imagination. In this spirit, I offer this history of medieval death and afterlife as more than a macabre exercise. My goal, rather, has been to provide a vista upon the distinctive life and society of the Middle Ages, and in particular to pry open a space for considering the complex cultural admixtures and discursive norms of the period. Traditions about death and the ancestors are exceptionally long-lived; they thus provide an excellent theme for tracking cultural inheritances through evolving social circumstances.

Afterlives is about the persistence of memory and the inevitability of loss. Collective representations of the dead, as Robert Hertz noted over a century ago,[9] provide an excellent purview onto cultural definitions of life. The dead provide a perfectly blank scrim or canvas upon which the living may project their deepest ideals, fears, and longings. From this perspective we might see the Death card as evocative of a set of lasting tensions perceptible throughout our medieval sources: between death and life; between the Christian church and imaginative motifs with pagan genealogies; and between surviving cultures and displaced ones. Yet ultimately these dichotomies become spurious. I have argued that the cultural and religious history of medieval Europe was one of creative synthesis and bilateral adaptation, rather than complete displacement and annihilation. The medieval Christian church, in seeking to promote its central teachings on the eternity of the soul and the certainty of future bodily resurrection, tolerated a broad range of collective representations of death and afterlife. During the period of active conversion, church leaders and lay communities collaborated in maintaining and reproducing any imaginative formation that suggested transcendence of mortality. Such traditions were ratified by the *Dialogues* of Gregory the Great, which constituted a foundational precedent for the Christian appropriation of motifs about ghosts and revenants. Thus pagan collective representations of revenants became a theological argument for the resurrection; the atavistic pagan motif of the army of the dead was transmuted into a folk theology of purgatory; folk traditions that associated the deceased with fertility and abundance were reformulated as commentaries on a retributive afterlife. Likewise, the ancient role of seer and psychopomp was recuperated by clerics in order

---

9. Robert Hertz, "Contribution à une étude sur la représentation collective de la mort," *Année Sociologique* 10 (1907): 48–137. See also Robert Hertz, *Death and the Right Hand*, trans. Rodney Needham and Claudia Needham (Glencoe, IL, 1960).

to offer insights into the world beyond the grave, and classical notions of ghostly possession persisted side by side with the more "modern" teachings of demonic possession. Missionaries, religious chroniclers, and clerics reinterpreted indigenous pagan traditions according to their own priorities, of course, and it is chiefly these reformulated versions, not the original ones, that we encounter in the written record. Yet the traces of their pagan past may readily be discerned.

In the thirteenth century things began to shift. Medical theorists were expanding their reach into natural philosophy, and their definitions of death aligned with an Augustinian understanding of death as an instantaneous event. As medicine became an increasingly influential way of understanding the death of the human body, it came to be utilized by juridical and administrative bureaucracies. Thus physicians' views of death were adopted by institutions of considerable power, and this form of knowledge came to be disseminated to a broader population through vernacular translations (e.g., lists of the mortal signs and literary references to them) as well as the behavioral modelings of coroners and doctors. The privileging of medical knowledge did much to shift the definition of death toward a more definitive pole, as a decisive and irremediable break with this world.

At the same time university-trained intellectuals, no longer needful of ghosts and revenants to teach about the afterlife to potential converts from paganism, also turned toward a more Augustinian vein of interpretation. Such thinkers rejected tales of the returned dead. This was not a universal shift: some clerics still found ghost stories useful for new teachings, most notably the doctrine of purgatory, which was only pronounced as doctrine at the late date of 1274. Yet despite various outliers, it is possible to detect a slow tidal shift about matters of mortality that began in the thirteenth century. More and more learned leaders began to argue against the belief that the dead might return to this world, interpreting such figures as, rather, demons in disguise. In some cases we can trace the dissemination of these new interpretations back down the social scale: the successful diabolization of Hellequin in vernacular French songs, for example; or the arguments of clerics with crowds of Florentine laity about the nature of possessing spirits; or debates over the reasons for certain cadavers' continued activity. Yet these three examples also show that the demonizing initiatives of intellectuals penetrated down the social scale with varying levels of success. In the first example cited above, that of Hellequin, a diabolic reframing was accomplished, whereas in the case of possession, most Italians resisted the suggestion that possessing spirits could not be ghosts. Similarly, socially stratified debates over the source of undead corpses' vitality ended in a stalemate.

Another theme of this book has been the significance of regional specificity. Ways of imagining the dead (which are essentially, of course, ways of imagining the future self) differed significantly in the septentrional and meridional spheres. Whereas the north focused upon the conditions under which a cadaver might potentially remain animate, the south abstracted the dead, conceiving of them as invisible and immaterial presences. These differences point, in turn, to the different cultures and forms of paganism that were indigenous to each area; when combined with Christianity, each produced its own alchemical admixture, resulting in a regionalized culture of mortality and afterlife. Medieval society was, thus, both unified and diverse, and much of the content that was variable may be traced to pagan antecedents. Local paganisms provided the template of a lasting medieval regionalism.

Conversely, however, it is important to note that some ideas with pagan genealogies became universal in the Middle Ages. Perhaps the best example is the notion of "good" versus "bad" deaths, a conceptual binary that is found in every region of medieval Europe and that was widely accepted by all cultural strata. In northern Europe to die badly, through violence and while still youthful, was to risk returning as an aggressive revenant. In the Mediterranean the bad death likewise opened a portal for postmortem return, though in a disembodied form for haunting or possessing. Yet Christian theologians endorsed this idea as well, in a line of pedigreed descent going back to Isidore of Seville in the seventh century. For teachers of Christian doctrine, to die badly was to risk departing with a higher burden of unexpurgated sin, which might imperil one's salvation. There thus was a vast cultural consensus surrounding this set of symbolic equivalences. Another notion that likewise garnered a broad endorsement was the presumption that the dead remained particularly attached to the location of their own remains. We see this in the revenant congregations of the north, which persisted as tomb dwellers rising up from their graves to worship in their local parish church, and in the communities of the dead haunting their own burial churchyards in southern France, who were regularly encountered by the *armariés*. Indeed, even the Catholic saints were particularly attentive to the location of their earthly relics, keeping watch on them from the world beyond, and images of the general resurrection fostered a deep sense of individual connectedness to burial place for the average believer.

The notion that death was only truly, finally complete after the dissolution of the flesh is yet another symbolic association that echoed throughout medieval society. We see it expressed both in northern revenant beliefs and in southern ghost beliefs: the dead would not rest until after the disappearance of their flesh. And of course, the gloriously incorruptible relics of the saints,

CONCLUSION

those very special dead, function within the very same symbolic economy. A final example of a pagan motif that became universal is the suggestion that mountains formed catchments for the dead. In northern Europe, as we have seen, whole societies of the dead lived underground in mountains; yet we also find such tales in Italy, particularly in connection with Mount Etna. Christian thinkers, of course, associated the mountainous realms of the dead with either hell or purgatory; thus mountains were visualized as correctional facilities for the collective dead in the Christian imagination, rather than as joyous postmortem societies, as pagans tended to view them. In sum, surely Christians from across Europe in the Middle Ages, of whatever social standing, had much in common with one another; yet the distinctiveness of local mentalities and of social stratifications should neither be minimized nor ignored. The tensions between the universal and the regional, the elite and the popular, are part of the multiplicity that makes the medieval period compelling.

This book begins with questions but it cannot end with answers. The problem of knowing death remains: we continue to struggle how to imagine the annihilation of the self. Many of the most successful film and television franchises of the past decade have featured the undead: ghosts, zombies, vampires. These entertainments plumb the nature of life and love, history and power, through plotlines featuring the animate dead returned among the living. In medical terms, modern human societies still struggle to define the border between vitality and mortality. We worry about the difference between brain death and body death, and we debate the use of medical machines that reach inside the human body in order to artificially sustain the vital signs of heartbeat and respiration.[10] We still revere certain bodies as symbolically charged and become attached to our ancestors' burial places.[11] We continue to use corpses for medicine as well, both in physicians' training and for organ harvesting, transplanting parts of the deceased into the bodies of the living in order to sustain them.[12] In an era when *Bodyworlds*—an ethically controversial exhibit of preserved, flayed corpses in active poses—is among the most popular attractions in the world, surely the fascination with the animate corpse cannot be said to be purely medieval. In sum, we have our modern relics and our contemporary revenants as we, too, try to imagine mortality.

---

10. Dick Teresi, *The Undead: Organ Harvesting, the Ice-Water Test, Beating-Heart Cadavers—How Medicine Is Blurring the Line between Life and Death* (New York, 2012).

11. Katherine Verdery, *The Political Lives of Dead Bodies: Reburial and Postsocialist Change* (New York, 1999).

12. Mary Roach, *Stiff: The Curious Lives of Human Cadavers* (New York, 2003).

INDEX

Page numbers in *italics* indicate figures.

Adam and Eve, 23, 25, 26–28, *27*, 30, 39
Adam of Bremen, 123–24, 138
Adso of Montier-en-Der, 122n21
Afonso Garcia (Guimarães spirit), 338–40
afterlife. *See* death and afterlife
"age class," dead as, 2–3, 59, 146, 299
age spectrum and closeness to death, 59–60
Aiken, Pauline, 82
Aix, murder in cemetery of church of, 134–35
Alcher of Clairvaux, *De spiritu et anima* (On Spirit and Soul), 73–74
Alès, haunting of widow of Gui de Corvo in, 269–70, 291–96, *295*, 299, 300, 301
All Souls' Day, 261, 279
al-Razi, Muhammed ibn Zakariya, *Book of Medicine Dedicated to Mansur*, 80–81
Amiel de Rieux, 265
ancestral dead: army of the dead and, 179; assistive techniques for, 4; conversion to Christianity and, 9, 10, 11–12, 14, 32–33, 114–15; cults of, 8, 120, 137, 140; cultural significance of afterlife and, 2–3; as *daimones*, 306; in Slavic and Germanic cultures, 110; spirit possession by, 306, 309–10, 327, 344; Visconti-Sforza tarot deck and, 348
Andreas Capellanus, *De amore*, 163, 180, 182–85
animals: reenfleshed after being eaten, 242–43; spirit possession by pig, 336
Antoine le Bon, Duke of Lorraine, *Hours of*, 225–27, *226*
Apocalypse of Peter, 52
approaching death and openness to afterlife, 128
Arab medical knowledge, 73, 74, 80–81, 82
armariés, 271, 273–80, 286, 298, 337, 351
army of the dead, 110–11, 157–205;
    Andreas Capellanus on, 163, 180, 182–85; in Anglo-Norman regions, 162–63; Augustinian versus Gregorian models of death and afterlife and, 163, 185–86, 188, 205; Christianizing accounts of, 179–85, 205; defined, 159; as demonic force, 163–64, 171, 187, 189–91, 194, 197, 199, 200; Étienne (Stephen) de Bourbon on, 161, 197–99; as *familia*, 165, 167, 172, 175, 178, 185, 188; female spirits ("good things") and, 160–62, 188, 191, 199, 242; Herbert of Clairvaux on, 163, 180–82; intersection of pagan and Christian views in, 16; leader of (Herlechin/Harlequin/Hellequin), 164, 166–67, 183, 200–205, *202*, *203*; Map, Walter, on, 163, 173–79; Orderic Vitalis on, 162, 163, 164–72, 177, 178, 179, 180, 201; pagan origin and associations, 158–59, 162–63, 165, 170–72, 176, 205; purgatorial associations, 16, 157, 163, 168, 185, 193–94; in *Roman de Fauvel*, 164, 200–205, *202*, *203*; in *Très Riches Heures de Duc de Berry*, 189, *190*. *See also under* William of Auvergne
Arnalda Riba, 279–80
Arnaud Gélis of Pamiers, 267, 269, 273–79, 280, 282, 286, 292.299–300
Arnold of Villanova, 107
ars moriendi genre, 5, 232, 294
Arthur and Arthurian legend, 147–48, 177, 197
Athon of Uzent, 275
Augustine of Hippo: *The City of God against the Pagans*, 42–43, 307n7; *Confessions*, 45; *De cura pro mortuis gerenda* (On the Care to Be Taken for the Dead), 44–48, 273n27; *De diversis quaestionibus ad Simplicianum*, 273n27; on demons

353

INDEX

Augustine of Hippo *(continued)*
and spirit possession, 307; Gregory the Great compared, 50, 54; Isidore compared, 60, 61–62; on postmortem return, 43–48, 334; on spirit medium of Endor, 271–72; thanatology of, 24, 38, 42–43, 63, 209; William of Auvergne influenced by, 188, 196

Augustinian versus Gregorian models of death and afterlife: army of the dead, accounts of, 163, 185–86, 188, 205, 207, 211–12; development of, 63–65; medical knowledge and, 107; popular culture in northern Europe and, 207, 211–12; separation of body and soul in northern versus southern Europe, 310; shifts between, 63–65, 349–50; spirit mediums and, 270, 297; Thietmar of Merseburg and, 131, 153

Autun, cemetery of, 128–29

"bad" death: evil or criminal dead, 214, 215–24, 233; excommunicated, 220–21, 223, 234, 251; suicides, 93, 237, 306. *See also* untimely/violent death

Baldwin of Pisa, 181
baptism, death without, 11–12, 236, 277
Bartholomew Iscanus, pentitential of, 236
Bartholomew the Englishman, *De rerum proprietatibus*, 59
Basel, Council of (1435), 251
Basil of Caesarea, 248
Beaucaire girl medium, 269, 270, 279–86, 290, 296, 299, 300, 301
Bede, *Ecclesiastical History of the English People*, 9–10, 57n68
Beltramo (spirit in *Miracles of John Gualbert*), 324, 328–30, 334
benandante, 271, 298–99, 300, 337
Benedict of Nursia, 51
Benet, Guillemette, 264–65
Bern, fraticello spirit medium of, 270, 296–98, 301
Bernard de Alazaic, 280
Bernard de Ribéra, 293
Bernardino of Siena, 311–12
Bernheimer, Richard, 170
Beutlerin, Magdalena, 68–72
bodies returning from the dead. *See* revenants of northern Europe
bodily resurrection. *See* resurrection of the body
body and soul, death as separation of, 72
body parts, using postmortem vitality from, 104–7, *106*

Bodyworlds (exhibit), 352
bog burials, 237
Book of the Miracles of Saint Foi of Conques, 150
Books of Hours. *See* manuscripts; *specific owners*
Brigit (niece of Thietmar of Merseburg), 133–34, 143
Brown, Elizabeth A. R., 241
Brown, Peter, 33n13, 37, 341
Brunissende of Pamiers, 274
Buda, Council of (1279), 251
Burchard of Worms: *Corrector*, 236, 243; *Decretum*, 236, 248, 249
burial mounds of German marches, 113–14, 148–49
burial practices, 113–14, 139, 240–42
burned and powdered human skull as medical treatment, 107
burning: as burial practice, 113–14, 139; of corpses of suspected revenants, 216, 218, 238; execution by, 319, 320, 323
burnt sacrifices, Thietmar of Merseburg on, 136–40

Caesarius of Arles, 33
Caesarius of Heisterbach, *Dialogus miraculorum*, 59, 147–48, 156, 211, 219–20, 232, 238
Cahors, Synod of (1206), 251
Canavesio, Giovanni, fresco of general resurrection (1491), 131, *132*
Canon Episcopi, 160
Carthage, Sixth Council of (401), 36
Cathars, 263, 264, 265, 290
Catherine of Cleves, Hours of, 84–88, *86, 87*
Celts, 64, 109, 246, 256, 340
charivaris, 200, *202, 203*, 204
Charlemagne, 122, 137
Chaucer, Geoffrey, 82–83
Christian tradition of death and afterlife, 17, 20, 23–65; for apostles and early Church, 25–31, 62, 304–6; army of the dead incorporated into, 179–85, 205; centrality of death and resurrection to, 6, 10, 19, 24, 25–26, 36; conversion to Christianity, 8–14, 32–33, 114–15, 122–26; *daimones* and spirit possession in, 304–8; as event versus process or narrative, 20–21, 37, 46–47, 54, 62, 186; funerary feasts and commemorations, 32–33, 115–16, 248; German marches, political and

religious context of, 121–26; Isidore of Seville and, 25, 48, 56–62, 64; martyrs and saints, 33–37, *35*, 46; medicine and theology, links between, 20–21; origins of death in creation and fall, 23, 25, 26–28, *27*, 30, 39; postmortem return, patristic denial of, 43–48, 63; in southern Europe, 255–56; spirit mediums and "witch" of Endor, 271–73; *spiritus*, concept of, 73–74; thanatology, patristic development of, 38–43, 62–63. *See also* Augustinian versus Gregorian models of death and afterlife; *specific church fathers*
Christina of Saint Trond (Christina Mirabilis), 66–68, 89
Chronicle of Lanercost, 153–54, 220–21, 233, 234, 250
Cluny: death ritual at, 91; mediation for dead at, 259–63
Clusone, Italy, Oratori dei Disciplini, outdoor fresco (fifteenth century), 247, *248*
coffins, animated corpses carrying, 215, *216*
Columba of Rieti, *Vita* of, 311
Constantine, lord of Torres, 181
Constitutions of Lanfranc, 218
conversion to Christianity, 8–14, 32–33, 114–15, 122–26
coroners and courts, investigations by, 93–95, 101–4
Cotard delusion, 186
courtly love literature, 182
creation and fall, origins of death in, 23, 25, 26–28, *27*, 30, 39
criminals: medical use of blood and body parts of, 105–7, 324; as revenants in popular culture, 214, 233; spirit possession by, 319–20, 323–24, 329–30
cultural pluralism in Thietmar of Merseburg, *Chronicon*, 120–21, 123, 127
Curtius, Ernst, 57

Dan the Proud (Danish king), 113
dancing: dance of death/*danse macabre* iconography, 5, 227, 247, *248*, 251–52, 347; of dead, 142, 146, 147, 153, 244–47, 251; of "good things," 161–62; of living, in cemeteries and churchyards, 32–33, 247–53
Dante Alighieri, *Divine Comedy*, 52, 54, 57n68, 151, 211
De Lisle Psalter, 228

death and afterlife, 1–18, 346–52; Augustinian versus Gregorian models of, 63–65, 349–50 (*see also* Augustinian versus Gregorian models of death and afterlife); in Christian tradition, 17, 20, 23–65 (*see also* Christian tradition of death and afterlife); cultural significance of, 2–6, 15–16; disembodied dead in southern Europe, 17, 255–57 (*see also* spirit mediums; spirit possession; spirits and ghosts in southern Europe); embodied return from the dead in northern Europe, 17, 109–11 (*see also* army of the dead; German marches; popular culture in northern Europe; revenants of northern Europe; Thietmar of Merseburg, *Chronicon*); as guide to cultural definitions of life, 349; as imagined experience, 1–2, 19–20; intersection of pagan and Christian views of, 6–8, 13–16, 349–52 (*see also* intersection of pagan and Christian views); medical knowledge of, 17, 66–107 (*see also* medical knowledge); regional specificity of, 351; tarot cards, iconography of, *ii*, 346–49
Death personified: Chantilly, France, Musée Condé, MS 146 (Jean Gerson, *Le Trésor de Sapience*, fifteenth century), 84, *85*; Clusone, Italy, Oratori dei Disciplini, outdoor fresco (fifteenth century), 247, *248*; in *Hours of Marguerite de Coetivy*, 229–31, *230*; Lavaudieu, Abbey of, St. André Church, France, fresco of Lady Death (1355), *22*, 23; Tarot card for Death, *ii*, 346–49
"Death Prognostic Man," 77–78, *79*
death rattle, 76, 81, 84, 99, 104
The Demon Lover (English folk ballad), 150
demonic interpretations
  of revenants: army of the dead, as demonic force, 163–64, 171, 187, 189–91, 194, 197, 199, 200; circumstances leading to, 207, 214–15; corpses, demonically possessed, 208–12; dancing dead, 246–47; doubts about/explicit rejection of, 214, 217, 218–19; by Thietmar of Merseburg, 141–44
  of shade of Samuel, 272–73
  of spirit possession: in Christian tradition, 304–8; corpses, demonically possessed, 208–12; in debate with

demonic interpretations *(continued)*
ghostly interpretations, 302–4, 307–8, 310–14, 341–45; medieval iconography of death and, 312–13, *313*; Nicholas of Tolentino, canonization testimonies for, 315, 319, 321; Our Lady of the Olive Tree in Guimarães, miracles of, 334, 338, 339, 342; in Raggiolo's *Miracles of John Gualbert*, 322, 323, 324–26, 328; socio-historical dimensions of, 341–45; transformation of spirits into demons, 338, 339, 340

demons: exorcism of, 320; in pagan and Christian tradition, 304–8

Dias, Mumadona, 330

disembodied dead. *See* spirits and ghosts

Długosz, Jan, 139

doctors and professionalization of death, 70, 71–72, 92–95

Doob, Penelope, 250–51

draugar, 212–15, 220, 224

dwarfs, 154, 167, 170–74. 177, 178, 201–4, *203*

Edwin (king of Northumbria), 9–10

Egyptian mummies, 105, *106*

Einherjar, 158

Eiriksmál ("Eirik's Poem," 954), 158

Ekkehard of Aura, 157–58, 161

embodied return from the dead. *See* revenants

Endor, spirit medium of (in 1 Samuel), 271–73

epilepsy, 89, 107

Ermengol de Béziers, *Breviary of Love*, *313*

Estêvão Domingues (Guimarães spirit), 332–38, 339, 340

Étienne (Stephen) de Bourbon, 147, 161, 197–99, 249; *De septem donis Spiritus Sancti* (On the Seven Gifts of the Holy Spirit) or *Tractatus de diversis materiis praedicabilibus* (A Treatise on Various Preaching Materials), 198

Etna, 52–53, 54, 148, 151, 177, 260, 261, *309*, 352

Eunapius of Sardis, 37

excommunicated, 220–21, 223, 234, 251

executed criminals. *See* criminals

exorcism: of demons, 320; medieval portrayals of death resembling, 312; of spirits, 320–21, 327

Eyrbyggja Saga, 148, 213, 223–24

fairies, 245, 246

familia, army of the dead as, 165, 167, 172, 175, 178, 185, 188

Farinerio, Buonaventura, 308, 310

Fasciculus Morum (Cluster of Customs), 83–84

feasts for and commemorations of the dead: dancing of living, in cemeteries and churchyards, 32–33, 247–53; early Christian tradition of, 32–33, 115–16, 248

Felicitas (North African martyr), 46

female revenants: as dancing dead, 244–46; "good things," 160–62, 188, 191, 199, 242

fertility and the dead, 4, 149–50, 176, 179, 245, 250

flesh and human vitality in northern European popular culture, 238–44, 351–52

Flos medicinae (Flower of Medicine), 75–77

Saint Foi of Conques, *Book of the Miracles of*, 150

Fournier, Jacques, and Fournier register, 267–69, 270, 273, 279, 286

Frederick II (Holy Roman Emperor), 148

funeral practices. *See* burial practices

Gdansk encounter with vagrant spirit, 199n86

Geary, Patrick, 2

Geoffrey of Burton, *Life and Miracles of Saint Modwenna*, 215–16, 223, 224, 233

Gerald of Wales, *Journey through Wales*, 249, 252

Gerard of Cremona, 80

Gerasene demoniac, 304–6

Germanic and Slavic cultures: army of the dead motif, origins of, 158–59, 162–63; Icelandic saga literature, 148, 212–15, 220, 223–24; process of separation of body and soul in, 310; revenants in, 109–10 (*see also* revenants of northern Europe)

German marches, 113–56; burial mounds of, 113–14, 148–49; burnt sacrifice by pagans of, 136–40; conversion to Christianity, 114–16, 122–26; cultural significance of burial customs in broader region, 113–16; map, *116*; political and religious context, 121–26; social life of the dead in, 144–51. *See also* Thietmar of Merseburg, *Chronicon*

Saint Germanus, hagiography of, 242

Gerson, Jean, *Le Trésor de Sapience*, 84, *85*
Gertsman, Elina, 252
Gervaise of Tilbury, *Otia Imperialia* (Emperor's Diversions), 147, 176, 246, 269, 280–90, 291
ghosts. *See* spirits and ghosts
giants, 166, 167, 170–72, 189, 200–201
Gil de Santarém, 93
Ginzburg, Carlo, 268, 271, 297
Gloterer, Paul, 69, 70
Gobi, Jean, 270, 291–95, *295*, 297, 299n116, 300
"good things," 160–62, 188, 191, 199, 242
Gottschalk (missionary), 123–24
Gower, John, *Confessio Amantis*, 182
Grateful Dead, legend of, 154–56, *155*
Gregorian model of death and afterlife. *See* Augustinian versus Gregorian models of death and afterlife
Gregory I the Great (pope), *Dialogues*, 349; army of the dead and, 185; spirit mediums and, 260, 262, 265, 292–93; thanatology of, 25, 48–56, 62, 63, 64; Thietmar of Merseburg and, 119, 131
Gregory of Tours, *Book on the Glory of the Confessors*, 128–29
Grettir's Saga, 213
Gualbert, John, *Miracles* of (Jerome de Raggiolo), 313, 321–30, 337, 344
Gui de Corvo, haunting of widow of, 269–70, 291–96, *295*, 299, 300, 301
Guillaume Fort, 264, 279–80
Guimarães, miracles of Our Lady of the Olive Tree in, 314, 330–40, *331*, 342
Guyénot, Laurent, 8–9

Harald (king of Denmark), 12, 115
Harlequin/Hellequin/Hellechin. *See* army of the dead
heads, corpses reburied without or with decapitated, 215–16, 236
heads on backwards, spirits with, 198, 199
hearts of corpses removed and burned, 216
Hélinand (twelfth-century poet), 229
Hellequin/Hellechin/Harlequin. *See* army of the dead
Helmold of Bossau, *Chronicle of the Slavs*, 138–39
Henri of Lausanne, 263
Henry I (king of England), 117
Henry II (king of England), 173, 178
Henry I the Fowler (Ottonian king), 117
Henry II (Holy Roman Emperor), 117, 123
Henry of Erfurt, 149–50, 153

Herbert of Clairvaux, 163, 180–82
heretical skepticism and dissent, 263–65, 277–78, 279
Hertz, Robert, 349
Hildegard of Bingen, 211
Hincmar of Rheims, 248
Hippocrates, Hippocratic corpus, and Hippocratic tradition, 74–75; *Aphorisms*, 74, 80, 81; Arab medical knowledge and, 73, 74, 80; "Death Prognostic Man," 78; *Flos medicinae* (Flower of Medicine), 75–77; *Prognosis*, 75; vernacularization of, 82, 84; Vincent of Beauvais, *Speculum naturale*, 78–81
Holy Innocents Cemetery, Paris: *danse macabre* fresco (1424), 229; flesh-eating soil from, 240
Hours, Books of. *See* manuscripts; *specific owners*
Hraban Maur, 154
Hughes of Durfort, 274, 277
Hughes of Rous, 274–75
Hutton, Ronald, 17

Icelandic saga literature, 148, 212–15, 220, 223–24
Ida of Louvain, *Life* of, 209–10
Indiculus Superstitionum et Paganiorum, 244n112
intersection of pagan and Christian views, 6–8, 13–16, 349–52; army of the dead and, 16; conversion to Christianity and, 8–14, 32–33, 114–15, 122–26; spirit possession and, 304–8, 321, 342–43; in Thietmar of Merseburg, *Chronicon*, 119, 120–21, 142–43. *See also* Christian tradition of death and afterlife; paganism
investigations by coroners, 93–95, 101–3
Isidore of Seville, *Etymologies*, 25, 48, 56–62, 64, 129, 232, 351

Janson, Henrik, 121
Jean, Duc de Berry, *Très Riches Heures* of, 189, *190*
Jean de Mailly, 210
Joan (miraculously resurrected by Thomas of Cantilupe), 95, 98, 99
John XXII (pope), 291, 293, 315
John of Gaddesden, *Rosa anglica sive rosa medicinae*, 89n49, 107
John of Gistyn, 100–101, 102
John of Mecklenburg, 138–39
John of Mirfield, *Breviarium Bartholomei*, 77

358 INDEX

Julian (Roman emperor), 37
Julius, Caesar, *Gallic War*, 136–37

Kieckhefer, Richard, 337
Kloczowski, Jerzy, 137

La Rossa, Anna, 298, 300
Lai du Trot, 182
"Last World Emperor" mythology, 121–22
Lavaudieu, Abbey of, St. André Church, France, fresco of Lady Death (1355), *22*, 23
Laxdaela Saga, 213
Lazarus, 30–31
Le Goff, Jacques, 151
Lewis, Ioan, 303
Lilium medicinae (Lily of Medicine), 75–77
Little, Lester, 234
livor mortis (lividity), 92
location of remains, attachment of dead to, 351
Louis IX (king of France), exhumation of, *35*, 35–36
Luque la maudite (Luca the Damned), 200
Luttrell Psalter, 224–25, *225*, 244
Lyons, First Council of (1254), 151
Lyons, Second Council of (1274), 293

Macer Floridus herbal, 75, 83
magpies, 227
Maifreda de Pirovano, 348
Mâle, Emile, 229
Malinowski, Bronislaw, 19, 21
Malleus Maleficarum (Hammer of Witches), 236
manuscripts
  Berlin, Kupferstichkabinett, Staatliche Museen, Inv. 78 B 12 (*Hours of Mary of Burgundy*), 215, *216*, 234, *235*
  Chantilly, France, Musée Condé: MS 65 (*Très Riches Heures de Duc de Berry*, 1416), 189, *190*; MS 74/1088 (*Hours of Marguerite de Coetivy*; fifteenth century), 229–31, *230*; MS 146 (Jean Gerson, *Le Trésor de Sapience*, fifteenth century), 84, *85*
  London, British Library: MS Add. 42130 (*Luttrell Psalter*, ca. 1325–40), 224–25, *225*, 244; MS Arundel 83 II (*De Lisle Psalter*; ca. 1310), *228*; MS Lambeth 444 (John of Mirfield, *Breviarium Bartholomei*), 77; MS Royal 12 B. III (Macer Floridus herbal, ca. 1070–1112), 75
  London, Wellcome Medical Library, MS 49 ("Death Prognostic Man," fifteenth century), 77–78, *79*
  Los Angeles, Getty Museum, MS 31 (*Vision of Gui;* 1475), 294, *295*
  Madrid, Real Biblioteca de lo Escorial, Provençal codex (Ermengol de Béziers, *Breviary of Love;* early fourteenth century), 312–13, *313*
  Münich, Bayerische Staatsbibliothek, MS Clm 15708 III (ca. 1478–89), 26–28, *27*
  New York, Pierpont Morgan Library: MS M.630 (Visconti-Sforza Tarot deck, ca. 1451), *ii*, 346–49; MS M.917/945 (*Hours of Catherine of Cleves*, 1434), 84–88, *86, 87*
  Paris, Bibliothèque Mazarine, exhumation of Louis IX (no catalog information), *35*, 35–36
  Paris, Bibliothèque Nationale de France: MS Français 146 (*Roman de Fauvel;* ca. 1316–20), 201–4, *202, 203*; MS NAL 302 (hours on Antoin le Bon; 1533), 225–27, *226*
  St. Petersburg, National Library, MS Fr. Fv VI #1 (Mattheaus Plateario, *Book of Simple Medicnes*, ca. 1470), 105, *106*
  Vatican City, Biblioteca Apostolica Vaticana, MS Borghes. 35 (Rituale Romanum), 210
  Venice, Biblioteca Marciana (Grateful Dead in Dutch Book of Hours, fifteenth century, no catalog information), 155, *156*
Map, Walter, *De nugis curialium* (Courtier's Trifles), 163, 173–79, 217, 219, 233, 234, 245–46, 260
Marguerite de Coetivy, Hours of, 229–31, *230*
Maria of Savoy, 348
martyrs. See saints and martyrs
Mary of Burgundy, Hours of, 215, *216*, 234, *235*
material wealth, of dead, 145–47
Matteoti, Giovanni, 302–3, 307–8, 310
Matthaeus Platearius, *Book of Simple Medicines*, 105, *106*
medical knowledge, 17, 20, 66–107; Arab transmission of, 73, 74, 80–81, 82; body parts, using postmortem vitality from, 104–7, *106*, 324; boundary between life and death, hardening of, 71, 88–89, 92–93; coroner and court

investigations, 93–95, 101–4; inert but intact bodies, 71, 88–92, 100–104; professionalization of, 70, 71–72, 92–95; Roger of Conway, 99–104; saints, miraculous resurrections by, 94, 95–99, 103, 104; *spiritus* or vital spirit as link between body and soul, 72–74; theology and medicine, links between, 20–21; triple deaths of Christina of Saint Trond and Magdalena Beutlerin, differences between, 66–72; vernacularization of, 82–88, *85–87*, 94–95; vital signs, 74, 90, 104. *See also* Hippocrates, Hippocratic corpus, and Hippocratic tradition; mortal signs

Mediterranean culture. *See* southern Mediterranean culture

mediums. *See* spirit mediums

Mellinkoff, Ruth, 201

memory, persistence of, 2, 349; army of the dead and, 182, 243; medical knowledge of death and, 73; spirit possession and, 304, 310, 319–21, 326, 341, 343–45; tarot cards and, 346, 348; Thietmar of Merseburg and, 118, 129, 130

mensae, 32–33

Merseburg Charms, 126

miraculous resurrections by saints, 94, 95–99, 103, 104

Modwenna, *Life and Miracles* of (Geoffrey of Burton), 215–16, 223, 224, 233

monasticism and spiritual mediation, 259–63

Monday, masses for the dead on, 145

Monica (mother of Augustine of Hippo), 45

Montserrat, dance of death fresco, 252

Moore, R. I., 262, 263

mortal signs: "Death Prognostic Man," 77–78, *79*; defined, 74; development of concept of, 74–82; livor mortis and, 92; putrefaction as sole sure sign of, 239–40; vernacularization of, 82–88, *85–87*, 94–95

Mount Etna, 52–53, 54, 148, 151, 177, 260, 261, *309*, 352

mountains, association of afterlife with, 53–54, 147–51, 157–58, 259–60

mummia, 105, *106*

necrologies, 4

necromancy, 28, 44, 73, 93, 306, 337, 2002

New Prophecy, 38

Nicaea, Second Council of (787), 7, 36

Nicholas (miraculously resurrected by Thomas of Cantilupe), 95, 97–98

Nicholas of Tolentino, canonization testimonies for, 313, 315–21

Nider, Johannes, *Fornicarius* (The Ant Hill), 69, 70, 270, 296–98

Northern Germanic and Slavic cultures. *See* German marches; Germanic and Slavic cultures

Notre Dame de la Bonne Mort, 232

Obodrites (Slavic group), 124

Odilo of Cluny, 259

Odin (deity), 16, 158

Olive Tree, miracles of Our Lady of (Guimarães), 314, 330–40, *331*, 342

Orderic Vitalis, 92n58, 163, 164–72, 177, 178, 179, 180, 201; *Ecclesiastical History*, 162, 164–65

ossuaries, 240–41

Oswald (king of Northumbria), 10

Otranto, Cathedral of, pavement mosaic of King Arthur (1163), 148, 177

Otto I (Holy Roman Emperor), *116*, 122

Otto IV (Holy Roman Emperor), 288

Our Lady of the Olive Tree in Guimarães, miracles of, 314, 330–40, *331*, 342

paganism: ancestral dead, cults of, 8, 120, 137, 140; army of the dead and, 158–59, 162–63, 165, 170–72, 176, 205; burnt sacrifice and, 136–40; conversion to Christianity from, 8–14, 32–33, 114–15, 122–26; *daimones* and spirit possession, 305–6; feasts for and commemorations of the dead, 32–33, 115–16, 161–62; flesh, vitality of, 242–44; German marches in eleventh century, political and religious context of, 121–26; spirit possession, 256–57, 305–6. *See also* intersection of pagan and Christian views

Paravacini Bagliani, Agostino, 241

Paris, Council of (1212/1213), 251

Park Katherine, 310

Parousia, 28, 30, 62, 243

Paschasius the Deacon, 54–55

Passagians, 263, 265

Paul and Pauline writings, 23, 26, 28, 29

Peltrara, Lucia, 298

Penitential of Theodore, 115

Pepin of Herestal (Frankish leader), 11

Perpetua (North African martyr), 39, 46

INDEX

Peter of Blois, 175–76
Peter of Bruys, 263
Peter of Duisburg, 139
Peter the Venerable *De miraculis libri duo* (Two Books of Miracles), 5, 194, 261–62, 263
Philip IV the Fair (king of France), 241
piaculum, 171–72
Pietro d'Abano, 89, 94
Pina-Cabral, João de, 14, 111, 340
popular culture in northern Europe, 206–54; common occurrence, revenants as, 231–32; dancing dead, 244–47, 251; dancing of living, in cemeteries and churchyards, 247–53; demonically possessed corpses, 208–12; evil or criminal dead, 214, 215–24, 233; flesh and human vitality, connection between, 238–44; funeral practices and, 240–42; Icelandic saga literature, 212–15; iconography of, *216*, 224–31, *225, 226, 228, 230*, 239; preventive measures against revenants, 215–16, 218, 222, 224–25, *225*, 234–38; shape-shifting dead, 222–24; untimely/violent death, significance of, 207, 232–34, 236, 238; violent and dangerous nature of revenants, 214, 215, 217–21, 225–27, *226*, 234–38, *235*; wandering dead, 215–22
popular culture in southern Europe, beliefs about spirits and ghosts in, 267–68, 298–99, 308–14
possession. *See* spirit possession
preventive measures against revenants, 215–16, 218, 222, 224–25, *225*, 234–38
Price, Neil, 114
Pseudo-Methodius, 122n21
psychopomps. *See* spirit mediums
purgatory: army of the dead and, 16, 157, 163, 168, 185, 193–94; Christina of Saint Trond and, 66–67; Cluniac mediation for dead and, 259–63; formalization of, 4; mountain, association with, 151; spirit mediums enquiring about, 289, 291–93

Radbod (Frisian ruler), 11–12
Raggiolo, Jerome de, *Miracles of John Gualbert*, 313, 321–30, 337, 344
Raoul/Ralph Glaber, 154, 159
Raymond of Saint-Foy, 263–64

Raymonde (cousin of Arnaud Gélis), 278, 279
al-Razi, Muhammed ibn Zakariya, *Book of Medicine Dedicated to Mansur*, 80–81
Redigast (Slavic deity), 139
Regimen sanitatis Salernitanum (Salernitan Health Regimen), 75–77
Relatio metrica de duobus ducibus (The Versified Story of Two Kings), 182
relics, 7, 24, 34–37, *35*, 46, 62, 105, 135, 243–44, 351–52
resurrection of the body: revenant/ghost stories as proof of, 51–56, 119, 129–31, 135–36, 144; skepticism and dissent regarding, 264–65
revenants of northern Europe, 17, 109–11; iconography of, *216*, 224–31, *225, 226, 228, 230*, 239; preventive measures against, 215–16, 218, 222, 224–25, *225*, 234–38; retribution or reward, providing, 154–56, *155*; social life of, 144–47. *See also* army of the dead; demonic interpretations; German marches; popular culture in northern Europe; Thietmar of Merseburg, *Chronicon*; violent and dangerous nature of dead
Reyneke (ghost in Henry of Erfurt), 149–50, 260
Richard de Fournival, *Conseils d'Amour*, 182
Richard of St. Victor, 57n68
Riga, Council of (1428), 115–16
rigor mortis, 92
Robert of Bellême, 165
Roger of Conway, 95, 100–104
Roger of Glos, 169
Roger of Wendover, *Flowers of History*, 89–90
Roman de Fauvel, 164, 200–205, *202, 203*
Romana, Francesca, 303
Rosa, María de Lurdes, 337
Rouen, Council of (1231), 251
Rudolf von Schlettstadt (Sélestat), *Historiae Memorabiles* (Memorable Histories), 140–43, 150, 219, 233–34, 237

Saint Patrick's Purgatory, Ireland, 151
saints and martyrs: cult of, 33–37, *35*, 46, 271; exorcisms at tombs of, 321; location of remains, attachment of dead to, 351; miraculous resurrections by, 94, 95–99, 103, 104; relics of, 7, 24, 34–37, *35*, 46, 62, 105, 135, 243–44, 351–52

Schmitt, Jean-Claude, 177
Schorbach, Lorraine, charnel house, 240–41
Scott, James, 127
secondary burial practices (ossuaries), 240–41
Seelenmutter, 271, 298, 300
Sforza, Francesco and Bianca, 346–49
shape-shifting dead, 222–24
sheepskin, dead human body compared to, 206
Slavic cultures. *See* German marches; Germanic and Slavic cultures
Snorri Sturluson: *Edda*, 242; *Heimskringla* (History of the Kings of Norway), 113–14, 116, 148
Snowball story, 223
social life of the dead, 144–51, 276
soul: body, death as separation from, 72; *spiritus* and, 73–74
southern Mediterranean culture: disembodied spirits and ghosts in (*see* spirit mediums; spirit possession; spirits and ghosts in southern Europe); process of separation of body and soul in, 310; religious skepticism and dissent in, 263–65, 277–78, 279
Speculum morale (attrib. Vincent of Beauvais), 47, 342n66
spirit mediums, 256, 259–301; *armariés*, 271, 273–80, 286, 298, 337, 351; Arnaud Gélis of Pamiers, 267, 269, 273–79, 280, 282, 286, 292.299–300; Augustinian versus Gregorian models of death and afterlife and, 270, 297; Beaucaire girl medium, 269, 270, 279–86, 290, 296, 299, 300, 301; *benandante*, 271, 298–99, 300, 337; Bern fraticello, 270, 296–98, 301; church teachings on medium of Endor and, 271–73; clerical appropriation, 269, 270, 286–90, 291–96; Cluniac system of mediation for dead, 259–63; community status of, 271, 278–79, 282–86, 290, 300–301; documented cases of, 266–72, *268*; Gui de Corvo, haunting of widow of, 269–70, 291–96, *295*, 299, 300, 301; Guillaume Fort on Arnalda Riba, 264, 279–80; possession compared, 303–4; purgatory, enquiring about, 289, 291–93; religious skepticism and dissent and, 263–65, 277–78, 279; *Seelenmutter*, 271, 298, 300; thanatology of spirits and, 266–67, 298–300

spirit possession, 256–57, 302–45; by ancestral dead, 306, 309–10, 327, 344; causes of, 311–12, 323–24; contours and geography of belief about, 308–14, *309, 321, 331*; exorcisms, 320–21, 327; by living persons, 336–38; medieval iconography of death and, 312–13, *313*; mediumship compared, 303–4; naming of spirit, 316–20, 332, 343; Nicholas of Tolentino, canonization testimonies for, 313, 315–21; Our Lady of the Olive Tree in Guimarães, miracles of, 314, 330–40, *331*, 342; in pagan and Christian tradition, 304–8, 321, 342–43; by pig, 336; in Raggiolo's *Miracles of John Gualbert*, 313, 321–30, 337, 344; socio-historical dimensions of, 341–45; untimely/violent death and, 308–9. *See also under* demonic interpretations
spirits and ghosts in southern Europe, 17, 255–57; potential violence and dangerousness, 255, 277; social life of, 276; thanatology of, 266–67, 298–300. *See also* spirit mediums; spirit possession
spiritus or vital spirit as link between body and soul, 72–74
Stephan of Ganvy, 101–2
Stephen de Bourbon. *See* Étienne (Stephen) de Bourbon
Stoeckhlin, Chonrad, 298
Strozzi, Alessandra, 308
suicides, 93, 237, 306
Summa contra hereticos, 265
Supplementum, 293
Sventovit (Slavic deity), 138
syncope, 89

Tacitus, *Germania*, 137, 237
tarot cards, ii, 346–49
Tertullian of Carthage, *Liber de anima* (Book of the Soul), 24, 38–39; on demons and spirit possession, 306–7; Gregory the Great compared, 49–50, 54; Isidore compared, 60, 62; on postmortem return, 43–44, 45, 46, 47, 48; thanatology of, 38–42, 63, 72, 209
Testard, Robinet, *106*
Theodoric (king of the Ostrogoths), 52–53
theology of death. *See* Christian tradition of death and afterlife

Thietmar of Merseburg, *Chronicon:* Arnaud Gélis of Pamiers compared, 275; biographical information, 117, 133; on burnt sacrifices, 136–40; cultural pluralism and, 120–21, 123, 127; demonic interpretations of revenants, 141–44; Deventer story, 133–36, 145; essential elements in ghost stories of, 143–44; intersection of pagan and Christian traditions in, 119, 120–21, 142–43; Magdeburg story, 133, 134, 135, 145; Orderic Vitalis on army of the dead compared, 164–65; political and religious context, 123, 124, 126; resurrection, revenant stories as proof of, 119, 129–31, *132*, 135–36, 144; Rudolf von Schlettstadt, *Historiae Memorabiles (Memorable Histories)* compared, 140–43; social life of the dead in, 144–47; Walsleben story, 117–18, 119, 126–29, 135, 136, 137–38, 145

Thomas Aquinas, 293

Thomas of Cantilupe, 95–99, 103, 104

Thomas of Cantimpré, *Bonum Universale de Apibus* (On the Universal Good of Bees), 67, 208–9, 210, 211, 212, 233–34, 238–39, 242, 246–47, 248

Thomas of Eccleston, 148

Thor (deity), 242

three living and the three dead, 4–5, 227–29, *228*

Tréguier, Statutes of, 251

Tres Riches Heures de Duc de Berry, 189, *190*

Trier, Council of (1227), 251

triple deaths, 66–72

triumph of death, 5, 247, *248*

Tundale's Vision, 78, 83, 89, 90

universal salvation, Arnaud Gélis of Pamiers on, 277–78, 279

untimely/violent death: army of the dead and, 158, 187, 191; in Christian tradition, 40, 44; Isidore of Seville on, 57–58, 60, 64, 232; of Jesus and martyrs, 7, 19, 24, 25, 34, 36, 64; popular culture in Northern Europe and, 207, 232–34, 236, 238; revenants in Germanic and Slavic culture and, 110, 129; spirit possession and, 308–9, 317; spirits/ghosts in Mediterranean culture and, 255, 304, 306, 320; Tertullian on, 39, 40–41, 44; Thietmar of Merseburg on, 129; universal beliefs about, 351; untimely deaths of healthy persons with no sign of violence, 88

Verdiana of Castelfiorentino, hagiography of, 319–20

Vincent of Beauvais: *Speculum majus* (Great Mirror), 78–80, 82; *Speculum morale* (attrib.), 47, 342n66; *Speculum naturale*, 60, 80–81, 82

violent and dangerous nature of dead revenants, 17, 110; army of the dead, 168, 188–89; popular culture in northern Europe on, 214, 215, 217–21, 225–27, *226*, 234–38, *235*; in Thietmar of Merseburg, 128–29, 135–36, 154–56

spirits/ghosts, 255, 277

violent death. *See* untimely/violent death

Visconti, Filippo Maria, 346, 348

Visconti-Sforza Tarot deck, *ii*, 346–49

vital signs, 74, 90, 104

vitality, postmortem: connection between flesh and human vitality, 238–44; medical use of body parts for, 104–7, *106*

Walchelin (in Orderic Vitalis's account of army of the dead), 165–71, 201

Waldensians, 263, 264

Walfrid (miraculously resurrected by Thomas of Cantilupe), 95, 96–97

Walsleben revenants, 117–18, 119, 126–29

Walter de Pirebrok, 99

watery places, disposal of corpses in, 237

Wends (Slavic group), 122–25, 137

Whyte, Florence, 252

Widukind of Corvey, *Deeds of the Saxons*, 117, 125n35

William (miraculously resurrected by Thomas of Cantilupe), 95, 97, 99

William of Auvergne, 23, 186
on army of the dead, 159, 161, 164, 185–97; Augustinian versus Gregorian models of death and afterlife and, 185–86, 205; as demonic force, 164, 187, 189–91, 196, 197, 199, 200; Étienne (Stephen) de Bourbon compared, 199; as illusion or actual, 192–97; *Roman de Fauvel* and, 204; systematic discussion of, 187–91; visionaries' reports of, 186–87

De universo (On the Universe), 47–48, 164, 186, 187, 219

on fleshly vitality, 239
on individual revenants in popular culture, 219, 231, 232, 234
William Durandus, *Rationale divinorum officiorum* (The Reasons for Divine Customs), 88, 135, 140, 148–49, 233
William of Glos, 169
William of Malmesbury, 231–32, 237
William of Newburgh, *Historia Rerum Anglicarum*, 217–19, 221, 222, 231, 233, 234, 238
William of Nottingham, 101–2

William, bishop of Orange, 288
Wulfram (Christian missionary), *Vita*, 11–12
Wulfstan (archbishop of York), 11
Wurzburg, Council of (1298), 251

Yorkshire collection of revenant tales (ca. 1400), 221–22, 224, 229, 233, 237

Zaroff, Roman, 124
Zeno of Verona, 302–3
Zita of Lucca, *Vita* of, 311

www.ingramcontent.com/pod-product-compliance
Lightning Source LLC
Chambersburg PA
CBHW020347170426
43200CB00005B/79